To Jacques

Dermot McCarthy

John McGahern and the Art of Memory

PETER LANG

Oxford • Bern • Berlin • Bruxelles • Frankfurt am Main • New York • Wien

Bibliographic information published by Die Deutsche Nationalbibliothek.
Die Deutsche Nationalbibliothek lists this publication in the Deutsche
Nationalbibliografie; detailed bibliographic data is available on the Internet at
http://dnb.d-nb.de.

A catalogue record for this book is available from the British Library.

Library of Congress Cataloging-in-Publication Data:

McCarthy, Dermot, 1948-
    John McGahern and the art of memory / Dermot McCarthy.
      p. cm. -- (Reimagining Ireland ; 23)
    Includes bibliographical references and index.
    ISBN 978-3-0343-0100-8 (alk. paper)
    1. McGahern, John, 1934-2006--Criticism and interpretation. 2. Memory
in literature. 3. Ireland--In literature. I. Title.
    PR6063.A2176Z793 2010
    823'.914--dc22
                                    2010029096

ISSN 1662-9094
ISBN 978-3-0343-0100-8

Cover image: Lake in County Leitrim, the setting for
That They May Face the Rising Sun, John McGahern's last novel.
Photograph © Dermot McCarthy 2007.

© Peter Lang AG, International Academic Publishers, Bern 2010
Hochfeldstrasse 32, CH-3012 Bern, Switzerland
info@peterlang.com, www.peterlang.com, www.peterlang.net

Printed in Germany

Contents

Acknowledgements

This book could not have been written without a sabbatical granted me by Huron University College. I am sincerely grateful to the Executive Board and the Principal of the College, Dr Ramona Lumpkin, and to Dean Trish Fulton for their support. Eamon Maher's belief in the merit of the book did not waver from first to final draft and without his enthusiastic encouragement I would not have completed the project. Finally, I owe the greatest debt of gratitude to my wife, Jacques, who with her usual cheer and support shared with me the frustrations and pleasures of writing a book on John McGahern at the present time.

Abbreviations

McGahern's Works and Editions Cited in the Text

AW	*Amongst Women*. London: Faber and Faber, 1990.
B	*The Barracks* (1963). London: Faber and Faber, 1983.
CE	*Creatures of the Earth: New and Selected Stories*. London: Faber and Faber, 2006.
D	*The Dark* (1965). London: Faber and Faber, 2008.
L 1974	*The Leavetaking*. London: Faber and Faber, 1974.
L 1984	*The Leavetaking*. Second edition, revised. London: Faber and Faber, 1984.
L	Because the texts and pagination of Part I of *The Leavetaking* are the same in both editions, all page references to Part I will be cited simply as (*L*).
M	*Memoir*. London: Faber and Faber, 2005.
P	*The Pornographer* (1979). London: Faber and Faber, 1990.
RS	*That They May Face the Rising Sun*. London: Faber and Faber, 2002.

CHAPTER ONE

John McGahern and the Art of Memory

The novelist Colm Tóibín, talking about the impact his father's death had on him when he was sixteen, said that writing was not a therapy that helped him 'to exorcize the demons within': 'It's almost the opposite ... [Writing is] the manipulation of hurt, the holding on to it. The things you could do with it now. And not letting it go because, God, what else is there? You almost solidify things by writing about it, rather than releasing.'[1] John McGahern was nine and a half years old when his mother died. The little boy was very close to her. Later, when he came to write about her in his fiction, he would describe her as his 'beloved' (*L*, 64), and at the end of his career, in a memoir, he would acknowledge her place at the heart of his whole imaginative life. For McGahern, however, that life was not so much a 'holding on to' the past as a struggling in its grip. McGahern's fiction is an art of memory and its greatest achievement is the liberation from the grief, guilt, and anger that entered his life with his mother's death. He wrote his way to that liberation by writing to understand his past and, ultimately, recover his 'lost beloved'.

Reading McGahern

Critical attention to John McGahern's fiction has focused primarily on its social realism. There has been excellent criticism dealing with McGahern's artistry and intellectual influences – most notably by Denis Sampson – but

[1]   Quoted in Michael Posner, 'Of Mothers and Sons and a father long gone', *Globe and Mail* (8 March 2007), R1.

his subject matter, prose style, and fictive world, even when they are seen to reveal the 'timeless' within a specifically Irish history, or to move 'From the Local to the Universal', as Eamon Maher's subtitle to his study of McGahern puts it, are nevertheless viewed in relation to a very specific social, cultural, and historical 'reality'. Thus, while Sampson has discussed the recurring 'archetypal patterns of experience ... centred in family life' in McGahern's fiction, most view McGahern as 'a social realist with a romantic bent' whose oeuvre composes 'the swansong of a disappearing civilisation ... the rural Ireland in which he grew up'.[2] If, as I believe, novels circulate within civil discourse as unique forms of knowledge providing 'special insight into the most important areas of social and cultural history',[3] such critical readings and judgments explain how – ever since the publication of *The Barracks* in 1963 – McGahern's novels and short stories have contributed so substantially to social discourse in Ireland.[4] However, it is not in that way nor in that context that I have read McGahern's novels in this study.

2   Denis Sampson, *Outstaring Nature's Eye: The Fiction of John McGahern* (Washington, DC: Catholic University Press, 1993), 31; Eamon Maher, *John McGahern: From the Local to the Universal* (Dublin: The Liffey Press, 2003), 99; see also Rianna O'Dwyer, 'Foreword', in James Whyte, *History, Myth, and Ritual in the Fiction of John McGahern: Strategies of Transcendence* (Lewiston, NY: Edwin Mellen Press, 2002), xi. For an overview of the critical tradition on McGahern's work, see David Malcolm, *Understanding John McGahern* (Columbia: University of South Carolina Press, 2007), 3–9. Patrick Crotty has argued that 'McGahern has never been in more than a very secondary sense a political writer .... His primary thematic interest is metaphysical'; that is, McGahern is 'concerned with the general conditions of being, with how life is lived and has to be lived' ('"All Toppers": Children in the Fiction of John McGahern', *Irish University Review* 35.1 [2005], 42).

3   Dominic Head, *The Cambridge Introduction to Modern British Fiction, 1950–2000* (Cambridge: Cambridge University Press, 2002), 1.

4   See, for example, Lori Rogers, *Feminine Nation: Performance, Gender and Resistance in the Works of John McGahern and Neil Jordan* (Lanham: University Press of North America, 1998), for discussion of McGahern's work in relation to women's issues during the period.

Eamon Grennan praises McGahern as 'the best cartographer of the physical and metaphysical landscape' of post-independence Ireland;[5] but if McGahern's body of fiction does compose – to echo another Irish 'cartographer' – a map of the conscience of his race, there is a map-within-the-map, hidden within its coded legend, that charts a private and singular terrain and records a personal journey through it. Without in any way challenging the social-realist dimension of McGahern's writing and its mimetic and moral significance within the larger, 'national' self-examination that has characterized much of Irish civil discourse over the last forty years, I want to argue that with his last work, *Memoir* (2005), McGahern himself invited a different if parallel view of his writing, a view, in particular, of the impetus behind the creative effort that shaped his story-making. A feature of the social-realist approach to McGahern's fiction is that its centrifugal perspective often looks out and away from the fiction to history, society, and some pre-existing discursive-ideological version of them. The fiction does engage these externals, of course, and McGahern as a result is undoubtedly a writer who changed the way his society saw itself, but a more centripetal criticism is needed to complement this socio-cultural approach by looking inwards to his works' internal and intertextual dynamics, and in particular, to how these may be interpreted in relation to the creative process, the narrative *poiēsis*, that produced the socio-historical reflection and discursive-ideological engagement so valued by the critics. To conclude from a reading of McGahern's work that the various father-figures in it, for example, represent 'the authority of the patriarchal society', while true in an abstract sense, is hardly helpful in this respect;[6] nor does it do full justice to the complexity of the characters or of the creative effort that produced them. More interesting is how McGahern's father-figures are all versions

---

5   Eamon Grennan, '"Only What Happens": Mulling Over McGahern', *Irish University Review* 35.1 (2005), 26.

6   Whyte, *History, Myth, and Ritual*, 143. The same can be said of Siobhán Holland's reading of McGahern's father-figures in relation to 'the tensions and instabilities that exist in an Irish patriarchal social matrix which is performatively constructed and vulnerable to resistance' ('Marvellous Fathers in the Fiction of John McGahern', *The Yearbook of English Studies* 35 [2005], 186–7).

of *his* father, Francis (Frank) McGahern; how the characters belong to a
continuous process in McGahern's writing that extends from *The Barracks*
to *Memoir* in which the son strives to come to terms with his anger and
hatred of the man who abused him as a child and adolescent, and who, just
the year before he died, McGahern said he believed he would have killed if
he had not left home when he did; and finally, it is more interesting to see
how, in each novel, there is a progress towards a final, triumphant exorcism
of that ghost in *Amongst Women* (1990) and *Memoir*.[7]

This is not to deny that 'McGahern's plotless novels and stories reveal
a lack of faith in the moral value of action, which can be related to the
disappearance of the clearly defined roles available in a traditional familist
society', nor that '[t]he pessimism of McGahern's fiction can be explained
as a sense of social and cultural isolation, a sense of not belonging to any
social world'.[8] But such readings are in danger of reducing a large and complex body of fiction to an allegorical monad, of connecting the work to a
version of the social-historical reality in which it was written, but in the
process disconnecting it from the creative life and *poiēsis* that produced it.[9]

---

7   McGahern makes the admission in Pat Collins' documentary, *John McGahern: A
     Private World* (RTE, Hummingbird/Harvest Films, 2005). For criticism that attends
     to the 'inner life' of McGahern's fiction earlier in his career, see Michael Foley 'The
     Novels of John McGahern', *The Honest Ulsterman* 5 (September 1968), 34–7; Richard
     Kearney, 'A Crisis of Imagination: An Analysis of a Counter-Tradition in the Irish
     Novel', *Crane Bag of Irish Studies*, ed. Mark Patrick Hederman and Richard Kearney
     (Dublin, Blackwater, 1982), 390–402; Karlheinz Schwartz, 'John McGahern's Point
     of View', *Éire-Ireland* 19.3 (1984), 92–110; and Denis Sampson, 'A Note on John
     McGahern', *Canadian Journal of Irish Studies* 2.2 (1976), 61–5, and *Outstaring Nature's
     Eye* (1993).
8   Whyte, *History, Myth, and Ritual*, 224, 21.
9   The contradiction between McGahern's lack of interest in plot and his belief that
     fiction should be 'life written to an order or vision' may derive from dialectically
     opposed aspects in his aesthetic and temperament: plot is inherently teleological, a
     chain of cause and effect planned or intuited to have intelligible meaning and felt
     significance, but this belies McGahern's sense of human experience as 'a series of acci-
     dents' without any clear point (see Rosa González, 'John McGahern' [Interview], in
     Jacqueline Hurtley et al., *Ireland in Writing[:] Interviews with Writers and Academics*
     [Amsterdam: Rodopoi, 1998], 45, 48). His 'weak' plots and indeterminate and circular

The passivity of McGahern's various protagonists might be better explored as a symptom of an inner condition, as complex gradations of an *acedia* whose causes are deep and whose effects are manifest, but whose causes are not primarily social even though the effects of the condition are evident in the protagonists' sexual and other relationships; instead of settling for the self-confirming circularity of pessimism induced by a sense of disconnection and disconnection brought on by a paralysing pessimism, or seeing his characters' flawed interiorities as a reflection of an external deficit, we might get closer to recognizing the real nature and magnitude of McGahern's creative achievement if we paid more attention to the inner voids in his characters, the missing 'centres' to their sense of selfhood. McGahern's fiction does present images of 'the Irish family' of the de Valera era as well as of post-revolutionary Irish *ressentiment*; it is true, as well, to say that he achieves a degree of the universal in these socio-historically specific images. But since the publication of *Memoir* it is very clear that the families in McGahern's fiction are all versions of *his* family, and the political and cultural disappointment and pessimism were his father's and his own, and it is McGahern's transformation of his own family particulars into a universal narrative art that merits attention. Ultimately, McGahern's achievement is paradoxical: the world of his novels remains far closer to that of a particular family than it does to any type of family, and yet it seems to mirror many. His families are so *real* because of the depth, intensity, and complexity of the emotions that inform his construction of them.

Critics have long noticed the repetitions of character, setting, circumstances and mood in McGahern's novels and short stories, and most have recognized that 'His books should be seen as part of a work in progress' because 'the same themes and settings recur but are dealt with in a different and a progressively more effective way'.[10] What *Memoir* helps us to see is

---

endings, therefore, are actually mimetic-expressive of a 'vision' of human experience that regards it as immanently significant if transcendentally blank. This is one way of interpreting the 'idea' to which he makes his re-invention and re-imagining of 'the ordinary [and] the boring' in human experience 'conform' (González, 'John McGahern', 45).

10   Maher, *John McGahern*, 3.

that the 'progressively more effective way' McGahern found to shape his
fictive world and articulate his core concerns was not exclusively artistic
nor even a completely conscious development, but a style and form that
developed in relation to a slowly evolving process of self-liberation from
the grief, guilt and anger that haunted him from childhood. 'What a man
essentially is', Northrop Frye wrote, 'is revealed in two ways: by the record
of what he has done, and by what he is trying to make of himself at any
given moment'; and '[i]t is the function of literature ... not to run away
from the actual, but to see the dimension of the possible in the actual'.[11]
McGahern's total body of fiction represents what he achieved as a writer,
but each novel represents what he was trying to make of himself at that
given moment in his life. In each case, the story-making involved his taking
what had happened to him and making something out of it, extracting the
possible from the actual. McGahern himself said that what he was trying to
reach through the process of writing was the joy and liberation that come
with understanding one's experience, *his* particular life.[12] Understanding,
it seems, was a kind of redemption for McGahern. For Frye, 'myth *redeems*
history: assigns it to its real place in the human panorama',[13] and McGahern's total body of work, when viewed as a single, continuous, imaginative
'project', possesses a mythopoeic quality. From *The Barracks* to *Memoir* the
poiēsis that shaped the fiction was shaping an understanding of the life that
would ultimately redeem the facts of that life by assigning them their 'real
place' in a vision, image, idea – or myth – of loss and recovery.[14]

McGahern said he wrote his memoir 'quickly' after finishing *That They
May Face the Rising Sun* (2002), motivated in part by 'the persistence of

11   Northrop Frye, *The Great Code: The Bible and Literature* (New York: Harcourt Brace
      Jovanovich, 1982), 49.
12   See Sean O'Hagan, 'A family touched with madness', *The Observer* (28 August
      2005), 16 June 2010, <http://www.guardian.co.uk/books/2005/aug/28/fiction.
      features3>.
13   Frye, *The Great Code*, 51.
14   Grennan recognizes 'a redemptive energy in the narrative itself' in McGahern's fic-
      tion; see '"Only What Happens,"' 19.

certain images',[15] and he obviously harvested his novels for much of the memoir's language of memory. Perhaps he did want us to see the memoir not as 'a historically accurate narrative but [as] a constructed one: a work of art, a fiction, even',[16] but to read the fiction and memoir together is to recognize not only the autobiographical sources of the novels and short stories but also, more significantly, the Orphic nature of McGahern's narrative poetics. *Memoir* casts an autobiographical light on 'The Image', the artistic credo McGahern first articulated in 1968, revised in 1991, and was still reiterating at the end of his life.[17] From tortured beginning to triumphant end, McGahern's career as a writer was a continuous quest to recover what, in 1968, he called 'the lost image', and in 1984, the 'lost world', but which are one and the same – the memory of the 'lost beloved'.[18] McGahern's recycling of passages from his fiction for his memoir suggests that years later they continued to carry a burden of meaning and importance for him – the truth he sought in understanding.

Denis Sampson argues that McGahern's 'goal as an artist' was not '"self-expression" or "imitation" but a constant effort to move from the lyrical to the epic and dramatic genres that the young Joyce argued were representative of the ideal progress of the artist'.[19] Self-expression *was* the core of McGahern's writing process, however, though as core, it was not evident from the surface of the finished artefact. McGahern told another

---

15   Collins, *John McGahern: A Private World*.

16   Stanley van der Ziel, '*Memoir*, by John McGahern', *Irish University Review* 35.2 (2005), 464.

17   See McGahern, 'The Image (Prologue to a Reading at the Rockefeller University)', *The Honest Ulsterman* 8 (December 1968), 10; 'The Image', *Canadian Journal of Irish Studies* 17 (1991), 12; see Maher, *John McGahern*, 152, and Whyte, *History, Myth, and Ritual*, 229, 231.

18   McGahern, 'The Image' (1968), 10; Eileen Kennedy, 'Q. & A. with John McGahern', in *Writing Irish: Selected Interviews with Irish Writers from the Irish Literary Supplement*, ed. James P. Myers (Syracuse: Syracuse University Press, 1999), 40. The 'lost image' and the 'lost world' are brought together in McGahern's revision of his credo in 'The Image' (1991), 12.

19   *Outstaring Nature's Eye*, 243.

interviewer, 'the writing comes out of oneself and not out of the place'.[20] If there is an epic quality to McGahern's oeuvre, and I believe there is, it is Dantescan: it is an oeuvre that performs a life-long quest to re-unite with a 'lost beloved'. The novels and memoir compose and express an Orphic imagination's purgatorial descent into memory, its hellish nadir, and its gradual ascent to paradisal vision. This is not to suggest any rigid Dantescan schema, but only that the writing process itself enacts a quest whose structure parallels Dante's paradigm. McGahern's first four novels – *The Barracks, The Dark* (1965), *The Leavetaking* (1974; rev. 1984), *The Pornographer* (1979) – alternate and vary in their 'infernal' and 'purgatorial' scenes and experiences; with *Amongst Women*, however, a breakthrough occurs with the 'Death of the Father', a death that closes the long and increasingly dark journey that began with the 'Death of the Mother' in *The Barracks*. But while McGahern's writing career is framed by these deaths, the second, the death of the father, is revealed to be the necessary condition for the resurrection of the mother. At the end of the memoir, when the reader comes to McGahern's remarks on his father's death, there is an almost palpable sense of release (*M*, 270–1), which may explain why *That They May Face the Rising Sun*, for all its use of setting and attention to natural detail, is tonally unlike anything McGahern had written before. McGahern's last novel *is* his paradisal vision. Characteristically earthly, earthy, human and humane, it is a vision inspirited and empowered by the Beatricean vision he describes in the closing paragraphs of *Memoir*. The Beatrice-like nature and function of the mother-image in the memoir are suggested by McGahern's description of the mother/son dream-image: 'When she died, I'd include her in all the Masses that I'd say until we were united in the joy of heaven, when time would cease as we were gathered into the mind of God' (*M*, 63). In terms of the mythopoeic structure of McGahern's total body of work, *That They May Face the Rising Sun* is the promised Mass he never said for his mother; it is a work that brings the rituals of confession, atonement, purification, and communion intrinsic in his fiction to a transcendent closure.

---

20   González, 'John McGahern', 41.

What dramatic energy is found in McGahern's writing is expressive of the inner tensions deriving from his sense of the story-making process as the shaping of personal experience into coherent narrative order. On more than one occasion McGahern asserted that 'it's been my experience that I've made my worst artistic mistakes by keeping too close to what happened'; life experience 'needs to be re-ordered. Reinvented in order to be true'.[21] *Memoir* reveals just how much McGahern's fiction is the story of his own life and how in novel after novel, story after story, he was shaping and re-shaping into narrative art the experiences that had moulded him. For Frye, the truth of a myth is inside its structure, not outside in the world. It may seem perverse to discuss John McGahern, the poster-boy for mid-twentieth-century Irish realism, in terms of myth, but the metaphor is heuristically useful in his case. Some may feel McGahern's novels lack plots, but in an Aristotelian sense, each is 'a complete action', a coherent process of becoming; and as a kind of *roman fleuve*, McGahern's total body of fiction does have a plot, a mythic plot whose total structure is as archetypal as the voyage of the sun, with a movement from darkness to light, solitude to community, grief to celebration, anger to forgiveness – a mythopoeia whose armature is the *poiēsis* of memory.

McGahern's narrator-protagonist in *The Pornographer* frustrated John Updike: 'We feel impatience with the hero and a frustrated suspicion that the real story occurred elsewhere'.[22] Whatever one chooses to call the 'real story' in a McGahern novel, be it the writer's life-experience, the narrative fiction drawn from that experience, or the process of transformation whereby the life-experience becomes a story, re-reading McGahern's body of fiction after reading his memoir, one finds a 'real presence' in the process of McGahern's narration itself, in what, very early in his career, he described as the quest for 'the lost image': 'the vision ... struggles towards the single image, the image on which our whole life took its most complete

---

21   Maher, *John McGahern*, 147. McGahern repeats the point about reinvention in the Preface to his last collection of short stories, *Creatures of the Earth*; see *CE*, vii.

22   Updike, *Hugging the Shore: Essays and Criticism* (New York: Knopf, 1983), 393; qtd. in Sampson, *Outstaring Nature's Eye*, 137.

expression once, in a kind of grave, grave of the images of dead passions
and their days …. Image after image flows involuntary now, and still we are
not at peace … straining towards the one image that will never come, the
lost image'.[23] *Memoir* makes clear that 'the lost image', like 'the lost world',
is the mother-image, the mother-world, and that the 'grave of the images
of dead passions and their days' where McGahern sought them is memory
and the unconscious, the personal labyrinth that he entered through the
portal of writing and traversed through the art of fiction. In the visionary
conclusion to *Memoir*, McGahern affirmed his mother's abiding presence
throughout his journey: 'I know that consciously and unconsciously she
has been with me all my life' (*M*, 272). In 'The Wine Breath', a story from
the appropriately titled 1978 collection, *Getting Through*, the protagonist,
a priest, realizes that his mother has been 'the mainspring' of his life and
that, since her death, 'it was as if the world of the dead was as available to
him as the world of the living' (*CE*, 112). The 'mainspring' of McGahern's
impulse to narrative is his memory of his mother's love, the torment of his
flawed farewell to her, the guilt of his broken promise to her, the anger at
the abandonment that her death seemed, and the horrors it condemned
him to suffer at his father's hands.[24]

McGahern's fiction transits the worlds of the living and the dead with
hermetic ease. As we know from Homer, the shades demand their cup of
blood before they will help the quester to advance on his way. McGahern's
poiēsis is very much a process of homage and descent, memory and interrogation. His admission in 1968 that 'still we are not at peace' is telling. It
would take McGahern over thirty years to find the way out of the labyrinth to the peace he sought. Patrick Crotty has observed that 'McGahern
emerges from the full range of his fiction as a writer powerfully engaged

23   McGahern, 'The Image' (1968), 10.
24   It is interesting to consider the way the mother-memory-'mainspring' connection
       might *inform* the metafictive image of 'setting' the clocks right at the end of *That
       They May Face the Rising Sun*. In a wonderful phrase that surely applies to McGahern
       himself, Sampson says the priest in 'The Wine Breath' 'becomes the artist of his
       own recovered self'; see Sampson, 'The Lost Image: Some Notes on McGahern and
       Proust', *Canadian Journal of Irish Studies* 17.1 (1991), 60.

with process, with the cyclical rhythms of birth, growth, copulation, and death, and with the sometimes fierce clashes of will that serve the instincts for sex and survival'.[25] But the 'process' that McGahern's fiction most engages and which informs and inflects 'the full range' of his fictive enterprise is the transformation of memory, grief, guilt, and anger; the trauma of loss; and the psychic toxins of *acedia*, doubt and despair.

Complicated Grief, Narrative *Poiēsis*, and McGahern's Art of Memory

Historically, the 'Art of Memory' refers to the 'method of *loci*' technique for memorizing a large body of material that was taught to would-be orators in the schools of classical rhetoric. The *loci* were actual locations in a building familiar to the student who was taught to 'place' the subject-parts of the speech in those locations so that the order of delivery would correspond to the order of a visualized walk-through of the building: as the speaker 'saw' each room in their mind, they would recall the idea or subject in the speech they had 'placed' there.[26] In the medieval curriculum, *Ars Memoriae* was included in dialectics as well as rhetoric. The phrase and the allusion it contains are appropriate for a discussion of McGahern's fiction because of the nature and subject of McGahern's creative activity, a 'speaking' that summons something housed in memory in order to re-place it in a house of fiction. McGahern's novels all have locations that are cognate with significant experiences in his own life: from the deathroom in the farmhouse in Aughawillan to the various rooms in the barracks (but especially his father's room), to the Dublin dancehalls, London pubs, and schoolyard in Clontarf, and eventually the lanes, fields and lakes of his beloved Leitrim.

25 "All Toppers,'" 43.
26 The classical study of the subject is Frances A. Yates's *The Art of Memory* (London: Routledge and Kegan Paul, 1966).

A parallel mnemonic system, the medieval *Ars Notoria*, coincidentally used an 'image' or other 'sign' as the key to memory, a practice not unlike the *poiēsis* McGahern outlines in 'The Image'.[27] I use 'the art of memory' to refer to the *conscious* dimension of the creative effort that works memory into narrative fiction and memoir; but in as much as that 're-collecting' shapes the images of memory and imagination into the order of art, it is itself shaped by unconscious imperatives and involuntary needs that, if it resisted, would compromise the truth of that art.

What I mean by *poiēsis* in this study is a particular grafting of meanings derived from Plato, Aristotle, and Heidegger. To Aristotle's sense of *poiēsis* as 'the process of making an artefact', I want to add that which Diotima describes in the *Symposium* as an action motivated by the desire to transcend the earthly round of birth and decay.[28] Both senses cohere in McGahern's narrative invention as the art of memory, an art that constantly laments the fatal even as it affirms the continuity of the human as the source of all value. Heidegger, drawing from Plato's discussion in the *Symposium*, picks up the notion of *poiēsis* as '*presencing*' and describes it as a 'bringing-forth': 'Through bringing-forth the growing things of nature as well as whatever is completed through the crafts and the arts come at any given time to their appearance'.[29] The Heideggerian sense of *poiēsis* is particularly helpful for understanding McGahern's search for the 'lost image' if we understand its location to be within himself, within his own condition of 'being-in-the-world'. 'Bringing-forth comes to pass only insofar as something concealed comes into unconcealment':[30] we should understand McGahern's

27 For a discussion of the *Ars Notoria*, see Mary J. Carruthers, *The Book of Memory: A Study of Memory in Medieval Culture* (Cambridge: Cambridge University Press, 1990).

28 George Whalley, *Aristotle's Poetics*, trans. and with a commentary by George Whalley; ed. John Baxter and Patrick Atherton (Montreal: McGill-Queen's University Press, 1997), 15–16; Plato, 'Symposium', in *The Great Dialogues of Plato*, trans. W. H. D. Rouse; ed. Eric H. Warmington and Philip G. Rouse (New York: New American Library, 1956), 99–104.

29 Heidegger, 'The Question Concerning Technology', in *Basic Writings*, ed. David Farrell Krell (New York: Harper & Row, 1977), 293.

30 Ibid.

art of memory as a process of unconcealment. For Heidegger, in artistic making the artist crosses over a threshold, moves from 'standing-within-oneself' to a condition 'outside-of-itself'. McGahern's admission to Denis Sampson that all his life he had been obsessed by the question of the Self and Other can be understood in this sense of the making of fiction as an 'ecstatic' project, a striving for a self-liberation that would place him outside the self that, paradoxically, is the matter of his art. It is possible to see the ultimate achievement of his art to be precisely that, the hollowing out of the self, the unconcealing that produces the 'ecstasis' of *That They May Face the Rising Sun*, the closest McGahern ever came to his Flaubertian ideal of being everywhere present in the work but invisible, like God in nature.[31] McGahern's version of this is his evolution from self-expression to self-projection.

The role of grief in McGahern's creative process, however, suggests that we might understand its 'presencing', 'bringing-forth', or 'unconcealment' in relation to the concept of 'encryptment' theorized by Nicolas Abraham and Maria Torok in their neo-Freudian revision of 'Mourning and Melancholia'.[32] In Freud's theory, the libido of the grieving individual, suddenly disconnected from its 'object', the loved one, withdraws into the ego and 'incorporates' the 'object-loss' as a psychic entity, in the process splitting the ego.[33] Normal grieving eventually leads to the expulsion of the incorporated object, and this frees up the survivor's libidinal energy to attach itself to a new 'love-object' in order to form a relationship with a new

31 Denis Sampson, 'A Conversation with John McGahern', *Canadian Journal of Irish Studies* 17.1 (1991), 15. McGahern told Maher that what he most admired about the American novelist, John Williams, was his 'method': 'His method is to go as far as possible from the self towards the other, and then find his way back through the self' (Maher, *John McGahern*, 147).

32 These ideas are not new to Irish studies. Maud Ellmann has used them to impressive effect in *Elizabeth Bowen: The Shadow Across the Page* (Edinburgh: Edinburgh University Press, 2003) and Linden Peach uses them in *The Contemporary Irish Novel: Critical Readings* (New York: Palgrave Macmillan, 2004). I am indebted to both critics' examples.

33 See Freud, 'Mourning and Melancholia', in *The Freud Reader*, ed. Peter Gay (New York: W. W. Norton, 1989), 586.

beloved. When this expulsion does not occur, mourning becomes melancholia and that which was incorporated by the ego 'turns' and incorporates it. Maud Ellmann's vivid example of this process is the pathology presented in Hitchcock's *Psycho*, 'in which the murderer's personality is taken over by the mother whose death he has denied'.[34] Abraham and Torok's version of Freud's libidinal 'incorporation' is that the process hollows out a 'crypt' within the ego in which the 'lost object' is buried alive. This encryptment within the ego of the object of its loss is what produces the 'haunting' of grief. Abraham and Torok call the encrypted figure the 'phantom': 'The phantom's periodic and compulsive return ... works like a ventriloquist ... within the subject's own mental topography'.[35] A healthy resolution of grief involves an opening of the crypt and the release of its secrets: when the lost object is recovered, it can be laid to rest. When grief is successfully worked through, incorporation is avoided and 'introjection' occurs; where incorporation leads to 'muteness', in introjection 'the ego articulates its loss in language, creating a verbal substitute for the lost object'.[36] In 'The Image', when McGahern theorizes his *poiēsis* as the search for the 'lost image', he is articulating an intuited need to move from incorporation to introjection in his life and writing. But what is significant is that he also admits a failure to achieve it – 'Image after image flows involuntarily now, and still we are not at peace'; moreover, as late as the 1991 version of the credo he allowed the admission of failure to stand. McGahern's 'lost beloved' is the 'phantom' encrypted within his fiction that his re-creation of the past as fiction ultimately confronts and liberates. The usefulness of this theory for reading McGahern comes from the verbal dimension of encryptment, which

---

34   Ellmann, *Elizabeth Bowen*, 121.
35   Nicolas Abraham and Maria Torok, *The Shell and the Kernel: Renewals of Psychoanalysis*, edited, translated, and with an introduction by Nicholas T. Rand (Chicago: University of Chicago Press, 1994), 171, 173; qtd. in Ellmann, *Elizabeth Bowen*, 121. We should remember this when we come to the uncanny passage in McGahern's last novel where McGahern's mother suddenly 'speaks through' the narrative voice – or Joe Ruttledge's, it is not clear which (see *RS*, 238).
36   Ellmann, *Elizabeth Bowen*, 198–9; see Abraham and Torok, *The Shell and the Kernel*, 128–9.

creates words to hide other words – 'broken symbols', which are symbols detached from their meanings.[37] We might think of encryptment and its broken symbol as what McGahern had to overcome if he was to achieve the 'understanding' that he believed came from 'getting the words right' and which he claimed to be the reason he wrote; 'I write to see. And the seeing is through language', he told James Whyte.[38]

Reading McGahern's fiction along with his memoir confirms the critical intuition that the long process of unconcealment that McGahern concluded with *Memoir* may have had something to do with the lingering effects of a pathologically severe grief. Complicated Grief (or complicated mourning) is the clinical term for 'normal' grief that worsens and extends over a long period; instead of achieving a natural resolution over time, the survivor's grief remains unresolved. The condition may continue for years.[39] Some of the symptoms of Complicated Grief that are reflected in McGahern's characterization of his protagonists and narrators are low self-esteem, the preoccupation with their own sadness, the loss of the ability to enjoy life, and the feeling that life holds no meaning or purpose.[40] The struggle with grief can be exacerbated by the kind of death or by the circumstances

37   See Nicholas Rand, 'Translator's Introduction : Toward a Cryptonomy of Literature', in Nicolas Abraham and Maria Torok, *The Wolf Man's Magic Word: A Cryptonomy*, trans. Nicholas Rand, with a Foreword by Jacques Derrida (Minneapolis: University of Minnesota Press, 1986), lviii–lix.

38   *History, Myth, and Ritual*, 13; see also Sampson, 'A Note on John McGahern', 62; Kennedy, 'Q. & A.', 40; O'Hagan, 'A family touched with madness'; Maher, *John McGahern*, 144, 145; *M*, 36, 203.

39   Psychiatrists and grief counsellors commonly approach the condition through the framework of John Bowlby's 'attachment theory'. See Bowlby, *Attachment and Loss* (New York: Basic Books, 1969); also J. Holmes, *John Bowlby and Attachment Theory* (London: Routledge, 1993).

40   'Emotional relocation requires that the bereaved form an ongoing relationship with the memories associated with the deceased, in such a way that they are able to continue with their own lives after the loss. Holding on to the past attachment rather than allowing the evolution of a new relationship with the memories of the deceased can hinder this task' (Jacques Duff, 'Grief and the Grieving Process', *Behavioural Neurotherapy Clinic*, 2005, 16 June 2010, <http://www.adhd.com.au/grief.htm>). Both Patrick Moran's and the pornographer's problems forming relationships that are

surrounding it. In McGahern's case, his sense of his 'failure' at the moment of farewell with his mother on her deathbed and the traumatically sudden and 'forced' removal from her and his home to his father's barracks before she died, compounded by his father's forbidding him to attend the funeral and burial, would have been sufficient to condemn any sensitive nine-year-old to a difficult grieving process. In his memoir, McGahern recounts how, before his mother's final illness, his father had tried to 'seduce' him into leaving her and his sisters and coming to live with him in the barracks at Cootehall. In the Collins documentary, he says he now understood this as his father trying 'to break up the bond' between him and his mother. If that feeling was present but unconscious in the child at the time of his removal from her presence at his father's orders, his father's further order that he not attend the funeral and burial could have solidified that feeling into a source of deep resentment.

Lack of closure not only complicates grief but, in a child's case, may extend it into adolescence; as an adolescent, he may consider that things will not get any better.[41] What McGahern describes as his experience as a child and adolescent in his father's house following his mother's death suggests an optimistic outlook would have been very difficult, to say the least. Moreover, in McGahern's case, the effects of the child's absence from the traditional rituals of closure at his mother's death may have been further complicated and intensified by the adolescent's decision to break his promise to her about becoming a priest. There is also something deeply suggestive about the congruence of this lack of closure in the boy's life, and his response to it, as recounted in *The Leavetaking* and *Memoir*; first, the child's imagining of the death, coffining, removal, funeral Mass, and interment; and then, the adult writer's formulation of an aesthetic based on the quest for the 'lost image'. A characteristic of complicated mourning is 'a prolonged yearning or searching for the deceased and a sense of rupture

---

free of the shadow of the dead mother-beloved suggest a failure of what the jargon terms 'emotional relocation'.

41   See V. E. Kandt, 'Adolescent Bereavement: Turning a Fragile Time into Acceptance and Peace', *The School Counsellor* 41 (1994), 203–11.

in personal beliefs'.[42] McGahern's search for the 'lost image', 'lost world', and 'lost beloved' may spring from this nexus of separation and disappearance: somewhere, she is still alive.[43] But I want to be clear: I am a literary critic and not a psychiatrist and I am in no way 'diagnosing' McGahern. Rather, what I am doing is proposing a paradigm which I believe is appropriate and helpful when considering those features of McGahern's life and writing which he himself clearly makes congruent. It is surely significant that all his novels look back; none is set in the exact period it is written. If McGahern suffered from Complicated Grief, I am not suggesting the condition continued for thirty-five years until the writing of *The Pornographer*, which I read as signalling an emergence from the shadow-world of the mother in his fiction. But I would suggest that in his art of memory he was at the very least working through his memories of years of lingering grief, guilt, and anger.

Reading the Novels

McGahern did not have to search for his subject matter as a novelist; as soon as he started writing, it found him. Episodes from the first novel he attempted, 'The End or the Beginning of Love', published in *X: A Literary*

---

42 Karen Kersting, 'A New Approach to Complicated Grief', *Monitor on Psychology* 35.10 (2004), 51.

43 'Disbelief is often the initial cognitive reaction to the news of a death, especially if the death was sudden. Although this response is usually transitory, it can persist and become denial, where the bereaved does not accept the death. Other cognitive responses include feelings of confusion, difficulty organising thoughts and preoccupation with the deceased, which may evoke intrusive thoughts of how the deceased died' (Duff, 'Grief and the Grieving Process'); see also J. W. Worden, *Grief Counselling and Grief Therapy: A Handbook for the Mental Health Practitioner*, 2nd ed. (London: Springer, 1991).

Magazine in 1961, became the basis of *The Dark*.[44] He told Shirley Kelly, at the end of his career, 'most writers don't choose their themes at all, the theme chooses them. That's certainly the case with my writing'.[45] *The Barracks* initiates the encryptment of the dead mother within the 'body' of McGahern's fiction and begins a process that will not be completed until *Memoir*. *The Barracks* is McGahern's Avernus, the portal-work that opens the way forward which, paradoxically, will always require his going back and down, deeper and deeper. In it, McGahern summons the shade of his mother, while at the same time strenuously disciplining the presence of the father, in order to engage, through the character of Elizabeth Reegan, in an extended imagining of a spirit and intelligence under assault. In Elizabeth's cancer McGahern encrypts the fatal 'wound' – 'the shame of intimacy' (*B*, 18) – that her choice of husband has made upon her. The recurring concern with time and eternity in McGahern's fiction that begins in Elizabeth Reegan's ruminations and continues through Michael Moran's epiphanic dumbfounding in *Amongst Women* to conclude in the mandala-like form of *That They May Face the Rising Sun* signals the preoccupation with death and loss, memory, and grief that centres his art of memory.

The Dark is a novel written in the 'Name of the Father'. The protagonist-son remains nameless in his own right throughout the story. McGahern's most explicitly confessional novel, its Augustinian braiding of the three persons of narrative voice into the trinity of sinner, confessor, and absolvent author also marks it as his most carefully engineered work. The enigma of McGahern's 'three-personed' narrator in this novel is a metaphor of the fragmented self that the narrative process struggles to suture, a dark allegory of the lowest circle in his personal hell. It is here that he confronts the man-monster at the centre of the labyrinth of memory, as well as its infernal consort, the shade of the broken promise to the dead mother. The world of *The Dark* is a world without joy or any hope of joy. The acedia

44   See McGahern, 'The End or the Beginning of Love: Episodes from a Novel', in *An Anthology from X: A Quarterly Review of Literature and the Arts, 1959–62*, ed. Patrick Swift and David Wright (Oxford: Oxford University Press, 1988), 153–63; also Malcolm, *Understanding John McGahern*, 29.
45   Kelly, 'The writing keeps the cattle in high style', *Books Ireland* (February 2002), 5.

that characterizes the protagonists in McGahern's later novels first presents itself here in the young Mahoney's melancholic resignation at the end of the novel, a resignation born out of the exhaustion of spirit and emotion that living in the shadow-world of the father has exacted. The philosopher Paul Ricoeur describes the *acedia* behind melancholy as a 'complaisance towards sadness' and suggests that the object of that complacency is actually 'the sadness of meditative memory', or more particularly, the debilitating effect of focussing on the relentless passing of time.[46] This debilitating consciousness of time recurs throughout McGahern's fiction in the motif of his protagonists musing on the absurdity of their circumstances and the pointlessness of acting in one way or another, an *acedia* McGahern expresses most poignantly in Michael Moran's bitterly rhetorical refrain, 'Who cares? Who cares anyhow?' in *Amongst Women*, but which he begins to explore with Elizabeth Reegan and the young Mahoney.

With the two versions of *The Leavetaking* and with *The Pornographer* McGahern made his 'turn' toward his great work of truth and reconciliation, and his first masterpiece, *Amongst Women*. What freed him to make his peace with the ghost of the father in that novel was the difficult resolution of his grief that he had worked out in the two novels that preceded it. Like a medieval diptych of the Virgin, *The Leavetaking* and *The Pornographer* compose McGahern's icon of the 'lost beloved'. The experience of loss that he theorizes in 'The Image' is encrypted in the multiple forms of leave-taking in the first (Patrick Moran's from his dying mother, from his career as a teacher, and from his motherland; also Isobel's from her father); in the second, pornography itself may be the most complex 'cryptonym' in all of McGahern's fiction, concealing not only the unresolved Oedipal love that haunts the pornographer's sexual predation and his relationship with the pregnant Josephine, but at the same time, as a metafictive metaphor, ironically drawing attention to the writing project itself. McGahern actually glimpses a version of what he seeks in this book's conclusion, where the aunt's funeral is a masked recovery of what the young Patrick – like the

---

46   Paul Ricoeur, *Memory, History, Forgetting*, trans. Kathleen Blamey and David Pellauer (Chicago: University of Chicago Press, 2004), 76.

young McGahern – was forbidden to attend. Both *The Leavetaking* and *The Pornographer*, however, end with weak images of recovery. Isobel and Nurse Brady, the new 'objects' of the protagonist-narrators' love, which has finally been freed from its entombment in the shadow-world of the mother, are unconvincing replacements. Brady pales, for example, against the full-blooded presence of the dying Aunt Mary, and Isobel, worried that Patrick will feel tied down by her, fails to intuit that he needs her to be the wings that will carry him, Dedalus-like, up and out of the island that has held him in thrall. These 'images' were sufficient enough, however, to free McGahern from the guilt of the broken promise, which then allowed him to turn back to the unfinished business of *The Dark* – and to finish it once and for all.

Amongst Women is McGahern's most critically acclaimed novel. The portrait of Michael Moran, his family, and their life at Great Meadow has achieved iconic status and is the favourite of those critics who value McGahern's art as a national allegory of the homogenous and unified society and culture they imagine 'de Valera's Ireland' to have been. If, as Ricoeur argues, 'It is the bipolar constitution of personal and community identity that, ultimately, justifies extending the Freudian analysis of mourning to the traumatism of collective identity', then reading *Amongst Women* as a national allegory is a consequence of the parallelism between personal and collective experience encountered in McGahern's fiction.[47] This leads to the question, if mourning can become melancholia for an individual, can a society/culture collectively fail to *work through* its grief and lapse into melancholia? However, not to deny McGahern's mimetic reflection of a larger, public, and collective world in *Amongst Women*, the 'sick historical memory'[48] that I find being healed most by McGahern's art of memory in

47   *Memory, History, Forgetting*, 78. Ricoeur continues, in language that is remarkably coincident with McGahern's themes of the 'lost beloved' and 'lost world': 'We can speak not only in an analogical sense but in terms of a direct analysis of collective traumatisms, of wounds to collective memory. The notion of the lost object finds a direct application in the "losses" that affect the power, territory, and populations that constitute the substance of a state'.

48   Ibid., 79.

this novel is personal and particular. More than once McGahern expressed his view that 'The novel ... is the most social of all art forms, as it is the most allied to the idea of manners and an idea of society' but that in Ireland 'There is no system of manners' and the family is 'a sort of interesting half-way house between the individual on one side and a larger society on the other hand, and one is not alone, and one is in a society but it's not a true society, since certain things will be tolerated within a family that won't be tolerated in a larger society'.[49] Instead of following these ideas in the direction of a national allegory, I tend to see a very specific family and a very specific 'lack of manners' behind them. The father-figures in McGahern's fiction, but especially Mahoney in *The Dark* and Moran in *Amongst Women*, represent an anti-social force, an uncivilized, unmannered, uncivil, and un-civilizing energy in dialectical conflict with the maternal-feminine. Hence the irony of Moran's situation: he does not feel himself 'blessed' to be 'amongst women', but 'cursed'. The death and absence of the mother in McGahern's novels results in the steady regression of the family as social microcosm to barbarism. The sons are Promethean rebels who must steal the fire of passion to make civilization elsewhere, to bring about a new world.

The end of history that *Amongst Women* records is the end of 'Father History' in McGahern's writing. And while there continue to be father-figures and significant history in *Memoir* and the final novel, the memoir is an illuminated capital, a mythopoeic reprise of the life-story told through the fiction, and *That They May Face the Rising Sun* is a work of transcendent memory. But while critical attention and praise have focused on the figure of Michael Moran, the epitome of the *acedia* that runs through McGahern's fiction, it is really the narrative voice that is McGahern's greatest achievement in *Amongst Women*. Its subtle, measured, eloquent and gracious balancing of understanding and judgment signifies the successful transition from incorporation to introjection in McGahern's reinventive remembering. The death of Moran finally lays to rest the ghost of the father in his writing. If grief and guilt inform the *poiēsis* of *The Leavetaking* and

---

49   Maher, *John McGahern*, 144; see also González, 'John McGahern', 42.

The Pornographer, it is anger and the desire for justice, hold-overs from the unfinished excoriation of *The Dark*, that return in *Amongst Women* to be refined, concentrated, and released into the grace of understanding. 'I hold no grudge. ... But I have a good memory', Luke tells his sister when she criticizes him for never visiting Great Meadow (*AW*, 143), and Luke, who is the narrator's 'alter ego' as well as the sublimated presence of McGahern in the novel, sums up in this statement the *terminus ad quem* of this subject in McGahern's writing. The beast is dead and buried at last.

In *That They May Face the Rising Sun*, McGahern-Theseus has put the labyrinth behind him and rejoined his beloved; McGahern-Orpheus has returned to a world of light in which the 'lost beloved' has been recovered *in* the light itself; and the Dantescan vision of a paradisal mountain is brought down to earth in the vision of a lake and shore, a town beyond, and on the horizon, the mountain home of the beloved. In *The Pornographer*, McGahern wrote, 'We master the darkness with ceremonies: of delight at being taken from the darkness into this light, of regret on the inevitable leaving of the light, hope as founded on the social and as firm as the theological rock' (*P*, 238). In these terms, McGahern's last novel is a 'ceremonial' work, a shepherd's calendar and book of common prayer, a paean to the love of place and the solace to identity that love of place can give the individual. In time it may come to be considered McGahern's second, if not even greater, masterpiece: for its dappled skies of light and shadow, and the mystery of the life beneath the surface of the lake; for the 'heron-priested' island at its centre, and for the spirits and humours of the centaurs, wise men, angels and fools that process round its shores. 'Sergeant Death' and his unfinished shed in Co. Leitrim have been placed where they are, adjacent to the house that fiction built with the art of memory on the rock of the social, because without their proximity that house would not be a true-built habitation and tabernacle of the 'Image'.

The enigma of memory is that it acknowledges loss even as it wins from it, as presence, what it knows will return as absence. Grief's poison and its antidote, memory is the *pharmakon*, the 'mystery' at the heart of McGahern's narrative art. The loss and recovery of the experience of 'presence' is at the centre of his fiction, and it is this 're-*presencing*' that is at the heart of his art of memory. The recovery of the past that McGahern sought occurred, ultimately, as the 'return' of the lost in the sense of the dividend that loss pays and that memory 'redeems'. *Memoir* should be read as a coda to his fiction. He says he wrote it 'to show how the journey out of that landscape became the return to those lanes and small fields and hedges and lakes under the Iron Mountains' (*M*, 260–1). The circular form so characteristic of his novels is a kind of 'body language', a 'homing instinct' that set his imaginative compass from the very beginning. On the surface, the journey his fiction charts is the socio-historical witnessing that many consider his pre-eminent achievement. But that map also 'covers' a different journey, a mission whose enterprise and ending do not become clear until his last two books: if the first, realistic map gives shape to the history McGahern lived through, the second reveals the contours of the myth – Orphic, Thesean, Dantescan – that he shaped out of that life. As coda, *Memoir* contains the code to the legend that McGahern affixed to his map of fiction. The point of identifying the autobiographical elements in McGahern's fiction is to understand better McGahern's creative process and the nature of his profoundly courageous personal achievement.

CHAPTER TWO

Orpheus Triumphant – Recovering the Lost Beloved: *Memoir* (2005)

For all McGahern's achievements and acclaim as a writer in the tradition of Irish realism, his memoir is an archetypal descent into memory that ultimately coheres as myth. The figure of the tyrannical, violent, narcissistic father emerges as the monster lurking at the heart of the maze who holds the family in thrall, while that of the dead mother, the 'beloved' whom the child in the man will mourn for the rest of his life, is a companion-spirit whose love is the thread that memory follows back to the light, to emerge triumphant and whole, but not before recounting a life spent entangled in the shadows of grief, guilt, and anger. As Gerald Mangan notes, McGahern's memoir 'discloses the well-springs of his fiction.'[1] Before its publication, what was generally known about McGahern's life was that he was born in 1934 and grew up with a number of younger sisters and brother in Leitrim and Roscommon; his father was a Garda sergeant and his mother a schoolteacher who died of cancer when McGahern was nine. It was known as well that before turning to writing full-time, McGahern had taught in a primary school in Clontarf, but after being dismissed from his position over the 'scandal' of his second novel, *The Dark* – a scandal that included his marriage to a divorced Finnish theatre director and translator, Annikki Laaksi – he had left Ireland for a number of years, living in London and Spain.[2] McGahern and Laaksi were divorced in 1969, and he returned to Ireland in 1970. After spending some time in Galway, McGahern bought a small farm beside a lake in Co. Leitrim, between Fenagh and Ballinamore, amid

---

1 Mangan, 'The Long Road Home', *Times Literary Supplement*, 28 October 2005, 26.

2 For Laaksi's account of their relationship and marriage, and McGahern's attitude toward the scandal over *The Dark*, see Conway, '"A calculating, control freak."'

the environs of his childhood.[3] What then followed were three decades of
writing and travelling, with stints as visiting professor or writer-in-residence
at various Irish, American and Canadian universities. With the publication of *Memoir*, however, the bones that had been scattered throughout
the fiction were gathered for a recollection that would provide the long
overdue 'rest from judgment'.[4]

The Work of Remembering-Mourning: Summoning the Image

In 'Remembering, Repeating, and Working Through', Freud discusses how
recalling a past trauma, particularly the death of a loved one, can be blocked
by repression and how this blockage can manifest itself as repetition-compulsion. In 'Mourning and Melancholia', he posits that an incomplete process of mourning may lead to melancholia, but that when the process of
mourning is complete, the ego becomes free and uninhibited. After he had
finished *Memoir*, McGahern told an interviewer: 'no matter how depressing the material, if it becomes depressing to write, or indeed, to read, it's
no good. I firmly believe that unless the thing is understood it's useless,
and that the understanding of it is a kind of joy. It's liberating'.[5] Not only
in his memoir, but in all his writing, McGahern wrote himself *into* understanding and *toward* self-liberation. His comment confirms our sense of
the writing process for him being heuristic as well as therapeutic, despite
his well-known antipathy to any notion of writing as therapy. (The latter

---

3   See Patricia Deevy, 'A light in the darkness', *Irish Independent* (30 December 2001),
     16 June 2010, <http://www.independent.ie/unsorted/features/a-light-in-the-dark-
     ness-512368.html>; and O'Hagan, 'A family touched with madness'.
4   In the Talmudic tradition of bone-gathering and reburial 'the bones were collected
     and deposited in chests. On that day, the son would grieve, but on the following day
     he rejoiced because his parent had now found rest from judgment' (Eliezer Segal,
     'From the Sources: Bare-Bones Burial', 16 June 2010, <http://www.acs.ucalgary.
     ca/~elsegal/Shokel/021219_Ossuaries.html>).
5   O'Hagan, 'A family touched with madness'.

should be understood anyway not as a rejection of a therapeutic *poiēsis* but rather as a rejection of 'unreconstructed' autobiographical fiction.) McGahern's belief that the writing process itself led to the understanding of the past that released him from it, offers another way of understanding his lifelong obsession with 'getting the words right'.[6] But to understand the 'rightness' of the language in exclusively aesthetic or stylistic terms would be to collude with McGahern's own repression of the imperatives concealed within his aesthetic pronouncements. For McGahern the memoirist and novelist, there were always two 'truths' he was preoccupied with 'getting right' – the truth of his beloved mother and the truth of his father. He told O'Hagan: 'I know that consciously and unconsciously she had an enormous influence on my life. [The memoir] was as much a way of acknowledging that as it was about my father's presence. If I am in any way successful, I think that both sides are given fair play'.[7] *Amongst Women* and the memoir brought to a conclusion his long struggle to understand his father; the memoir and *That They May Face the Rising Sun*, each in its own way, express the 'joy' that McGahern said understanding brings, and together, his last three books represent the final stages of the self-liberation that his art of memory achieved. McGahern had written his way to these final stages by *working through* the grief and guilt he felt over his mother and his anger at his father.

For the philosopher, Paul Ricoeur, 'it is as a work of remembering that the work of mourning proves to be liberating'.[8] It does not seem too far-fetched to read the oft-noted repetitions of character, setting, situation and mood in McGahern's writing as a form of repetition-compulsion symptomatic of an incomplete process of grieving and the guilt and anger associated with it. The goal of the work of mourning is the liberation of the self from the other or object of love that preoccupies it and that self-liberation is only possible if there is a 'just' recognition of the other who was loved and now is lost. The necessity of such a recognition of the other

---

6   Ibid. See also Maher, *John McGahern*, 144, 145.

7   O'Hagan, 'A family touched with madness'.

8   Ricoeur, *Memory, History, Forgetting*, 72. My approach to McGahern's memoir and to its significance in relation to his body of fiction has been shaped very much by a reading of Ricoeur's work.

underlies McGahern's concern throughout his career with 'getting the words right', which for him was always more a truth to 'vision' than a truth to fact. Discussing the difference between writing fiction and memoir, McGahern told O'Hagan: 'There is not the same freedom in the memoir as there is in the novel. Fiction needs to be imagined. Even events that actually happened have to be reimagined', whereas '[w]ith a memoir you can't imagine or reinvent anything'.[9] It is the nature of McGahern's 'reimagining' of his life that needs attention, the nature of the process that produces the fiction; what he means by 'reimagined' is 'remembered'. For McGahern, memory is a form of imagination, and his art of memory is his reformulation of the 'vision' of memory into the 'image' of his narrative fiction. The life *is* reimagined as it is written from memory into fiction, in the process discovering the understanding that the visionary image holds. McGahern also told O'Hagan: 'One thing you find out while writing a memoir is what an uncertain place the mind is'.[10] Memory falters, imagination struggles, and the desire to 'get it right' has as much to do with feelings as facts. The truth McGahern writes towards, the 'right' he obsesses over as a writer, in the fiction as well as the memoir, is as much the righting of wrong as the accuracy of fact, a moral and human truth as much as documentary realism.

For McGahern, as for Ricoeur, 'the meaning of human existence is not just the power to change or master the world, but also the ability to be remembered and recollected in narrative discourse, to be *memorable*'.[11] *Memoir* is a *hommage* to a beloved, his mother, that memorializes her through 'the inventive power of language' and the capacity of narration to re-structure 'clock-time' in a way that 'humanizes' it.[12] In the memoir McGahern transforms the beloved into the spirit of place, which explains the profound love of place that imbues *That They May Face the Rising Sun*. McGahern did not turn away from the centring force of his earlier work for his last novel; quite the contrary, the beloved remains omnipresent but in a form that is no longer a cause of mourning but of burgeoning

9   O'Hagan, 'A family touched with madness'.
10   Ibid.
11   Ricoeur, 'The Creativity of Language', in *States of Mind: Dialogues with Contemporary Thinkers*, ed. Richard Kearney (New York: New York University Press, 1995), 218.
12   Ibid.

celebration, no longer an absence that haunts, but a presence that enlivens.[13] At its publication, McGahern said that 'all the writer can do is write what he has to write at the time. Of course ones [*sic*] vision of life changes. There'd be something wrong with a person if he didn't change at all'.[14] The 'vision' of life we encounter in *That They May Face the Rising Sun* could not arrive until McGahern had undergone the process of 'change' that made it accessible. Nor is it that in his earlier work he was not yet able to break out from under the shadows of his past; for each work was in itself part of the breaking out by its *working through* the grief and guilt.

For Ricoeur, 'The duty of memory is to do justice, through memories, to an other than the self'.[15] McGahern denied that there was any dimension of judgment in his memoir: 'judgment has no place in the writer's trade'.[16] But while he may have thought he was writing on a plane of detachment, as with his fiction, there is a palpably forensic quality to his witnessing. *Memoir* is a work of justice, judgment, and self-judgment; judgment of the Ireland of his youth and early adulthood, the Catholic Church, the Irish State, the national schools and its teachers, but most definitely there is judgment of his father.[17] Without such judgment there could be no understanding. The overwhelming intertextual character of *Memoir* in relation to the novels and short stories signifies how the writing itself – the words he found or dredged up for the stories – composed a single continuous search for understanding and self-liberation. The memoir describes how he brought himself to the point where he could write *That They May Face the Rising Sun*, his masterwork of praise and celebration, a writing that took twelve years.

---

13   The title of the novel is explained within it (see *RS*, 282); the explanation, however, recalls McGahern's memory of his mother linking Easter and the sun as well as his attempt as a baby to walk into the sun (see *M*, 11–12).

14   Kelly, 'High Style', 5.

15   *Memory, History, Forgetting*, 89.

16   O'Hagan, 'A family touched with madness'.

17   McGahern admitted that his sisters thought he had been 'too easy' on their father; see O'Hagan, 'A family touched with madness'; Tom Adair, 'Darker side of Irish charm', *The Scotsman* (10 September 2005), 16 June 2010, <http://www.arlindo-correia.com/101105.html>.

Summoning the Image: Beginning the Remembering/ Remembering the Beginning

McGahern told O'Hagan, 'A memoir is tricky because one was itching to alter it so that it conforms to a certain vision, but one is stuck with what happened'.[18] And yet *Memoir*, in its total shape, and in its climax, does compose a vision. Moreover, at the outset of his career, the acclaimed realist seems to have understood himself as a kind of 'visionary'. In 1968, McGahern sited 'the image' at the centre of his creative process, which he described as the shaping of 'vision' into 'image': '[vision] struggles towards the single image, the image on which our whole life took its most complete expression once, in a kind of grave, grave of the images of dead passions and their days ...'.[19] The career of the novelist is thus a serial imagining, fashioning image after image in the quest to produce an *eikon* of the 'vision', of 'the one image that will never come, the lost image'.[20] In his 1991 version of this credo, McGahern defines the 'vision' as 'that still and private world which each of us possesses and which others cannot see'; then, in 2002, McGahern told Eamon Maher: 'you couldn't have the image without memory'.[21] What *Memoir* makes clear is that in 1968 what McGahern was referring to, more unconsciously than consciously, as 'the image on which our whole life took its most complete expression once' but which now is hidden 'in a kind of grave', was the image of the beloved, the lost mother. By 2001, McGahern could see this and admitted to Patricia Deevy: 'sometimes I think that maybe the long and complicated journey of [my] art may be a simple activity to try to recover that world that I lost at her death. But I don't know that. One writes because one needs to, and it's an

---

18   O'Hagan, 'A family touched with madness'.
19   McGahern, 'The Image' (1968), 10.
20   Ibid.; see Ricoeur: 'the *eikon* contains within itself the other of the original affection' (*Memory, History, Forgetting*, 51).
21   McGahern, 'The Image' (1991), 12; Maher, *John McGahern*, 146; see also, Whyte, *History, Myth, and Ritual*, 231.

instinct, and though I've done nothing else for the last 40 years much, I still don't understand it'.[22]

McGahern said that following his mother's death the move from the farm to his father's barracks 'was my first experience of the world as a lost world and the actual daily world as not quite real'.[23] For Sampson, 'The phrase "the lost world" ... indicates the significance of memory as a means of restoring reality to the world'.[24] But what McGahern's *poiēsis* strives to 'restore' is the presence of the mother *in* her image in his world: 'the lost image' and the 'lost world' are the mother and mother-world. In *Memoir* when McGahern describes his reunion with his mother following her first hospital stay, he writes: 'it was as if my lost world was restored and made whole and given back' (*M*, 60; see also 66–7). At the outset of his writing career both 'the lost image' and the 'lost world' are buried in the 'grave of the images of dead passions and their days', that is, in the unconscious and in memory. In 1968 McGahern admitted that he was 'still ... not at peace' and he allowed the statement to stand almost thirty years later. The writing process itself was his way of searching for that 'peace'. In 2002 he told Maher, 'I think that when a writer finishes a book, he has dealt in images and rhythms, and out of the material the book is shaped finally – the last thing a writer does is shape it ...'.[25] In the memoir, as in the fiction, McGahern's 'shaping' is nothing less than his re-constitution of the 'lost world' and recovery of the 'lost image' in the form of the *eikon* of the beloved.[26]

Memoir is framed by a remembered and then a fantasized image of the son and mother walking the Leitrim countryside. Both these scenes reprise the work's central memory-scene of their walk to Ollarton's farm (*M*, 63–4). Taken together, they compose an iconic triptych that makes clear that the most important images McGahern 'shaped' in the memoir are versions of 'the one image' that haunted all his writing. The imagined reunion with

22   Deevy, 'A light in the darkness'; Maher considers 'the lost world' in McGahern's fiction to be the society and culture of vanishing rural Ireland (*John McGahern*, 5).

23   Eileen Kennedy, 'Q. & A.', 40.

24   *Outstaring Nature's Eye*, 5.

25   Maher, *John McGahern*, 152.

26   'To remember is to have a memory or to set off in search of a memory' (Ricoeur, *Memory, History, Forgetting*, 7).

the beloved-mother at the end of *Memoir* is not so much the abolishment of time and memory as their apotheosis. McGahern told González that 'all autobiographical writing is by definition bad writing unless it's strictly an autobiography. Writing, fiction especially, is life written to an order or vision, while life itself is a series of accidents'.[27] It is appropriate, then, that McGahern ends his memoir with the apotheosis of autobiography – the salvation of fiction.

The memoir's opening paragraphs are archetypal, symbolic, metafictive, mythopoeic. The recollection begins with the soil but ends with the recollecting man, a quasi-journalistic quickly morphing into a poetic voice – 'Rich crops of rushes and wiry grasses keep the thin clay from being washed away' (*M*, 1): the sudden surge of *technē* – alliteration, assonance, sibilance, internal rhyme, iambic-spondaic variation, as well as the echo of Kavanagh's 'Clay is the word and clay is the flesh'[28] – asserts the presence of the narrating consciousness. In the opening paragraph the act of describing the past becomes a declarative inhabiting of it. The recollecting self re-enters the 'green tunnel' (*M*, 2) of childhood, an image that suggests both birth-canal and maze (see *M*, 3). As the paragraph grows, it becomes progressively more and more 'literary'. The reader encounters vividly nominative language; metaphor, rhythm, repetition; an evident orchestration of crescendo and counterpoint; the catalogue of flora, fauna and fragrance; and the elegiac finale of 'these fields have hardly changed at all since I ran and played and worked in them as a boy' (*M*, 1), with its echoes of Wordsworth and Dylan Thomas, all of which convey a palpable sense of the writing itself *becoming* the remembering, not in the sense of over-writing memory but rather of expressing in its very nerves and sinews the sense of Wordsworthian amazement that the recollecting mind experiences when the past it conjures suddenly *appears* before it. McGahern's memory and observant imagination run over the beloved landscape and release the spirits of place and past, and ultimately, the image of the beloved herself.[29]

27   González, 'John McGahern', 45.
28   Patrick Kavanagh, *The Complete Poems*, ed. Peter Kavanagh (Newbridge: The Goldsmith Press, 1990), 79.
29   For a discussion of landscape as 'mnemonic device', see Jan Vansina, *Oral Tradition as History* (Madison: University of Wisconsin Press, 1985).

The Happy Memory and 'the lost image': The Walk to Ollarton's

The opening paragraphs of *Memoir* engender what Ricoeur describes as the 'small miracle of recognition', the effect of which 'is to coat with presence the otherness of that which is over and gone. In this, memory is re-presentation, in the two-fold sense of re- : turning back, anew'.[30] There is, of course, a cognitive dimension to the simultaneous 'turning back' and 'anew' that Ricoeur describes, a 're-cognition' akin to what Eliot describes in 'Little Gidding': 'And the end of all our exploring / Will be to arrive where we started / And know the place for the first time'.[31] McGahern's 'recognition' of the beloved landscape awakens a knowing that moves from familiarity to the valued 'understanding' that he said was his motive for writing; it also ushers in the first of three 'happy memories' that coordinate the memoir as a whole: a generalized memory of walking the lanes and roads with his mother, a specific memory of walking with her at night to a farm for milk, and the fictive or projected 'memory' of a mother-and-son reunion.[32] *Memoir* coheres around these three passages of recollection, recognition and joy, three 'happy memories' which compose, in effect, a three-fold recovery of 'the lost image'/'lost world'.

The first 'happy memory' is a recollection of the three-year-old's experience of walking with his mother to her school in Lisacarn. McGahern credits the attendant spirit of his mother with affording him the 'deep peace' (*M*, 4) that such 'spots of time' in his beloved Leitrim landscape provided him. In this first scene, a rational, self-conscious, self-reflective voice – 'I must have been … I suspect … no more than' (*M*, 4) – tempers the admission-confession of the irrational experience; but at the same time, the 'truth' of that experience goes unquestioned. To the rational mind, the past *is* lost; yet there have been instances when 'the actual lane and the lost

---

30 Ricoeur, *Memory, History, Forgetting*, 39.

31 Eliot, *The Complete Poems and Plays* (London: Faber and Faber, 1969), 197.

32 Ricoeur writes: 'it is 'a "happy" memory, when the poetic image completes the work of mourning' (*Memory, History, Forgetting*, 77).

lane [became] one for a moment in an intensity of feeling ... without the usual ... pain and loss' (*M*, 4). Ricoeur's remarks about the 'curious parallel ... between the phenomenology of memory and the phenomenology of imagination' bear on McGahern's equivocation here:

> a specific search for truth is implied in the intending of the past 'thing,' of what was formerly seen, heard, experienced, learned. This search for truth determines memory as a cognitive issue. More precisely, in the moment of recognition, in which the effort of recollection is completed, this search for truth declares itself. We then feel and indeed know that something has happened, something has taken place, which implicated us as agents, as patients, as witnesses. Let us call this search for truth, faithfulness.[33]

There is perhaps no better expression of this sense of the recognition that memory can bring, or of the understanding McGahern sought through the *poiēsis* of image and vision, than his metaphor of 'the actual lane and the lost lane becoming one'. In each of the 'happy memories' that McGahern recounts the reader is made to 'feel and indeed know that something has happened, something has taken place' in McGahern's life that he is searching to recoup; his 'search for truth' in the memoir is an act of 'faithfulness' to his own life, and in particular, to the two figures who most shaped it – his mother and father.

The first 'happy memory' foreshadows the second, the memory of the walk to the Ollarton farm with his mother which I believe is *the* 'lost image' that haunts McGahern's fictive making and centres his art of memory. It dates from a crucial and critically short period in the young boy's life when he recovered the *original* 'lost world', the prelapsarian state in which he was his mother's only child and the object of her undivided attention:

> We walked to Ollarton's with a can for milk. ... The happiness of that walk and night under the pale moon was so intense that it brought on a light-headedness. It was as if the whole night, the dark trees, the moon in the small lake, moonlight making pale the gravel of the road we walked, my mother restored to me and giving me her free hand, which I swung heedlessly, were all filled with healing and the certainty that we'd never die. I was safe in her shadow. (See *M*, 63–4)[34]

---

33   Ibid., 54, 55.
34   The walk to Ollarton's became the 'walk to Priors' in *The Leavetaking*; McGahern recycles significant language and imagery from Patrick Moran's recollection for his

The whole passage from which this excerpt is taken is numinous; the event religious, ecstatic; the memory, sacramental. Jungian archetypes of moon-mother-anima and the unconscious abound.[35] The description of the clear, cold night, the pale moon, the pool, quarry and lake, the 'avenue of great trees' and the approach to the light of the barn – builds to the 'communion service' of the milk. Later in the memoir we learn that his mother hoped McGahern would become a priest, and in this passage, perhaps, we read where he discovered on the level of the unconscious, at least, his vocation to be a priest of life, to give worship in and through his art to the mundane mysteries of daily life amid bird, beast and flower, an ordination he celebrates most gloriously in his last novel. Here his mother teaches him the posture of attention and respect that later will centre his art; his image of her also prefigures her role in his life as silent, abiding presence, a presence he signals by the echo in this passage of the 'extraordinary sense of security, a deep peace, in which I feel that I can live forever' that he described coming upon him while walking the lanes around where he lived (*M*, 4). The 'healing' and 'certainty' McGahern recalls feeling when he was in his mother's presence compose the lost 'peace' which haunts all his fiction. This memory-image is at the core of the myth of abject loss and ecstatic

---

own in the memoir (compare *L*, 64). Note how the 'shadow' image used here in relation to the mother-figure differs from the equivalent passage in the novel, where Moran uses the image for his father (see *L*, 49).

35 There is much in *Memoir* that invites a Jungian reading. Here, however, I will only draw on Jung's comment regarding the anima to suggest an ambiguity in the narrator's statement that 'I was safe in her shadow': 'To the young boy a clearly discernible anima-form appears in his mother, and this lends her the radiance of power and superiority or else a daemonic aura of even greater fascination. But because of the anima's ambivalence, the projection can be entirely negative. Much of the fear which the female sex arouses in men is due to the projection of the anima-image. An infantile man generally has a maternal anima; an adult man, the figure of a younger woman' (C. G. Jung, *The Archetypes and the Collective Unconscious*, trans. R. F. C. Hull. 2nd ed. Bollingen Series XX. Princeton, NJ: Princeton University Press, 1968, 200. The figure of the beloved-mother is as potentially dangerous as that of the ogre-father. Jung's remarks about the relation between negative anima-projection and 'the fear which the female sex arouses in men' are worth considering in relation to the characterization of the narrator-protagonist in *The Pornographer* and particularly the psychodynamics of his relationship with Josephine. See also Whyte, *History, Myth, and Ritual*, 199, 224–5.

restoration that the memoir constructs; moreover, its centring role and position in the sequence of three happy memories is an example of how it is the structuring impulse within narration itself that leads us to story-telling to make order and sense from the past and in doing so 'acquire an identity'.[36]

It is important to see how the three 'happy memories' work together and in doing so how they 'work for' McGahern. The memory of the walk to Lisacarn foreshadows the actual recollection of the walk to Ollarton's, and that recollection is then 'projected' into the dream-image that con-cludes *Memoir*, the paean to the beloved-mother who 'never really left us' and whose love was always present 'like a hidden strength' (*M*, 271–2). The language and imagery in this passage echo the memoir's beginning, but what begins as an image of the past ends here as a prospective of desire. McGahern has moved from 'memory that repeats' toward 'memory that imagines'; in the latter, recollection searches out the lost time, the misplaced self, and pulls free of the gravity of forgetting.[37] In McGahern's case, what he seems to have searched out are the 'happy memories' of the beloved and their obverse, demonic contraries, the images of guilt and trauma – specifi-cally, the image of the leave-taking that haunts and the image of the father that terrorizes him. Writing, for McGahern, moves against this current, which is not just the current of time and forgetfulness, but also the current of repression. The circular form of *Memoir* is an upward spiral, a movement from loss to hope. The dream-image that concludes it is the climactic turn of what McGahern describes in *The Leavetaking* as 'the long withdrawing tide of memory becoming imagination' (*L*, 45). In the walk to Ollarton's passage and the climactic dream-image, the *poiēsis* of memory completes the work of mourning through the 're-*presencing*' of the 'lost beloved'. And

36   Ricoeur, 'The Creativity of Language', 222.
37   Ricoeur, *Memory, History, Forgetting*, 25, 27. McGahern's passage has affinities with a passage he quotes from Ó Criomhthain's *An tOileánach*: 'My mother used to go drawing turf when I was eight years old, so that she could have me at school. I hope that she and my father ... will inherit the blessed kingdom and that I and every single person that will read this book will meet up with them again in the island of paradise'; see McGahern, 'What Is My Language?' *Irish University Review* 35.1 (2005), 11.

if 'the actual lane and the lost lane [become] one for a moment in an intensity of feeling ... without the usual ... pain and loss', so absence becomes presence when the mother's voice blends with her son's in the italicized excerpts from her letters which precede the dream-image (see *M*, 271–2). *Memoir* ends mythopoeically with McGahern completing his Orphic descent into the 'grave of the images of dead passions and their days' and successfully recovering 'the lost image' he mourned most. The agency and instrument of that descent are the same memory-imagination and narrative invention that produced the fiction. Indeed, in the way he tells his 'life-story' in *Memoir* McGahern replicates the process of self-fashioning that, at its deepest level, the writing of fiction always provided for him.

'In dreams begins responsibility'

The closing paragraphs of *Memoir* do not describe a memory of the beloved but rather a triumphant willing of her image into a form of redeemed and redeeming presence that brings the novelist his long sought 'peace': 'It is here, in this search for the one image, that the long and complicated journey of art betrays the simple religious nature of its activity: and here, as well, it most sharply separates itself from formal religion'.[38] Remembering becomes invoking, a summoning of vision. Writing for McGahern was always such an action, the searching for the lost faith, the absent beloved, the time before. Dream, with its connotations of desire and image, futurity and past, what may be hoped, imagined, and anticipated, and what has been lost, haunts and reminds, is crucial to the *working-through* in *Memoir*. The dream metaphor encodes the image of desire that by his own admission drives his creative life. The memoir describes two conflicting dreams and the young McGahern's choice between them becomes a source

---

38   McGahern, 'The Image' (1991), 12; this passage also helps to clarify the meaning of resurrection and the symbol of the rising sun in McGahern's last novel.

of significant guilt. First, there is the mother's dream for her son, which sees the boy growing up to become a priest and dedicating his Ordination Mass to her, after which she will live with him as his housekeeper (*M*, 63, 99, 109–10). This dream cunningly resolves the Oedipal conflict by having the son replace the father as the mother's partner, but through a spiritual strategy rather than patricide. McGahern emphasizes that while it was his mother's dream that he become a priest, he so deeply internalized her desire that 'it was impossible to tell to whom the dream belonged' (*M*, 62). The second dream, the adolescent boy's own, of becoming a writer, clearly contradicts the first but McGahern's use of 'vocation' to describe his desire links them (*M*, 212), suggesting that his dream of the writing life, which becomes in practice a masked form of life-writing, will perform a secular version of the forsaken ceremony of the Ordination Mass. Each of these dreams claimed McGahern, and the memoir discloses how his life became a conflict between competing responsibilities; this in turn explains the patterns of repetition that structure his work, because even as the writing career advanced the second dream, the writing process itself was a continuous act of atonement for his broken promise to the first. The guilt associated with his mother's dream for him became encrypted in *his* dream of his mother. It is the latter which 'inflects' the search of the narrator-protagonists in both *The Leavetaking* and *The Pornographer* for a 'beloved' to replace the 'first beloved' – a search which Annikki Laaksi, McGahern's first wife, might say reflected McGahern's own: the search for a wife who would fulfil the son's dream of living with his mother as 'housekeeper'.[39]

The way McGahern uses the memoir to negotiate a resolution of these competing dreams and their responsibilities is critical for the work's mythopoeic achievement. 'Without the promise that one day I'd say Mass for her I doubt if I would have been able to resist my father when he wanted to take me out of school' (*M*, 272; see also 204): this helps us understand the complexity of the guilt that McGahern had to expiate through the act of writing and the career that he describes as a form of priestly vocation: 'I did, in the end, answer to a different call than the one she wished for me,

---

39   See Conway, '"A calculating, control freak".

and followed it the whole of my life' (*M*, 272). The masterstroke in this climactic and concluding passage in the memoir is the way it gathers into a singular coherence the earlier image-memories of the beloved mother as a spirit of place and self-confidence with that of muse-like inspiration for the career as a writer. Keeping his promise to himself saved him; breaking his promise to his mother made him the man he had to become to be whole. The language at the very end of the memoir repeats, literally, the language of the first 'happy memory', just as the description of the dream-walk also repeats language and imagery from the memoir's beginning. The language is testamentary: it admits to his mother's forgiveness and blessing, for breaking and keeping the promises that made him. *Memoir* is McGahern's ultimate expiation of this paradoxically enabling guilt. The narrative's circular form magically contains and transforms the mother's shadow, transforming it in the final paragraphs into life-warming light. Gloriously, the 'lost image' is found: 'She never really left us' (*M*, 271).

But the 'happy memories' have their demonic opposites and McGahern's faithfulness also must face the darkness of the past before it can turn to the rising sun. The most poignant episode in the memoir is McGahern's account of his mother's death and the wound that the loss of the beloved was for the child, a wound that scarred him more deeply than the later physical wounds he suffered at the hands of his father. The darkness of this memory derives from more than her dying, however; it also comes from the boy's sense that he failed or betrayed her at this crucial moment in their relationship (see *L*, 75 and compare *M*, 129, 134). It is this, perhaps the deepest scar in his psyche, that McGahern confesses in the memoir, and what is remarkable is that the pages in which he relives the experience (*M*, 122–35) are not *new* writing at all, but taken, much of it word for word, from *The Leavetaking* (*L*, 70–82). There is no more compelling evidence in the memoir, and there are many other such instances of recycled language from the fiction, that McGahern's novels and short stories were indeed masked autobiography, despite his stated lack of respect for such writing; in fact, unless we consider *Memoir* a work of fiction, the re-use of the writing from *The Leavetaking* for this crucial segment of the memoir suggests that, in McGahern's case, the distinction between fiction and autobiography is less than meaningful: the shaping of life into narrative art that he claimed had to occur is the same in the novels as in the memoir, and the 'truth' is the same. This wholesale rehearsal of the novel in the memoir suggests that in relation to this core experience in his life the memoir itself is the 'second leavetaking' (*L*, 72), the return to her room he felt incapable of making at the time. The repetition also exposes the oxymoron in the novel's title: when he left that sick-room McGahern took with him a burden he would spend his writing life unpacking and repacking in his fiction.

The complexity of the pain that the confession of the leave-taking purges is signified by McGahern's description of his behaviour, in both the fiction and the memoir, as an 'abandonment' of his mother. The horror behind this term is not just his sense that he had betrayed her, but that his behaviour linked him with the cowardice and selfishness of his father, who stopped visiting his wife during the last stages of her illness. It is also possible to see McGahern reading back into his account of the failed leave-taking a presaging of the other act of filial unfaithfulness, his break-ing his promise to become a priest and becoming a writer instead. At the time of his mother's funeral he recalls thinking that he would atone for his actions by realizing his promise to her: 'One day I would make every-thing up to her by saying Mass for her' (*M*, 134). He never does, of course, and the language of 'life and pleasure' that he uses in *The Leavetaking* (*L*, 85) recurs in the memoir when he describes his rejection of his mother's dream for his own: 'Instead of being a priest of God, I would be the god of a small, vivid world' (*M*, 205). Later, he adds: 'The guilt I felt at turn-ing my back ... on the death in life that was the priest's choice and on that dear promise to say Mass ... I was able to partially resolve by telling myself that teaching was my mother's profession and was sometimes called the second priesthood' (*M*, 208). Clearly, it was his own dream that 'set me free' (*M*, 205); his mother's would have imprisoned him even more in the shadow-world of 'death in life' which the mother-world became following her death through the unresolved guilt and incomplete grieving which the failed leave-taking came to symbolize.

In the memoir McGahern represents his mother as close to nature and a naturally pious, sensitive, loving woman who believed in the Catholic God, if not necessarily his priests, and who abhorred violence of any kind. When it moves to deal with the guilt of the leave-taking and the broken promise of the priesthood, the memoir painfully enacts a faithfulness that exorcizes as well as praises and celebrates this strand of McGahern's identity. *Träume* soon give way to trauma and a series of images that offset the 'happy memories' of the mother, set as they are in the nightmare world of the father. As McGahern finally 'outs' his father as a selfish, narcissistic, fickle, unpredictable, violent and sexually abusive tyrant, exorcism gives way to excoriation. A monstrous figure of bullying authority, repeatedly represented in his Garda sergeant's uniform, the father becomes a not so subtle synecdoche for the oppressive symbolic order of a State that turned the whole country into a barracks (see *M*, 29, 32).

While McGahern explicitly acknowledges that the difference in his feelings towards his parents to a degree 'conforms' with a classical Oedipal conflict (*M*, 9), his 'first memory' (*M*, 12) of his father comes in an order that seems more than chronological after his description of his mother's revulsion at the 'routine' violence endemic in the school system at the time, the bullying of women teachers by the male inspectors, and the 'punitive' Irish language policy that was forced upon 'all the children of the State' (*M*, 8). The sequencing links his father, the world of the barracks, and the State into a demonic 'Father-world' in stark contrast to the natural beauty and tenderness of the soon-to-be-lost world of the mother.[40] The first memory itself sees McGahern as the victim of his father's violent will: irritated by his son's baby-curls, but angered more by the attention the baby was receiving from his wife and his own mother, he set about shearing the lamb after locking the protesting and visibly upset women in another room. His assault on the terrified child occurs in a dark hallway, a setting that contrasts with the 'green tunnel' and 'lost lanes' of his mother's world, and

---

40 Later in the memoir McGahern explicitly links the 'licensed' violence and systemic abuse students suffered from their teachers to the violence that characterized domestic relationships, citing 'sexual sickness and frustration' to be at work in both (*M*, 18). Both forms of violence are embodied in father-figures, the teachers who were representatives and employees of the paternalistic state and national religion, and the paterfamilias (see *M*, 18). This informs McGahern's later speculation about the combination of violence and sexual abuse that characterized his father's evident personality disorder.

throughout the ordeal his father is in uniform (*M*, 9). This is only the first of many horrors McGahern suffered or witnessed his siblings suffer at his father's hands. An even more gruesome incident, which McGahern links explicitly with his symbolic 'beheading' as yet another ceremonial 'execution', occurs when his father uses a knife to remove scabs from the little boy's face (*M*, 23). By the end of *Memoir*, the reader can only wonder how McGahern avoided a life in therapy; that he did points to the therapeutic effects the making of fiction must have provided. Writing about the same fictive family under slightly different names and circumstances over and over again in the novels and short stories was the working-through of the life that had formed him; in *Memoir* he gives to this life the shape of an archetypal myth of death and rebirth.

The hair-cutting and scab-removal foreshadowed years of brutal beatings and sexual abuse at his father's hands. McGahern was required to share his father's bed and the abuse took the form of late night 'massages': 'Looking back, and remembering his tone of voice and the rhythmic movement of his hand, I suspect he was masturbating' (*M*, 188).[41] McGahern believes the violence and the abuse were connected: 'During the beatings there was sometimes the same sexual undertow, but louder, coarser' (*M*, 188). All the children were made 'to feel a burden and to feel ashamed' (*M*, 157), but McGahern's abjection must have been the deepest, compounded as it was by the wound of his mother's death, his sense of guilt over the failed leavetaking, and the humiliation of the sexual abuse and beatings he took from his father. McGahern captures the utter desolation of a child brutalized by a bullying adult in the infamous opening chapter of *The Dark* – the most traumatic passage in all his writing, and the original experience still haunted him in *Amongst Women* (see *AW*, 112). But there is a significant difference between the later scene in *The Dark*, in which young Mahoney stands up

---

41   See the image of the detumescent strap, 'the leather hanging dead in his hand' (*D*, 10), at the end of the horrific opening episode in *The Dark*. If *The Leavetaking* was the novel in which McGahern confronted his guilt towards his mother, *The Dark* was the novel in which he began to exorcize his anger and shame over his father's sexual abuse and physical brutality; compare *M*, 188 and *D*, 19–22, but also 'Coming into his Kingdom' in *Nightlines* (*N*, 36) and *AW*, 38–9.

to his father and threatens to hit back if he continues with his assault, and the original incident as told in *Memoir*, where McGahern describes an almost hysterical, passive-aggressive resistance (compare *D*, 36–7 and *M*, 190–1). It is interesting how the style of resistance to his father in this turning-point moment in his adolescence resembles the way McGahern behaves years later during the censorship scandal over *The Dark* and his bullying by Archbishop McQuaid, which ultimately cost him his teaching job. Then, too, McGahern did not run away, but did not fight either – he simply stood and took the abuse (see *M*, 250–2).[42] Seen together, McGahern's victimization by both 'father-figures' subtly links familial and institutional abuse within a bullying Irish State.

It must hurt to wish your father in hell; at least, by becoming an atheist, McGahern avoided that kind of self-damage. The words McGahern writes over his father's death in his memoir, however, seem uttered on the edge of a chasm that some might sense is slightly sulphurous, even though the language seems little more than a shrug at the Great Unknown: 'Though I have more knowledge and experience of him than I have of any other person, I cannot say I have fully understood him, and leave him now with God, or whatever truth or illusion or longing for meaning or comfort that word may represent' (*M*, 271).There is a world of hurt in that shrug. The significant imbalance in the memoir between the single paragraph that records his father's death and the dozen pages devoted to his mother's and its aftermath is found in the fiction as well, with the lengthy treatment of Elizabeth's dying in *The Barracks* and of the mother's death in *The Leavetaking*, contrasting with the brief, though still uncannily powerful, notation of Moran's passing in *Amongst Women*. McGahern's account of his father's death in *Memoir* is profoundly dismissive, a paradoxically perfunctory gesture that reminds us that the real work of exorcism had been accomplished already in *Amongst Women*. In the memoir, mythopoeia reconstitutes that exorcism in archetypal terms.

---

42   Compare Patrick's explanation for returning to Dublin in the first version of Part II of *The Leavetaking*, when McGahern first dealt with this experience in his writing (*L* 1974: 161).

As *Memoir* begins, the narrow lanes and hedges with high banks become the 'maze' (*M*, 2) of the past, the labyrinth of memory and imagination where McGahern's fictions waited to be found: scattering, linking, wandering, arriving, the torque in the memoir form is provided by an unrelentingly centripetal force, the return and search, which is all the while in a dialectical struggle with the centrifugal desire to escape the horrors he knows he will have to confront. This sense of memory as a labyrinth and recollection as a quest suggests that, while the memoir will include both 'found' memories and 'sought' memories, the latter will carry the burden of McGahern's *poiēsis*.[43] The labour of imaginative memory entailed in the process of writing the memoir is a working at something that needs to be addressed, faced, expunged, namely, the monster at the centre, the composite shadow of his mother's death and the failure of his leave-taking, and the penal tyranny of his father. These are linked in the memoir (as in *The Leavetaking*) by the narrative fact that the father 'steals' the children away from the dying mother and takes them to the barracks with him – in other words, he is implicated in the poignant failure of the son's farewell – leaving her prematurely entombed in the farmhouse that he has emptied of furniture, family, and love. In a sense the father-figure in the memoir *is* Death and stands opposed to the mother who is Life: 'In nearly all things they were opposites' (*M*, 47). McGahern recalls feeling 'a strange foreboding' as a child when his mother told him her nausea was no more than 'early morning sickness', and then adds, 'I felt the same fear when my father was in the house' (*M*, 22–3). This anecdotal linking of death, pregnancy, and the father in the memoir is developed more elaborately in the fiction, however, as the narrator in *The Leavetaking* imagines his father pressuring his mother to have sex following her return from hospital, even though the doctor has warned them that another pregnancy could reactivate the cancer (*L*, 65); the child that is born is called 'the cancer child my brother' (*L*, 72).

---

43   See Ricoeur, *Memory, History, Forgetting*, 4. For McGahern's own view that 'involuntary memories are more true because they surprise us, evading will and habit', see Whyte, *History, Myth, and Ritual*, 231.

In the opening paragraphs of the memoir McGahern's maze does not seem to be Theseus' labyrinth of challenge and opportunity, but it is. At first, the lanes and paths and hedges seem only the honeycomb of nostalgia and re-entering the 'green tunnel' seems no more than Ricoeur's or Eliot's turning back that is prelude to seeing anew. But the honeycomb suddenly becomes a wasp's nest: 'A different view of these lanes and fields is stated by my father' (*M*, 2). The figure of his father pointedly enters McGahern's text as a voice of contradiction, a pole of negative energy in relation to the son; it is the baying of the minotaur.[44] What the reader gradually discovers is that the memoir is indeed a version of Theseus' story, as it is of Oedipus' and Dante's, and that at the centre of the labyrinth there is a lost 'Image' of love and beauty. The goal of this quest is to free the 'Image' from the monster-miser that has stolen it and thereby free the questing narrator's future from the shadows of his past. The 'Image' is the memory of the mother but the memory of the mother is also the thread – 'the love she gave ... was there like hidden strength' (*M*, 272) – that the storyteller uses to enter and exit the horrors of his past, the world of the man-monster father, the 'nay-sayer' patriarch whose venom and negativity run like an open sewer through all McGahern's writing. McGahern's title for the American edition of his memoir, *All Will Be Well* (2005), evokes the myth of memory that informs all memoir. Memory as a form of the Orphic imagination that recoups a 'lost world' is evident in the memoir's gradual disclosure of its narrator-protagonist's quest to recover the body of the beloved at the centre of the labyrinth, which he does when he banishes to oblivion the monster hoarding it with little more than a shrug at the end.

---

44 Remembering McGahern's remark that 'my father's secrecy was practically pathological' (*M*, 57), we should recognize that contradiction can also point to repression; his presentation of 'my father's refusal of the past' (*M*, 49) sets the father-figure at odds with the memorial impulse of the memoir, which thus becomes the son's *speaking against* the darkness and silence that the father embodies.

'In the beginning was my mother': Memory, Truth, and Myth

In a 1992 interview with James Whyte that McGahern 'revised ... for publication' in Whyte's book ten years later, McGahern was asked about the
role of the dead mother in his fiction:

> JW: At the back of all your novels, there is a dead mother. ...
> JMcG: That's true. My mother died when I was nine.
> JW: Is there a sense in which all your characters are trying to come to terms with
> that situation?
> JMcG: I don't know. What I do know is that personal therapy has no place in art.
> Art has to conform to an idea or a way of seeing. Self-expression is always bad writ-
> ing. It's one of the fascinations of art ... that the more the material is worked into
> an artifice, the more true feeling is set free. ... The truth or a version of the truth is
> much more likely to be found in working the material through this circuitous artifice
> than by straight speaking.[45]

McGahern's 'I don't know' seems disingenuous. By 2002, with *That They
May Face the Rising Sun* behind him and the memoir well under way, was
he still in the dark about the deepest sources of his *poiēsis*? Surely not, as his
more forthcoming admission to Patricia Deevy in 2001 suggests. Although
his claim 'that personal therapy has no place in art' now seems contradicted
by what the memoir shows about the fiction – and the memoir is as *artistic*
as any of McGahern's novels[46] – McGahern's antipathy to 'self-expression'
was perhaps a reaction against the *passive* stance towards the life experience that the confessional mode seemed to represent for him, a narrative
stance that would, quite troublingly, re-enact the posture of the victim
he was forced into throughout his childhood and adolescence. There is a
moment in McGahern's 2005 interview with Sean O'Hagan that speaks
to this directly: "'I never felt a victim," he says, calmly. "To be a victim is a
failure of intelligence. One becomes responsible for one's own life, however

45   Whyte, *History, Myth, and Ritual*, 227, 235.
46   See, for example, Van der Ziel, '*Memoir*'.

difficult that life may be'".[47] What the creative life of the writer seems to have meant most for McGahern is a profoundly personal and very specific kind of empowerment, the power 'to create a world in which we can live: if not for long or forever, still a world of the imagination over which we can reign', rather than to live for long and forever under the tyranny of the Father, subject to what he calls in 'The Image' (1991) 'the whole mortal game of King'. McGahern's oft-repeated emphasis on the necessary trans-formation of experience into art expresses his lifelong need to free himself from the thrall of the past by turning the experiences that shaped him into something that *he* reshaped in the story-world, not just consciously, into meaningful and pleasing formal order, but consciously and unconsciously into a path out of the labyrinth of grief, guilt, and anger. The world of imagination that McGahern sought to create and reign over through the art of narrative was not an escapist world or egotistical fantasy but the world of memory. If, as Ricoeur writes, 'the meaning of human existence is not just the power to change or master the world, but also the ability to be remembered and recollected in narrative discourse, to be *memorable*', then McGahern's Eliot-like belief that art must transform personal emo-tion into the '*significant* emotion' of art does not mean for McGahern what it meant for the early Eliot, an escape from or transcendence of the personal.[48] What McGahern's pronouncements in the Whyte interview and in 'The Image' (1968, 1991) articulate is his belief that only through the making of narrative can truth and understanding be extracted from the world of material fact, and only in memory can the dead complete the full meaning of their lives.

In the memoir, although the 'shadow' of the mother is a positive image in one passage (see *M*, 64), the shadow she casts is ultimately that of her absence and the grief suffered by the son, as well as the guilt from his feel-ing that he had failed the test of the leave-taking. The other shadow in his life is of course that cast by his father and the narrator must shed both.

47　O'Hagan, 'A family touched with madness'.
48　Eliot, 'Tradition and the Individual Talent', in *Selected Prose of T. S. Eliot*, ed. Frank Kermode (New York: Harcourt Brace Jovanovich, 1975), 44.

Memoir ends with the death of the father and the 'return' of the mother in the dream image, and McGahern's last novel, *That They May Face the Rising Sun*, ends with McGahern's appropriation of the Christian myth of resurrection to serve his own art of memory. The 'truth' of the passage recording his father's death is less the truth of fact than the mythic significance released by the fact when it is 'placed' at that point in the narrative, a placing which clearly reveals the writer's shaping of the life into story. Like the death of the ogre in a fairy tale, the meagre paragraph that records his father's passing is followed immediately by the return of the beloved – or the resurrection of the dead – in the apotheosis of the original 'happy memory' as a triumphant vision. It is as if the Father was the obstacle all along, the rock in front of the tomb, that 'grave of images', that the memoirist finally manages to roll away to recover the lost 'Image' of his beloved. It is in this way that the memoir is a work of remembering that completes the work of mourning, and the liberation of the self from the shadows of grief, guilt and trauma that results from this process has been achieved, according to McGahern, through the intercession of the beloved in his life. The image of the mother at the end of *Memoir* is a figure of resurrection, a resurrection willed and instantiated by the power of an Orphic imagination. When McGahern admits that 'In the beginning was my mother. The only way that life could be continued with her was through prayer' (*M*, 203), it is no casual allusion. The mother is most certainly the *Logos* in the memoir and McGahern's re-writing of the evangelist is a revelatory appropriation. In a sense all McGahern's words up to the closing paragraphs of the memoir have composed one prayer, beads on a rosary of secular mysteries repeating the formative events and characters in the life-myth he has narrated.

   Memoir is a fascinating gloss to the novels and short stories that allows the reader to identify specific connections between the fictive and autobiographical worlds and to consider how all McGahern's writing, when read as an organic whole, composes a continuous mythopoeic effort to work through his life using the compensatory powers of the imagination to shape experience into the pattern of myth, ultimately, the sublimation of the personal in the universal story of fall and redemption. Although *That They May Face the Rising Sun* may seem to stand apart from the previous five novels, McGahern's last novel makes eminent mythical sense in relation to the cycle that begins with the 'Death of the Mother' in *The Barracks* and ends with the 'Death of the Father' in *Amongst Women*. That cycle provides the propulsive torque that transforms McGahern's oeuvre into the comic spiral it now can be seen to achieve, escaping the downward, tragic circuit it would otherwise assume. All the novels from *The Barracks* to *Amongst Women* occur in the autumnal-winter father-world; *That They May Face the Rising Sun*, McGahern's shepherd's calendar, revolves around the mythos of spring and in it McGahern finally recovers the briefly enjoyed mother-world of his childhood. Metaphorically, the landscape is the main character in *That They May Face the Rising Sun* because the spirit of place that centres the story-telling, the still-point at the hub of the narrative wheel, is the mother-world whose recovery McGahern re-enacts in the memoir.

McGahern took the title for the American edition of his memoir from the *Revelations of Divine Love* of Dame Julian of Norwich: 'Sin is behovely, but all shall be well and all shall be well and all manner of thing shall be well', where 'behovely' means necessary, useful, purposeful.[49] Clearly, the shaping myth that informs his narrative is that of salvation and the redeemed life: wrong-doing, suffering, error, hurting and being hurt, compose the meaning of a life that is both uniquely personal and timelessly universal. The most important feature of McGahern's mythopoeia is his use of story-telling and a growing body of fiction to *work through* the full cycle of fall and redemption.[50] McGahern might have encountered the

---

[49]   Julian of Norwich, *Revelations of Divine Love*, Ch. 27, trans. Grace Warrack. *Christian Classics Ethereal Library*, 16 June 2010, <http://www.ccel.org/ccel/julian/revelations. xiv.i.html>.

[50]   Whyte's view that McGahern's 'enabling myth' is that of 'a fall from a lost world of social harmony in which unity of artistic vision was possible' (*History, Myth, and Ritual*, 1) is only half the story; McGahern's 'lost world' is not 'social' or centred by a putative 'artistic vision'. From the evidence of the memoir, McGahern's ideal world was always minimally 'social' because it was a society of two – mother and child. The social world that composes the fallen condition of the fiction is that of the family itself – which McGahern always saw as a microcosm (see McGahern in Whyte, 233).

lines from Dame Julian in Eliot's 'Little Gidding', for the epigraph points
the memoir as project in the same direction that *Four Quartets* explores;
indeed, immediately before he quotes the medieval English mystic, Eliot
writes a passage of profound relevance not only for the memoir but for
McGahern's whole writing life:

> This is the use of memory:
> For liberation – not less of love but expanding
> Of love beyond desire, and so liberation
> From the future as well as the past.[51]

In relation to the text that follows it, McGahern's quotation of 'Sin is
behovely' comes to have a sense similar to Eliot's 'Garlic and sapphires in
the mud / Clot the bedded axle tree' in 'Burnt Norton': *Memoir* progresses
from 'the sodden floor' where son and father, 'the boarhound and the boar
/ Pursue their pattern as before', until finally, through the intercession of
the Beloved, all are 'reconciled among the stars'.[52]

---

51   Eliot, *Complete Poems and Plays*, 195.
52   Ibid., 172.

CHAPTER THREE

Reflections of the One Thing: *The Barracks* (1963)

McGahern's first published novel tells the story of the final months in the life of Elizabeth Reegan. Married to a domineering and bitter Garda sergeant, step-mother to his three young children, she finds herself thinking more and more as her health deteriorates about her past as a nurse in London when she had an affair with a young doctor who killed himself, and trying to make sense of her life and marriage and how she has ended up where she has. In comparison with the books that follow it, what strikes one immediately in this novel is how much McGahern minimized his own presence as the little boy, Willie Reegan. The focus is on the character of the step-mother, first and foremost, and then the father. *The Dark*, *The Leavetaking*, and *The Pornographer*, all have young, male protagonists, and even *Amongst Women* gives more prominence to young Michael and the absent Luke, than McGahern does to Willie. His first task, it seems, setting out on the writing path, was to orient himself to the magnetic pole of his imaginative world, the image and memory of the dying mother, the 'lost world' that he would recover only in his last novel and that he could only reach by writing his way through the long darkness that descended upon his world with her loss. In his second novel, therefore, *The Dark*, we see McGahern identify his imaginative world's emotional and moral antipode, the tyrannical father, the monster figure whom the son must overcome in his struggle toward individuation. All McGahern's novels show protagonists struggling from darkness toward light, the light of self-understanding and self-possession to which he pays inchoate homage in this *ur*-figure of the dying mother in his fiction, and these poles and the energies and emotions that run between them form the axis of memory that centres and vivifies his writing.

While McGahern admitted that the setting and events in the novel derived from his childhood experience, he emphasized that the characters were 'imagined', and in particular, claimed Reegan to be unlike his father because he is comparatively uncomplex and 'far more attractive' (*M*, 245). In the memoir McGahern remains silent about the mother-figure but the autobiographical origin of all the characters is clear. Willie is ten years old, McGahern's age when his mother died.[1] The dying Elizabeth Reegan, however, is Willie's step-mother, and Francis McGahern did not re-marry until McGahern was in his late teens. In the memoir McGahern says that he and Agnes McShera, his step-mother, became instant adversaries (*M*, 207) and he describes her as his father's 'terrier' (*M*, 219).[2] In *The Barracks* there are traces perhaps of McGahern's feelings about Agnes in the narrator's statement that Elizabeth knew the children did not love her, but there is a truth also, presumably, in her feeling that 'At least ... they did not hate her' (*B*, 8,10). When McGahern has Willie contrast Elizabeth and his dead mother, Elizabeth may seem old to Willie because McGahern is really drawing on his image of the much older Agnes and contrasting it with his memory of his mother. What is interesting is how the characterization expresses a dialectic of concealment and revelation that allows McGahern to look back at his mother, paradoxically, by looking through the image of the woman who replaced her. What McGahern achieves in his first novel is a simultaneous return and distancing that allows him to re-imagine his mother's dying while at the same time not yet look fully at it or at his own role in it. Thus, at the centre of *The Barracks* as the

---

1   John McGahern was born 12 November 1934; his mother, Susan McManus McGahern, died 28 June 1944, a little over four months shy of his tenth birthday.

2   This sheds some light on the characterization of Rose in *Amongst Women* (see *AW*, 69), who seems presaged in Elizabeth's thought that Reegan regards her as merely his 'housekeeper' (*B*, 13). Elizabeth's family opposed her marriage to Reegan (*B*, 15); Rose's too would discourage her marriage to Moran. Both women return from years of working in England. Elizabeth married Reegan to escape a life drudging for her mother and brother (*B*, 15); while her relationship with Reegan has paid decreasing dividends, she does admit to sometimes experiencing 'the rich feeling of care and love' (*B*, 56), of being needed, from the children.

beginning of McGahern's narrative quest for the 'lost image', 'lost world' of the beloved, is the complex encryptment of McGahern's mother in the character of Elizabeth, an occlusion all the more complicated because she is masked by the character's identity as step-mother.[3]

The Excitement of Discovery: Elizabeth Reegan

The Barracks coheres around the passages in which McGahern imagines Elizabeth thinking her way towards her death. Even before her diagnosis, he describes her growing sense of her life as lacking 'purpose and meaning' (*B*, 49). McGahern's initial approach to imagining his mother's dying is to have Elizabeth react to her fear of death as the erasure of the value of her own existence, her achievements, responsibilities, desires. The sudden flood of a sense of her own insignificance brings on an existential 'panic' (*B*, 49) which begins the paradoxical process of her feeling, simultaneously, both increasingly separated from the life going on around her and yet plummeting rapidly toward the source of the life-force itself. She questions her motives for marrying Reegan and admits to herself that she was desperate and perhaps had deluded herself about him. Their relationship has failed because she has held back; but she has held back because 'she had always been essentially free' and comes to wonder 'Was this why it

---

3   For a discussion of encryptment, see Jacques Derrida, 'Foreword', in Nicolas Abraham and Maria Torok, *The Wolf Man's Magic Word*. Another interesting moment that connects *The Barracks* with *Amongst Women* and McGahern's use of the step-mother character occurs when Willie encourages a reluctant Elizabeth to take a holiday and attend a cousin's wedding in Dublin; his unthinking but innocent outburst shocks her, and she goes to her room to recover; an uncharacteristically sensitive and appreciative Reegan chastises Willie (*B*, 35–6); in *Amongst Women*, it is Moran who utters the hurtful line (*AW*, 69), and instead of salving the wound he opens, the result is that both he and Rose descend into a 'deepening blindness' (*AW*, 72) to each other, a blindness Elizabeth Reegan also senses in her and Reegan's relationship.

had failed?' (*B*, 104) When McGahern describes the Reegans as 'tied in the knot of each other' (*B*, 156), the pun subtly expresses the bond that denial and repression can fasten. But the moment is more complex than this because in imagining Elizabeth thinking this, McGahern is imagining/acknowledging for his mother a 'freedom' of spirit from the ogrish husband who ultimately abandoned her. The character's expression of self-doubt conceals a contradictory content – the author's unconscious affirmation of his mother's 'essentially' unpolluted separateness from the man who was unworthy of her.

This first effort at introspection is unproductive (*B*, 50) and what follows is a series of episodes of 'despairing reflection' (*B*, 57). The themes of change and control provide McGahern's characterization and the character's self-analysis with their coherence. What is also noteworthy is the degree and quality of the interiority that McGahern constructs for the character. It is a realism that respects the character as a woman with a mind and feelings beneath the appearance of the domestic labourer that her world sees. But we might also consider that McGahern's realism is his most effective mask, concealing the profoundly complex and painful psychological forces at work in the fiction. For Roger Garfitt, McGahern's 'realism is all the more effective because it takes place within a central, metaphysical concern, and because that concern creates a perspective.'[4] That 'concern' and 'perspective' arise within McGahern's construction of the character, 'Elizabeth' – which he said was 'as much a way of looking as a character'[5] – but they also express McGahern feeling his way through grief using storytelling to weave self-expression and fictive creation into a Janus-like looking back to the trauma and ahead to new creation. A core entanglement of the personal and the fictive seems present in McGahern's construction of Elizabeth's oscillation between despair and resolve, fear and indifference, sadness and joy; specifically, what he explores in his presentation of her evolving state of mind is the paralysis that can overcome the spirit when the individual

4   Garfitt, 'Constants in Contemporary Irish Fiction', in Douglas Dunn, ed., *Two Decades of Irish Writing* (Cheadle: Carcanet Press, 1975), 224.
5   Kennedy, 'Q. & A.', 40.

faces something that seems inevitable or beyond their capacity to resist. Suspecting breast cancer, Elizabeth vacillates between giving up and waiting for the disease to kill, and setting about making sense of her life and self before it is too late (*B*, 72). (Her procrastination will reappear in the character of Kate Moran in *The Leavetaking*.) Elizabeth's panic is her fear that she will die before she has had time 'to gather the strewn bits of her life into the one Elizabeth' (*B*, 72) and the character's anxiety is also the novelist's, whose task is to create the character, and even if she remains an un-unified subject, to gather the fragmented self into a coherent image of incoherence. McGahern does not approach the characterization of his protagonists from any sense of ontological crisis, however; the 'crisis of the subject' we encounter in his novels is not a vertiginous *loss* of identity so much as a nausea that results from feeling the *surfeit* of identity that builds from complicated mourning, guilt, abjection, and anger, and that, for the writer, only *poiēsis* can alleviate.

As Elizabeth turns to face the possibility of dying from cancer and to question what she has made of her life, an involuntary memory of her affair with Halliday suddenly focuses her attention. The character stops to 'listen' (*B*, 85) to memory and in doing so enacts a dimension of the introspection that has created her. Elizabeth's openness to memory as a source of knowledge or understanding is an important feature of her character and the most important clue to her metafictive role as the 'surrogate artist' in the novel.[6] In the symbolic code of McGahern's memoir, the gnostic character of memory places it in the world of light, not darkness. For McGahern, memory is the medium of the imagination. Elizabeth's posture of attentive listening is similar to how McGahern recalls his mother's attitude of openness to the moment in *Memoir*. In the scene following her interview with Dr Ryan, when she begins to panic at the thought of her life being over, Halliday surfaces in Elizabeth's consciousness because, as a figure of existential despair, he represents a perspective and response to her situation that part of her is attracted to, as she was attracted to Halliday himself. She had met him in London when 'suddenly, one morning, the first morning

6   See Sampson, *Outstaring Nature's Eye*, 17.

of the world, she had woken up to herself' (*B*, 87). Halliday 'appears' on
the screen of Elizabeth's memory because she had heard him pose the
same basic questions in the midst of his own despair, but ironically, his
effect on her is a parody of the closing of his own mind as a result of the
nihilism that, like a cancer within him, had eaten away at his will to live
(*B*, 90). Elizabeth's recollection of their failed relationship ends with her
asserting herself *against* her suicidal lover yet again in her mind: 'She was
alive and being was her ridiculous glory as well as her pain' (*B*, 94). With
this McGahern has Elizabeth articulate the first step toward the light of
understanding that illuminates her final hours; the passage presages a sentiment McGahern articulates beautifully many years later in his memoir:
'We grow into a love of the world, a love that is all the more precious and
poignant because the great glory of which we are but a particle is lost almost
as soon as it is gathered' (see *M*, 36).

What McGahern constructs in Elizabeth's relationship with Halliday
is central to what he eventually expresses through his characterization of
her. Denis Sampson argues that 'Halliday is the closest McGahern comes
to implanting a "lost image" in a novel which is then echoed throughout,
not only in ideas or in its central place in the character of Elizabeth but
... in the form of the novel also'.[7] To see the structural isomorphism of
Halliday as 'lost image' to Elizabeth, and Elizabeth as an image of the lost
mother for McGahern, is also to begin to see the Oedipal dynamics in
the parallel triangulations of Halliday, Elizabeth, and Reegan and McGahern, his mother and father. It is possible to see the origin of Halliday in
McGahern's belief that his mother had had other men interested in her
– and she may have been more than just interested in other men – before
she married Francis McGahern (see *M*, 54). Halliday thus represents a
lost alternative to McGahern's own past; so, in this sense, he *had* to die: in
the anachronistic time-zone of the psyche, Halliday was killed by Reegan,
the father-in-waiting, the Father Time that would also take Susan McGahern from her lover-son. As a figure of narcissistic despair and nihilistic
acedia Halliday is the prototype of the pornographer, the protagonist of

7   Sampson, 'The Lost Image', 61.

McGahern's fourth novel. But he is also an image of the lover who fails to keep the beloved, and he and Elizabeth are a mirror-inversion of McGahern and his 'lost beloved'. Despite its horrible yet banal denouement, when Elizabeth remembers her affair with Halliday it remains the highpoint of her life. Indeed, her time with him was the one and only true 'holiday' she has ever had; her life since London has been the drudgery of her service either to her family or to Reegan. Further, it's possible to see her 'happy memory' of her time with him as a sublimated 'prototype' of the happy memories in McGahern's memoir. The joy Halliday brought into Elizabeth's life was not eradicated by the sadness he also caused. Halliday symbolizes the paradoxical holiness of every day, the mystery of the mundane but also of the coexistence of beauty and horror in the banal eventualities that consume our days and that occasional epiphanies intensify but do not explain. If there is a truth McGahern seems convinced of from the outset of his writing life, it is that he must bear unequivocal witness to both sides of the coin of experience, the mind-numbing, spirit-breaking drudgery of human existence, the self worn 'down to its own dead impersonality' (*B*, 188), and the equally undeniable truth of the human spirit's ecstatic affirmation of its own in-dwelling reality.

This is how the meaning of Elizabeth's relationship with Halliday is related to her spirituality and her love of the forms of Catholic ritual. The latter are, in essence, occasions in which Elizabeth witnesses the world of everyday sensory experience – indeed, experiences her very senses – to be exalted. The meaning of Christ's life to her is its ennoblement of the mundane, the sanctification of the human; ironically, this also explains how Halliday may function as a Christ-figure for Elizabeth: both are fatal sufferers with whom she now identifies – 'Christ on the road to Calvary, she on the same road; both in sorrow and in ecstasy ...' (*B*, 194–5). At the climax of the novel, as Elizabeth thinks her way toward her death, Halliday's voice again rises from her memory and in remembering what he meant to her she recovers the self-control that her affair with him had forced her to grasp. Recalling Halliday's confession, 'I used you so as not to have to face my own mess', Elizabeth wonders if she married Reegan for the same reason (see *B*, 209–10). This sentiment also prefigures the world of sexual predation in *The Pornographer*. But Elizabeth was no Galatea to Halliday's

Pygmalion; she knows that what he had evoked from her for himself she had shaped into what she needed for herself, 'she and he reflections of the one thing' (*B*, 211). Halliday, not Christ, was Elizabeth's ironic saviour because he awoke in her the capacity to look at the irresolvable nature of human being and not turn away into despair, a capacity that Halliday himself did not possess. What McGahern imagines for Elizabeth, what his characterization shapes her into, is a vision and voice of stoic resignation and existential courage. The imagery and rhythm of this passage foreshadow the passage in the memoir where McGahern describes the cycle of human life and consciousness (*M*, 36). In both, the absence of palliative dogma and clerical cliché is noticeable.

McGahern develops Elizabeth as a character whose experience has brought her to a disciplined passivity, a Buddhist-like openness before a nothingness she now senses is everything. Elizabeth's epiphany is the first of what becomes a characteristic turning-point or defining insight for the protagonists in McGahern's fiction, with one exception and one transcendent variation. Mahoney's decision to reject university and head for Dublin at the end of *The Dark*, Patrick Moran's resignation to his dismissal in *The Leavetaking*, the pornographer's decision to commit himself to a future with Nurse Brady in *The Pornographer*, all these decisions entail the characters facing an unknown future in a posture of wilful humility, a self-assertion that is, paradoxically, an attempt to curb the ego's need to dominate the unknown and colonize the unknowable. The exception, significantly, is Michael Moran in *Amongst Women*, whose death arrives without him ever sensing the grotesqueness of his self-ignorance. McGahern based Moran on his own father, of course, the model for all the aggressive, violent, narcissism found in his fiction. The transcendent variation from this pattern is found in McGahern's last novel, which has no protagonist but whose narrative voice and overarching vision express and embody the same quietist, celebratory humility before the facts of life.

When McGahern has Elizabeth feel 'for a moment pure, without guilt', with 'no desire to clutch for the facts and figures of explanation' (*B*, 211), he is describing her very close to her death; it is the same time that he returns to in both *The Leavetaking* and the memoir. To what extent, then, is his construction of Elizabeth's final self-possession an expression of his own need to feel 'without guilt', to get beyond grief, to achieve the self-forgiveness that would allow him, eventually, to 'smile', like Elizabeth, at the whole mystery of it all – to 'see', as he does at the end of *Memoir*, his mother smiling at him – forgiving and forgiven? 'That was the way it must be' – but in 1963 could not yet be – and so, 'here in this lonely room it ran its course in her cursed life' (*B*, 212); and so it would for McGahern. Elizabeth Reegan's 'lonely room' is Kate Moran's deathroom in *The Leavetaking* and both are Susan McGahern's upper room in the farmhouse in Aughawillan. It would take McGahern forty years and five more novels to complete the redemptive process his story-telling begins in *The Barracks*, working through his memories of the beloved's death, his failed farewell, and the descent into the gulag of grief, guilt and his father's tyranny until he could achieve the impersonal vision of *That They May Face the Rising Sun*.

In the penultimate chapter of *The Barracks*, McGahern rounds out his characterization of Elizabeth and her oscillation between despair and joy, paralyzing fear and liberating praise; in the process, he expresses his own thoughts and feelings about life and death. The acquiescence to 'this sense of mystery' which seems to anchor Elizabeth in her last days is an affirmation of McGahern's own humanist-existentialist values and beliefs at the outset of his writing life. His representation of Elizabeth's thoughts about her death in relation to the big picture is part of his working through the meaning and meaninglessness of his mother's death and of his guilt over the 'broken promise' of the priesthood. In this sense, the scene in which Elizabeth remembers rejecting the priest who tries to browbeat her into joining the Legion of Mary is a symbolic sanction of McGahern's rejection of the priesthood in a way that cancels the promise or at the very least opens it for re-negotiation, and his construction of Elizabeth's consistently spiritual but anti-clerical perspective has the effect of softening his guilt, casting the image of the lost mother as a figure who would understand her son's choice of 'life, life and life at any cost' (*B*, 202) as an artist, over the entombment of the self that the priesthood came to represent for him. Mysteriously, irrationally, in the midst of her pain and despair Elizabeth feels the desire to affirm (*B*, 215). This may have been McGahern's instinct as man and artist at this point in his life, too, but it would take him decades of writing to write his way to affirmation. And when he did, it would be an affirmation of life, not an affirmation of an afterlife at the expense of the world of human experience.

In his memoir McGahern admits that his mother's 'deep religious belief' made her 'unreachable' to both her husband and son (*M*, 47), and the novelist may have transmuted this characteristic into Elizabeth Reegan's separateness as she lies dying, the making of the fiction shaping the auto-biographical in a way that delivers the benefits of self-expression as well as the benefits that result from shaping the autobiographical into the fictive. By the time he wrote *The Barracks*, McGahern no longer believed in what his mother believed; unable to share that faith, he makes Elizabeth spiritual but not religious in the conventional Irish Catholic sense. For example, she participates in the nightly ritual of the rosary but gives no observance to the daily pealing of the Angelus; when she sees the Sacred Heart lamp on the mantelpiece, she is repulsed by its ghoulish colour and declines to light it as the children come inside because she knows it will deflate the high-spirits of their after-dinner play. Waiting in the hospital before her surgery, she regards the priest who visits her on his rounds as her equal in life-knowledge, not her superior (*B*, 118). She recalls the confessional's lack of mystery for her because she could not get past the scent of the flesh and blood man on the other side of the screen (*B*, 157–8) and she refused to join the Legion of Mary because of her revulsion at such 'organizations', refuting in the process the priest's patronizing assumption of power over her (*B*, 163). We are told that Elizabeth had never lived inside the 'magic circle' of unquestioned or absolute belief; and when, in her desperation, phrases of prayers automatically come to her lips, they sound 'dishonest' and uttered by someone else (*B*, 123). When she asks God to soften her pain, however, it is the narrator who suddenly seems to intrude upon the free interior discourse to describe the impulse as desperate, and McGahern's presentation of Elizabeth's attitudes towards the Catholic clergy and the church is very much a projection of his own (see *B*,123 and compare *M*, 201, 203).

As the priest gives her the Last Rites, Elizabeth 'flinches' at the touch of the oil for it reminds her that all that she valued in life came to her through her senses (*B*, 216). Here, through Elizabeth, McGahern articulates his own humanist, artistic credo: 'The whole of her vital world was in herself, contracting or going outwards to embrace according to the strength and direction of her desire, but it had nothing to do with what some one else thought or felt' (*B*, 218). Elizabeth is indeed, finally, the 'surrogate artist' in the novel, a figure of the inner voice that struggles to speak its own truths, to embrace and share experience, to dwell fully in the beauty and absurdity, acknowledging the unique reality of every life, its incomprehensible significance amid the awesome indifference of the universe. The priest comes to be her anti-type, someone who has abandoned the challenge of individuation and the prize of individuality to settle for the rote truths and trite nostrums of a powerful and complacent institution, and McGahern makes clear his scorn for the 'intolerant lunacy' of his kind and for the institution that breeds such 'knaves and fools' (*B*, 219). McGahern's most ironic trumping of the clerical by the artistic occurs when he describes Elizabeth's attitude to the rosary shortly before her death. The literal and denotative meanings of Catholic prayer are hollowed out of the form to leave a ritual that is no less spiritual, a rhythm and music Elizabeth fills with her 'need to praise and celebrate' (*B*, 220). As McGahern describes it, Elizabeth's rosary sounds like a lyric poem. Indeed, McGahern's presentation of Elizabeth's mental processes seems to present what he had come to feel himself by the time he left school, 'that reflection on the mystery of life was itself a form of prayer, superior to the mouthing of empty formulas' (*M*, 202).

The historian Roy Foster has noted that 'the traditional image of the Irish Catholic mother began to be eroded from the early 1960s, well before the Women's Liberation Movement'.[8] In *The Barracks*, a central feature of McGahern's construction of Elizabeth Reegan's character is her fight to maintain her dignity as a free-thinking, independent woman who during her ultimate confrontation with the facts of life and death refuses to give in either to inner despair or to societal pressures and expectations. Consequently, McGahern's first novel is an important harbinger of the fragmentation of the Catholic *habitus* that characterizes the last thirty years of the twentieth century in Ireland, and even though McGahern's body of work generally presents, in Foster's words, 'the picture of an Ireland before the women's movement, before the Celtic Tiger, before prosperity,

---

8   R. F. Foster, *Luck and the Irish: A Brief History of Change from 1970* (Oxford: Oxford University Press, 2008), 40.

before everything that the last thirty years [have] brought', it is nevertheless
a picture that contributed significantly to the civil discourse that formu-
lated the 'transformation in cultural expectations, based not only on a new
confidence in the wider world but also on the rejection of old authoritarian formations: patriarchy and the Catholic Church'.⁹ The challenge for
McGahern in this respect was to characterize Elizabeth in a way that both
paid homage to some of his mother's qualities and strengths – including
her religious beliefs and spiritual sensibility – but at the same time created
a character that 'lived' freely in *his* evolving fictive world; ironically, the
source of that independence in the authorial imagination entails expressing *through* the character thoughts, feelings and attitudes that his mother
would have found objectionable. For example, when Elizabeth thinks that
the question of an ultimate reality is simply irresolvable and not worth the
headache (*B*, 177), this is McGahern projecting and not the mother he
recalls and represents in *Memoir*. However, Elizabeth's love of flowers and
the sensual delight she takes while picking blackcurrants or smelling roses
show McGahern's use of characterization as both a homage to his mother
and a way of imagining her in the situation of her dying, but through the
filter of his own developing attitudes:

> a total love was the only way she had of approaching towards the frightful fulfilment
> of being resonant with her situation, and this was her whole terror and longing. She
> could love too much, break the vase, cast herself on the ground, and be what she was,
> powerless and helpless, a broken thing; but her life with these others, their need and
> her own need, all their fear, drew her back into the activity of the day where they
> huddled in their frail and human love, together. (*B*, 152)

---

9   Ibid., 63, 37. Crotty describes the critical perception of *The Barracks* and McGahern's
     second novel, *The Dark*, as 'a literature of protest ... exposing the cruelties and pri-
     vations of Irish rural life at mid-century' with, in particular, a 'pitilessly clear-eyed
     apprehension of the inadequacies and hypocrisies of Catholic Ireland' ('"All Toppers,"'
     42). For a discussion of the decline of the authority of the Catholic Church in
     Ireland since 1970, see Foster, *Luck and the Irish*, Ch. 2, 'How the Catholics Became
     Protestants', and Tom Inglis, *Moral Monopoly: The Rise and Fall of the Catholic Church
     in Modern Ireland* (Dublin: Dublin University College Press, 1998).

This is a major passage in the novel where McGahern achieves a synthesis of characterization and self-expression. For Sampson, memory provides Elizabeth with a salving balm against the chaffing of the present and even possesses an 'innate power to restore belief in an essential self outside time'.[10] Elizabeth's use of memory, along with an almost visionary sensitivity to both natural beauty and quotidian universals, are the centring qualities in McGahern's characterization. But of course the memory and vision are McGahern's and his characterization of Elizabeth is a projection of childhood witness, imaginative recollection, and the existential view of the human individual he was developing in the early 1960s. As Elizabeth observes her fellow patients, their visitors, and the rituals of 'entrance and departure', she recognizes and affirms the paradoxical value and significance of every individual life (*B*, 136). Sensing the gravity of her situation, that the mastectomy has only bought her a little more time, her mood swings violently from post-operative elation to deepening gloom.

The Shame of Intimacy: Sergeant Reegan

Despite his disclaimer, McGahern's construction of Sergeant Reegan, from beginning to end and in almost every detail, from the 'patrols of the imagination' he logged into the station record-book (*B*, 105; see *M*, 34) to his do-it-yourself shoe-repair, bears all the hallmarks of his father's life, character and personality as he describes them in his memoir. Reegan fought and led men in the War of Independence and afterwards was among the first recruits taken into the new police force (*B*, 109; see *M*, 48); years later, he shares his model's disillusionment with the 'new Ireland.' (A similar background and resentment are given to Moran in *Amongst Women*.) Like McGahern's father, Reegan is a thin skin wrapped around a bladder of self-pity (*B*, 11–12). Wife and children live in a constant state of anxiety and

---

10   *Outstaring Nature's Eye*, 50.

fear of the man. In the opening lines of the novel, they are restless and on edge not because of the darkness but because they know the bad weather will have put Reegan in a foul mood. As he awaits his father's arrival, Willie's face is drawn and his voice strained (B, 7).[11] Reegan must dominate and his domination must be openly acknowledged. Ironically, he tells the children that education should develop independent thinking (B, 17), and yet he expects them to parrot his views and clichés and toe his solipsistic line of authority. Obsessing over his run-in with his superintendent, Quirke, when he speaks, Reegan's voice pierces the kitchen quiet like a splinter of glass (B, 20). Like Elizabeth and the children, the other policemen tread warily in his presence.

Another feature of Reegan's character that McGahern took from his father was his inability to face the reality of his wife's illness. When he hears the diagnosis, Reegan wants to run away (B, 110); McGahern's father did (M, 112, 121). As Elizabeth's condition worsens, Reegan becomes more and more obsessed with Quirke; desperate to resign before he is cashiered, Reegan becomes more self-centred and even less attentive to his ailing wife: 'she'd have to collapse before he'd ever notice now' (B, 189). In a passage like this, the repressed animus that fuels McGahern's characterization of Reegan, but which for the most part he keeps under wraps, breaks out; the conscious or unconscious restraint that attempts to keep the character at a distance from his father falters, and a passage a few pages after this suggests that it has been a moment of authorial intrusion upon the narrative voice. McGahern presents Elizabeth affirming her respect and admiration for Reegan's vitality, his brute energy, and monomaniacal devotion to his egotistical dream (B, 192); this admiration and respect are bound up with her love for him, which in large part rests on the memory of her original physical attraction. But as we shall see, this linking of sexual desire and death is a nexus of grief and anger throughout McGahern's writing.

What McGahern describes in the Reegans' marriage is how disparate threads of circumstance and personality have pulled over time into a taut, intractable knot of habit, ever-diminishing expectations, and increasing

---

11   See *Memoir* (22–3) for a similar description of McGahern's barracks world.

regret. After being diagnosed, Elizabeth briefly thinks that if only she and Reegan could face the facts together perhaps they might open up to each other before it was too late, but in bed that night 'silence lay between them like a knife' (*B*, 111). For both, it seems, any gesture of openness towards the other risks a self-wounding. Their closest moment in the novel comes, ironically, when Reegan's misanthropy drives him into 'inarticulacy' and his frustration suddenly converts into sexual desire for Elizabeth who, herself exhausted by the illness and the effort of trying to manage her husband's unhappiness, is grateful for 'the animal warmth and loving kindness .... It didn't have to mean anything more than that' (*B*, 181).

McGahern seems to have constructed Elizabeth and Reegan out of the love and animosity he felt towards his mother and father. At the same time, the *poiēsis* seems to perform an attempt to fathom his parents' relationship; to imagine, from the vantage-point of his own adult experience, the quality of the relationship he witnessed as a child, rather than to create characters who break free of their models. What is also clear in retrospect is that the construction of Reegan released McGahern for – or perhaps drove him on to – the exorcism of *The Dark*. Reegan is not a monster like the elder Mahoney of that novel, but the potential is clearly present. Essentially, McGahern constructs both as men who lack imagination; their self-consciousness is so extreme that it overwhelms whatever capacity they have for recognizing the presence and inherent value of another human being. When Elizabeth tells him she may have cancer, Reegan immediately thinks of his own 'bad luck' (*B*, 99). Like Mahoney in *The Dark*, and Moran in *Amongst Women*, Reegan is a narcissist who is incapable of change or growth and who as a consequence is forced to survive off the continually diminishing capital of his own ego. Misers of the spirit, these fathers count every penny of emotion spent in any exchange and then, convinced they have overpaid, try to snatch some back. After narrating the episode of his run-in with Quirke, Reegan recoils at his emotional exposure to the others and 'the shame of intimacy ... started to nag him to desperation' (*B*, 18). But there is no comfort either when he turns inward to brood (*B*, 19).

Reegan is even thrown off-balance when touched by the generosity of another's happiness. On the train to Dublin for her operation Elizabeth recalls the lost but still real happiness of past Christmases with her family, and she burnishes the memory into a rejuvenating 'spot of time'. But her beaming face discomfits Reegan; this is not how a 'defeated woman' should act (*B*, 115). His consciousness like his emotions seems arrested between the inchoate and childish (*B*, 116). Like Moran, Reegan carries a grudge against life because it hasn't given him what he wanted, and over the years he has come to visualize the source of that withholding in the tricolour of the new state and to project his animosity into the hated figure of Superintendent Quirke.[12] His monolithic sense of his oppression by the very state he fought to create blinds him to his own oppressive behaviour. Believing that the money he can make from selling turf will not only pay for Elizabeth's hospital expenses but also allow him to resign from the police force and buy a small farm, Reegan drives his children as hard as himself, insensitive to the excessive hardship he is imposing on them, even after Elizabeth speaks up against it.

One might ask, however, why – apart from showing the behaviour that his circumstances and his poisoned character (*B*, 108) have led to – McGahern does not expose and explore the inner workings of Reegan in the same way he imagines the inner life of Elizabeth. There does seem to be a resistance. Or perhaps at this first stage of his writing life the remorse and guilt of the grieving imagination took priority over other emotional imperatives like the expression of anger, shame, and even hatred. The metaphor of a poisoned selfhood recurs later when Elizabeth thinks how she has spent her marriage precariously managing Reegan's violent volatility and then recognizes the ironic boon this pays when her increasing ill-health begins to prey on her mind: 'it prevented her from dwelling on herself, one poison counteracting the other' (*B*, 185). Reegan's reluctance to break from his frenetic physical life and look inward is aligned with his and Elizabeth's fear of 'scraping down to the cores of personality' (*B*, 153). He is almost a different man when potato-seeding time comes and he spends long days

---

12   The representation of the 'new Ireland' ushered in with independence in *The Barracks* continued throughout McGahern's career, with passages in *Amongst Women* and *Memoir* expressing the same criticisms; see *B*, 28; see also 208–9; compare *AW*, 5, 88 and *M*, 32, 48–9.

at manual labour, but his good spirits are the fumes of a narcissistic fantasy and bought at the expense of the children (*B*, 109). Significantly, there is one characteristic that Reegan and Elizabeth seem to share – the desire to be free (*B*, 71, 110). And perhaps even more important is that both seem to feel relationship with another as an encroachment upon that freedom, although in Elizabeth's case, it is possible that this feature of her character is a projection by McGahern based on his view of his parents' marriage. Reegan's desire to be free is expressed primarily in his dissatisfaction with his job and his desire to be loose of authority (*B*, 110).

An important distinction McGahern draws between Elizabeth and Reegan is her spirituality and his hollowness, and as already noted, her spiritual sensibility is another facet of her characterization that links her to McGahern's mother. The Mass may have become for her an empty form (*B*, 53), but McGahern constructs her as a character with a highly developed spiritual sensibility for whom the life story of Christ and the liturgical rituals that commemorate it, especially those of Holy Week, are profoundly significant.[13] Reegan, on the other hand, possesses a mind incapable of prayer (*B*, 18). Like McGahern's father, whose religion was all costume drama and dress parade, rules and regulations, Irish opera (see *M*, 47; 105, 135–6), Reegan is preoccupied with the visible signs of piety rather than spiritual substance. It is as if there is no interiority to his religious observance but only an exaggerated participation in the rituals so that his observance will be observed. His behaviour in church is a way of evoking a public recognition similar to the respect he demands when in uniform. It is the same with

---

13   Maher remarks that 'It is [Elizabeth's] spirituality, her unflinching faith that provides her with some limited solace. Elizabeth is the most religious of all McGahern's characters. She has a huge attachment to rituals and ceremonies' (*John McGahern*, 18). McGahern's characterization, however, does not develop Elizabeth as a figure of faith in the conventional sense of a practicing Irish Catholic of the 1940s or 1950s; rather, her spirituality is constructed quite explicitly in terms of an intuitive belief in the sanctity of the natural world and of the human person. The Christ she contemplates is more good man than god. Grace Ledwidge also recognizes McGahern's distinction between faith and spirituality in his construction of the character; see 'Death in Marriage: The Tragedy of Elizabeth Reegan in *The Barracks*', *Irish University Review* 35.1 (2005), 102.

the motif of the nightly rosary. From early in the novel it is a daily domestic convention more than meaningful spiritual exercise, but for Elizabeth it is at least a time for escape to the privacy of her own thoughts and the nourishment of memory.[14] The narcissistic image of Reegan at prayer is less than subtle: he kneels before a mirror (*B*, 33, repeated 185) and worships his own image, the god of home and barracks, the lord of all he surveys. For Reegan – as for Moran in *Amongst Women* – the nightly rosary is a way to end his day by imposing his will on others.[15] The rosary at bed-time along with the ritual of his morning shave, at which he is 'served' by the children like mock-altar boys to his parodic celebrant, function like the lowering and raising of the flag at a colonial outpost, with Reegan the beleaguered and increasingly bitter administrator surrounded by savages and half-wits who cannot see, let alone comprehend, his wasted potential.

Reegan's inability to pray, his attraction to mirrors, and his apparent inability to access an interior self are all significant; the latter, in particular, is a feature that recurs in all McGahern's subsequent father-figures. McGahern's description of Reegan eating his breakfast in the same void of self-consciousness as he says the rosary is masterful. The 'total blankness' (*B*, 45) of Reegan's state of mind recalls the description of Sheila waking him and his return to consciousness as if returning to the planet. For a moment he has no idea who she is (*B*, 43). It is as if Reegan is a shell inhabited by an alien being that enters and vacates his body, animating the hollow man in ways that are inscrutable to those around him.[16] As he slowly becomes aware of Elizabeth's presence, he cannot ignore that his bovine self-absorption in the mastication of his food while she has been speaking to him has given

14   Later, it must be noted, Elizabeth *does* recall the prayer ritual in more positive terms (see *B*, 220).

15   See Antoinette Quinn, 'A Prayer for My Daughters: Patriarchy in *Amongst Women*', *Canadian Journal of Irish Studies* 17.1 (1991), 86; also Siobhán Holland, 'Re-citing the Rosary: Women, Catholicism and Agency in Brian Moore's *Cold Heaven* and John McGahern's *Amongst Women*', in *Contemporary Irish Fiction: Themes, Tropes and theories*, ed. L. Harte and M. Parker (Basingstoke: Macmillan, 2000), 70–1.

16   McGahern uses the metaphor of Reegan as a reluctant actor who impersonates what he cannot be; in his memoir, McGahern describes his father with the same metaphor (compare *B*, 70 and *M*, 226).

some offence (*B*, 45); then, ironically, after she admits she needs to see the doctor, he blurts out "'You don't look well" ... with unthinking cruelty' (*B*, 46). Reegan, however, looks well; in fact, he's 'shining' (*B*, 47). And that seems to be what matters in the world of the barracks. Reegan does begin to worry about Elizabeth, however, or rather, about himself in the event of losing her; his sense of his situation immediately summons the image of his first wife and the thought that Elizabeth might die comes into his mind only in the form of the 'ludicrous' idea that life might deprive him of two wives (*B*, 47).

The motif of the rosary connects *The Barracks* to the later *Amongst Women*. In his first published novel McGahern is unequivocal in his description of the ritual's utter hollowness (*B*, 33; see *M*, 15). The second time he describes the family praying he extends his point, emphasizing that the prayers 'never assumed light of meaning' but were 'as dark as the earth they walked' (*B*, 73). The light and dark imagery looks ahead to McGahern's second novel and introduces a symbolism that is central to his writing when considered as an expressive project and mythopoeic process. In *Memoir* there is a 'wisdom' passage that provides an important gloss on this passage in *The Barracks* and the dark/light symbolism in his fiction in general:

> We come from darkness into light and grow in the light until at death we return to that original darkness. Those early years of the light are also a partial darkness because we have no power or understanding and are helpless in the face of the world. This is one of the great miseries of childhood. Mercifully, it is quickly absorbed by the boundless faith and energy and the length of the endlessly changing day of the child. Not even the greatest catastrophe can last the whole length of that long day. (*M*, 36)

The powerlessness of children is a recurrent theme in McGahern's writing, represented not only by their physical weakness and vulnerability to violent abuse, but also by the fear and suffering in which being 'in the dark', or more precisely, in McGahern's case, being 'kept in the dark', can result.[17] Darkness is not just the unknown but the *feeling* of not knowing; knowledge and understanding bring joy, and to escape from being kept

---

17 Crotty describes the world of *The Barracks* as one 'where children have a deeply ingrained understanding of their secondariness' ('"All Toppers,"' 45).

in the dark is the way to self-empowerment. In his memoir, McGahern explicitly juxtaposes his father and mother by connecting his father not only to the darkness of unknowing but also to the oppressive manipulations of secrecy (*M*, 35). In the period leading up to the death of their mother, Francis McGahern intensified his tyranny over the children by keeping them 'in the dark' concerning her whereabouts and the reason for her absence (*M*, 37). McGahern's second novel, which deals with the nightmare world of childhood and adolescence under the rule of his father, is titled simply *The Dark*.

The fear of being 'gathered into a total nothingness' (*B*, 71), which leads Elizabeth to resist her desire for emotional comfort from Reegan, should be understood in relation to this light/dark symbolism. For McGahern, identity, it would seem, is a process of gradual self-gathering, a cohesion and coherence of self-consciousness in relation to others and the world that is shaped by and from experience, memory and imagination, but it 'is lost almost as soon as it is gathered' (*M*, 36). The 'gathering' Elizabeth resists is her own undoing. McGahern's construction of Elizabeth Reegan is a meditation on a dying person's sense of the imminent erasure or scattering of the self that her life has gathered, her subtraction from 'the great glory' (*M*, 36) in which, with all of its joys as well as disappointments, she comes to see her life participating – the kind of insight, it should be pointed out, McGahern will make a point of informing us that Michael Moran was incapable of having (see *AW*, 179). Indeed, from this point on in the novel, Elizabeth's interior monologues increasingly show her 'precious and poignant' (*M*, 36) love for the world she is leaving. This aspect of the characterization, like the intensity of McGahern's representation of the horrors of the 'father-world' in *The Dark* and of lingering guilt and pain in *The Leavetaking*, renders his assertion that 'Not even the greatest catastrophe can last the whole length of that long day' of childhood less than convincing (*M*, 36); rather, McGahern's fiction provides overwhelming evidence that the shadows cast by the long day of his childhood stretched well into his adult years. Indeed, it is possible to see McGahern's writing activity itself, in its complex synthesis of memory and imagination, as a reversal of the Isis-Osiris roles of myth, a lifelong (self-) gathering of the scattered memories of the 'lost beloved' into the iconic presence or Image of the 'lost world' or 'the great glory of which we are but a particle' (*M*, 36), a psychological and artistic process that is not completed until the visionary reunion described at the end of *Memoir* and the sublation of the beloved in the recovered 'mother-world' of *That They May Face the Rising Sun*.

What also begins in *The Barracks* is McGahern's use of the rosary as vehicle to bring out the hollowness of the State religion's and the religious State's sanctimonious ennoblement of woman and the family: McGahern's shaping of the narrative for ironic effect is evident when he describes Elizabeth coming out of her exhaustion, pain, and memory of being hurt by Willie's outburst, to hear Reegan 'sing-songing' the litany to the Blessed Virgin.[18] McGahern's language, however, suggests that Reegan is really in a 'tranced' worship of his own idolatrous image, and the reference to 'The Dedication of the Christian Family' only amplifies the irony (*B*, 36). McGahern elicits a different ironic effect when he closes the second chapter with another rosary scene. Before Reegan begins 'the Mysteries' that organize the prayer, he surprises Elizabeth by offering the prayers 'for a special intention'; for a moment she is overwhelmed with a sense of being loved; he is thinking of her; but the moment passes: 'She had no means of knowing. He wouldn't tell and she could never ask' (*B*, 73). For McGahern, the greater mysteries are obviously the joyful, sorrowful, and glorious incidents, shared or not, in the lives of human beings. Elizabeth's attention is on the earthly mystery of the human heart, her own and Reegan's, not on any transcendental truth, but she has no hope of answer.

In Elizabeth Reegan McGahern imagines the mental life – the thoughts and feelings – of a character by drawing from his childhood recollections of his mother in the months leading up to her death, but also from what he could imagine as an adult about his mother's feelings toward her husband and his father. The life in the barracks and her relationship with Reegan and the children provide the context for Elizabeth's thoughts and feelings about life, daily routine, the past, the meaninglessness of it all, and

---

18   For a reading of Elizabeth as a hopelessly defeated and abject victim of her husband and her society, with Reegan being a representative of the patriarchy that Church and State give institutional authority to, see Ledwidge, 'Death in Marriage'.

the equally undeniable, intuitive truth that our most direct access to joy is through the ephemeral glory of simple things. The writing articulates a process of empathic imagination – an attempt to think and feel oneself into another's dying – as well as of imaginative recollection; the characterization, in Elizabeth's case, is a synthesis of homage, grief, and praise, but also an expansion of mourning into self-expression as McGahern uses her interior monologues to articulate his own developing views on life, religion, relationship, and sexuality. If Elizabeth is, as McGahern himself described her, 'as much a way of looking as a character', then her perspective is a prismatic refraction of McGahern's own memory and imagination. If we can see her, as Sampson does, as 'a surrogate artist for whom memory is centrally important', 'an artist-narrator of her own life',[19] it is because the making of her character provided McGahern with 'a way of looking' back to the past, his mother, her dying and death, his father, and his childhood, as well as at what he had seen of life since then. Although there seems to be no 'agenda' as such with regard to the characterization of Reegan, in relation to McGahern's memories of his father, the sergeant is hardly the 'uncomplicated', 'more attractive' figure McGahern suggests he is in *Memoir*. It is now clear that the characterization of Reegan was the beginning of a process and generated a specific imaginative momentum that led inescapably to the subject matter of *The Dark*.

McGahern's management of the narrative voice and the characters' perspectives in *The Barracks* serves a self-expression that oscillates between the poles of absolute uncertainty and certain absolutes. The narrator's reference to 'the ferocious ruthlessness of life' that can make desire seem 'ludicrous' (*B*, 16)[20] and 'the desperate satisfaction' of absolute uncertainty and the absolute mystery of others (*B*, 62) are sentiments that recur in the later novels and here, rather than focalizing inner feeling or thought, seem to enter the narration from a vantage-point outside the character. The narrator's description of Elizabeth's spirituality as a 'wonder' in the face of an ultimately unknowable world (*B*, 165) combines McGahern's adult recollections of his mother's natural piety and his own deepening agnosti-

19   *Outstaring Nature's Eye*, 17.
20   Compare 'the stupidity of human wishes' in 'Christmas' (*CE*, 25).

cism. It is possible to see McGahern projecting into the characterization when the narrator has Elizabeth think about her failure to fathom Reegan's strangeness (*B*, 64). Many years later, McGahern would admit the same thing about his father (see *M*, 271). Also, the surprising rhetorical force of the phrase 'the shame of intimacy' (*B*, 18) in the description of Reegan's sense of exposure following his account of his run-in with Quirke, draws attention to the narrative voice as much as it informs us about the character; the phrase seems disproportionate for the scene and to what we know about Reegan at this point, and is perhaps the intrusion of memory and a sublimated expression of the 'shameful intimacy' forced upon McGahern by his father which he will turn into fiction in his next novel and describe in detail in his memoir.

When Reegan suddenly asks Elizabeth how she is feeling, her impulse is 'to fall into his arms and give way to starved emotions'; but she holds back: she wants them both to 'stay in some measure free' (*B*, 71). McGahern's construction of Elizabeth's life of feeling, her emotional character and point of view, her understanding of the two very different men that she has loved, Reegan and Halliday, is what shapes the complex heart of the novel. But being 'fair' to Reegan must have taxed him as well. Recognizing and respecting his mystery as a human being must have chafed the painful memories of the man who shadowed the novelist's construction of the character. Elizabeth's desire for 'control' and 'private order' reflect the need on McGahern's part to maintain his distance from the darkness that, in a sense, he was trying to write himself out of, so that *he* 'might stay in some measure free'. Writing his way back to the beloved, for McGahern, was also the way forward, away from the jailer and the cell that had dominated his childhood and adolescence. And when McGahern describes Elizabeth looking at Reegan's unhappiness and feeling some responsibility for it, because somehow she had failed to find out what it was he really wanted from her, what she was supposed to know even if he didn't, but had no idea or intuitive sense what it might be, how she could make him whole and free him from the eagle tearing at his liver (*B*, 175–6) – one cannot help think that, in imagining this feeling for his character, McGahern was actually describing, consciously or unconsciously, what *he* had come to feel growing up with his father.

The Lost Image

As Elizabeth's condition worsens and her spirits swing more violently between despair and elation, McGahern's characterization becomes its most complex amalgam of memory, imagination, and self-projection. When Elizabeth tries to write a letter to a nurse-friend from her London days to invite her to visit her, she realizes that to be honest would mean writing 'about herself ... her relationship with Reegan ... her heart gone weak, the cancer, the futility of her life and the life about her, her growing indifference. That was the truth she'd have to tell' (*B*, 187). Three times McGahern has her attempt to articulate her feelings, but each formulation proves unsatisfactory. First she writes, '*Things get worse and worse and more frightening*', but that was hardly the whole truth; she judges her second attempt, '*Everything gets stranger and more strange*', to be just as misleading, as well as suggesting 'a faint touch of craziness'; her final effort, '*Things get better and better, more beautiful*', while it 'reached praise of something at last', seems no 'more false or true' than her first two attempts and leads her to give up trying to express her feelings in words (*B*, 187). The burden of this meta-narrative episode is as much McGahern's as his character's. The poles of despair and ecstasy spark in Elizabeth a sense of the world becoming increasingly uncanny, 'stranger and more strange', and in trying to imagine the growing storm in the mind of the dying woman, the darkening clouds of fear and despair, the sudden clefts of clarity and ecstatic beauty, the *poiēsis* leads McGahern to inhabit the mind of an other who is also his mother. As he imagines Elizabeth beginning to take leave of her world, McGahern is also writing his way back to the leave-taking that never occurred between himself and his mother. The fiction summons the language of the 'lost world', the words that went unspoken between son and mother and mother and son, a closing of a circle that had been left broken, and so, open, paradoxically, to both regret and promise. The struggle against despair; the drive to be honest and accurate and to express both the horror and the joy, the sense both of blank emptiness and of supervening grace that can attend perception of innate yet accidental beauty in the world; the urge to acknowledge, lament and celebrate in a way that each does not diminish or obscure the reality and truth of the other – characterize McGahern's story-telling from the outset of his career. The 'strangeness' of the world that Elizabeth increasingly senses is not due to any estrangement from it, nor to an alienating unfamiliarity; rather, what McGahern gradually describes Elizabeth experiencing derives from his imagining of his mother's intuitive gnosis of the life-force in nature, an imagining that is really a projection of a voice within him that is intermittently articulate throughout his fiction and fully 'outspoken' in his memoir and last novel.

In the penultimate chapter of *The Barracks*, bed-ridden after a heart attack, Elizabeth realizes that she will never again perform the daily rota of domestic chores that she had felt to be 'the drag and burden of their lives together' but which now she hears as 'a wild call to life; life, life and life at any cost' (*B*, 202). The chapter is a combination of dialogue and interior monologue. Elizabeth has become the fixed point around which Reegan, the children, and the other policemen circle as they go about their routines. Her immobility conceals the tidal surges of desire and epiphanic joy within her, as well as the frantic squalls of fear and despair that cloud her thinking as she nears the end: "'Sometimes meaning and peace come but I lose them again, nothing in life is ever resolved once and for all but changes with the changing life, calm had to be fought for through pain, and always when it was given it was both different and the same, every loss had changed it, and she could be sure it never came to stay, because she was still alive["]' (*B*, 204). The passage begins in Elizabeth's interior voice but then McGahern seems to lose focus (as well as the terminal quotation mark) and allows the narrative voice to merge with it; this devolution of the fictive first-person into the masked subjectivity of the third-person narrator is symptomatic-expressive of the fragility of McGahern's 'control' here; the narration comprises an imagining that is really a remembering, a re-visionary 'seeing for the first time' what the nine-year-old child saw but could not have understood or imagined at the time.

A similar synthesis of imaginative recollection and empathic projection informs McGahern's construction of Elizabeth's 'spots of time', passages where he achieves an access to the beloved by imagining an image of how and what she loved. In the first such moment, McGahern allows Elizabeth the kind of epiphany he will not repeat until he reprises the technique, with an even sharper irony, in *Amongst Women*. She recalls the glorious summer day when she first met Reegan. Coming out of a church, where she had been unable to say any 'formal prayer' (*B*, 14), she saw a farmer pass by atop a cart loaded with hay – a figure out of the 'eternal' world of the seasons – and he acknowledged her with a commonplace about the weather but 'it came to her as a prayer of praise, she never had such long-ing to live for ever' (*B*, 15). The impulse to 'natural' prayer succeeds where the sense of formal duty remains inert; the lust for life triumphs over the routines and forms of religious authority. McGahern's construction of the moment is both a homage to his mother's love of life and the beginning of his development of Elizabeth's spiritual independence and rejection of religious convention.

A similar conjunction of elements occurs in the second 'spot of time' which comes as Elizabeth is helping the children with their homework:

> She felt she was part of their whole lives as they worked. She watched them for a few minutes in a perfect wonder of peace. Then she went to the window to touch the heads of the daffodils with her fingers. The sun had gone down close to the fir-tops across the lake. The level glare stained a red roadway on the water to the navigation signs and the grass of the river meadows was a low tangle of green and white light. It came so violently to the window that she'd soon to turn away, spelling the word Willie had asked her in inarticulate wonder. (*B*, 62–3)

McGahern's memories of his schoolteacher mother helping him with his homework flow into this scene where the mother-figure releases the son's 'inarticulate wonder' into expression (see *M*, 66). Spelling the word for him she models the future novelist's challenge to articulate the sense of 'wonder' at life that was his mother's legacy to him. This use of the 'spot of time' in the novel is profoundly expressive of the nature of McGahern's narrative *poiēsis*. Recollection and epiphany, moments when 'the great glory' is glimpsed and the darkness of unknowing gives way to the light of understanding, are generated by a process of imaginative recall and narrative construction that recover the past even as its reconstitution confirms its loss.

The 'Image' lives only in the *mythos* and Elizabeth's almost Augustinian sense of existence as dispersion – 'the human body is undone'[21]– is counterbalanced by such moments, as when she remembers Christmases past – 'What did it matter that it had all slowly broken up and separation had come before even the first death? It didn't matter, she must affirm that – it made no difference! Only her happiness mattered. She'd been given all that much happiness and she wanted to praise and give thanks' (*B*, 115).[22] Make the feminine pronouns masculine and this passage could serve as an epigraph to McGahern's whole career as a writer, a career which is rooted in the trauma of loss and separation but which steadily works toward the affirmation of an original happiness and concludes in praise and gratitude. Throughout that career, the function and power of memory to focus self, self-esteem, and self-presence, and to provide the continuity of the self-in-time and the continuance of value against the dark that threatens to obscure or erase it are at the centre of McGahern's making of fiction.

The denouement of *The Barracks* describes Reegan's collapse following Elizabeth's death. He neglects his duty and achieves a pyrrhic victory over Quirke by resigning before he can be suspended. The significance of the final image of the children drawing down the blinds as they did in the opening chapter does not close the narrative circle so much as draw attention to the emptiness now at its centre; the echo of the beginning accentuates the hollowness of the family without the mother-figure present. *The Barracks* establishes the lost mother as the centring absence of McGahern's fictive world. The pastoral round that haunts the novel's form is corrupt. 'All the years were over now' (*B*, 232); the expectation of cyclical renewal is arrested and the narrative ends blankly, with no sense of Reegan's or of the children's future. The form of *The Barracks* approaches the downward

---

21   See Ricoeur, 'The Creativity of Language', 220.

22   The impulse to 'praise' that is such an important aspect of McGahern's characterization of Elizabeth is an imperative force within his own development as a writer. Elizabeth's desire 'to praise and give thanks' recalls her response to the farmer's expression about the summer day as 'a prayer of praise' (*B*, 15), as well as the passage in which the narrator praises her: 'Her woman's days had no need of change. They were full and too busy, wanting nothing but to be loved' (*B*, 21).

spiral of tragedy, but the novel has no tragic hero or heroine. Its power derives from the fragmented synergy of myth and realism which gives to its story of a dying beauty and bridled beast an aura of gathering but as yet unshaped gravitas.

The narration of Elizabeth Reegan's dying in *The Barracks* marks a first stage in McGahern's working through the memories of the grief and guilt that his mother's death brought upon him. However, it is not until his third novel, *The Leavetaking*, that McGahern deals explicitly with these feelings in a section that he later 'recycles' in *Memoir*. In *The Barracks*, when Elizabeth tells the children that she is going to hospital for tests, their reaction is to remember when they lost their mother, but what McGahern describes as *their* memories are the same as Patrick Moran's in *The Leavetaking* and his own in *Memoir*. Interestingly, in his first fictional 'treatment' of these painful memories, McGahern diffuses the sense of individual guilt that dominates the later accounts by describing all three Reegan children playing outside during their mother's funeral and asking the two fisherman to take them out on the river (*B*, 102–3). The details are identical in the later novel and memoir except that, there, it is the solitary young boy, Moran/McGahern, who pleads with the men to take him along, and looking back, the memory is part of the pain of his sense of having failed his mother at the moment of farewell. Perhaps not yet ready to write about such painful feelings, or perhaps first needing to acknowledge his mother's experience before he turned to his own, in *The Barracks* the burden of McGahern's creative effort is an empathic imagining of the character's state of mind as she faces death, an imagining that may mimic the inner world of his own grieving, even as the writing objectifies the loss and externalizes the process as a form of mourning. What this recollecting-imagining also involves is a coming to terms with the otherness that shrouds the beloved when she is lost to the loving survivor. The imagining of Elizabeth Reegan is McGahern's first effort at letting go, of *allowing* his mother to die, if still on *his* terms. What these terms are is important because they enable him to move on to the next stage in writing himself free of grief and its memories. Elizabeth's sense of being alone and abandoned at the end – by Reegan, the children, and Mrs Casey (*B*, 212) – is McGahern's first recording of his sense of his own mother's abandonment by his father (see *M*, 117) – something for which he seems never to have forgiven him; but it was also a first step towards the confession of his own sense of culpability. In *The Barracks* McGahern obliquely accords his mother a victory over the despair that otherwise would paralyse him, a despair and paralysis he will not exorcize until *The Pornographer*.[23] In this way, he imagines her victory over his father, the man who abandoned her, but also over the father-in-him, the son who also betrayed her. It is important to recognize the combination of mimesis and expression in the process, the construction and management of the character in a realistic fiction, and the working-out of the conscious and unconscious agendas that narrative *poiēsis* attempts.

---

23   Sampson describes *The Barracks* as 'a study of the personal qualities that counter despair with endurance and serenity' (*Outstaring Nature's Eye*, 35); he also recognizes that the novel is 'shaped ... by memory' ('The Lost Image', 60). What I am suggesting is that the despair being 'countered' is the writer's and the imagining-writing is the grief-work that counters it.

CHAPTER FOUR

In the Name of the Father: *The Dark* (1965)

The opening chapter of *The Dark* is the most harrowing in all of McGahern's fiction. Flawed or complex, an overly ambitious experiment in symbolic meta-narrative or simply written too quickly, as McGahern himself suggested (*M*, 249), his second novel contains some of his most powerful and affective writing. The first and third chapters alone set it apart from his other works. *The Dark* braids three subjects – adolescent sexuality, the uncertainty of vocation, and paternal abuse and its effects – into an ambiguously open-ended portrait of self-awakening and self-assertion. The continuities within the discontinuities between it and *The Barracks* make clear that it is a coded sequel to his first novel. Roscommon has been replaced by Leitrim, the barracks by a farmhouse, and a truculent Garda sergeant by a farmer-patriarch of ogre-like monstrosity, but the dead mother of the first novel remains dead and the peripheral young boy, Willie, has become the unnamed protagonist-narrator. If McGahern's first novel is about the dying mother, his second is about the son who must continue without her. Willie Reegan's younger sisters, Una and Sheila, have become Joan and Mona, the protagonist's older siblings, based on McGahern's sisters, Rosaleen and Breedge. Even more than in *The Barracks*, the intertextual relations between *The Dark* and McGahern's memoir attest to the autobiographical nature of the fiction and the continuing drive to exorcize the past that informs his act of writing. In *The Dark*, two aspects of the latter have drawn particular critical attention: a narrative voice that modulates through all three persons for no clear programmatic reason and a conclusion that seems inconsistent with much of the preceding action.

'Your blood and mine': Fee, Fie, Foe, Fum
– Symbolic Rape, Seduction and Abuse

The Dark begins with the scene of a father terrorizing his adolescent son.

> 'Say what you said because I know.'
> 'I didn't say anything.' (*D*, 7)

This opening exchange is a parody of the confessional interrogation that provides the novel with its narrative drive and organic form. Mahoney, the father, reaches for his shaving strop and orders his son to go upstairs with him. His brutally ironic promise to teach him a lesson introduces the theme of learning in the novel, developed in the boy's use of education to escape his father's tyranny and the construction of Mahoney as a demonic inversion of the parent as loving mentor-teacher.[1] Mahoney's choice of a bedroom for his classroom is also darkly significant. He wants an audience and the boy's younger sister, Mona, is in bed. He forces the boy to remove his clothes in front of her. McGahern's language transforms the father into a rabid beast: 'a white froth showed on his lips. ... The belt twitched against his trousers, an animal's tail' (*D*, 8). At this point the scene turns into a symbolic rape.

Like all rape, the assault is about power and powerlessness. The narrator describes the father getting 'pleasure' from ordering his son to strip (*D*, 8). The 'pleasure' is all the more ominous as he orders the boy to kneel in a chair and bend over: 'On your mouth and nose. I'll give your arse something it won't forget in a hurry' (*D*, 9). Naked and whimpering, the terrified boy waits for the lash but it never comes because the father's aim is to terrorize, demean, degrade, and break his spirit in front of his sister. Terrified, the boy loses control of his bladder. When he tries to move, Mahoney threatens but does not strike. Instead, his 'measured passion'

---

1   For a scene in which McGahern describes his own father's authoritarian pretensions in this regard, see *M*, 196–7.

spent, a detumescent, red-faced Mahoney merely stands and looks down at the boy he has humiliated, his son, 'the leather hanging dead in his hand' (*D*, 10).[2] After this horrific opening, we are told that all three children had set themselves against their father and as much as possible shut him out of their lives (*D*, 11).[3]

Being forced to share his father's bed means the boy must end every day by sleeping with the ogre who has made his day a misery. Some nights, however, a different horror unfolds: 'The worst was to have to sleep with him the nights he wanted love ...' (*D*, 17). The vicious symbolic rape of Chapter One is followed in Chapter Three by a disgusting parody of seduction. Although the voice is that of a focalized third-person, already one can hear the more 'personal' dimension that will enter the novel with the first- and second-person narrators, when the anonymous protagonist becomes the narrator-protagonist. The scene is presented in much more detail than the psychological 'beating' of the opening pages but its power derives as much from its rhythms as from its disturbing details: a noxious suspense is created as McGahern describes the boy listening to his father undressing, the delay before he gets into bed, then the burning match held to his face; but suspense gives way to a sickening despair as the boy realizes his ruse is ineffectual and he resigns himself to his father's will: 'Hatred took the place of fear, and it brought the mastery of not caring much more' (*D*, 17–18).

The 'seduction' begins as Mahoney apologizes for waking him, includes him in a shared sense of grievance at being confined to the farm, and suggests a meal in town.[4] We are told that these crude blandishments are a

---

2   In his memoir McGahern speculates that his father got a sexual pleasure from beating him and his sisters (*M*, 188); the masturbatory quality to Mahoney's actions here recurs more explicitly in the 'seduction' scene of Chapter Three.

3   Mahoney's recurring complaint of being ignored by his children is drawn from McGahern's father (compare *D*, 11 and *M*, 192), as is his isolation (see *M*, 159–60) and the game the children play mocking his mantra, 'God, O God, O God ...' (*D*, 15, 28, 48, 105; compare *M*, 156, 191). Being forced to attend Mahoney as he mended one's shoes is also drawn from McGahern's childhood (see *D*, 32 and *M*, 158).

4   It is important to recognize the structural pattern to the irony that McGahern begins to build into the novel at this point. The promises of 'tea in the Royal Hotel' and 'a new suit' (*D*, 20) are part of Mahoney's 'seduction', his getting his way and

familiar prelude; listening to his father's repulsive prattle, the boy knows 'there were worse things in these nights than words' (*D*, 19).⁵ It is soon obvious what the 'worse things' may be as Mahoney questions the boy's love for him, cajoling him into kissing him: 'The old horror as hands were put about him and the other face closed on his, the sharp stubble grown since the morning and the nose and the kiss, the thread of the half-dried mucus coming away from the other lips in the kiss' (*D*, 20). The travesty of paternal love is heart-breaking: 'Your father loves you', Mahoney whispers, while his hands 'begin to move in caress on [the boy's] back, shoving up the nightshirt ... the voice echoing rhythmically the movement of the hands', until

> ... The breathing quickened.
> 'You like that. It's good for you,' the voice breathed jerkily now to the stroking hands.
> 'I like that.'
> There was nothing else to say, it was better not to think or care .... It was easy that way except for the waves of loathing that would not stay back. (*D*, 20–1)

When a sated Mahoney forces yet another good-night kiss and falls asleep, McGahern again draws attention to the semen-like track of spittle left on the boy's lips by his father's mouth (*D*, 21). 'Loathing' is repeated five times in this scene which, with the abuse scene of the opening chapter,

---

having his pleasure. We should remember this when he eventually does take his son to town, years later, to celebrate his having won a university scholarship. McGahern makes quite clear that Mahoney does it so he can brag in public; that is, it is for *his* pleasure, not the boy's, a pleasure that remains narcissistic and masturbatory (see *D*, 153). Insensitive to his son's embarrassment and discomfort as he parades him from shop to shop, the emotional pattern of Chapter Three – 'loathing' followed by exhausted resignation – is repeated as the boy's shameful resentment gives way to an ironic 'You are marvellous, my father' (*D*, 160), ironic because of the echo in 'marvellous' of the 'The heavy blankets were marvellous and warm after' the sexual abuse of Chapter Three (*D*, 23).

5   The echo of Reegan's sense of 'the shame of intimacy' (*B*, 18) in the boy's reference to 'the dirty rags of intimacy' (D, 19) links the father-figures in McGahern's first two novels.

introduces us to the horrors Mahoney visits upon his son, but also to the motif of hatred that McGahern builds to describe the boy's feelings toward his father.[6] It is these repeated expressions of hatred, loathing, and repulsion, along with the powerful images of Mahoney's mistreatment of his children, that make the apparent reconciliation between son and father in the closing pages of the novel seem arbitrary and unconvincing. A careful reading of the ending of the novel, however, reveals explicit echoes of the sexual abuse scene in Chapter Three, and it is the irony that this generates that renders the final state of the protagonist's mind less than clear.

What is clear, however, from *Memoir*, is that the details of the physical and sexual abuse in *The Dark* were drawn from McGahern's own experiences as a child and adolescent. The ceiling-boards the boy counts while waiting for his father to come to bed are the same as those in McGahern's father's bedroom in the barracks: it is the same room, the boy lying in bed pretending to be asleep is McGahern, and Mahoney is McGahern's father. In the memoir, however, McGahern is explicit: 'Looking back, and remembering his tone of voice and the rhythmic movement of his hand, I suspect he was masturbating' (*M*, 188). In the winter of 1963–4 when he wrote *The Dark*, McGahern was already 'looking back', and writing what he did was a necessary step toward the more explicit exorcism of the memoir thirty years later. A peculiar effect of the protagonist's anonymity in *The Dark* is that it makes him a shadow of his father, a self-in-waiting, 'young Mahoney', 'Mahoney junior', a self that must find a way out from under the shadow that is stifling him. In Jungian terms, if *The Barracks* is a novel of the anima, *The Dark* is a novel of the shadow. The shadow-figure, Mahoney, is all that the son fears and loathes but must come to acknowledge and accept as part of himself if he is to escape the paralysis, the sickness of will that blights his adolescence, and make his break for freedom. It is in these terms, perhaps, that the problematic 'reconciliation' between father and son that ends the novel might be seen, a conclusion that is as ambiguous and open-ended as it is rooted in the writer's unconscious, perhaps, or in that intermediate

---

6   For explicit references to the boy's hatred of Mahoney, see *D*, 18, 21, 29, 35, 37, 43, 44–5, 115, 150, 153, 185; for his sisters' hatred of their father, see *D*, 15–16, 28, 37.

zone where character and author, the construct of consciousness and the ghosts of memory and the unconscious, make their deals. For certainly, from the horror of the opening chapters through to the end of the novel, there is little evidence of a growing change of attitude in the son toward Mahoney, who himself remains consistently brutal and the source of all the darkness in the story-world.[7]

The Name of the Father Is Darkness

The powerlessness of children and the abuse of parental power, a theme McGahern introduces in a minor key in *The Barracks*, becomes a major theme in *The Dark*. Mahoney is a tyrant; where power should be legitimized by authority, his authority derives solely from his physical power to threaten, beat, coerce and abuse his children: 'They all got beatings, often for no reason ...' (*D*, 11). In the opening chapter, the description of Mahoney's voice 'grinding' away at the boy conveys the man's character and method of relentlessly breaking down the spirits and bodies of his children – a character and behaviour drawn from McGahern's own father.[8] To read

7   For Whyte, Mahoney is as much a victim as his son for 'he is clearly a victim of his environment' (*History, Myth, and Ritual*, 38), but McGahern's text unequivocally presents Mahoney as a brutal victimizer, the source of whose vile animus is 'the dark' that emanates from the core of his character; to identify that source as 'a society in flux' traduces the very spirit and vision of McGahern's work; see also, Holland, 'Marvellous Fathers'.

8   The litany of abuse McGahern and his sisters suffered growing up forms the depressing core of the paradoxically triumphant *Memoir*: see *M*, 6, 23, 29, 68, 151, 153, 157–60, 186–7, 190–1, 197–9, 233. That *The Dark* would be banned as pornographic because of its depiction of adolescent masturbation will always be a sad reminder of just how late into the twentieth century the institutionalized, malignant hypocrisy of Church, State and society continued in Ireland. In Chapter One, after he dresses himself, the boy runs outside to the lavatory at the back of the yard; this is clearly drawn from McGahern's memories of the barracks at Cootehall (see *D*, 10, 38, 116 and *M*, 29).

the opening chapters of *The Dark* after reading *Memoir* leaves no doubt that McGahern was setting out in this novel to 'deal with' his memories of his father, who at the time, in 1963, was still very much alive and a potent shadow in his life.

But if Francis McGahern was the 'anti-light' that the novelist transformed into the tyrannical deity of his second novel and symbolized in its title, the force of continuous opposition to the illumination of life by love and generosity, 'the dark' of the novel is not what he describes in *Memoir* when he writes 'We come from darkness into light and grow in the light until at death we return to that original darkness' (*M*, 36). The 'dark' that McGahern embodies in Mahoney belongs to the child's experience of being 'helpless in the face of the world' (*M*, 36), but it is not the darkness of the world itself. It is the depravity, corruption, and evil of a man who brought up his children, in his son's words, 'in near starvation and violence and slavery' (*M*, 229). In *Memoir*, McGahern repeatedly associates his father with darkness and secrecy. The effect is a symbolic duality of father-darkness and mother-light (see *M*, 203). McGahern's anecdote of trying to walk into the sun as a baby foreshadows the old man's sunlit recovery of the 'lost beloved' in the conclusion of the memoir (see *M*, 11–12, 270–2). But with his father, 'There was ... something dark or forbidding in his personality' (*M*, 226) – indeed, his secretiveness was 'practically pathological' (*M*, 57; see also *M*, 35). 'A life from which the past was so rigorously shut out had to be a life of darkness' (*M*, 271), and this rejection of history was a trait McGahern would develop in the figure of Moran in *Amongst Women*. In the memoir McGahern recounts how, when he was little more than six, his father tried to coax him to leave his mother and sisters at Aughawillan and go to live with him at the barracks in Cootehall; the little boy evades and resists until his father gives up, ordering the boy not to tell his mother about his request. McGahern writes that there was something about his father's invitation that was 'too dark and shameful for speech' (*M*, 108).

McGahern's characterization of his father in *Memoir*, more than thirty years after his construction of Mahoney, shows how the narrative process in *The Dark* was not only a 'working out' of the writer's thoughts and feelings but an attempt to understand the man his father was. McGahern records how over the years he had heard people describe his father as an actor, and while he sensed a truth in the metaphor, it was never clear to him; but writing the memoir he came to see his father's role-playing as an aspect of his need to control others while concealing and protecting himself (see *M*, 226, 227). In *The Dark* McGahern draws on his father's 'theatricality' (*M*, 69) to present Mahoney's solipsism and self-interest in a scene where, drunk and unable to find anything to fault his children with, he berates them for being an unappreciative audience at the performance of his life (*D*, 128). More a buffoon than a Lear, Mahoney's bathetic 'improv' reeks of self-pity and ends with scorn for those he wants to impress. He is much more pleased with his 'turn' before the captive audience in the Royal Hotel, when he takes his son out to celebrate his scholarship. The performance is pure narcissism and the boy realizes he is merely a 'prop' in his father's egotistic pantomime: 'He was playing a part in Mahoney's joy ... celebrating Mahoney's joy ... not his own' (*D*, 153). At the novel's close, when Mahoney arrives in Galway to 'help' his son choose between university or a job with the E.S.B., he arrives 'full of a sense of drama. ... He'd play in it to the last' (*D*, 183). Again Mahoney's ego upstages his son's, but as he realizes that encouraging his son to remain at university might involve *him* in some expense, the puff quickly goes out of his bumptiousness and the curtain drops on the play (*D*, 184). (McGahern will reprise this feature of his father's character in Moran's handling of Sheila's dream of becoming a doctor in *Amongst Women*.) McGahern's use of the 'actor' motif for Mahoney is a long way from the more psychological complex use of the metaphor to describe his father in the memoir; it remains at the superficial level of exposing the man's hollowness and in this sense it builds from his characterization of Reegan in *The Barracks*.

Dreams, Vocations, and Cold Feet

The figure of the absent mother is not prominent in *The Dark* but her three appearances at the beginning of the novel are still significant. (The only other reference to her comes, also significantly, on the last page of the novel.) In the opening chapter Mahoney mentions her to shame the boy for swearing (*D*, 7), and then, after the assault in the bedroom, she comes into the boy's consciousness as a fragment of memory breaks through into his ordeal, the 'Day of sunshine he'd picked wild strawberries for her on the railway she was dying' (*D*, 10). The horrors of living with his father seem to have eclipsed the horror of his mother's death, so much so that there is a muted accusation of abandonment in the memory, as if in her absence she enables the abuser. This first memory is a version of McGahern's *ur*-memories of being with his mother and walking the lanes and roads with her that he recounts in *Memoir*. Pathetically, it recurs at the beginning of Chapter Three as the boy waits in terror for his father to come to bed (*D*, 17).[9] The third reference to the dead mother comes at the end of Chapter Five when the protagonist recalls the promise he made to her to become a priest but which he now feels unworthy of carrying out (*D*, 33). McGahern's breaking of his promise to his mother in favour of his own sense of vocation as a writer becomes a central theme in his next novel, *The Leavetaking*.

The reason the boy feels unworthy of fulfilling his promise is his guilt over his developing sexuality. The way McGahern develops, indeed drama-tizes, the relation between vocation and sexuality in the novel is complex but coherent, and related to the confessional use of the second-person narration. In *Memoir* McGahern describes how as a child he took up his mother's dream for him to become a priest (*M*, 62). In *The Dark* the boy remembers promising his mother that one day 'I'd say Mass for her' (*D*, 33;

---

9   A similar conjunction of a father's sexual abuse of his son and the son's memory of the dead mother occurs in McGahern's short story, 'Coming into His Kingdom' (see *N*, 36).

see *M*, 99). But what becomes clear is that the dream of a clerical career is as much a dream of a life free of his father. From McGahern's description of his mother's dream for him in his memoir it is possible to see that when writing *The Dark* he transferred specific memories of his mother's fantasy to the character of Mahoney. However, when Mahoney tells his son that he had dreamed of him as a priest so that he could sell the farm and move in with him (*D*, 45–6), McGahern is not only parodying his mother's dream of being his housekeeper (*M*, 63) by recasting it as Mahoney's self-serving fantasy; by shifting it to the loathsome Mahoney, he is already setting up the clerical dream for rejection.[10]

In Chapter Five McGahern suddenly switches to first-person narration. The boy of the first four chapters is now an adolescent narrator-protagonist. Moreover, we are thrust without preamble into the adolescent's sexual fantasy-life. But by having the first-person narrator describe the latter as 'a dream of flesh in woman' (*D*, 30), McGahern not only connects him through the use of the dream image to the third-person narrator of the previous chapters but also juxtaposes the clerical dream with its powerful competitor. In *Memoir* McGahern describes his adolescent development as a conflict of dreams, between his mother's, which he had promised her he would realize, and the vocation that displaces it, his own dream of becoming a writer. The conflict becomes a choice between the death-in-life of the priesthood or the life of the body of the writer in the world (*M*, 208). *The Dark* configures the difference in vocations in the same terms (see *D*, 56, 77, 83, 127). In Chapter Five, after masturbating, the narrator goes downstairs to study; as he takes up his books a memorial card for his mother falls out, sparking his memory of his promise to her (*D*, 33).

---

10   This scene is also significant in relation to McGahern's manipulation of narrative voice. Chapter Eight returns to the third-person voice after the dramatic shift to the second-person in Chapters Six and Seven. The narration in Chapter Eight is focalized through the point of view of Mahoney, so that when the boy fails to respond to his fantasy, Mahoney, like Reegan in *The Barracks*, is embarrassed and resentful of his self-exposure (see *D*, 46). Note that he regards his son as 'the other'; the locution captures the adversarial view of life and paranoid narcissism that drive Mahoney's emotional and material miserliness. It also links Mahoney with Michael Moran, who scorns the 'mere Other' (*AW*, 178).

Chapter Five also introduces the theme of confession. It occurs comically as the boy imagines himself having to confess the enormity of 'one hundred and forty impure actions with myself' in the month since his last Confession (*D*, 31). But in Chapter Seven the sacrament is treated more seriously, as, indeed, 'a judicial process in which the penitent is at once the accuser, the person accused, and the witness, while the priest pronounces judgment and sentence'.[11] Confession is thus a 'self-examination', and the function of the second-person voice in *The Dark* is to facilitate the 'confessional' motive that drives the story-telling. On a psychoanalytical level, the novel is McGahern's first admission of the broken promise to his mother and his search for self-forgiveness in the absolution of narrative, and the broken promise may itself be interpreted as a 'broken symbol' of the beloved encrypted in McGahern's narration. McGahern describes the atmosphere and mood in the church as the penitents queue 'to judge themselves' (*D*, 39), and the use of the second-person voice gives a particular intensity to the scene and produces a dizzying effect of present-pastness and past-presence in the verb forms (see *D*, 40). For the boy, to confess is 'a kind of death' (*D*, 40), and although this is followed by a comic-histrionic fantasy of the last moments of a condemned prisoner in Mountjoy prison, the boy seriously believes that successful commission of the sacrament will result in the death of the sinful self and its rebirth as a self delivered from guilt by the grace of penance. But this 'almost ecstasy' (*D*, 42) is suddenly truncated by the figure in the boy's life who embodies the very 'fear and darkness' (*D*, 42) that he seeks relief from, his father. Before he can complete his act of penance, Mahoney interrupts to tell him he is taking too long and a sudden 'wave of violent hatred' (*D*, 43) breaks over him. Mahoney's effect upon the boy's state of mind is to dispel 'the state of grace' and pull him back into the world of 'mechanical' obedience to his father's power.[12]

11   Catholic Encyclopedia, 'The Sacrament of Penance', 16 June 2010, <http://www.newadvent.org/cathen/11618c.htm>.

12   The parallels between this whole stratum of narration, action, characterization, and theme and the second and third chapters of Joyce's *A Portrait of the Artist as a Young Man*, particularly the final movement of Chapter Three, are extensive and deep. Like Stephen, McGahern's narrator-protagonist will reject a future as a priest to become a

The boy's clerical ambitions take another fall in Chapter Ten. Alternating between weeks of self-transcending prayer and weeks of manic self-abuse, he is worn down by what seems merely an effort to avoid inevitable failure; but more importantly, his spirit flags because the sacrament of Confession no longer delivers the 'ecstasy' it once did (D, 53–4). The low self-esteem and sense of personal unworthiness produced by years of abuse exacerbate the boy's confusion: instead of recognizing a natural and healthy call to life, he sees a lack of self-control, behaviour unacceptable in a future priest. In a further ironic use of the confessional setting and interrogation, McGahern has the boy fantasize about being a priest listening to a young woman confess to fornication. The fictional interrogation quickly deviates into self-titillation, but what McGahern uses the scene to show is the boy's ongoing self-interrogation with regard to his sense of vocation. It is clear that he has a greater hunger for the warm bread of human flesh than the unleavened joy of the Host. With the summer fast approaching, during which he is expected to make his decision about the priesthood, he begins to think of the choice of the priest's life as the end of choice (D, 55–6). McGahern presents the boy's dilemma as a choice between apparently opposed forms of knowledge: the knowledge of life, embodied in woman, and the knowledge of God. Both seem to promise a consummation that is self-consuming. The boy's fear of committing to the Odyssean quest for the beloved – symbolized by his 'dream' of Mary Moran as his future wife (D, 57) – is that it could degenerate into a 'drifting death from hole to hole'; but he also thinks that if he were to choose the priest's life, 'All your life would be a death in readiness for the last moment when you'd part your flesh and leave' (D, 56). Opting for spiritual safety, however – which is picked up later in the theme of financial security as the purpose of education and the goal of life (D, 102, 136, 173) – seems a form of cowardice or bad faith, like Pascal's wager, for the boy is also less and less sure of the essential truth of the 'professional' religious life. Participating in the annual Corpus Christi procession, he is attracted by the promise of

---

writer, but his reasons for rejection will be more Oedipal than Luciferian, setting out for Dublin, rather than Paris, to search for the beloved he needs to fill the loveless void at his centre, rather than for the distance he needs to construct the conscience of his race.

security that belonging to the cult offers and fantasizes that someday he will be in the position of the priest-celebrant (see *M*, 201–2). However, he holds back because, ironically, belonging to such a community seems so exclusionary and estranging (*D*, 58). Nor is the sense of exclusion that censors his fantasy of a future life spent at the centre of communal worship just the consequence of a sense of unworthiness caused by his failure to live his adolescent life pure in thought and deed; the boy also has doubts that there is anything behind the veil. McGahern is repackaging Elizabeth Reegan's self-interrogation as an adolescent boy's wondering about absolutes. The chapter ends with the boy realizing, like Elizabeth, that 'It was impossible to know', and adrift in uncertainty (*D*, 58–9).

The complication of the boy's vocational choice reaches a crisis when he visits Father Gerald, a cousin of his dead mother. The priest has been an irregular mentor in the presence of a persistently hostile Mahoney. Both the priest and the boy understand the summer visit will bring the question of the boy's future to a head, and it does; however, the crisis that occurs is more complicated and more surprising than the boy could have expected and composes the turning-point in the novel. While daring and provocative, particularly in relation to the Ireland of the early 1960s, McGahern's resolution of this stage of the boy's search for freedom makes sense in relation to the issues he has set in play in the novel – sexuality, vocation, and abuse and its consequences.

Joan, the boy's sister, has been put out to work for a draper in Cootehill near Father Gerald and before he takes him to the rectory, the priest and the boy stop in on her. The boy realizes something is wrong immediately and is troubled when Joan tells him that 'It's worse than home' (*D*, 63); but there is no opportunity to ask her what she means. The disturbance caused by Joan's appearance and behaviour, however, is the first of series of disquieting moments in the chapter which McGahern uses to build toward the crisis in the chapter that follows. When they arrive at the rectory, the boy is surprised to learn that the priest's housekeeper is not the expected middle-aged woman but a sixteen-year-old boy like himself. Then, after a late-night snack during which Father Gerald expresses his exasperation with 'John's' lack of taste, as evident in his arrangement of the knick-knacks on the mantelpiece, the priest tells him about his stomach surgery years before and casually unbuttons his trousers and pulls up his shirt and vest to display his scars. A medley of unsynchronized clocks chimes away as the priest concludes his bizarre and unsavoury 'spelling' lesson (*D*, 65).[13]

McGahern devotes three chapters to the events of the night of the boy's arrival at the priest's house. Chapter Twelve begins with Father Gerald showing him to his room and another awkward moment when the priest lingers in the doorway. Significantly, the boy's first thought is that the priest is going to try to kiss him good night like his 'cursed father' (*D*, 67–8). McGahern wastes no time in having the boy feel uncomfortable and apprehensive, and his immediate association of the way the priest makes him feel and what his father used to do to him cannot help but undermine the priest in the reader's mind. This is confirmed when Father Gerald suddenly does return to the boy's room and gets into bed with him.

McGahern's deft and dramatic combination of suggestion, understatement, echo and ambiguity in this scene deserves close attention. At first, after an 'uneasy' exchange of 'good nights', there is a sense of danger averted, but then McGahern begins to build a sense of suspense as the narrator-protagonist describes the view outside his window, then imagines his father's house and those asleep in it, which apparently prompts him to recall Joan in town and her disturbing behaviour earlier in the day; with this circling back to the issue of possible sexual abuse McGahern keeps the possibility we had thought averted still within the textual horizon. The narration also circles back to the view of the church graveyard outside the window, and this inspires the next cycle in the boy's thoughts. McGahern's use of the second-person narrative voice here is particularly effective in capturing the reflective, interrogative nature of the boy's self-dialogue, accentuating once again the confessional paradigm that underlies the narration throughout the novel; it also conveys the adolescent's developing powers of imagination and self-projection. We have already seen these in his capacity for sexual fantasy, but here we see the same powers turning the boy's late night thoughts beside the graveyard into a meditation on death, and a tacit identification with the restless, wandering souls of the dead (*D*, 69). The image of the dead rising from their graves to approach the house

---

13   The same wall of clocks reappears in Jamesie Murphy's house in *That They May Face the Rising Sun* (98–9).

where he is sleeping sends the boy into a tightening spiral of fear, but what is important is McGahern's language, which subtly anticipates the next scene in the drama. The boy's fascination with the figure of the priest as a man like any other but with a supernatural power to absolve guilt is crucial for understanding his reaction to what he judges to be Father Gerald's failure to respond appropriately to his 'confession'.

Having frightened himself, the boy is paralysed because he knows there is no escape (*D*, 69–70). This is the first echo of the abuse scene in Chapter Three, which began with the boy lying in bed waiting for his father. From this point on the echoes become even louder as the priest enters his room (compare *D*, 70, 17–18) and 'soon suspicion grew in place of the terror, what could the priest want …, the things that have to happen' (*D*, 70). The theme of powerlessness recurs as the boy acquiesces to the priest's request to join him under the covers – 'what else was there to say' (compare *D*, 18). As before, when the priest lingered at the doorway saying good night, the boy thinks he knows what is going to happen. McGahern's language is an explicit reprise of the earlier description of the terrified, desperate boy feigning sleep as his father approaches his bed. As the tension mounts, McGahern takes the scene to the apparently obvious and inevitable next stage. The boy's repeated responses to the priest's questions and 'roving fingers' – 'Yes, father' – are a grotesque turn on his replies to 'Daddy' in Chapter Three (*D*, 71; compare *D*, 20).

But at the very moment when the reader, like the boy, expects the obvious to occur, McGahern takes the scene in an unexpected direction. Father Gerald says he has come to have a 'heart-to-heart' about the boy's future and his forcing the question of vocation on the boy is described in language that ironically makes it seem more offensive than any physical assault. As the boy expresses his uncertainty about studying for the priesthood before he has had some experience of the world, Father Gerald turns the conversational to-and-fro into a pointed interrogation about the boy's sexuality. Intuiting the reason behind his reluctance to commit to the religious life and being an experienced confessor, the priest's interrogation echoes the earlier confessional scenes in the novel. As the episode reaches its climax the meaning of the boy's earlier thought of the figure of the priest as a man of flesh like him but with the 'power to pardon' (*D*, 69) becomes clear; for having confessed his behaviour, doubts, and sense of unworthiness to Father Gerald, the boy now looks for two elements in the priest's response – divine forgiveness and human understanding. At first, the boy believes he hears what he needs to hear and is exultant; the language explicitly echoes the confessional scene in Chapter Seven (compare *D*, 73, 42–3). But if the first element of the desired response has been heard, he is disappointed in the second. When he asks the priest, who is lying in bed beside him with his arm around his shoulders, if he had ever struggled against sin at the same age, thinking the priest's bed manners invite and promise a mutual openness, the boy is quickly made to feel that *he* has gone too far. More than disappointed, he feels hurt, then angry, as the priest patronizes him with impersonal images of playing football, going to dances, self-control, and growing into a 'good' and 'normal' life as a priest. The boy rages inwardly at the way the priest has abused him, not physically, like his father, but even more insidiously, by oppressing him with his bogus superiority (*D*, 74).

While what would have raised eyebrows about this chapter in 1965 is its flirting with the suggestion that Father Gerald is homosexual or paedophiliac or both, the real 'risk-taking' here is McGahern's careful treatment of the homoerotic dimension of the boy's evolving sexuality at this time in his life. At the beginning of the scene the boy is obviously afraid the priest is going to behave like his father and it is clear from the way he has written the scene that McGahern wants the reader as well to think that this might be the case; but the boy's fear is soon submerged in the emotions that are released by his 'confession', when the 'joy' he feels moves him to be even more open with the priest in whose embrace he is now apparently comfortable. At this point, we might consider an alternative ending to the chapter in which Father Gerald responds as the boy 'hopes', admitting in a frank and open manner to his own sexual urges, youthful masturbation, doubts about his worthiness to be a priest, and so on, eventually touching the boy in a gesture of sexual intimacy. The point I am making is that such a 'turn' in the novel would not have contradicted anything in terms of the characterization of either the boy or Father Gerald to this point. Nor would it have meant that the novel would then have to become the ground-breaking 'gay' novel of contemporary Irish fiction. What McGahern has developed in terms of the boy's profound need for love, sensitivity, and the self-confirmation that comes with emotional reciprocity between people would make such a scene and moment credible in narrative-dramatic terms.

McGahern does not take the novel and characters in this direction, however, even though the scene and language do allow a faint homoerotic note to be heard within the boy's quiet rage at the end: 'What right had he to come and lie with you in bed, his body hot against yours, his arm about your shoulders. Almost as the cursed nights when your father used stroke your thighs' (*D*, 74). (Consider what that 'Almost' almost expresses here.) The reason, presumably, is that from the outset McGahern has developed the boy's character's growth in terms of his struggle towards the right vocational choice by showing him trying to understand his own developing sexuality while at the same time struggling to find his way through the tortuous labyrinth of his father's abuse. In this respect, when Father Gerald declines the boy's invitation to reciprocate personal honesty with personal honesty, he displays the 'separateness' of the priestly life that the boy had before understood as a mark and guarantee of spiritual privilege, especially at the time of death and judgment; but now he sees it for what it is, an insincere brotherhood, a false fellowship, masking an unwarranted superiority and a hollow secrecy. Now he thinks he sees Father Gerald for what he is – the class-conscious, anal, and fussy calibrator of the social hierarchy he expects the boy to maintain in his turn (*D*, 65). He will be forced to revise his judgment, of course, in Chapter Sixteen, but it will still be too late.

If 'loathing' of his father and of himself was the residue of the abuse in Chapter Three, after Father Gerald leaves 'anguish', 'rage', and 'shame' (*D*, 75) engulf the boy and lead him, significantly, to masturbate for the first time in three weeks, but this time in a manner that really does approach 'self-abuse'. The paragraphs that begin Chapter Thirteen are some of the most effective in the novel for the way McGahern uses the second-person voice to capture the recollective-empathic older self looking back on the younger, understanding, acknowledging, suffering with, and forgiving. The voice builds from the plaintive 'What right had he ...' into an increasingly frenetic phantasmagoria of chiming clocks, moonlight, and interchanging ceilings, the bed and bedroom in Father Gerald's house fusing with those in his father's (see *D*, 75–6), then gradually the rhythms slow and the pulse of the prose confirms the return of self-control by the chapter's end. But when the priest left his room at the end of Chapter Twelve, McGahern had brought the boy to the brink of decision, the decision that all McGahern's protagonists make – to choose the life of the body and of the world, which in terms of its autobiographical basis, was McGahern's own choice of the life of the teacher-writer, the artist as secular priest whose solitude is the sacrifice that brings about the communion and fellowship of art, a choice that flows from the same feeling the boy describes when watching the Corpus Christi procession. Rather than raising the Host, however, McGahern's 'burden' (D, 58) will be the responsibility of truthful witness, the celebration of *all* of life's glorious, sad, light, dark and grey mysteries of the everyday and eternal, the unchanging and never-the-same.

What happens between the boy and Father Gerald completes the braiding of the themes of sexuality, vocation, and abuse that McGahern's characterization and emplotment have been weaving from the beginning. However, although this marks a turning-point in the boy's sense of vocation as well as in his attitude towards clerical authority in matters of his future well-being, it is only the first part of a two-stage experience. In Chapter Thirteen, the boy feels he has 'chosen' to reject the priesthood, but this is a negative choice and in a sense one that he feels has been forced upon him not just by the fiasco of the previous night, but by the confusion of 'the night and room and your father' (D, 77). Nor is the confusion dissipated when he serves Mass in the morning. The service is dream-like, and the metaphor is sharply ironic, denoting the blunting of reality by ritual rather than sanctity, but also the loosening of the maternal dream of his becoming a priest. He is inattentive during the mystery of the transubstantiation, the heart of the sacrament, and only focuses on where he is and what he is doing when he has to stay back from taking communion because of his state of sin. As if to confirm this turning-point, McGahern has the boy later dream of married life, complete with house and children (D, 82), but once again the boy's obsession with death and judgment obtrudes, and for the first time in the novel we realize that the ghost that has come from the graveyard to add to the boy's confusion is that of his dead mother – *and* McGahern's, of course. If he were to love a woman, he would be vulnerable to loss if she were to die, as his mother did. A priest, he thinks, by choosing

God is safe from such grief because 'he'd given up happiness ...' (*D*, 83). It is clear that to have chosen the priesthood for the reasons he would have chosen it is as much a mistake as not choosing it for the reasons he has marshalled; both are negative choices. Ultimately, he is going to have to make a *positive* choice and he turns toward that when he is called out of himself by suddenly remembering his sister.

Joan's tale of sexual harassment by her employer is the catalyst to action the boy needed. Here is someone who desperately needs his help and he makes the immediate decision to take her back home. She is afraid of Mahoney's reaction (presumably she has been sending him money), but the boy comforts her.[14] As exhausted as he is in both body and nerves, when he returns to the rectory the boy is determined to stand up to Father Gerald. He tells the priest he is taking Joan home the next day, that her employer had molested her, and that he is no closer to making up his mind about the priesthood. The call of life is too strong and the boy is unwilling to enter the religious life without first having some experience of the world. Father Gerald suddenly lets down his guard, admitting the religious life does not get any easier after ordination and that the Church is changing as Ireland becomes more and more bourgeois. The boy's disappointment from the previous night makes him all the more receptive when the priest now surprises him with his candour (*D*, 100). Ironically, the 'grace' he now experiences moves the boy closer to seeing his future no longer in terms of the negative choice of either/or, the religious life or the aimless 'drift' of freedom; rather, a secular life and a religious career, while different paths,

---

14   The autobiographical basis of the ensuing events is clear from McGahern's account in the memoir, where he tells of bringing his sister, Rosaleen, home from an intolerable situation in Cootehill. Rosaleen was afraid of their father's reaction and the boy's reassurance of Joan is a weaker version of McGahern's description of his words to Rosaleen (*M*, 186). McGahern's aggressive tone is explained a few pages later when he recounts the confrontation between him and his father in which he had 'stood up' against his abuse (*M*, 190–1). A few weeks later McGahern again came upon his father beating one of his sisters and shouted at him to stop; when his father hit him, McGahern found himself at a breaking point (*M*, 191). McGahern condenses the two incidents in the novel (see *D*, 35–6).

are responses to the 'one call to struggle and sacrifice' (*D*, 100).[15] Father
Gerald's plain-speaking and personal directness move the boy deeply. The
priest to whom he had gone for help in choosing a vocation has actually
helped to set him free and to avoid the great mistake he would have made by
choosing the religious life. By the time he arrives home with Joan the next
day, he has made up his mind. He tells Mahoney he will not be a priest.

'A child can become infected with unhappiness': Dissecting the Infected Self

Almost half of *The Dark* is narrated from a second-person point of view
which should be understood as inflected by both a retrospective temporality
and a 'confessional' ethos.[16] It is important to recognize that the second-
person voice is a confessional instrument in the novel. It first appears in
Chapter Six, immediately after the third-person voice of the first four
chapters has been dramatically displaced by the first-person narrator of
Chapter Five, as a kind of narrative fission in which the confessional 'I' of
Chapter Five, the chapter that recounts in vivid detail the boy's masturbation, divides, becoming the penitent 'you' and the narrator-confessor who
addresses 'you'. The second-person voice is that dimension of the recollective self that interrogates the 'suffering sinner' and by doing so not only
constructs the confessional narrative but advances the self-understanding

---

15   In his memoir, McGahern recalls a young priest whose sermons on love, humility
      and charity had a great impact on him as an adolescent. McGahern used this priest's
      description of prayer for Father Gerald's words to the boy here (compare *D*, 101 and
      M, 202). At this point in *The Dark* McGahern is certainly remembering the nature
      of his own adolescent belief (see *M*, 202–3).

16   For other discussions of this feature of McGahern's narration, see Maher, *John
      McGahern*, 63; Sampson, *Outstaring Nature's Eye*, 69, and 'Lost Image', 62; Karlheinz
      Schwartz, 'John McGahern's Point of View', *Éire-Ireland* 19.3 (1984): 92–110; and
      particularly, Van der Ziel, '"All This Talk and Struggle"'.

that is a pre-requisite for the self-forgiveness that emerges as the narration's ultimate achievement.

For Sampson, McGahern's use of all three persons in the narrative voice achieves 'a composite portrait of the state of becoming, the drama of the formation of identity'.[17] If one is reading McGahern's novels as a *roman fleuve* of memory, grief, and the search for the 'lost beloved', however, the significance of the shifting narrative voice is best understood in relation to the *retrospective* nature of the narration and what Ricoeur describes as the 'strong relation' that fiction has to the past: 'Narration preserves the meaning that is behind us so that we can have the meaning before us. There is always *more* order in what we narrate than in what we have actually already lived.'[18] The power of the narrative imagination to give order, unity and coherence to past experience in effect transforms time itself by making it an extension of the experiencing self rather than an external force oppressing the self in its weakness. Eamon Maher writes that '[McGahern's] characters look back towards the past in an effort to understand what they have become – in order to make sense of their future'.[19] This is certainly the case with Elizabeth Reegan in *The Barracks*, but what is remarkable in *The Dark* is that McGahern has given expression to this defining feature of his recollective imagination at the level of narrative form. Recollective narrative is, in a sense, the re-possession of time in order to inhabit it, to humanize it, and in doing so, achieve the self-possession that is a prerequisite for stable identity. What McGahern's shifting narrative voices in *The Dark* show is not so much the formation of a self as a writer trying to gather and organize memories into a *story* of the formation of a self. The form very much draws attention to the process of making form. It should be noted, however, that the 'self' of the protagonist-narrator that emerges at the end of *The Dark* is still too fluid, amorphous, 'in process' to represent any achieved form of identity.

17　*Outstaring Nature's Eye*, 17–18.
18　See 'The Creativity of Language', 221–2.
19　*John McGahern*, 62.

The narration of *The Dark* is an expressive tour de force that initiates a process of confession and self-forgiving that is not completed until McGahern revises *The Leavetaking* (1984). The shift to the first-person voice in Chapter Five occurs as McGahern has the narrator describe his masturbatory activities. The first-person injects an immediacy and energy into the narration, and allows a rare sense of humour to be heard as the narrator imagines confessing 'one hundred and forty impure actions' to an astonished priest (*D*, 31). At the same time, the first-person voice evokes a stronger sense of emotional turmoil, disappointment and shame when, at the end of the chapter, the narrator despairs of fulfilling his promise to his mother. But this shift to a greater interiority, or at least the kind of interiority the first-person entails, was apparently not something McGahern felt he wanted to continue. The shift to the second-person voice in the next chapter can be interpreted as a conscious adjustment of the *confessio*. To begin with, it opens a rhetorical distance between the narrator and the protagonist (*D*, 34) and establishes the protagonist as a character on the same level as 'the others'.[20] But at the same time, the second-person voice's direct address to the character, 'you', fixes that distance by stabilizing the relationship between the narrative voice and the character. The nature of that relationship is more than that of an older self looking back on a younger, although that is certainly part of it; implicitly, it is the classic relationship of the confessor to the penitent (a relationship presented explicitly in Chapter Seven). Beginning in Chapter Six, what McGahern does with the second-person voice is to re-shape the ritual interrogation of the sacrament into a confessional narrative which seeks that grace of understanding which is self-forgiveness, a grace that comes dropping slow, but even so, touches the boy in the epiphany he experiences at the end of Chapter Thirty. It is as if the self that acted is being reviewed by a later self that can look back upon itself as one of its 'others'. From the perspective of the retrospective self, the earlier self is now a *fictive* self, an image, a construction of memory and the language of recollection. If 'What is lost in experience is often salvaged in language',[21] then what McGahern's use

20   Compare the opening paragraphs of Chapter Six with the account in *M*, 190–1.
21   Ricoeur, 'The Creativity of Language', 228.

of the second-person voice conveys most palpably – especially when the novel is read in relation to the memoir – is the dialectic of memory itself, the past and its imaginative reconstitution as narrative. The second-person voice is implicitly dialogic: the narrator of Chapters One through Four becomes the narrator-protagonist of Chapter Five, only for that hyphenation to hypostasize in Chapter Six. Whatever self-understanding and self-autonomy are achieved in the novel emerge from this narrative fission.

What actually breaks in Chapter Six is the boy's capacity to endure his father's brutality towards his sisters:

> He swung her by the hair. Her feet left the ground. He started to swing her round by the dark hair ....
>
> You'd watched it come to this, hatred rising with every word and move he made, but you'd watched so many times it was little more than habit. Then her heels left the ground and swung, the eyes staring wide with terror out of the face, and the screaming. You couldn't bear any more this time. (*D*, 35)

The rhythm and repetition in the prose are palpably expressive. The element of confession in the episode – the boy not only opposes his father's authority but also threatens violence against him if he continues (*D*, 36) – is couched in the explanatory-exculpatory tone of the climactic 'You couldn't bear any more this time'. The scene presents an act of filial rebellion against an unjust patriarch that foreshadows the son's finding an authority within himself that will ultimately displace that of the father; moreover, the moment is described explicitly in a way that *interprets* it as an event in a larger narrative; following the crisis everyone recognizes things will never be the same in the house and family. McGahern constructs this moment as a turning-point in the narrative of the emergent self of the protagonist, just as many years later, in his memoir, he reconstructs the original moment as a turning-point in his own story (see *M*, 191). But while successfully standing up to his father is a momentous advance in the boy's struggle with his external circumstances, his struggle against his inner demons, who are empowered to a great extent by those external circumstances, is ultimately the more difficult.

An important dimension of the confessional paradigm and how it functions is intimated in Chapter Seven. The scene in the church mirrors the narration as it dramatizes the confessor-penitent dialogue. But what is important to recognize is how a sense of *sharing* in the character's experience is conveyed through the second-person voice's quality of narrating an ongoing present (see *D*, 40). Through this sharing, in effect, the narrative voice functions as the priest-confessor who takes upon himself the burden of the penitent's sin, a 'relief' that is soon felt by the boy in the scene (*D*, 42). Moreover, the relief is nothing less than a resurrection, and it is possible to see in this moment of death and rebirth the underlying myth that is nurturing McGahern's *poiēsis*, the death of the old self and birth of the new, the resurrection of the past as a story of a timeless present. In this way the confessional 'transaction' in Chapter Seven adumbrates the desired movement of the novel as a whole, or at least the desire that moves within the novel's evolving form – a form McGahern returned to for *Memoir*, whose subtitle could have been *The Dark Revisited*. As noted already, McGahern ends the chapter dramatically by having one 'moment' violently displaced by another as Mahoney's interruption of his son's act of penance assaults the boy's fragile beatitude. Considering the embryonic delicacy of the boy's independence and self-assertion, as well as the ambiguity of Mahoney's presence and the boy's feelings towards him at the end of the novel, this counter-moment at the end of Chapter Seven also seems to encapsulate the larger rhythm in the novel's psychological ebb and flow, for there is a sense of incompleteness at the end of *The Dark* that could also be described as a feeling of interruption, of a frustrated or blocked progress.

What is significant, of course, is not just the number of chapters given to each narrative voice, but the groupings and moments of disjunction between them.[22] It is because the effect of changing the narrative voice *is* so disjunctive that the technique is so effective. The shift back to the third-person in Chapter Eight, after the confessional scene of Chapter Seven, is all the more effective because the narrative voice is surprisingly focalized on Mahoney instead of the boy, and suddenly draws us closer to the character we have found so repulsive by bringing us into his experience of making

---

22   There are thirteen chapters narrated in the third-person (1, 2, 3, 4, 8, 9, 11, 17, 24, 25, 26, 27, 31), most often focalized on the boy; fifteen narrated in the second-person (6, 7, 10, 12, 13, 14, 15, 16, 18, 19, 20, 21, 28, 29, 30); and three in the first-person (5, 22, 23).

himself vulnerable to his son's rejection. The shift back to the second-person in Chapter Ten 'makes sense' in that the chapter's return to the confessional theme picks up from Chapter Seven, and the second-person voice is crucial to the way McGahern develops the boy's inner struggle by merging his preoccupation with sex and the growing crisis of the question of vocation. The self-interrogation of the confessional voice becomes accusatory only to modulate into the excusatory and consolatory. The tacit dialogue between the old self and its retrospective other (*D*, 54–6) not only brings out the boy's growing doubts about his vocation (*D*, 59) but also the power of the 'dream' of life that was displacing 'the fear of hell' in his mind (*D*, 56). The conjoined themes of sexuality and vocation in Chapter Ten are brought to a crisis and climax in Chapters Twelve through Sixteen, all of which are also narrated in the second-person. With the return to the third-person voice in Chapter Eleven to recount the boy's journey to Father Gerald, McGahern provides a frame for this turning-point movement in the novel.

The narrative power of the middle movement of the novel derives from the way McGahern uses the second-person voice's combination of rhetorical question and confessional interrogation to 'enact' the boy's inner dialogue with an intensity that mimics interior monologue (*D*, 82–5); there is a dramatic impact as well in the way the second-person voice takes the reader through the process of the boy's initial disorientation and dismay, then disappointment and anger, at Father Gerald, and then his surprise and gratitude for the 'total generosity' (*D*, 102) he feels he has experienced when Father Gerald finally speaks to him in an honest and non-patronizing way at the end of the visit. Moreover, the process of self-analysis that the second-person voice narrates results in an important moment of insight at the end of Chapter Sixteen. Exasperated by Joan, the boy vents his frustration on her and then suddenly recognizes something about himself: 'it was only with someone simple and weak you were able to be violent ...' (*D*, 105). His self-consciousness and self-analysis mark his difference from his father, even as he tacitly recognizes that he shares with him a capacity for violence against another, even someone he loves. Psychologically, it makes perfect sense, then, that he should summon the image of that violent man to turn the moment around and expel the demon that momentarily possessed him, and he leads Joan into the children's secret game of mimicry-mockery of their father's 'God, O God, O God' lament (*D*, 105).

The second grouping of chapters narrated in the second-person voice (Chapters Eighteen through Twenty-One) covers the period in which the boy studies for his final school exams. Having decided against the priesthood, his goal is now a university scholarship. In the first half of the novel, the boy's repeated bouts of masturbation undermined his sense of worthiness for the priesthood; the motif they form, however, is more than hormonal. The boy's sexual fantasies evoke a larger sense of eros than sexual intercourse, a desire to embrace life in the world and to live free of the constraints embodied in the small rooms, oppressive relationships, and confining expectations of the home life depicted in the novel. In the second half, the boy's masturbation occurs in a different context, namely that of his preparation for the all-important exams which will determine his future prospects, but the function of the motif remains the same. He masturbates when the tension caused by the school-work, the pressure he and others have placed on him, and his continuing uncertainty as to what he really wants to do with his life, becomes too much.[23] The first half of the novel ends with his rejection of the priesthood; the second ends with him rejecting university, both of which symbolize safe, cloistered, *institutional* lives spent under the gaze and within the narrow circuit of an oppressive authority. Indeed, in terms of image and scene, both are presented as versions of 'the father's bed' and the boy's escape from that bed in all its forms is perhaps the central symbol of freedom in the novel.

23   For a view of masturbation as a metaphor in a national allegory, see Mark Storey, "'Bewildered Chimes": Image, Voice and Structure in Recent Irish Fiction,' in *Across a Roaring Hill: The Protestant Imagination in Modern Ireland*, ed. Gerald Dawe and Edna Longley (Belfast: The Blackstaff Press, 1985), 162.

A Kind of Happiness and a Kind of Terror: The Inconclusive Epiphany

For some readers, the ending of *The Dark* is seriously flawed.[24] However, if the boy's actions and apparent manner toward his father at the end are examined closely, they do not necessarily contradict the earlier parts of the novel. Indeed, the explicit echoes of the latter undermine any sense of a fundamental change in the boy's deep-seated hatred of his father, a hatred that has been expressed continuously in the text. What emerges in the closing lines, rather, is a sense of calm based in a kind of emotional fatalism, a recognition that what has happened is now history, undeniable, unforgettable, horrible, but at last, behind him; the paramount point is that what the boy thinks and feels he thinks and feels because he is now absolutely certain his life with his father is over. He is escaping. At first reading, perhaps, the problematic moments – for example, when the boy thinks 'You are marvellous, my father' (*D*, 160), at the end of Chapter Twenty-Six, and 'I wouldn't have been brought up any other way or by any other father' (*D*, 191), in the closing lines of the book – do seem to be either grossly dishonest or egregiously mismanaged. However, the dishonesty and the awkwardness may be the character's and explained by his situation and emotional-psychological condition at the end of the novel. Moreover, McGahern may himself have provided us with clues as to how to read such moments ironically. When the boy thinks 'You are marvellous, my father', the reason it is so jarring to the reader is not only that the sentiment flies in the face of absolutely everything we have learned about the boy, his father, and their relationship, but also because it clashes more immediately with the scenes preceding it in the chapter. And it is the latter

24   John Cronin, for example, finds 'an inconsistency of character and incident' (see Maher, *John McGahern*, 28–9). Maher finds 'the general confusion that surrounds the hero's decision to abandon university and to suddenly reconcile himself with his father' to be exacerbated by some 'unusually awkward' prose, but adds that 'It is important to note that the point of view used throughout most of this novel is that of a confused child' (29).

clash that makes it particularly ironic, and one of a series of ironic moments in which the boy's feelings toward his father seem to be changing. 'You are marvellous, my father', in fact, echoes the first such moment in the novel, in Chapter Nineteen, when the boy thinks 'No matter what else, he had at least the beauty of energy' (D, 122). Of course, so do cancer cells. The hyper-euphemistic 'No matter what else' should not be ignored here.

Irony is an effect of structure, of course, and the irony in these moments points to an emotional reflex, and the reflex to the trace elements of love that survive in the underlying love/hate that is the boy's relationship with Mahoney. The structure is a two-step sequence: a negative feature of Mahoney's character is revealed, then the boy seems to think something positive about him, but that is undercut by the preceding incident. In Chapter Nineteen, the narrator-protagonist recounts an instance of Mahoney's Christmas spirit, his sudden notion to be generous to the boy's teachers. Mahoney's idea is to make the Brothers a gift from his stock of potatoes. (The reader will remember the painful scene in Chapter Four in which the brutish Mahoney forces the children to dig up the potatoes in the rain, a scene that connects him both to Reegan in *The Barracks*, and the Francis McGahern of the memoir.) The boy knows the Brothers would prefer whiskey but that by giving potatoes Mahoney can avoid the disagreeable experience of actually parting with cash (D, 120).[25] The scene with Mahoney, the boy, and Brother Benedict is full of irony at Mahoney's expense as well as some self-criticism of the boy for his sense of shame and embarrassment, and it is important to note in this respect that this is an instance where the second-person voice is clearly that of the older self looking back on the younger. The irony is clear; but it also seems that it is the retrospective narrator who is inflecting his representation of himself as character (inserting 'taciturn and withdrawn' [D, 122], for example) and so it is not clear at all that the point of view of the grudging acknowledgement of Mahoney is the boy's at the time *or later* when recollecting the incident. What is clear is that throughout the novel Mahoney's most damaging effect upon his

---

25   For the version of this incident in his memoir, where Brother Benedict is Brother Placid, see *M*, 170.

son is emotional. When he places first in his exams, the boy's response to the letter of praise he receives from Brother Benedict is pathetic, reflecting the damage to his self-esteem from the years of Mahoney's cruel and brutish treatment (*D*, 122–3). McGahern also makes it clear that Mahoney's change in attitude to the boy's studying for the scholarship exams is driven by self-interest.

When the boy finishes school and turns to work on the farm while waiting for his exam results, there does seem to be a change in tone, introduced with a subtle double-beat at the end of Chapter Twenty-Three: first, an elegiac recognition that a time of life has ended; then the boy looks out to the world beyond his room (*D*, 146). It is a minor-key expression of the 'consciousness of the mystery' (*D*, 101) that McGahern's later fiction will explore, particularly *That They May Face the Rising Sun*. The change in mood and view to expectation and externality is complemented by the shift back to the third-person narrative voice for the four chapters that present the boy working with his father, the news of his winning the scholarship, celebrating in town with Mahoney, and the departure for university (Chapters Twenty-Four through Twenty-Seven). After months of intense study, the boy throws himself into physical labour on the farm alongside Mahoney and working together leads to his recognition of the bond between them (*D*, 148). And at long last Mahoney openly praises his son: 'There's nothing the two of us mightn't do together' (*D*, 148, 150).[26] But the praise is ambiguous. The boy can see that Mahoney is not the man he was, the brutal and violent miser who had made his children's lives an emotional and physical torment, and that the son will soon surpass his father in strength (see *D*, 150). Like the earlier fantasy of retiring as his son the priest's housekeeper, Mahoney's praise recognizes a good thing when he sees it, unpaid labour. The boy's acknowledgement that 'They shared something real at last' only confirms the lack of any positive emotional bond between them in the past; it also suggests that Mahoney can only relate to the boy in anything like normal human feelings of respect and appreciation now when he has him,

26   The latter is a version of a favourite saying of McGahern's father (see *M*, 216, 220) and McGahern uses it again for Moran in *Amongst Women* (108).

literally and psychologically, on his own ground. Until now, everything about the boy has been 'other', alien and alienating to Mahoney, who was threatened by his son's intelligence, sensibility and academic talent. The apparent softening toward Mahoney is less a change in the boy's underlying feelings about his father than a sign of a new confidence developing in him as a result of his physical maturation, growing strength, and academic achievement; moreover, the tenuous bond the boy's statement seems to acknowledge is short-lived: it breaks in the next chapter.

The description of Mahoney's celebration of the boy's winning a university scholarship follows the same ironic pattern. Even as he presents an apparently different Mahoney in these chapters, McGahern reminds the reader of the earlier narcissistic monster of abuse and violence. The undercutting begins as Mahoney is described behaving 'in the manner of a drama' (D, 152) and then of usurping the leading role; instead of allowing his son centre-stage, Mahoney reduces him to a supporting role in his own performance. When he takes him to Curleys for new clothes and shoes and declaims to all present the reason for his largesse, the boy is once again ashamed and 'Hatred swept against Mahoney' (D, 153). The result of the performance is that the store-keeper praises Mahoney, which of course is the point of the performance.

A more serious undermining occurs at the beginning of Chapter Twenty-Six, when Mahoney takes the boy to the Royal Hotel for dinner. The echo of the seductive promise Mahoney used to soften the boy up for his abuse in Chapter Three darkens an already darkening scene (see D, 156, 158, 19). As he continues to draw attention to himself, 'Resentment grew with hot embarrassment' in the boy; and when he asks Mahoney to be quiet, it is clear that 'there was no union between them' (D, 157), which erases any sense that the bond intimated in Chapter Twenty-Four has developed into anything lasting. This is an important statement in the novel because it quietly points to the profound paradox underlying not only *The Dark* but all of McGahern's writing about the father-figure: hatred *is* a bond. There *is* a complex union between Mahoney and the boy, far more negative than positive, and what the novel ultimately achieves, as self-expression on McGahern's part, is like the effect of insulation around copper wire. The charge or 'load' can be transmitted without the threat of shock. The narration shapes the potentially destructive power of emotions like grief, guilt, hatred, and shame, in conjunction with the positive emotion of love into a constructive process of confession and testament. Mahoney's behaviour at the hotel is yet another form of 'brute force' to get his own way (*D*, 157). Considering all we have seen in Mahoney's treatment of his children, one can only hope that the irony McGahern loads into Mahoney's advice to his son 'to learn to have more confidence in yourself' and to 'stand up for your rights' (*D*, 158) was as satisfying to him as it is noxious to the reader. Mahoney's blindness is total, his solipsism abysmal, and their common core is captured poignantly in the boy's *unspoken* complaint about Mahoney's contemptuous treatment of their waitress: 'She's a person too' (*D*, 158). The boy is 'speaking up' for himself as well, even though he is not speaking out. Yet another echo of Chapter Three is heard when Mahoney begins to preach his sanctimonious cant that whatever has happened between them is not important because all that matters is that 'We still love each other after all the years' (*D*, 159; compare *D*, 19). The enormity of the void that is within him in place of self-consciousness, self-analysis and self-judgment resounds in his grossly hypocritical 'That's what Christ preached' (*D*, 159). The remark brings the boy's nerves near to breaking. It is clear that nothing significant is changing in his relationship with Mahoney, nor will it from here to the novel's end. Thus, when Mahoney makes his tired joke as they cycle past the graveyard, the boy's grudging acknowledgement, 'You are marvellous, my father', contains a very strong sense of 'you're unbelievable!' The language is quite ambiguous: the boy '*wanted* to laugh with him and say, "You are marvellous, my father"' (*D*, 160, my emphasis), but he didn't. Just as he didn't speak his mind over his father's treatment of the waitress. The final line in the chapter reflects the same emotional confusion that McGahern presents in the closing lines of the previous chapter when he describes the boy feeling an 'uncomfortable but half-pleased centre of praise' (*D*, 155). Emotional confusion and uncertainty plague the boy to the end of the novel. Even as he is about to leave the misery of Mahoney's house for university in Galway, when he says goodbye to his father at the bus-stop his inability to say what he wants to say is presumably because he does not sufficiently *feel* it (see *D*, 163). The 'one absolute compulsion to praise or bless' (*D*, 163) recalls the dying Elizabeth Reegan of *The Barracks*, but we should not expect the boy to possess her resources nor to be able to expunge his life's accretion of bitterness. His desire to transcend the real time of his farewell in 'some vision' (D, 163) of forgiveness and reconciliation is reported here as a failure, another delusive dream. The final episodes in the novel, set in Galway city and presenting the boy's rejection of university, are framed by chapters narrated in the third-person (Chapters Twenty-Seven and Thirty-One), but in the penultimate chapters, McGahern returns to the second-person narrator to complete the novel's confessional project. The 'you' that is addressed at the end of the novel is an 'other' self who loses – or rather, abandons – yet another dream. The almost staccato-like effect of the repeated second-person pronoun captures the way the strange setting and novelty of being alone assault the boy's sensibility and nerves. His fantasies of self-determination and sexual fulfilment, which he believes have come together in the dream of the university, seem on the point of realization, but then evaporate. McGahern presents the boy's disillusionment as a reaction to the blatant materialism of student ambitions and professorial counsel.[27] But the boy's ultimate withdrawal from the university is really just that, a *withdrawal*, a recoiling not so much out of moral repulsion or intellectual disagreement with the increasingly job-oriented ethos of the modern university, but rather out of fear, insecurity, and a lack of confidence compounded by the same vocational uncertainty that has hounded him since childhood. It is also important to recognize that what McGahern shows in this ultimate action and condition of the protagonist is the effect of the kind of childhood and adolescence he lived under the rule of his father, for what is clearly paramount is the boy's desire to be free of Mahoney. If he has any discernible sense of a future it is in medicine, but that degree will not be covered by his scholarship and the prospect of having to turn back to Mahoney for support is 'frightening' (D, 174).

27   The students' obsession with economic 'security' (D, 172, 173) recalls Father Gerald's remarks about the new bourgeois Ireland that was changing the Church (D, 102), as well as, ironically, Father Bull Reegan's retreat sermons on the importance of 'success' (D, 136). The boy's rejection of a university education reflects McGahern's own conclusion at the same time in his own life that 'the university could not give me what I wanted' (see M, 243).

Standing outside a dance, where he hopes to meet a girl, any girl, he thinks he is finally about to realize the dream *he* has chosen – life – over his mother's – the priesthood. But he loses heart and runs away. His loss of nerve is the beginning of the end of his university dream, and when he takes the offer of an interview with the Electrical Services Board in Dublin, he is running away again. The boy sees it as running toward freedom, but McGahern makes it clear that what he means by this is freedom from Mahoney (*D*, 178–9). The E.S.B. offer puts the boy in a situation where he will have to make an immediate decision and when a professor arbitrarily throws him out of the lecture hall in order to set a precedent for class discipline, the boy takes the expulsion as a sign that he was not meant to stay. He wires Mahoney for his 'consent' presumably to avoid any future recrimination, and consequently has to endure one more performance by his father before he is finally set free of him. It is the boy who now manipulates Mahoney by playing to his character and raising the possibility that he would have to contribute money if he were to remain at university. The boy has made up his mind but lets Mahoney think he is playing a role in the decision. True to his character, Mahoney takes his show on the road and performs the role of concerned parent to a public gallery – in a restaurant, then with the boy's landlady, and then with a policeman in the street. It is a repeat of the celebration day at Curleys and the Royal and arouses a similar 'cold and hidden fury' in his son (*D*, 185). Finally, they decide to seek the advice of the Dean of Residence.

The interview recalls a more famous one in *A Portrait of the Artist as a Young Man*, where Stephen decides against a future with the Jesuits, and then experiences the epiphany on the beach where he commits himself to a future as a writer. The difference between the scenes is instructive. In *The Dark* the boy is acting falsely, presenting himself before the Dean for advice when he has already made up his mind, but it is his decision to bring Mahoney into the matter which has put him in the charade that results in him having to present himself to the Dean as weak and indecisive. The Dean senses the boy's bad faith and the boy feels his contempt as he advises him to try for the E.S.B. job. McGahern's version of the Joycean epiphany comes as the boy leaves the campus with his father, seething inside, feeling he has been judged by the Dean as mediocre and inadequate, feeling 'defeated'. The quality of the moment and the nature of the turn in the boy's feelings are completely convincing for the character that McGahern has constructed. The boy knows that what he needs is a new beginning and his only chance of that is a life independent of and distant from Mahoney. Working for the E.S.B. is meaningless in itself; it is simply a means to achieve that new beginning. What has become clear in the boy's mind is that he is less interested in finding economic 'security' than in discovering an inner 'authority' (*D*, 188). As yet the boy is a long way from achieving this, but McGahern has already presented it in his fiction. The desire for 'a calmness even in the face of the turmoil of your own passing' (*D*, 188) links the boy with the figure of Elizabeth at the end of *The Barracks*, who ultimately did achieve such an inner authority. And what McGahern describes the boy looking forward to here – and at this moment in the text it seems obvious that the 'person' addressing the 'you' of the character is McGahern addressing himself – is actually an expression of McGahern looking back, in terms of his writing and of his own life, to the 'lost image' – recollected and imagined – of his own mother.

The Dark could have ended with Chapter Thirty, but as with *The Barracks* McGahern chooses to end the novel with a return to its beginning. The conversation about the boy's leaving for Dublin that occurs in Chapter Thirty-One could have been placed *before* the weak epiphany in the last paragraph of Chapter Thirty. This is a weak epiphany befitting the character, completely convincing in its conjunction of 'terror' and 'unclear recognition' (*D*, 188). Anything more optimistic or less guarded would ring false, out of tune with what has preceded it. But it is an awakening none the less and a convincingly modest joy tinged with apprehension. How could it not be, given all that we know of the boy? It will take a lifetime to outgrow the crippling sense of 'unworthiness' he has ingested from his father, the deformation of spirit and emotion that Mahoney's influence has caused (and that resonates, quite horribly, in McGahern's use of 'touching' in the passage), and to grow into the 'authority' of an individuated self.

If the circular movement of *The Barracks* produces a 'flat', non-projective, future-less effect, with the image of the children drawing down the blinds one of occlusion and entombment, the ending of *The Dark*, while not quite the upward spiral of comedy, is more positive and future-looking, if also restrained and ambiguous.[28] Chapter Thirty-One describes the boy and his father in bed at the rooming house and the allusion to the horror of Chapter Three is explicit: 'Memories of the nightmare nights in the bed with the broken brass bells came, and it was strange how the years had passed, how the nights were once, and different now ...' (*D*, 189). Even though the nights are 'different now', the effect of reminding the reader of the nights of abuse dashes any suggestion that the boy has forgotten them or that there can be any true reconciliation. So, too, with Mahoney's prayer-like repetition of self-exculpation, 'There was good times and bad between us ... but it's not what counts much' (*D*, 190): this echo of the 'brute force' of Mahoney's emotional bullying in the Royal Hotel scene (*D*, 159), which itself echoes his 'seduction' of the boy in Chapter Three, makes clear that with regard to the fundamental feeling and relationship between son and father, nothing changes on the deepest level from beginning to end in *The Dark*. Mahoney's professions of love are never more than thinly veiled pleas to his victim to pretend that nothing much wrong ever happened, that the little that did is all forgiven, and that he has been a model father who has raised a model family. Gratitude is in order.[29] The boy's replies sound mechanical, the exchange a hollow antiphon, and this is corroborated by his outright *lie* when Mahoney reminds him of the 'good day' they had at the Royal. 'I enjoyed that day very much' (*D*, 191), the boy replies, when we know he spent most of the time embarrassed, angry and silently raging at his father. The boy is only saying what he knows Mahoney wants to hear. The terse responses that simply repeat Mahoney's words back to him recall the little boy's replies after the abuse in Chapter Three, when all he wanted was to go to sleep. It is no different here. Mahoney is almost pleading with

28   Maher remarks that 'the circular nature of existence ... is a constant preoccupation' and 'the wheel trying to come full circle ... a recurring symbol' in McGahern's writing (*John McGahern*, 47, 62). *That They May Face the Rising Sun* is the best illustration of both points, although it is *Memoir* that reveals the solar cycle and the sun itself to be the primary symbolism in McGahern's fiction.

29   The irony of allowing Mahoney to 'excuse' himself of his shortcomings by suggesting 'It might have been better if your mother had to live' (*D*, 191) must have been particularly self-lacerating for McGahern.

the boy to say he holds no grudges. When the boy says, 'I wouldn't have been brought up any other way or by any other father' (*D*, 191), the only way the novel allows the reader to interpret this is as bitterly ironic. The last chapter also sees McGahern return to the third-person narrator of the opening chapters, a narrative voice that now confirms the ironic cast of this final exchange: 'It seemed that the whole world must turn over in the night and howl in its boredom, for the father and for the son and for the whole shoot, but it did not' (*D*, 191). There is more 'good bye' in the boy's final 'good night' and a sense that he simply wants the man to shut up.[30]

The father's bed as the place of abuse and abasement is introduced in Chapter Three of *The Dark*. In Chapter Twelve, the boy is forced to share his bed with another 'father' and the echoes of the earlier chapter are explicit. The sequence with Father Gerald ends with the boy breaking free, ironically, of what emerges in the novel as the 'temptation' of the priesthood. Finally, in the last chapter, the boy finds himself back in bed with his father. This time, however, for all the troubling echoes of the previous scenes, he seems to have broken free not only of the temptation of an academic future, but also, finally, of the man of darkness himself. There are thus two 'cycles' or movements in *The Dark*, both ending with the achievement of a *negative* freedom: in the first half of the novel, the rejection of the priesthood; in the second, the rejection of the university.[31] What the protagonist achieves by the end of the novel is at best a freedom *from* that has yet to evolve into

---

30   Some might feel that McGahern *does* lay some groundwork for interpreting the clos-
      ing scene as a reconciliation earlier in the novel, for example, in the closing paragraph
      of Chapter Twenty-Four, but the passage only confirms that 'Hatred and contempt'
      (*D*, 150) were the dominant emotions in the son's relationship with his father, and
      'incomprehension' remains his final feeling toward Mahoney, as it was McGahern's
      toward his father (see *M*, 226, 271).

31   Sampson describes the structure of the novel as 'a double movement: towards auton-
      omy of the self, this impulse being associated with choice, and towards the relin-
      quishing of self-assertion in the face of an impersonal reality, or darkness, of which
      the father is the dominant image' (*Outstaring Nature's Eye*, 69). Neither the novel's
      title nor the figure of Mahoney point to an 'impersonal reality', however, but rather
      to McGahern's loveless home life in which the father embodies a brutal will-to-
      power.

a freedom *to* or *for*. The most devastating and far-reaching effect that the long reign of terror of Mahoney's brutal will has had upon his son, has been upon the boy's own will. At the end of *The Dark* there is no sense that he is anything more than a damaged refugee of what Riggs and Vance, using the euphemistic sociological jargon of our times, describe as 'a dysfunctional Catholic family', heading for an uncertain future in the big city.[32] His condition, in fact, is exactly what McGahern turns to explore in the *acedia* of the protagonists of *The Leavetaking* and *The Pornographer*. Each of the boy's three dreams in *The Dark* – the spiritual dream of becoming a priest, the erotic dream of sexual consummation and marriage, and finally, the academic dream of a university degree and career – contains a 'mystery' at its centre: the mystery of Christ, the mystery of the body, and the mystery of truth. When he rejects the priestly vocation the boy turns from the mystery of Christ to the mystery of the body, which he thought university life would reveal (see *D*, 124). By the end of the novel, the protagonist has been disillusioned of all three dreams and the 'mystery' that he is advancing toward is implicitly the writer's craft, which in McGahern's case, coheres in the triangulation of all three needs – the spiritual, erotic, and intellectual.

---

32 Pádraigín Riggs and Norman Vance, 'Irish Prose Fiction', in *The Cambridge Companion to Modern Irish Culture*, ed. Joe Cleary and Claire Connolly (Cambridge: Cambridge University Press, 2005), 263.

Breaking the Moulds – Part I: *The Leavetaking* (1974; rev. 1984)

McGahern considered the writing of his third novel to be a turning-point in his career: 'I would actually have stopped as a writer unless I had broken out of my own moulds in *The Leavetaking*'.[1] In 1979, five years after its publication, he told Denis Sampson: 'it was actually a book I had to write'.[2] It seems, however, that the process of 'breaking out' remained unfinished and was not completed until, taking advantage of a proposed French translation, McGahern revised the second part of the novel for a new edition in 1984. In his 'Preface to the Second Edition' McGahern explained that he felt the way he had presented the figure of 'the beloved' in the original version of Part II had prevented the work from achieving 'that inner formality or calm, that all writing, no matter what it is attempting, must possess' (*L* 1984: [5]). What needs to be recognized, however, is that whether or not the revised version of *The Leavetaking* does achieve the 'inner formality or calm' McGahern desired, it was the writing of *The Pornographer* that in large part 'enabled' the revisions that finally 'broke the moulds' of the early writing.

But what might that mean? What makes the two versions of *The Leavetaking* when taken together such a 'breakthrough'? What were the 'conscious risks'[3] he told Denis Sampson he took while writing the story of Patrick Moran, the young, recently married schoolteacher who spends the last day of his short-lived career recalling his life and the events leading up to his dismissal, from the death of his mother when he was a child to his

---

1   Quoted in Sampson, *Outstaring Nature's Eye*, 110.
2   Sampson, 'A Conversation', 15.
3   Ibid.

marriage to Isobel, an American he met in London? What was McGahern 'attempting' in this writing? He continues the confessional mode of *The Dark* but practises it at an even deeper level of *poiēsis*. The experiment with narrative voice continues with the use of a first-person narrator-protagonist whose narration moves in and out of reveries of memory, like the gulls that swoop in and out of his focus as he supervises the playground during his last day as a teacher. The cyclical rhythms that again shape McGahern's narrative form intensify this sense of reverie. The two parts of the novel circle concentrically around the last day and night Patrick and Isobel spend in Ireland, with each part ranging out from that narrative present into different periods in Patrick's past – his childhood and the death of his mother, in Part I, and in Part II, his romantic-sexual experiences leading up to his leave in London and his affair with Isobel, their marriage and brief return to Dublin.[4] The significance of the circular form is suggested by Isobel's account of the 'painful going inwards' (*L* 1974: 133) of her experience in psychoanalysis, and by McGahern's linking of this movement to the 'tidal' rhythm of his own narrative practice in Patrick's recognition of the eventual subsuming of memory by imagination.

McGahern's use of autobiographical material in this novel is as prominent as in *The Dark*, but he draws on his childhood rather than adolescence, remembering what he saw of his parents' marriage but also imagining their courtship, his mother's life as a single woman, and his father's childhood. As well he draws on his years in Dublin when he taught school, wrote *The Dark*, took a year's leave of absence from teaching, met and married his

---

4   Michael J. Toolin's complaint that minor characters like Isobel's father and even
     Isobel herself are 'either ill-focused or implausible' (qtd. in Maher, *John McGahern*,
     39; Maher adds Patrick's parents) might be qualified by this sense that the substantial-
     ity of character, like that of landscape and setting, is a function and reflection of the
     quality of the reverie – the stream of consciousness – that composes the narration.
     We should not expect the kind of three-dimensionality of character that a tradi-
     tional third-person narrator typically provides. Isobel's father is more developed in
     the 1974 version of Part II; in his revision, McGahern sharpens the focus on what is
     most important about this character in terms of Patrick's point of view and attitude
     towards him and his relationship with Isobel.

first wife, Annikki Laaksi and, following the publication of *The Dark* in May 1965, was fired from his teaching job that September. (*The Pornographer* represents a second culling of his Dublin years.) Patrick Moran's recollections in Part I build relentlessly toward 'what I did not want to look on' (*L*, 31),[5] the climactic account of his mother's dying and the last time he saw her, the scene of his farewell in the upper room of the farmhouse in 'Aughoo' (the Aughawillan of McGahern's childhood). To write this scene in his character's past, McGahern had to confront the deeply traumatic memories of his own childhood that had 'moulded' so much of who he was.

The autobiographical core of *The Leavetaking* is the death of McGahern's mother, and in it he addresses her explicitly as 'my beloved' (*L*, 64) for the first time in his fiction. It is through the synthesis of the figure of the dead mother and the living lover-wife that the novel, as a total image, attempts to establish a myth of loss and recovery: Patrick's account of winning his beloved/Isobel from the clutches of her sinister, incestuous father in Part II balances the story of his loss of the beloved mother and fall into the clutches of his father in Part I.[6] Part II of *The Leavetaking* forms a sequel of sorts to *The Dark* in that Patrick Moran's life in Dublin continues the 'search for personal authority'[7] that saw the young Mahoney set out for the city at the end of that novel, and Part I deals with the death of the mother that goes untold in *The Dark*. On a deeper level, *The Leavetaking* continues the previous novel's preoccupation with the broken promise, a preoccupation that has now morphed into the need for atonement. In the opening line of Part II, 'One day I'd say Mass for her' (*L* 1974, 1984: 85), Patrick Moran articulates word for word the young Mahoney's guilty

5   Because the texts and pagination of Part I are the same in both editions, all references to Part I will be cited simply as (*L*).

6   Sampson argues that 'although an autobiographical or confessional aura surrounds ... Patrick Moran, it is objectified through an intricate and complex fiction' (*Outstaring Nature's Eye*, 111); one might say, however, that in the character and narration of Patrick Moran, McGahern's autobiographical-confessional *poiēsis* is objectified in a subjective fiction.

7   Sampson, *Outstaring Nature's Eye*, 119.

memory in the earlier novel (*D*, 33). Patrick's story is very much a realization of the 'dream of flesh in woman' (*D*, 30) that supplanted the young Mahoney's dreams of the priesthood and university, just as the plot of *The Pornographer* realizes the boy's fear of that dream becoming a life of 'drifting death from hole to hole' (*D*, 56). In *The Leavetaking* McGahern not only continues to examine his life through the writing process, he also makes the interrelation of memory and imagination an explicit theme in the novel (*L*, 35, 45). Already McGahern seems to envision 'the completed circle' of his artistry as the 'total obliteration' of memory by imagination (*L*, 35), a sublation of the self that he achieves in his last two works, *Memoir* and *That They May Face the Rising Sun*.

We are told that before she married, Patrick's mother, Kate McLaughlin, lived with her sister, May, who ran a shop across from the railway station in an unnamed town where their unmarried brother, Michael, drove a taxi (*L*, 40); Kate and May lived above the shop and Kate taught in a convent school. Their older, married brother, Jimmy, lived and worked on the family farm in the nearby Iron Mountains (*L*, 61).[8] McGahern's mother's maiden name was McManus and her sister, Maggie, kept a shop across from the station in Ballinamore, where their brother, Pat McManus, drove a hackney for some years (see *M*, 72); their brother, Jimmy, who was as successful a scholar as Susan, worked the family farm (*M*, 45). While she lived with Maggie, Susan McManus taught in a convent school in nearby Lisacarn (*M*, 52). Patrick describes 'a natural antipathy' between his father and his aunt (*L*, 45, 58); McGahern records a similar dislike between his father and his aunt Maggie (*M*, 14–15). Like McGahern's, Patrick's father was a Garda sergeant who, once Kate McLaughlin had accepted his proposal, prolonged their 'eccentric engagement' (*L*, 39) for a number of years until she wrote to him to break it off; this results in the sergeant driving immediately from Monaghan to Kate's school to chastise her for her decision and bully her into a 'quick' wedding (compare *M*, 52–5). After they are married, he takes against her family, constantly nagging her that they are 'spongers' (*L*, 52), which McGahern also describes his father doing (*M*, 68–9).

8   Kate's surname and family home in the Iron Mountains link her to McGahern's mother (see *M*, 44).

In the novel, McGahern appears to use only the bare details of his family history and experience, whereas thirty years later in the memoir he is more forthcoming about the emotions involved. For example, Patrick describes how, when he was two years old, his father cut off all his baby curls in a pique of jealousy over the attention given to him by his mother and grandmother (*L*, 47–8); in his memoir McGahern presents the incident as a much darker revelation of his father's jealous and violent character (*M*, 9–10). Conversely, in the memoir the incident of an infant McGahern crawling through the hedges in search of the sun and getting lost and falling asleep in a ditch ends with a lighter touch than in the novel, which has Patrick's grandmother scolding him (compare *M*, 11–12 and *L*, 48).[9] When Patrick goes by train and bicycle to visit his father at the barracks, his father meets him halfway between Drumshambo and Cootehall and they ride the rest of the way together (*L*, 49). But in the memoir, McGahern's father couldn't be bothered riding out to meet his son, and McGahern's account describes the anxiety he felt as he tried to find his way to the barracks as well as his sense of his father's untrustworthy character (*M*, 102–5). A similar toning down occurs when Patrick tells how, at the end of his stay, his father tried to talk him into leaving his mother and sisters and living with him in the barracks (*L*, 50–1). In the memoir, this episode is given more context, making it appear as a 'temptation' or another example of his father's 'seductive' nature when he sets out to get something he wants (*M*, 105–8). The details and outcome are the same in both accounts but the memoir ends much more strongly with 'a look of hatred in his eyes' that McGahern 'came to know ... well' (see *M*, 108).

9   In the memoir, the anecdote develops the symbolic motif of the sun, ultimately a symbol of his mother's love, and a symbolism that is continued in the title and imagery of his last novel. In *The Leavetaking*, this incident is followed by an account of the grandmother putting the baby's finger into the fire to teach him a lesson (*L*, 48), which is not repeated in the memoir. Patrick's grandmother is based on McGahern's paternal grandmother – as the incidents concerning the folk-remedy for whooping cough (*L*, 48–9; *M*, 12) and the visit to the hospital in Carrick-on-Shannon when she was dying make clear (*L*, 49; *M*, 14–15).

Late in his career, McGahern claimed that 'all autobiographical writing is by definition bad writing unless it's strictly autobiographical'.[10] In 1979 he told Sampson: 'I have found that the most serious mistakes I have made were ... when I have actually stuck close to the way things happen. Very seldom have I done that .... The way I got sacked and the way that sacking is described in *The Leavetaking* really have got nothing to do with one another. I mean that day with the bell that happens in the novel; that day never happened in my life'.[11] By this standard, assuming that the memoir is 'strictly autobiographical', or at least not fiction, much of McGahern's fiction is 'bad writing' because, as a reading of *Memoir* makes clear, for much of it he 'actually [*has*] stuck close to the way things happen[ed]', and the description of the sacking in *The Leavetaking*, for example, is closer to the account he provides in his memoir than his remarks to Sampson suggest.[12] But it is the spirit more than the details of the original experience that informs McGahern's re-creative imagination and which his writing seeks to give 'the grace of ceremony'.

The Grace of Ceremony

At the outset of his career, McGahern described the purpose of his writing to be the bringing of a 'private world' to life as an artistic 'vision': 'The vision, that still and private world which each of us possesses and which others cannot see, is brought to life in rhythm – rhythm being little more than the instinctive movements of the vision as it comes to life and begins its search for the image in a kind of grave, grave of the images of dead passions and their days'.[13] In 1979, with *The Leavetaking* and *The Pornogra-*

---

10   González, 'John McGahern', 45.

11   Sampson, 'A Conversation', 14.

12   In the novel Patrick returns to Dublin with Isobel; McGahern went back on his own (see *M*, 250).

13   'The Image' (1968), 10; repeated in the revised version in *Canadian Journal of Irish Studies* 17 (1991): 12. McGahern used 'vision' in the same sense with Sampson: 'The

pher behind him, McGahern told Sampson: 'Each person lives in his own isolation and out of that the particular is given the grace of ceremony, is given the grace of the general.'[14] The shape of McGahern's 'private world' and the 'moulds' he sought to break through by writing *The Leavetaking* are one and the same. From the beginning there is a clear sense of McGahern's creative effort as an instinctive 'drive' to bring (back) to life the 'lost beloved'; indeed, the Orphic 'search for the image in a kind of grave' is the mythic core of all McGahern's writing.

In the 'Preface to the Second Edition' of *The Leavetaking*, when McGahern says that he came to realize that the second part of the novel needed 'to be reformed' (*L* 1984: [5]), we might understand this as his feeling that 'that still and private world' from which the fiction issued was still inchoate, not yet fully transformed into a narrative order (or 'rhythm') which would mark real progress in the quest for the 'lost image.' The most significant revisions McGahern makes to Part II, in this respect, are his removal of the explicit allusions to the dead mother. As a result, the 'revised' Isobel is less under the shadow of the dead beloved of Part I than in her 1974 incarnation. The first version of Part II may have 'lacked that distance, that inner formality or calm' that McGahern aspired to because the writing was still too close to the emotion that was driving the *poiēsis*, because he was still writing within the experiential moulds that had shaped *him*.

The 'grace of ceremony' for McGahern is the order of art, a secular, Yeatsian more than Proustian protocol by which the 'terrible beauty' of the commonplace is arranged artfully in a way that quietly celebrates 'the rich horn' of experience; it is the benediction of attention to the universals encoded in the everyday acts of living and dying, an attention that raises the individual life to the coherence of a compensatory idea. But most

---

final shape of any work is won out of the material ... And that shape is won out of the argument between the vision, the authorial presence, or whatever it is called, and the material' ('A Conversation', 17). In the mid-1990s, McGahern told Rosa González: 'I think a writer writes out of his private world, and that is more or less shaped by the time one is twenty, twenty-one or twenty-two. Everything that happens to you, changes you, but ... that private world is essentially shaped and one always works on that' ('John McGahern', 42).

14   Sampson, 'A Conversation', 13.

importantly, it is the 'ceremony' of writing itself that promises McGahern the access to the grace he most craves – the self-control that masters grief, the storied balm that salves the wound deep in the self; as he writes in *The Pornographer*, in language that looks back to his second novel: 'We master the darkness with ceremonies' (*P*, 238). McGahern believed strongly that 'Writing, fiction especially, is life written to an order or vision, while life itself is a series of accidents … It has to be re-invented or re-imagined, and I think that's because it has to conform to an idea.'[15] The making of the fiction, for McGahern, is thus the metamorphosis of the 'vision' emanating from 'that still and private world' of memory into an 'idea' enlivened by the 'rhythm' of its fictive reformation, an 'idea' manifested in the work as a total image, and it is this transformation of 'vision' into image – and specifically, the image of the 'beloved' – that seems to have been the source of his dissatisfaction with the original version of Part II of *The Leavetaking*.

In the 'Preface' McGahern explains that he set out to write the two parts in different styles that would capture the way 'the remembered "I" comes to us' but 'that more than "I" – the beloved' disappears into mere 'reportage'; his intention was to find a way to make 'these disparates … true to one another' (*L* 1984: [5]). McGahern is actually drawing on the language of his narrator-protagonist in the novel here, from a passage he added to the revised Part II (see *L* 1984: 143), and in doing so ironically erases the distinction between writer/character when he merges the 'voices' of novelist/narrator. And what has to be recognized is that, psychoanalytically, for McGahern/Patrick, the Other, the beloved, is a composite figure of loss that comprises both his mother and his lover(s): the echo of Arnold's 'Dover Beach' – 'Ah, love, let us be true / To one another!' – unmasks the attempted disguise of the beloved/lover as 'these disparates' of the subjective/objective voice.[16]

---

15   González, 'John McGahern', 45.

16   McGahern's choice of metaphor in his interview with Eamon Maher is also relevant here. He explains the 'idea' behind *The Leavetaking* in the same language he uses in the 'Preface' and the Sampson interview but phrases the last point differently: 'to see if the two things could be *married* or joined at the end' (*John McGahern*, 146; my emphasis). McGahern's remarks about Self and Other in the Sampson

McGahern describes the flaw in his original effort as deriving from the fact that 'I had been too close to the "Idea"' behind the novel, namely, the 'the irredeemable imprisonment of the beloved in reportage' (*L* 1984: [5]). But the 'Idea' to which McGahern felt too close may have been, rather, the 'search for the image in a kind of grave' that he described in his 1968 credo; for the image of the 'lost beloved' entombed in memory and kept alive by grief dominates the first part of *The Leavetaking* and haunts the first version of Part II. What the impulse to revise may signify is a tension between the writer's conscious 'Idea' and an unconscious need. The two-part structure of the novel suggests an attempt to separate the past from the future, to formally take leave of the past, to break free of its 'mould', but this is at odds with the failed leave-taking actually described in Part I and the ghostly presence of the beloved/mother in Part II.[17] McGahern's

---

interview need to be taken with more than a grain of theoretical salt. They begin well – 'I happen to think that the person cannot emerge from the Self, and that the Other, which is the beloved object, does speak in a different language to the Self' – but quickly become incoherent: 'The life of the Other had to be left there in its own language, and that own language is an artifact, and actually its formlessness is a chosen formlessness, so that it's not in itself formlessness' ('A Conversation', 15, 16). Not surprisingly, Sampson asks McGahern to explain 'How … you capture the formlessness in a work of fiction and leave it that quality of formlessness?' Neither *The Leavetaking* nor *The Pornographer* is a narrative form of formlessness, whatever that might be, and McGahern cannot explain; instead he seems to try to distract the interviewer by changing the subject to the nobility of attempting the impossible: 'If something is impossible, that is all the more reason for attempting it. You might not get it right this time, but if you know that you are going to get something right, then one almost has a duty not to do it, because one is no longer dealing with the unknown' (Sampson, 'A Conversation', 16).

17 Sampson reads both *The Leavetaking* and *The Pornographer* as 'portraits of the artist' (*Outstaring Nature's Eye*, 13) and recognizes that, in *The Leavetaking*, 'The mother's shadow from which, on one level, as teacher, [Patrick] wishes to be freed, is an ambivalent presence in his life because she has a key role in the formation of his artistic sensibility' (Ibid., 122). As with *The Dark*, however, the text of *The Leavetaking* gives no indication that the protagonist is a future writer. Escaping from the ghost of his mother is, however, at the centre of Patrick's story and the language of freedom in the novel is knotted around the linked figures of the dead mother and the women

remarks in the 1979 Sampson interview and the 1983 'Preface' suggest that
the Other is overwritten by the language of the Self when objectified as
'reportage' but McGahern's revisions to Part II seem a conscious effort to
excise that ghostly presence. The title, *The Leavetaking*, refers not just to
the traumatic scene from Patrick's childhood that still haunts him; there
is a sense in which it comes to refer to the desire of the 'lost beloved' to be
set free of the son's grief, to be let go. Formally, the two-part novel simultaneously separates and bridges the Self and beloved Other, an illogical if
completely understandable desire. The narrative form is ironic, dialectical,
and the explicit allusion to Arnold's elegiac 'Dover Beach' in the closing
pages sounds the doom that permeates its tale of a failed homecoming that
is a cipher for a marriage that failed, on one level, perhaps, because it was
a failed reunion with the 'lost beloved'.

'In the beginning was the Word .... And the Word was made flesh,
and dwelt among us', writes the evangelist (John 1.1, 14); and McGahern,
appropriating that voice at the end of his life, wrote: 'In the beginning was
my mother' (*M*, 203): her love was the light that illumined her son's world,
and then she died, and the world fell into shadow, into the dark, and 'The
only way that life could be continued with her was through prayer' – or, as
he ultimately discovered, through the writing life that became a search for
the 'lost beloved' in words that transcended the grieving self. *The Leavetaking* is a novel in two parts in two senses: it is a work in two sections issued
in two versions that are actually two stages in an ongoing process; and it is
the second edition that is the pivotal work in McGahern's career because
it marks the paradoxical turn away from the dark, inner world of his grief
toward the rising sun of the redeemed beloved of vision. The 1974 version
of the novel is a work that, for all its 'conscious risks', remains trapped in
the dark of his first two novels. It is the 1984 version of the novel that
breaks the moulds of those early works and if McGahern thought he could

---

he seeks to displace her as 'the beloved'. In the original version of Part II Patrick feels
that while the black-haired girl who has jilted him 'had given me a death instead of
a love ... [nevertheless] ... it had taken the sexual death to burn out the first death,
and give me my life late but at last' (*L* 1974: 108), the 'first death' being that of his
mother.

not have written *The Pornographer* without first writing *The Leavetaking*, he could not have revised *The Leavetaking* without having written *The Pornographer*, because it is in *The Pornographer* that he first achieves 'that distance, that inner formality or calm, that all writing, no matter what it is attempting, must possess'. In terms of the story McGahern was telling *himself*, in his 1979 interview with Sampson, he cast *The Leavetaking* as the novel in which he wrote himself free of the shadow of his grief.

The Long Goodbye – *The Leavetaking*, Part I: 'I had not loved her enough'

The first 'leave-taking' presented in the novel is Patrick's farewell to teaching. There is, however, a connection between his abandoning his career for the woman he loves and his sense that he abandoned his first beloved, his mother, when she was dying, when he acknowledges that 'Her dead world comes to life in my mind as I drift ... on a tide of memory' (*L*, 25). When McGahern later re-shapes the latter image into 'the long withdrawing tide of memory becoming imagination' (*L*, 45), we may sense that the narrator-protagonist's reverie is as much an unburdening in order to travel more lightly into the future as a stock-taking of his nine years in his mother's profession. For leaving teaching needs to be understood in relation to Patrick's attempt to set to rest the guilt that haunts him from 'betraying' his mother and not becoming a priest.[18] Becoming a teacher was following in his mother's footsteps in a rather sinister sense, following her into her

---

18   Her 'dream' of being Patrick's housekeeper (*L*, 27–8) is a reprise of Mahoney's in *The Dark* (*D*, 45–6) but is drawn from McGahern's memory of his own mother (*M*, 62–3, 99–101, 109–10); McGahern also re-uses the conversation between Patrick and his mother (*L*, 25–6) in his memoir (*M*, 63, 101; compare also *L*, 29 and *M*, 118) and draws from the description of Father Gerald's church and rectory in *The Dark* – e.g. the clocks, apple garden, and cemetery, for some of the imagery here. The scene where Patrick walks up the railway tracks to visit his cousin Bridget Kiernan and

'dead world' not as the Orphic hero but as an act of self-sacrifice, a self-entombment in the shadow-world of guilt and grief.[19] The images from the failed leave-taking in the upper room that haunt Patrick attest to the larger lack of closure that the scene contributes to, as well as to the failure to expiate his guilt and move on from his grief.[20]

What the novel records, then, is the turning-point in McGahern's own life when he left teaching to become a full-time writer. In the novel, Patrick expresses a strong revulsion at his memory of his mother's fantasy of him as a priest and his childish compliance with it (see *L*, 28). The awkwardness in the passage reflects the resistance of the still grieving and guilt-ridden son to the impulse to break free of the *abnormal* darkness of the 'dead world' of the mother that 'comes to life' in his mind. It is as if McGahern, through Patrick, was saying 'enough is enough. Time to let the dead die and the living live'. The imagery suggests that the continuing bond between the dead and the living is too tight a leash upon the living, too rigid, an emotional calcification that, considering McGahern's later use of Wordsworth's riddle, 'The child is father of the man', is threatening to abort the unborn adult in the child; 'the need of the chain to lengthen and grow strong in normal darkness' (*L*, 28) suggests the author's recognition of a normal guilt and grief but also that what Patrick has endured is *not* normal: his memory of his mother's sickroom is 'more vivid' than his immediate surroundings (*L*, 28). What disgusts Patrick about the memory now may be his childish self's acquiescence to the clerical dream. He no

---

she pushes him to face the possibility of his mother's dying (*L*, 31–4) is also re-told in the memoir. (Bridget is based on Bridie Keegan; see *M*, 120–21).

19   Sampson notes the 'central ambiguity' of the mother's 'dead world' being 'more real in some vital way than the "coffin" of the schoolroom present' (*Outstaring Nature's Eye*, 120).

20   For Maher 'It is sometimes difficult to ascertain what is so special about Patrick's relationship with Isobel. Why is she so special ...? What leads him to get married in full knowledge of the negative consequences it will have on his career. I don't think any of these questions are adequately answered' (*John McGahern*, 39); but Patrick *must* leave teaching if he is to begin to escape the shadow of his mother and Isobel is the beloved who must displace her in his mind if their marriage is to succeed (just as he must displace her memories of her father as well as whatever residual attraction to him she still feels).

longer shares his mother's beliefs (see *L*, 25, 69). It is also noteworthy that he is being fired because of the power the Church has over the school system and thus the polysemy of 'leave-taking' extends from the mother and the teaching career to 'Mother Church' as well.[21]

Patrick's account of his mother's first bout with cancer, her sudden departure for hospital in Dublin, and the children's move to their father's barracks is the same as McGahern's in *Memoir* (compare *L*, 63–4 and *M*, 25, 58–9). The account of her return, however, is different in the novel, summarized in three paragraphs, whereas in the memoir, McGahern celebrates what were clearly some of the happiest memories of his life. In the novel, Kate comes from hospital to the barracks for a few days, and then takes Patrick back to the farmhouse with her. In the memoir, McGahern's mother went from hospital to her sister's shop in Ballinamore and resumed teaching; the farmhouse at Corramahon was still being put in order. McGahern makes a point of mentioning that his father appears not to have gone to see her following the mastectomy (*M*, 60). The two days mother and son spend in the house alone in the novel are a whole week in the memoir. In the novel, Patrick feels 'my beloved was home, and I was alone with my beloved' (*L*, 64; see *M*, 60), and three decades later McGahern repeats this word for word in his memoir, except to remove the repetition of 'my beloved' (*M*, 62). It is during this week while they are alone together that Susan McGahern told her seven year old boy how in hospital, after meeting a woman whose son was a priest, she formed her dream of his becoming a priest, a fantasy she repeated to him so often 'it was impossible to tell to whom the dream belonged' (*M*, 62). McGahern suggests that the power the dream held for him was not so much in the image of becoming a priest as in that of living inside an exclusively maternal world (*M*, 63). In *The Leavetaking*, McGahern makes the dream more definitely Patrick's mother's and in his memoir, he admits that even as a child he knew that there was something else happening in his playing up to his mother's fantasy, a boy's attempt to charm his beloved into remaining at the centre of his life and world (see *M*, 109).

21   As an adult Patrick now resents that he had to purchase his mother's love with the coin of catechismic dissembling (see *L*, 25).

Patrick ends his recollection of this happy time with a brief account of walking with his mother one night to a nearby farm for milk. It is a fictive version of the central 'happy memory' McGahern later describes in his memoir, and while the image of the 'lost world' McGahern presents there is more elaborate and impassioned, what is significant in the novel is the assuagement of memory by imagination in the image of healing (*L*, 64; compare *M*, 63–4). The intensity in the passage illuminates the cryptic language of the paragraphs that begin Patrick's turn to 'what I did not want to look on': 'Loss and the joy of restoration, sweet balm of healing: already that shape must have been on all the faces bent over their books in this the classroom of the day. What a little room it would be without memory of the dead and dead days, each day without memory a baby carriage in the shape of a coffin wheeled from the avenue of morning into night' (*L*, 64).[22] The imagery echoes 'what a coffin this schoolroom would be without the long withdrawing tide of memory becoming imagination' (*L*, 45); experience and its memories are all that fill the void between birth and death, giving 'shape' to the formlessness of existence. Patrick has come to a point where he accepts that his life has been shaped 'as naturally in its element as the trees that lean away from the sea' (*L*, 64), imagery that McGahern repeats twice more during Patrick's account of his mother's death at the end of Part I. This recalls the kind of resignation to circumstances that characterizes young Mahoney in *The Dark*; indeed, Patrick's earlier admission to his wife about the emotional climate of his childhood (*L*, 44) is similar to Mahoney's abject acceptance of his years of abuse at the hands of his father. In *The Leavetaking*, however, McGahern provides some background for this attitude: Patrick is his mother's son, although his passivity *does* seem to chafe against a formless but nevertheless growing will.[23] The dynamic in McGahern's outlook, the tension between one's life being shaped by circumstances and the individual attempting to shape it

---

22   The image of the baby pram in the shape of a coffin returns as the centrepiece of the elaborate 'plan' Maloney outlines in *The Pornographer* (*P*, 127–8).

23   Patrick's description of himself (*L*, 48) also recalls McGahern's description of the Reegan children as pawns (*B*, 23).

for himself or herself is central to his preoccupation with narrative as the shaping of the 'image' out of experience. The work of art, the shaped fiction, the completed circle of story, assert human presence in time, maintain memory as history.

Amidst all this use of memory, the novel also shows Patrick's 'memory becoming imagination' when he imagines his mother as a teacher and then her attempt to end her engagement. Later, he imagines the conception of his brother, 'the cancer child' (*L*, 72), so described because Patrick believes the pregnancy 're-activated' his mother's disease. Perhaps the most poignant instance of this modulation occurs when, in the midst of recalling his mother dying in the upstairs bedroom, Patrick consciously decides to *imagine her remembering* something he believes would have given her pleasure. The (con)fusion of memory and imagination here parallels the fusion of novelist and narrator already observed in the 'Preface.' Patrick 'recalls' a summer afternoon during haying time when Kate was home on holidays from boarding school. Her father sent her from the field to get a new emery stone he had saved to sharpen the scythe. Both parents warn her to be careful with 'the delicate black stone' (*L*, 68). The passage quickly takes on the tone of a fairy tale and is uncharacteristically explicit in its psycho-sexual notation. The cool grass under her bare feet, the form-fitting shape and heft of the phallic stone in her grip, 'brought a wildness to her blood'. She stops to play, rolling the stone up and down the side of a haycock until she pushes too far and it falls over the other side and breaks. Patrick confesses that he likes 'to imagine' his mother re-living this moment in the mountains of her youth many times as she lay alone and dying in the upper room of the farmhouse (*L*, 68–9). It is a strange memory for Patrick to wish for his mother: why would he imagine the memory of an accident due to negligence, which presumably would have caused some upset and disappointment to her parents, to have been a source of pleasure to her as she lay dying? This tells us more about him than about her past. The memory has the aura of a dream and many of its features call out for symbolic interpretation. The description of the heat, landscape and stone is charged with pent up sexual energy. The figures of the father and mother, and the daughter charged with a specific errand whose failure to perform her responsibility is due to a combination of disobedience and carelessness, as if some wandering god, the Pan whose hardened 'hooftrack' broke the stone, had distracted her, are like characters in a folktale. The act of transgression itself seems a scene in the theatre of the unconscious, where age and youth, authority and independence, responsibility and play, virginal innocence and erotic impatience are all held in a delicate balance that suddenly breaks, ushering in irrevocable, undeniable, permanent, and unfixable consequence. Freudian phallic symbol, Jungian symbol of the integrated self, the broken stone may also symbolize the son's obsession with his mother's sexuality and his knowledge that it would lead, ultimately, to her own 'breaking' – as well as his.

The shift from memory to imagination in *The Leavetaking* recalls the transitions in narrative voice in *The Dark*, for as he imagines his mother and father, Patrick's narration passes into an extended third-person voice; however, this instability of the apparently realistic frame which McGahern has constructed with the first-person voice only marks a shift in the nature of the reverie that characterizes Patrick's stream of consciousness. Patrick himself frames the first instance by introducing it with a sententious existentialist comment about the irreversibility of chance (*L*, 35). He imagines his mother working late in her classroom and being seen by Mother Mary Martin, who questions her about a religious vocation. Patrick imagines the question awakening his mother to the possibility of such a life and moving her to write to the policeman who has kept her waiting over a seven-year engagement.

In his memoir McGahern admits that he does not know the reason for his mother's extraordinary decisiveness in returning the ring and ending the engagement: it could have been because she had heard the stories about other women or because of family pressure over the length of the engagement, or perhaps someone else had caught her eye (*M*, 54). In the novel, McGahern uses these details of his parents' relationship but extrapolates from them in order to give Patrick's mother an altogether different motive for ending the engagement – the desire to pursue a life of independent self-fulfillment. Patrick's mother is an image of Susan McGahern but one informed or inspirited by McGahern's projecting back into his 'memory' of his mother an idealization of her as an unmarried woman before she became the partner of the man who would transform her life and then re-shape her son's after her death. At the same time, McGahern represents his father's behaviour in more definite terms; in the novel, the 'rumours' that he mentions in the memoir are presented as Kate's apparent knowledge that her fiancé was having 'a riot of affairs elsewhere' (*L*, 39). These paragraphs in which 'Patrick' imagines his mother shimmer in narrative transparency. We recognize that the third-person narrative voice describing Kate is, of course, a ventriloquial projection of the first-person narrator-protagonist, and yet the imagining that has displaced memory is a doubly compounded fiction, with author and character seemingly becoming interchangeable.

Memory becoming imagination is the nature of McGahern's narrative art. Patrick's memory becoming imagination is thus not only the product of McGahern's memory becoming fiction, but also a metafictive reflection of the process that involves not only extrapolation from memory but also the shaping of autobiographical fact into personal mytheme. For example, McGahern says that he never knew for certain the details of his father's family's background but only 'rumours' of illegitimacy and his grandmother's abandonment (*M*, 16). In the novel, however, McGahern takes these rumours and makes them the basis of an embedded story in which Patrick, claiming to repeat what he heard his father tell, describes his father's childhood poverty (*L*, 52–6), and in doing so, goes a considerable way toward explaining how his own father's character and personality became so deformed. (Throughout the account Patrick speaks in his father's voice, another significant bifurcation of his own first-person voice.) This is a powerful instance of how making life into fiction can lead to a kind of understanding that is not forthcoming if the writer sticks closely to what he knows to be the 'facts'. In *Memoir*, McGahern can find no meaningful explanation for his father's behaviour, other than that his nature always was or somehow became mean-spirited, selfish and cruel.[24]

---

24   Another example of Patrick's memory becoming imagination as a result of McGahern's is when Patrick thinks of the time his father brought him a dog (*L*, 56). In his memoir, McGahern describes the details in six lines (*M*, 88); in the novel, Patrick's account of his father's arduous journey takes three pages and includes stops at a pub and at his sister-in-law's shop (*L*, 56–9). Compare also the account of Patrick accompanying his mother on the train to Ballinamore to do her Christmas shopping (*L*, 59–63)

When McGahern has Kate try to explain to Mother Mary Martin that she uses poetry in her teaching because she regards poetry as an openness to 'the great mystery of life itself' (*L*, 38), McGahern is using the character to articulate his own outlook on life as well as to pay homage to his mother.[25] But in his imagining of Kate McLaughlin's 'passivity', her reluctance to take charge of her life but rather to 'drift' or let circumstances 'shape' it for her (*L*, 39), McGahern seems to be addressing a source of something in his own character: the drifting image recalls the young Mahoney's fear in *The Dark* (*D*, 56, 84) and, as already noted, the 'shaping' metaphor is a central image in McGahern's moral and aesthetic vocabulary. Moreover, by having Kate admit that before she accepted her husband's proposal she was intending to enter the convent and take vows, but that her procrastination meant that she was vulnerable to his stronger will (*L*, 40), McGahern not only provides a lineage for his own problematic passivity but also for his rejection of a clerical life for a life in the world. Once again the imagination here is assuaging memory.

But what is *McGahern's* imagination 'doing' when he has Patrick imagine his father and mother the morning after their wedding night, his father feeling both anxious and peeved as he looks across the breakfast table at his enigmatically smiling wife who is slowly coming to terms with her changed condition by 'trying to change the sheets and blood and sexual suck of the night into a sacrificial marble on which a cross stood in the centre of tulips and white candles' (*L*, 42)? Is the imagination intruding to forgive and redeem the 'fallen' mother for giving herself to the hated father? Or is there even an unconscious element of 'shared' exasperation with the contortions of a religious sensibility that has to deodorize the natural with sanctimony? As Patrick imagines his mother thinking about 'it', obviously 'it' is the focus of *Patrick's* imagination, and 'it' is clearly not marriage but

---

and McGahern's in *Memoir* (71–2). Both novel and memoir contain a description of the interior of Aunt Maggie's shop in Ballinamore, as well as descriptions of Hughie McKeon, the conductor-guard on the train, and Mary, who worked for Maggie.

25   Kate's reference to the mystery of life also recalls Elizabeth Reegan and is evidence of that character's source in McGahern's recollections of his mother (see *B*, 59, 64, 192, 211).

sexual initiation and the loss of virginity, and perhaps by extrapolation, the beginning of the sexual 'accidents' that will lead not only to his own birth, but ultimately, her own death (see *L*, 42).

The ruptured hymen also signals a break in the narrative membrane as the first-person voice suddenly 'returns' and McGahern brings Patrick back into the foreground only for him to imagine the beginning of his parents' sexual life in a way that merges an imagined past and his own present. In the narrative present, in the classroom on his last day at the school, Patrick remembers that following their arrival in Ireland, he and Isobel had followed in his parents' footsteps when they had climbed Howth hill (*L*, 43). This is a complex moment and it completes a cycle in Patrick's narration that is a profoundly significant reflection of McGahern's art of memory.

Beginning with Patrick's contemplation of the parallel worlds of the present and 'the world of memory becoming imagination', McGahern shows memory becoming imagination when Patrick imagines the scene between his mother and Mother Mary Martin and its consequences, leading to the breakfast scene and his parents' decision to climb Howth. McGahern then shows imagination becoming memory as Patrick, unconsciously, grants to what he has just imagined the authority of remembered 'fact' by linking it to a memory of what his mother told him, an authority that then serves to establish not only a coincidence in time of past and present, but more ambiguously, between the two pairs of newlyweds (*L*, 43). This apparent acceptance of the presence of the past in the present echoes Patrick's earlier acknowledgement of the intrusion of the 'dead world' of his mother into his mind as well as McGahern's own identification of the goal of his Orphic quest as the 'grave of the images of dead passions and their days'. But what is also wonderful about this passage is the suddenness with which the narrator asserts the authority of the present *against* that of the past by having his newer memory of feeling his wife's evident comfort in her own sexual skin as they climbed together *displace* the memory and imagination of his mother (see *L*, 43). The image of the dead hovering or looming over the lives of the living 'in fashions that had ceased' (*L*, 43) suggests a continuing presence but also an unbridgeable separation between past and present. Isobel actually expresses a sense of the uncanny in the occasion and what her words describe is the paradoxical sense of the past haunting

the future, with the implicit threat of foreclosing its possibilities by imposing its fears and inhibitions on the present. McGahern 'frames' Patrick's
memory/imagining of his parents' marriage with a conversation between
newlyweds who both want their marriage to be *unlike* anything their parents had. The wind blowing on Isobel's face throughout their conversation
connotes a hope of change, but when they notice the seawater stained with
effluent and then see the sewage flowing from the city out into the bay,
this hope is undercut by the suggestion that the future is already polluted
by the past, a possibility Patrick and Isobel seem naively insensitive to as
they raise their glasses later in the pub.

   But there is a sense in *The Leavetaking* that narration itself is *disinfect-
ing* for the narrator. By constructing Patrick's mother as a deeply religious
woman who allowed her sense of a spiritual vocation to be overridden by
a proposal of marriage simply because she was a procrastinator, someone
as passive as she was sensitive, imaginative, and gentle, McGahern subtly
shapes Patrick's narrative of 'betrayal' in a way that ultimately exonerates
him. And because the details of Patrick's life and his mother's death are so
clearly based on those of McGahern's and his mother's, the exoneration
is more than an effect of emplotment in the conventional sense; for the
emplotment in *The Leavetaking* belongs to a process of self-making that
extends throughout McGahern's writing, from *The Barracks* to *That They
May Face the Rising Sun*, in which the shaping of fiction is the struggle to
grow toward the light of understanding that McGahern describes as the
purpose of life (*M*, 36). Patrick's mother once had a sense of vocation, but
after accepting a proposal of marriage, this lapsed and weakened during
her protracted engagement; then, suddenly, she recovers it and attempts
to break off the engagement with the intention of resuming that vocation. For the second time, she is dissuaded from the religious life and so
becomes a married woman and mother. Learning this when we do gives
a definite edge to Patrick's later statements to Isobel about his mother's
wish for him to live her dream. Patrick admits that his mother set out to
use him to make up for her own weakness of will, to succeed vicariously by
sacrificing his life to a clerical career to atone for her own failure. The tension between 'my own life' and '[her] dream for my life' (*L*, 45) in Patrick's
account of things is central to the novel and to the complex symbolism of
'leave-taking' in it. The tension is also central to understanding what's 'in

play' in McGahern's *poiēsis*, what the story is 'attempting', working over and working out in terms of the story's autobiographical roots.

The association of sex and death in McGahern's writing is explained in *The Leavetaking* when, in another instance of memory becoming imagination, Patrick imagines his father pressuring his wife to have sex even though the doctor has warned them that pregnancy will likely reactivate her cancer. It is a connection McGahern repeats in his memoir (*M*, 77); and when McGahern has his narrator-protagonist announce, 'I turn to memory and images out of my own life to imagine the night that she conceived' (*L*, 65), while 'she' refers to Kate Moran the psychoanalytical double-dealing of the 'I' and 'my own life' is undeniable. The 'memory and images out of my own life' are *McGahern's* recollections of his mother's last pregnancy and the birth of his only brother, Frankie, as *Memoir* makes clear (*M*, 93). The scene Patrick describes is voyeuristically seen; there is no memory to become imagination but only imagination filling in the blank of senselessness. Patrick 'counts back' from the birth of 'the cancer child my brother' (*L*, 72) in late October to date his conception to the night in the previous winter when his father arrived with the whippet (*L*, 65).[26] The way that he imagines his father pressing his reluctant wife for sex clearly constructs the sergeant as the cause of the cancer's recurrence and so, indirectly, as his wife's killer: 'He meant to be careful, but moving in the warm dark flesh of the woman the male urge to *inflict* the seed deep within her grew and it was too late when he pulled free' (*L*, 65; my emphasis).[27]

From this point on, the novel turns back from imagination to memory. Everything to do with Patrick's mother's final illness and death is found in McGahern's memoir, much of it simply 'reprinting' the text of the novel.[28] One of the most important details that McGahern draws on from

26   This adds further meaning to the striking image of 'a baby carriage in the shape of a coffin' (*L*, 64). Later, Patrick refers to his brother again as 'The child of her cancer' (*L*, 81). McGahern's brother, Frankie, was born November 9, 1943 (*M*, 93).

27   Sexual desire is a fatal flaw in *The Leavetaking* and in his memoir McGahern describes it leading all three McManus girls to make bad choices in partners (see *M*, 44).

28   Compare the description of Kate's morning-sickness on the way to school, the arrangement for a substitute teacher, the doctor's house-calls and her brother, Michael's, visits (*L*, 65–6) with McGahern's memories in *Memoir* (118–21); also, the description of

his memory of this terrible time in his life is that throughout his mother's final illness and death she was cruelly abandoned by his father. Like Susan McGahern, Kate Moran dies alone in an upstairs bedroom in an empty house with only her nurses in attendance (*L*, 68–9). Her cowardly husband refuses to attend her deathbed, and even sends hired men with a truck to remove her children and furniture shortly before she dies (*L*, 69–72; compare *M*, 122–4). McGahern seems never to have forgiven his father for this and references to his abandonment of his mother compose a sad and bitter motif in the memoir (see *M*, 112, 122, 128, 227, 246; also 42).

The Passion of Complicated Grief

When he came to recount his mother's death in his memoir, McGahern re-used the thirteen pages from the end of Part I of *The Leavetaking*. There are a few differences in details and some re-ordering of paragraphs and sentences, but otherwise the accounts are the same.[29] The major difference is

---

Nurse O'Neill and May's pleading with her to come to tend Kate (*L*, 67–8) is based on Maggie's efforts to find a nurse for her sister (*M*, 119).

29   In the novel, there is a priest in attendance: Kate's cousin (who recalls Father Gerald in *The Dark*, the boy's mother's cousin) administers the Last Rites and remains to comfort her as everyone leaves (*L*, 69, 71–2); there is no priest present in the memoir. There are subtle differences in the description of the lorry's arrival and Michael's/ Pat's response to the note and excuse sent by Sergeant Moran/McGahern (*L*, 70; *M*, 123). In the novel, McGahern's description of the sound of the men beating apart the rusted pieces of the iron beds is particularly effective; it elicits Michael's contempt for his brother-in-law (*L*, 71), and later he swears as he repeats the remark (*L*, 72); in the memoir, McGahern does not identify the man who swears (*M*, 123). The motif of the noisy hammering in the novel comes to symbolize Sergeant Moran's obnoxious presence even in his absence and the severing force of his will, something that links him both to the Mahoney of *The Dark* and Moran in *Amongst Women*. In the novel, Patrick stands in the garden outside during all this activity until the nurse calls him in (*L*, 70–1); McGahern describes waiting outside and 'hating' his little sisters for

how each account *functions* in the larger work of which it is a part. Patrick's experience of his mother's dying, her death, his sense of abandoning and then betraying her, and his feelings of grief and guilt afterwards – all this is a necessary and meaningful prelude to the experiences he recounts in Part II; it is especially necessary for understanding his relationship with Isobel and his decision to return to Ireland in order to be formally fired from his teaching job. By ending Part I with the moving description of the little boy's suffering, and particularly with the explicit language of its closing paragraph, McGahern clearly establishes the frame within which he intends Part II to be read, and also shows the 'mould' that has shaped his narrator-protagonist's character; at the same time, he tacitly announces that what Patrick will narrate in Part II will be the experiences since his mother's death which have led him to the point where he is about to break out of this mould which has all along been the 'dead world' of her shadow.

'She was gone where I could not follow', Patrick recalls feeling (*L*, 76), a lament McGahern repeats in his memoir (*M*, 129). The account of the

---

being so oblivious to what was happening (*M*, 123–4). When McGahern came out of the house, he remembers his uncle's silent gesture of compassion; in the novel, Michael meets Patrick outside the room and greets him with the same gesture but speaks to him (compare *M*, 124 and *L*, 71). As they all pile into the lorry, the reference to 'the cancer child my brother' in the novel (*L*, 72) is revised to 'the baby' in the memoir (*M*, 124). The drive to the barracks and the sight of the sergeant in uniform waiting for their arrival are the same, except that there are three other guards and two of their wives in the memoir. Patrick admits he knew his father was lying when he said he could not come to the house himself because he had used up all his leave and follows this with explicit recrimination and Patrick's image of his father's 'mouth' recalls the repulsive Mahoney's kisses (*L*, 73). The incident of Patrick dropping a coin so he could look up a woman's dress recurs in the memoir (*L*, 73; *M*, 126). McGahern 'corrects' the time of his mother's death by thirty minutes (see *L*, 74; *M*, 127). The description of Moran leading the children in the rosary (*L*, 74) echoes that of Mahoney in *The Dark*, and McGahern repeats it in the memoir (*M*, 127), including the father's threat when the little girls start giggling (*L*, 75; *M*, 128). The choral lament of the women that sends Patrick to hide in the cupboard beneath the stairs is also repeated in the memoir (*M*, 128), as are their remarks about the children not going to the funeral, the boy's attempt to avoid going to Sunday Mass, and his discomfort when he is made to go (*L*, 76–8; *M*, 129–30).

leave-taking in *Memoir* is no less important in McGahern's story of his life than it is in the story Patrick Moran tells, but – and this is the important difference between the early fiction and the later memoir – in the novel, the loss of the mother casts a shadow which Patrick must escape if he is to move forward into the light of a life with a new beloved; whereas in the memoir, the loss of the mother inspires the life-quest which culminates in her recovery in its climactic final paragraphs, where McGahern, Orpheus-like, sings her back from the shadows of memory into the full sunlight of imagined presence. What comes through in the novel is an underlying romance archetype; what evolves in the memoir has a mythic reach. Both versions convey the horror and confusion of the situation for the little boy, but in the novel the effect of the repeated image of his mother's eyes is ambiguous. 'She held me still in her eyes' (*L*, 71) is wonderfully suggestive, connoting a spectrum of meanings, from the mother's heroically compassionate attempt to calm the little boy whose pain and panic she can sense, to the more complex and sinister suggestion of being gripped and stifled. The memoir revises the image to a more neutral and single instance of 'Her eyes were fixed on my face' (*M*, 124). Likewise, the fear of becoming 'lost' (*L*, 71) first evokes the obvious sense of the boy on the verge of becoming overwhelmed by the enormity of the event, of his wanting to grab hold of the leg of the bed as the tidal wave of grief looms over him; but from another angle it is his mother's kiss that disorients him and sparks the urge to run away, that draws him toward the vertigo of self-loss and the desperate anchor of the deathbed. Staying forever in that room is impossible, but becoming lost in the cycle of complicated mourning is quite possible for child and adult alike. The memoir too conveys a sense of danger in the moment, of the growing boy becoming imprisoned in his absolute love for his mother, petrified by the enormity of the loss, unable to grow naturally free of it because his satisfaction of his need of her has been abruptly cut short and incomplete, and the need to be free of her has not yet been allowed to form and lead him toward independence. The description of the others being unable to remove him from the room is ambiguous (*M*, 124): would they be unable to separate him because he wanted to stay in the room with her forever, or because whether he wanted to or not, in one sense he *would* be buried alive with her if he followed the impulse to stay rather than run.

A significant, and quite poignant, difference is that in the novel McGahern's little boy does say a final goodbye; in the memoir, he does not. Perhaps this is because the novel does set out to tell a story of self-liberation, whereas the memoir sets out to construct a myth of self-recovery. Or perhaps it is further evidence that from the outset McGahern, consciously or unconsciously, used the writing of fiction to redress the incompleteness of life. Outside, waiting for the truck to leave, Patrick feels drawn back to the 'deathroom' (*L*, 72). His language, in another context, could serve an erotic agenda and is another sign that McGahern's novel is the story of a young man growing free of the shadow of a 'lost beloved' so that he can be free to pursue his relationship with her replacement. The mother's gaze has already become an accusatory, if not yet punitive, haunting; and the horror the boy senses is beyond his understanding (*L*, 72), if not his intuiting. In his memoir, however, McGahern tones down this passage considerably; there is no haunting, no sublimated eros, no horror (*M*, 124).

Patrick remembers how he spent the hours leading up to the funeral imagining the details of his mother's body in the farmhouse before its removal to the church, and then the ritual of the funeral; and throughout, he describes a sense of guilt growing within his grief: 'She must have felt that I too had abandoned her .... I had not loved her enough' (*L*, 75; compare *M*, 129). His feeling 'that I *too* had abandoned her' makes Patrick feel he has behaved like his father. In the memoir McGahern allows the admission of guilt to stand, but tones it down as he reorders the sequence of regret and memory. In the novel, Patrick feels regret first and salves it with bittersweet memories of the walk to Priors for the milk, of helping her wind wool, of her being ill when they walked to school and his not knowing that it was the beginning of the end. And then guilt and shame begin to encumber the grief (*L*, 76). In the memoir, McGahern edits the list of memories but ends with the same question: 'What must she have thought when she heard the lorry leave?' (*M*, 129; compare *L*, 76)

In *Memoir*, McGahern makes very few changes to the description of Patrick's imagining the mourners coming to view his mother, the closing of the coffin, the removal and its arrival at the church; and on the day of the funeral, his frantic behaviour as he imagines the ritual of the funeral Mass, hiding beneath the laurel bushes, staring at the hands of the clock, and then, when he knows it is over, trying to escape onto the river with two passing fisherman – must signify his recognition that when he wrote the novel thirty years before he had 'gotten it right'. That is, when he wrote *The Leavetaking* he had confronted and worked through the trauma of his mother's death, and when it came to treat the same experience in the memoir, he judged the 'truth' of his fiction to be the truth of his life. In the novel, however, when Patrick imagines his father, aunt and uncle kneeling beside the bed before his mother was placed in the coffin, he expresses his sense of needing to be there (*L*, 78). McGahern does not repeat this in the memoir, but he does repeat the boy's anguish as he imagines the end of the funeral service (*L*, 80; *M*, 133). His imagination could not provide closure for the boy, and recalling that when he came to write the novel must have reopened the wound, necessarily perhaps, for it to be cleansed of the poison that had festered; and then when he came to 'cover' the events again in the memoir, that writing seems to bring a final resolution, a confession and atonement that is a prelude for the climactic 're-union' of son and mother that is celebrated at the end of the memoir.

In the novel and in his memoir, McGahern presents the failed leave-taking as the boy's foreshortened and incomplete farewell to his mother before he is taken away with his siblings to the barracks. But a clue to the full composition of this trauma is, paradoxically, hinted at in *The Barracks*, in language which, while it initiates the *poiēsis* of mourning that in varying degrees characterizes all of McGahern's writing, is notable for the ways it occludes the personal even as it expresses it. In *The Barracks*, we are given no information about Reegan's first marriage, other than that his wife died in childbirth – an interesting refiguring of the details that prefigures the theme of sex, pregnancy, and death in *The Leavetaking* and *Memoir*. The detail in the early novel that recurs in the later novel and memoir that stands out, however, because the bedroom scene and the removal to the barracks are missing, is the episode of the children's playing outside during their mother's funeral and pleading with two fisherman to take them out on the river. McGahern has the children recall that they were prevented from seeing the coffin or hearse or attending the church or cemetery (*B*, 102). Like the repressed, what is only mentioned in passing in McGahern's first novel *returns* more strongly in the later novel and memoir. It is the lack of closure from the failed leave-taking – from the botched farewell in the bedroom and from not seeing his mother at peace, from not seeing the coffin, the hearse, and being at the church service – that haunts McGahern's protagonist and the memoirist himself. And of course, his father is responsible: McGahern's fictive and real fathers separate the child from his dying mother and forbid him from going to the funeral to say good-bye. In *Memoir*, he remembers the intensity of his need to see the grave and to kneel in prayer beside it and describes going back to Aughawillan on his own to do so the following summer (*M*, 42). This lack of closure would have been a significant factor in McGahern's Complicated Grief. In the novel, after the men have refused to take him fishing on the river with them, Patrick returns to the house to meet the mourners and endure once again their choric performance of sympathy; he remembers being 'in awe of them' because they had seen his mother in the coffin and had been at the graveside, while he could attend only in his imagination. Patrick remembers thinking 'A terrible new life was beginning, a life without her ...' (*L*, 81–2; compare *M*, 135). In the memoir, McGahern repeats this passage almost word for word, but with the difference that the phrase 'terrible new life' has a meaning and impact for the reader of the memoir that are much greater and more vivid than in the novel. Also, in the memoir McGahern inserts a memory of feeling 'ashamed' of his desire to go out on the river with the men after he realized that not only had he let his mother down at the leave-taking but now she would never see him say Mass (*M*, 134). Significantly, in the novel at this moment, Patrick does *not* remember his promise to his mother to become a priest. Part II opens with this theme, but McGahern constructs Patrick in Part I as *already* having absolved himself of that betrayal, and as Part I ends, the final paragraph tells the reader how to approach the second part of Patrick's story, which will recount his decision to become a teacher rather than a priest, and then his search for a beloved. The final paragraph also makes clear that Patrick's narration itself is part of the process of his self-liberation.[30]

---

30   Speaking of the scene where Patrick pleads with the men to take him with them fishing on the river (*L*, 81), Sampson writes: 'He has exorcized his grief and desolation and has turned to "the glittering lake, the calm oar strokes" ...' (*Outstaring Nature's*

Earlier Patrick described his life following his mother's death as 'shape[d]' by that 'shadow' (*L*, 71), but he hopes that, with Isobel, and once he is free of his teaching job, his 'life would have made its last break with the shadow, and would be free to grow without warp in its own light' (*L*, 82). This explains how, for Patrick, the narrative of the leave-taking – the act of telling it – is an attempt to finally bury the past. He did not want to be a teacher but entered the profession as a result of the 'shadow' of his mother that had fallen over his life. His classroom has always been connected to her and the 'dead world'. His passive-aggressive approach to his firing is an accurate reflection of his personality in this sense. It is his way of breaking out from under the shadow of the past into the light of the future. Part I of *The Leavetaking* ends with Patrick – and McGahern – finally looking at 'what I did not want to look on' (*L*, 31) and makes clear, of course, that looking at that is the whole point of the novel. Moreover it is the act of narration itself, or the synthesis of conscious and unconscious processes from which the narration issues, that is both the act of 'looking at' his mother's death and the instrument of 'vision' that summons and confronts 'the horror of a second leavetaking' (*L*, 72), a confrontation that is psychoanalytical both in process and product. *The Leavetaking* is McGahern's most deeply 'confessional' novel and the scenes at the end of Part I compose a kind of 'passion play', a series of emotional tableaux that illuminate the son's grief and guilt. Earlier, McGahern has Patrick remark, 'I find myself telling my love' (*L*, 45) about his parents' honeymoon, as if we are meant to read the whole narrative as addressed to Isobel, as his way of explaining to her who he is, and why he is the way he is, but there is a sense embedded in the phrase that he is telling his wife about the nature of his love for his 'beloved mother', for as he admits, 'I had but the one beloved' (*L*, 80; see *M*, 133).

Eye, 125). The boy remains desolate for the next while, however, and his grief is still a potent emotion in his twenties, inflecting his feelings towards women and infecting his relationships with all his lovers. All McGahern's early protagonists – even Elizabeth Reegan – display the characteristics of Complicated Grief and it is not until *The Pornographer* and then *Amongst Women* that McGahern seems to have written his way out of this condition or his memories of it.

We should see in this tug-of-war between the living and the dead a reflection of the ambiguous dialectic within McGahern's creative life, expressed in the confluence of 'shadow' and 'shape' in the imagery of the final paragraph in Part I (see also *L*, 10). 'Shadow' evokes the 'shade' of the mother, the ghost that haunts the son, crying out for the resuscitating blood of sacrifice, an absence-presence that distorts his love and life. 'Shape' evokes the artistic act, the form-making, part-and-whole fitting together labour of the craftsman. The shadow of the past does shape the present, as the unconscious can distort the conscious mind, and the successful work of fiction for McGahern must be a product of conscious artistry and an openness to the unconscious shaping that attends it. Shadow and shape, dead mother and son, dead beloved and living, unconscious and conscious, past and future, grief and guilt and the need to move beyond them – the form of *The Leavetaking* derives from this structuring tension at the centre of McGahern's making of fiction.

The Long Goodbye – *The Leavetaking*, Part II: Vision and Revision

In the 'Preface' McGahern explains the original idea behind the novel's two-part structure and his judgment that he had failed to realize it. But while he explains why he believed it necessary to revise Part II, he does not explain how the original Part I would still 'fit in' with a Part II he claimed to have re-written 'from scratch'; presumably a radically revised Part II would affect the shape of the whole book.[31] The revisions range from complete excision of scenes, paragraphs, sentences, phrases and words to re-ordering and re-phrasing and the insertion of completely new writing, and the reasons for the changes soon become clear. The opening sentence, 'One day I'd say Mass for her', repeats word for word the young Mahoney's

---

31   See Eileen Kennedy, 'Q. & A.', 9.

guilty recollection in *The Dark*, and is the same in both editions. Here is the original version of the important first paragraph that follows:

> Through the sacrifice of my life to the priesthood I'd redeem the betrayal of her in that upstairs room. For years I promised it to her memory that, 'One day I'd say Mass for her'. I'd lift the chalice in anointed hands on the altar and in the lonely rooms of presbyteries I'd be faithful to her, but when the time arrived for me to make that sacrifice I failed her once again. I wasn't able to renounce the longing to enter the mystery of the lovely and living flesh of woman, and out of guilt I chose second best. I followed her footsteps to the Training College. In some country school I'd teach out my days. If I was lucky I'd find a girl lovely as she was whom I'd love and live with in the heart of the country. It seems all far away from this last day in the classroom: a confused child's world of guilty dreaming. (*L* 1974: 85)

Here is the revised version:

> I felt I had betrayed her in that upstairs room. Through the sacrifice of the Mass I would atone for the betrayal, but that in its turn became the sacrifice of the dream of another woman, became the death in life, the beginning only in the end. That way I would make good her dream. That way I would deny her death with my living death. That way I would keep faith. But I was not able to keep faith. The pull of nature was too strong, taking its shape in sweet, sickly dreaming. I had not the strength to make the sacrifice. I could give up all dreams but the dream of woman. (*L* 1984: 85; compare *D*, 30.)

At first, the changes seem primarily stylistic. The revised version is not just less wordy, the voice is more restrained, the tone clipped, and the rhetorical patterning gives the impression of emotional control even though the content remains confessional. It is soon noticeable, however, that the stylistic house-cleaning alters the quality of the narrative voice itself; ultimately, what McGahern is doing bears little relation to the rationale of the 'Preface' and seems more a straightforward repairing of self-image. But the core of the revisionary project in the second half of the novel is really the careful re-shaping of the presence of the dead beloved, and of the narrator-protagonist's relationship with her. The sense that 'I failed her once again' is not as strong in the 1984 version, and there is a difference between 'redeem' and 'atone', as there is between 'the sacrifice of my life to the priesthood' and 'the sacrifice of the Mass'. The first version describes a greater sense of hope for a life salved by ritual, but also of that religious devotion as a barely repressed erotic ambiguity: 'I'd be faithful to her'. Hence, the apostasy-betrayal is erotic-sexual as well as religious and emotional-moral: he could not 'renounce' his desire for 'other women'. However, the decision to become a teacher is described as an Orphic search for a simulacrum of the 'lost beloved': he will follow in the latter's footsteps, looking for 'a girl lovely as she was', life with whom, even though she will be 'second best', nevertheless will be better than the celibacy of a mourning priest.

The Composite Beloved

Patrick's fantasy is to achieve a future life that will be a version of the lost 'world' of his past (*L*, 64). The 'guilt' he feels, however, is as much Oedipal – expressed unconsciously, perhaps, in 'a confused child's world of guilty dreaming' (*L* 1974: 85) – as it is emotional and moral, caused by memories of the botched farewell and broken promise; it has influenced not only his choice of the 'second best' profession but also of a 'second best' beloved in Isobel. The 'sweet, sickly dreaming' (*L* 1984: 85) of the revision is less forthcoming than the original 'guilty dreaming', and seems to come from the author's reaction to the overheated passion and unbridled sentimentality of much of the language describing the sex and emotions in the 1974 version of Part II. Significantly, McGahern excises the fantasy of the 'girl as lovely as she was' (*L* 1974: 85) from the 1984 text and reverts to the language of *The Dark* and the young Mahoney's more explicit characterization of the priesthood as death-in-life, even as he cuts out the Lawrentian earnestness of 'the longing to enter the mystery of the lovely and living flesh of woman' (*L* 1974: 85), which also echoes the language and narrative voice of the previous novel. But 'the dream of *another* woman' (*L* 1984: 85) still develops the sense that there is a dimension of the guilt and the broken faith that is sexual-erotic. However, it is not so much that the speaker *wants* another woman (which he does) as that he *wants to love* and *be loved by* another woman. McGahern describes Patrick's grief and guilt impelling him into a parody of an Orphic quest. This search for a new beloved who will be the lost one in 'another woman' is clearer in the original version when Patrick pronounces that in his first romantic relationship at the Training College, 'I found her again' (*L* 1974: 85), 'her' being the dead beloved, his mother. McGahern drops this from the revised edition, although he does retain Patrick's explicit identification of the girl with his 'lost beloved', 'the girl with the emery stone' (*L* 1974: 86; *L* 1984: 86–7). In the first version, Patrick's passion is clearly an unhealthy inversion of his grief. The repetition of 'my love' (*L* 1974: 88) ironically confuses even as it identifies the dead mother with the new beloved; the relationship is indeed more 'dangerous' than Patrick knows. (The revised version replaces the first 'my love' with 'my mother' and the second with 'this attachment' (*L* 1984: 88), the latter in particular injecting an awkwardly 'clinical' tone that reveals the severity at times of McGahern's revisionary impulse.)

    After only a few pages it is clear that this is a different Patrick Moran – a different voice, more superego than ego, more self-consciously reconstructing himself than consciously giving himself to the process of self-recovery – than that we encounter in Part I and in the original version of Part II. The revisions seem intended to 'discipline' the extent and intensity of the original confession, which is not surprising considering that the revisionary process entails seeing the first text differently. In 1974 Patrick recalls the 'sweet ecstasy of first love' (*L* 1974: 88); a decade later, that romantic-Dionysian 'ecstasy' is toned down into a more prosaic 'drunkenness', the 'love' into 'infatuation' (*L* 1984: 88). In the original version of this relationship, the unnamed girl is clearly just a normal young woman who is not yet ready for a serious relationship, whereas Patrick is far from normal and thinking marriage within hours of their first meeting. His 'infatuation' is self-propelled and needs almost no fuel from the other to sustain its ascent into fantasy; he receives very little encouragement anyway, and when she breaks with him, she thinks she is doing so before anything has really started. McGahern's revisions are more generous towards Patrick. Even though Patrick still comes across as trying much too hard, McGahern removes the description of his last meeting with the girl as 'the plea and the rejection' (*L* 1974: 91). Most significant is the fact that McGahern excises two paragraphs which contain language explicitly linking Patrick's obsessive desire for the young woman with his memory of his mother. Recalling the evening they 'broke up', Patrick thinks:

> The afternoons at the Kingsway, the dark of the cinemas, the long white dress of taffeta were but as hour-marks on a wall with the paintbrush that measured the change of my longing from her as she lay dying in that upstairs room to a young and lovely woman, about to enter her life. (*L* 1974: 91)

This uncanny confusion of the death bed and the lover's, of past and present, like the juxtaposition of the young woman 'ripe' for sexual activity and procreation and Patrick the twenty-year-old man-'child', sexually ambitious but, paradoxically, psychologically prepubescent, is an emphatic reminder of what should be clear from Part I of Patrick's story: his emotional maturation has been arrested in a relationship with a dead beloved whose death trapped him in a lost childhood.[32] In retrospect, Patrick sees this first romantic love as the beginning of the shift from his 'longing' for (re)union with his dying mother, a longing which had drawn him into her 'dead world', to a desire for 'a young and lovely woman, about to enter her life'. The shadow imagery that follows this passage is less than coherent, unless there is coherence in its ambiguity. Patrick presents himself as recognizing on that night, when he was a heartbroken twenty-year-old, the shadow of his mother fall from the girl who had just rejected him. But does this mean the shadow fell *away from* her, in the sense that she was set free from its pall in him, or that he suddenly realized that *she cast* the same shadow as his dead mother over him because he was seeking in her a confusion of mother-love and sexual love? The fact that he describes himself running away from 'the shadow and the country dream it withered' (*L* 1974: 91) suggests the latter; but earlier in the paragraph he refers the 'change' in

---

32   This paragraph makes clearer the significance of the reference in Part I to the girl with the black hair in the nearby girls' school (*L*, 25), and reinforces the psychological importance for Patrick of his leaving his school and profession; the shadow of his mother will haunt him as long as he remains there, in a sense, through the presence of her first surrogate, a presence which underscores the link between his choice of teaching and his inability to grow beyond his grief and guilt.

his longing for the mother to a longing for the girl, as if the latter was the way out of the shadow-world of the mother and toward 'life' for him. The sinister sense of the shadow imagery here also derives from the image he describes seeing as he watched the girl walk away from him to her house, seeing 'her shape climb to her mother's dark shape in the doorway .... Both shapes merged ...' (L 1974: 91). The girl's shadow-shape merges with her mother's which consumes it like a greater, original darkness; the imagery suggests entrapment in a sinister domestic darkness. But whose mother is really standing in that doorway?

Another interpretation of this shadow imagery is that it signifies the trailing cloud of grief that attends loss. Patrick's mother's shadow fell upon him when he lost her to death; his guilt and grief haunt him constantly. Now, a version of that shadow approaches as he loses the girl he had thought would be his new beloved, and McGahern describes Patrick wracked by grief over her as well. McGahern's revisions to the paragraph in which Patrick describes his grief over breaking up with the girl removed language that added some clarity to his shadow imagery. Patrick is haunted by her memory until he finds himself staring at her photograph and senses the image become lifeless: 'We know leaving the house of the dead that the person we came to look on a last time has totally fled us and lives only among the shadows of memory' (L 1974: 92). The revised version of this reduces the moment to 'I was looking at celluloid that merely looked back. There was not even the sense of persons missing from empty spaces that will never be filled that way again' (L 1984: 91). Both versions present the reader with links to the mother-beloved via the girl but the first version is more echoic of the source of the intensity of that connection in the sinister house of shadows that encrypts the dead beloved.

In his revisions, McGahern deletes the description of Patrick's Dublin pub and dancehall life following this disappointment. He also edits Patrick's description of his affair with the older woman who tutors him in the 'dignity' of sexual intercourse (L 1974: 92). She is named Elinor in the first version, and he addresses her as 'my love' (L 1974: 93) after their first coupling; in the revised version, she is an anonymous widow whose children are away at school. It is most significant that she is a *mother* who *teaches* Patrick about sex in a relationship that he knows is temporary but whose end will *not* be felt by him as the dreaded experience of loss. The revised description of their affair is less sexually explicit, less romantic-sentimental, less self-exposing, and so the changes dramatically alter the quality of the first-person voice and hence the reader's sense of the character of the narrator-protagonist. On this point, it is important to remember, perhaps, that when McGahern came to revise Part II of *The Leavetaking* he had recently written *The Pornographer*, and it is reasonable to expect that what he 'worked through' and achieved in that novel affected how he re-read his previous novel and how he approached the act of revision. McGahern told Eileen Kennedy that writing for him had always been 'a way of seeing,'[33] and *The Pornographer* would have led him to see the 'love story' of the second half of *The Leavetaking* differently; after *The Pornographer*, the sexual explicitness of the first version of Part II, for example, might have seemed embarrassingly *de trop*, even though it had been necessary if McGahern was to get to the point where he could write a novel like *The Pornographer* and complete the 're-orientation' that the two novels, taken together, achieve.

Patrick's relationship with Elinor gives him the self-assurance to begin a series of one-night stands before tripping again into the 'calamity of love' (*L* 1974: 94); the latter is the catalyst for his taking a leave of absence from his teaching job. The woman he picks up in a dancehall remains nameless in both editions. Patrick is attracted by her confident, sensual movements on the dance floor even though he senses a hardness bordering on cruelty in her manner (*L* 1974: 94). (In the revision, McGahern changed his mind about the cruelty [*L* 1984: 92]). Once again, Patrick falls quickly, feeling a 'magic' in her physical presence (*L* 1974: 95), and they begin a sexual relationship on their first date; and once again McGahern either curtails or removes altogether the sexual explicitness of the first version of the affair. Like Patrick, she has been disappointed in love, and the turning-point in their affair comes when she hints that what she wants is marriage and children and he fails to respond. She immediately begins to change toward him; the sex becomes merely athletic and eventually routine (*L* 1974: 98).

---

33   Kennedy, 'Q. & A.', 6.

Then their roles reverse: he now worries she will not accept his proposal, and he is caught by surprise when she suddenly ends the relationship and takes up with her previous lover. '*It has happened all over again*', Patrick thinks (*L* 1974: 101), 'it' being the loss of the beloved and the dream of a shared future. The previous version of this dream was with the country girl he met at Training College, but it is important to remember that the *original* dream was that of the boy growing up to become a priest with his mother as his house-keeper.[34]

The two versions of Patrick's post-mortem on this relationship are worth comparing. In the first, after describing the torment of jealousy and imagination he felt following the break-up, Patrick concludes that what he was actually suffering was 'the loss of my own life': 'The morning of the hammering apart of the sections of the iron beds in the upstairs room, the more gentle night of the dead end of the moonlit road over Allen, grew clear: they were times when my own gradual death ... was made present by the torture of the loss of the self I had imaged on to the other' (*L* 1974: 104–5). By returning to Patrick's memory of the morning of the leave-taking told in Part I, McGahern explicitly links his recent experiences of romantic loss with his 'primal' experience of loss and grief. But McGahern also has Patrick rationalize the intensity of his feelings by theorizing that the loss of the other was felt so deeply because what he was experiencing was 'the loss of the self I had imaged on to the other'. The revised version condenses this passage, but more significantly, drops the allusion to the death of the mother and changes the metaphor of loss from death to a game or wager: 'I had transferred the dream of my own life to another, and had lost. ... Through losing, I had stumbled on the bitter truth that she was the one irreplaceable world everybody is, but which we feel only ourselves to be' (*L* 1984: 99). While the revision removes the explicit linking in Patrick's mind and feelings of his memory of losing his mother and his

---

34   The same emotional structure and cycle can be found in the stories 'My Love, My Umbrella' and 'Parachutes'; in the former, the loss of the beloved is a projection of one's own future death (see *CE*, 66, 68) and the dialogue in the break-up scene in the latter is similar to that in the novel (see *CE*, 151).

grief over the 'loss' of the two women he has been involved with, the link is still present in a coded form.[35] The rephrasing of 'irreplaceable being' (*L* 1974: 105) as 'irreplaceable world' derives from another passage in the first edition in which Patrick describes the torment of recognizing places in the city associated with his lover as 'the world I had lost' (*L* 1974: 105). The 'lost world' for McGahern was his childhood world with his mother.[36] His experience of her death became the template of all loss for him and this is what he confronts in the novel through Patrick's recollection and confession. The dialectic that drives the invention might be understood as the passivity of grief in thrall to the 'lost world' and the struggle to break free of the paralysing belief that the lost world is 'irreplaceable'; the latter, moreover, is an important aspect of the nihilism, despair, and *acedia* that torment the protagonist in *The Pornographer*.

The first version of Part II of *The Leavetaking* makes clear that the loss of the mother that Patrick describes in Part I haunts his attempts at relationship in Part II. In the following passage, which McGahern also dropped from the second edition, it is the shadow of the dead mother that seems to infiltrate Patrick's language and make it so ambiguous. Having asked for and received a leave from his school, he has gone to London and taken a job in a pub in South Kensington. Heart-broken, he also feels 'free': 'She had given me a death instead of a love, but it had taken the sexual death to burn out the first death, and give me my life late but at last ... Only if I was lucky would I find what I was searching for, a friend and a beloved in one, and she would not be young' (*L* 1974: 108).[37] 'She' is the tall, dark-haired, gay but cruel woman whose memory haunts and torments Patrick. He had asked her for love, but too late, and she had given him a 'death' instead. So, in a way, had his mother. The parallel with his 'failure' to hold on to his first beloved is as obvious as the year's leave from school is another kind of leave-taking; where the first is indelibly linked in his mind with the

---

35   The 'hammering' motif is not dropped so much as relocated; see *L* 1984: 143.

36   See Kennedy, 'Q. & A.', 5.

37   Although this passage is dropped for the second edition, the 'friend and beloved' theme is still raised by Isobel (*L* 1984: 108) as it was in the first edition (*L* 1974: 116), although it is not developed as much.

'upstairs room' of the farmhouse, the more recent leave-taking is caused by his desire to escape the rented room he associates with his passion for the lost lover. The greatest ambiguity is in the statement that it took a 'sexual death' to excoriate 'the first death'. In terms of Patrick's narrative history in the novel, 'the first death' is that of his mother. We know that he sought her replacement in his first romantic attachment, the fellow student at Training College, and then, in the woman who has just rejected him. Each time, however, he was cast back into the misery of loss. Now he feels that he has reached the nadir of self-loss, a death that can only be followed by a re-birth, 'late but at last'. His new dream is to find a woman who will offer him the succour and security of the maternal as well as the strangeness and passion of the *inamorata*. Significantly, the only attribute Patrick already knows this dream-woman must possess is one shared by his mother: 'she would not be young'. He might have added, she would not have black or dark hair, for when the tall, fair-haired Isobel walks into his pub, it is clear she is the one. But it is her American nationality and background that most signify the break with the previous pattern of desire that she appears to represent.

Yet for all the novelty of her character in Patrick's story, there is an uncanny connection between Isobel and McGahern's previous narrator-protagonist, the young Mahoney, and of course, with McGahern himself: all three share similar experiences of sexual abuse. Isobel describes how one night when she was eight her father had come into her bed and masturbated against her (L 1974: 131). In the revised version Isobel is twelve, but otherwise the details are the same and in both versions she explains her adult relationships with men as distorted by her feelings for her father (L 1974: 132). Isobel's account of her experience with psychoanalysis is longer and more detailed in the first edition. The scene of abuse she describes recalls those in *The Dark* and *Memoir* and her admission to Patrick that she consciously set out to 'break out of my breakdown' (L 1974: 131) through psychoanalysis parallels McGahern's 'use' of the writing process to confront 'the lies and violence' (L 1984: 117) of his own childhood. In Patrick's case, he, too, is struggling to break out of his brokenness, to put his own versions of 'a guilty love' and 'a false life' behind him. What is fascinating is how McGahern develops Isobel as a gender-mirror-inversion of Patrick's filial-sexual confusion and of his own history of sexual abuse.

In the first version of Part II, Patrick's mother's shadow casts its pall over him on his way to his registry wedding, but McGahern excises the allusion in the second edition: 'Much of the past came to disturb me as I prepared to go to the registry office ... she too had one day walked down the aisle looking the picture of death. Belief was as blind, I thought, as grief, one worn away by habit, the other becoming a habit' (see the whole passage, *L* 1974: 159).[38] By removing this passage McGahern further erases the pattern of connections in Patrick's mind between Isobel and his mother that is present in the first version of the novel and builds the impression that Patrick has broken 'the blind chain' (*L* 1974: 159) of Complicated Grief that has bound him to the dead world of his mother through his 'following' her into the teaching profession. In the deleted passage, the 'link' (*L* 1974: 159) he believes he has broken is the chain of religious belief that connected him to her: by marrying a divorced woman, Patrick formally broke with the Catholic Church, and as he tells Isobel afterwards, set in motion the ending of any teaching career in the Republic of Ireland (*L* 1984: 142; see *L* 1974: 160–1). But the more powerful 'link' is to his mother and it is not at all clear that this *has* been broken. The day of his wedding, Patrick remembers his paternal grandmother's description of his mother 'looking the picture of death' at her wedding '*too*' (*L*, 42; my emphasis), clearly linking Isobel with his mother in his mind. Recognizing that his grief has become an unconscious 'habit', however, *is* a potential turning-point in Patrick's attempt to move beyond its shadow.

On his return journey to Dublin in the first edition McGahern has Patrick meet Isobel's father on the train. They have a meal together, Patrick shocks Evatt by telling him he and Isobel are married, and they argue when Patrick challenges him about his treatment of his daughter. It is an important scene because of what it suggests is 'encoded' in McGahern's construction of the Patrick-Isobel-Evatt triangle, and so when McGahern cuts it from the revised version, one of the circles leading to the 'inner circle' of the novel is lost. Patrick describes the 'shock of horror' he feels when he

---

38   McGahern married Annikki Laaksi in a registry office; see Kennedy, 7. The image of the circular journey of life from the 'original darkness' (*L* 1974: 159) of the sea is perhaps the source of the important passage in McGahern's memoir (*M*, 36; see also *B*, 73).

first sees his father-in-law in the dining car (*L* 1974: 162). Evatt is another father-monster, an archetypal figure of romance, a devouring ogre like Mahoney in *The Dark* and Moran in *Amongst Women*. The motif McGahern constructs around the character – he is obsessed with eating and has a habit of 'stealing' food from the plates of his dining companions – seems to come out of a Freudian fairy tale and makes him both ogre-like and infantile. He has preyed upon Isobel her whole life, distorting and perverting her love for him, giving and stealing back, charming her with his good looks and keeping her in thrall by his 'magic', deceit and deception; now that he has 'lost' her to Patrick, he is both pleading and petulant, accusing Patrick of stealing her by trickery and lies, as if she were his 'treasure'. Patrick admits being 'obsessed' with Evatt and 'for a while I'd be seeing him everywhere' (*L* 1974: 162). The confrontation in the dining car has an aura of romance and fantasy as Evatt seems to blow up and then deflate during the exchange (*L* 1974: 164). Like an evil sorcerer Evatt tries to overpower Patrick, 'fixing me all the time with those great eyes' (*L* 1974: 162), but now that they are safely married, Evatt's power is spent. Significantly, Patrick describes this father-adversary in the struggle to possess his new beloved as, in essence, the past; but we should by now recognize that, psycho-symbolically, Evatt's sinister power has a much longer provenance in McGahern's *poiēsis*.[39]

39   Isobel's account of her father's life as a married 'gigolo' (*L* 1974: 111) is more detailed in the first version of the novel. He is a much more obnoxious, even sinister, character in the first edition. When she tells Patrick about her father's anger after she had spent the night with him, she says 'he's been trying to pimp me off on for years ...' (*L* 1974: 123, 127); McGahern's revision tones this down considerably (*L* 1984: 112). McGahern also shortens the scene in which the father takes Patrick to dinner and deletes altogether the important scene where they meet on the train. In the 1974 version Isobel is much more forthcoming about her relationship with her father and its incestuous propensities (*L* 1974: 128) and how she acted these out in a relationship with a married man her father's age (*L* 1974: 118). Originally, Isobel's mother left her husband and daughter and never saw them again (*L* 1974: 126); McGahern's revisions make her a more sympathetic character with whom Isobel remains close to throughout her childhood and adolescence (*L* 1984: 114). In the revised version Isobel's medical-student husband, Jason, is devastated following her abortion and by her decision to divorce him (*L* 1984: 116), but it is Jason who goes to her father

When he first thought he recognized him on the train Patrick says he was 'Paralysed between my will to see and a natural flinching from unpleasantness' (*L* 1974: 162), an ambivalence found in all McGahern's protagonists. The sexually abusive father-figure evokes fear and horror and Patrick's 'defeat' of him by using a combination of 'aggression and irony' (*L* 1974: 163) gives the scene a resonance and circle of symbolic reference that extend beyond its immediate and literal scope. Symbolically, Patrick's confrontation with Evatt functions as the confrontation with and escape from his own father which is missing from Part I, but which, in a sense, McGahern had already described in the young Mahoney's story in *The Dark* and would repeat again later in his memoir. Evatt is another father who would keep Patrick from his beloved, as his own father had done by forcing him to abandon his first beloved in the upstairs room and again by forbidding him from attending her funeral. Like the other father-figures in McGahern's fiction, Reegan, Mahoney, and Moran in *Amongst Women*, and like McGahern's own father, as he describes him in his memoir, Evatt is hollow, a black hole of narcissism and parasitical greed. And just as the young Mahoney, Luke Moran, and the McGahern of *Memoir* come to see through these vicious parodies of masculinity, Evatt's son-in-law ultimately sees through him (*L* 1974: 164–5).

---

for help arranging the abortion and her father 'stage-manages' it in both versions, sleeping in the hospital with his daughter (*L* 1974: 129–30; *L* 1984: 116). Isobel tells Patrick that although the pregnancy was unintended, once pregnant, she 'wanted' the child (*L* 1984: 116); whereas in the first edition she is simply 'interested' in having it (*L* 1974: 129). Originally 'disturbed and depressed' by what he hears (*L* 1974: 130), in the revised version Patrick expresses no opinion, listening to Isobel's account of her father, husband, and the Brazilian novelist she takes up with after her divorce (whose name, Roberto Leonelli, is dropped from the revision), her time in analysis in New York, and her sex life after her break-up with Roberto, following a second abortion (*L* 1984: 117, which is not in the original). Patrick listens to Isobel's story with mounting arousal (*L* 1984: 118). In the first version he proposes and Isobel accepts immediately (*L* 1974: 137); in the revised version the proposal is less direct, as is her reply (see *L* 1984: 119).

In place of this long episode the revised edition describes Patrick alone
on the train and thinking confidently about his situation and future; the
result is that the revised text makes 'conclusive' what is still very much 'in
process' in the first edition:

> My mind was as full of shapes as the racing wheels of the train beneath my feet and
> they all kept returning to the one shape. ... Eventually the beating apart of those rusted
> sections of the iron beds would claim its certain place. I did not find it depressing.
> The very contrary. The acceptance of that end gave the strength to make that summer
> last a whole life long whether it ran to three days or forty years. (*L* 1984: 143)

The abstract image of 'the one shape' extends the motif established in
Part I, where it refers to the effect the image of the dying beloved and his
memory of their forced sundering had in shaping his life up to this last
day at the school (*L*, 71, 82); it also expands it to admit the image of the
relationship to the new beloved, an expansion which Patrick foresees as
displacing the old image and relegating it to a place in his mind subordinate
to that occupied by the new love in his life. 'The acceptance of that end'
clearly announces an evolution in, if not even the end of, the son's grieving,
and the belief that his relationship with Isobel will lead to his life being
'reformed' (to use the word McGahern uses to describe the revision process
in his 'Preface'). The relationship between 'reforming' and 'reshaping' in
the revisionary process is evident here when we realize that the thematic
image-motif of 'the beating apart of those rusted sections of the iron beds'
in this new passage is actually a relocation of 'the hammering apart of the
sections of the iron beds in the upstairs room' from the excised paragraphs
describing Patrick's post-mortem on his failed romantic relationships (*L*
1974: 104–5), in which the image functions to connect Patrick's three
beloveds in a continuity of loss. In the revised version of Part II, however,
the image is reformed and reshaped to support the sense of Patrick's grief
finally coming to an end.

The critical question, of course, is whether or not we find this newfound 'acceptance' and guarded optimism in a 'reformed' and 'revised'
Patrick convincing. In this respect, the image of 'the one shape' should also
be interpreted as cognate with 'the single image, the image on which our
whole life took its most complete expression once ... the lost image' that

McGahern described as the *telos* of his artistic quest.[40] The intertextual connection between them reminds us of how specific extra-textual forces can impinge on the pre-existing text in the revision process. All that revision entails – excision, alteration and re-ordering of existing text, and the insertion of new writing – reflects the need to 're-form' the text to satisfy an altered authorial perspective and intention and should remind us of the *disciplinary* dimension of revision, the 'reform' in re-shaping. Thus the revised version of this moment in the text is in both senses a 'reformation' of this point in Patrick's life and as such possesses a metafictive dimension. Patrick is narrator and character; McGahern, the author, changed his mind about the original version of the narration of the love story in Part II. What seems clear is that he was not satisfied with its relation to the 'love story' in Part I.

The language McGahern uses in the 'Preface' to explain his *original* intentions is drawn from the paragraph McGahern inserted into the *revised* version of Part II in place of the scene between Patrick and his father-in-law on the train: 'The whole dear world of the beloved comes to us with the banality of news reports, while our own banalities come to us with the interest of poetry. It did not seem right. The contrary should be true, but it would be as impossible to reverse as to get trees to lean towards the sea' (*L* 1984: 143). The echo of the earlier passages describing the inescapable impact of his mother's death upon his character (*L*, 71, 82) links Patrick's sense of the force of circumstances being as impossible to withstand as the forces of nature with his Paterian belief in the self as the 'solitary prisoner'[41] of a consciousness ontologically incapable of penetrating the absolute

---

40 McGahern, 'The Image' (1968), 10.
41 'Experience, already reduced to a swarm of impressions, is ringed round for each one of us by that thick wall of personality through which no real voice has ever pierced on its way to us, or from us to that which we can only conjecture to be without. Every one of those impressions is the impression of the individual in his isolation, each mind keeping as a solitary prisoner its own dream of a world' (Walter Pater, 'Conclusion', in Adams, *Critical Theory Since Plato*, revised edition (New York: Harcourt Brace Jovanovich, 1992), 642. McGahern emphasizes this sense of inescapable solipsism when Patrick recalls how, when Isobel told him about her childhood, he 'had to

otherness of the other: 'She was breaking free with me while I was joined to that small mute woman coming out of hospital. I could suspect but not know. I could ask her but there would be no point, not even if she knew' (*L* 1984: 143). What is made clearer, indeed, explicit in the revised version is the psycho-symmetry of Isobel and her father, and Patrick and his mother, 'that small mute woman' he is still 'joined to'; but hidden within this, as well, is the sexual abuse of the young Mahoney/McGahern by his father. What Patrick *intends* as 'the one shape' about to unify (in) his life is the merging of the dead and living beloveds; in effect, the experience at long last of the return of his love for and from a beloved in a way that completes the broken circuit of his childhood. The dead beloved is and is not the 'irreplaceable being' (*L* 1974: 104), 'irreplaceable world', (*L* 1984: 99) he thought and felt her to be. Isobel cannot replace her but will. This is why he can say that he is finally laying to rest his memory of the failed leave-taking. And yet, he seems still 'joined to that small mute woman coming out of hospital', and, it seems appropriate to add, to the memory of the father who crawled into *his* bed, if we see McGahern continuing his own story in Patrick's, just as Patrick's seems to continue by 'framing' – as prequel and sequel – young Mahoney's in *The Dark*. The repetition of language between the novel and the 'Preface' also connects Patrick's voice and McGahern's and destabilizes the *para*textual quality of the 'Preface', almost closing the distance between author and narrator. But this ironic act of self-plagiarism is itself a metafictive symbol of the dialectic of occlusion and revelation that energizes *The Leavetaking*.

In retrospect, McGahern says in the 'Preface', he came to see the 'crudity' of his original plan for the novel when he saw, ironically, that he had been *too* successful; he had buried the 'other' too deeply in the 'reportage' of Part II because he was 'too close to the "Idea"' (*L* 1984: [5]). But what *is* the 'Idea' that, looking back, he felt he had been too close to? If McGahern's art of memory enables the return of the repressed, revision most certainly involves the return of a disciplinary consciousness upon the already expressed. Is it, perhaps, because the novel *does* 'conform to an

translate' the images 'into my own' before they were 'clear' (*L* 1984: 143; compare *L* 1974: 121).

idea or a way of seeing' that McGahern felt so compelled to revise it?[42] Perhaps the problem was that the novel was an expression of a *need* as well as an 'Idea', as much unconscious as conscious, expressed in the allusion to the 'irredeemable' condition of the beloved. Then the flaw in the original version of Part II would have been in the execution, as McGahern suggests, but not in the way he describes. The intense, impressionistic world of the 'I' is successfully communicated in Part I, which McGahern lets stand in its original version. The world of the beloved other in Part II would better have been narrated in a third-person voice if McGahern really wanted to communicate its 'irredeemable imprisonment ... in reportage'; but by continuing in the confessional mode of Patrick's first-person narration, McGahern hobbled any conscious intention to achieve 'that inner formality or calm' (*L* 1984: [5]) by facilitating the continued access of his story-telling to its unconscious imperatives, the 'personal therapy' and 'self-expression' he rather obsessively objects to but which his writing so obviously enacts. The real problem is that the 'beloved other' of Part II is really the 'other beloved', haunted quite clearly, in Patrick's narration, by her original in Part I. It is the *composite* nature of the beloved in the novel and the continuity of feeling in the relationships that McGahern's revisions seem most intended to reform and reshape. The irony is that there is really very little 'circuitous artifice' in McGahern's writing and what there is, paradoxically, is still a form of 'straight speaking'.[43]

Walking the Path of the Dead

The 'Idea' behind *The Leavetaking* would seem to be an attempt to atone for a sense of wrong done, to admit guilt and receive forgiveness; on a deeper level, it is the need to recover the 'lost beloved', to shape grief into a symbol of the 'lost image' that the 'circuitous artifice' of the sacrament of

---

42 Whyte, *History, Myth, and Ritual*, 235.
43 Ibid.

art will transform, like the bread and wine of the Mass, into the real presence of the beloved; and finally, it is the 'Idea' that 'the circuitous artifice' of love can recover the 'lost beloved' in a new love that cherishes the bride's individuality, paradoxically, as a light made brighter by the shadow it casts out. The future of the lovers at the end of both versions of *The Leavetaking* is vague, but in the first version it is more palpably threatened both by the shadow of the dead beloved and by the predatory patriarch, Isobel's father. As he leaves the school for the last time, Patrick thinks how what he is doing parallels what Isobel has done in leaving Evatt: 'We'll build our changing lives together outside the father and the world I now leave' (*L* 1974: 180). His leave-taking from the school is thus bound up not only with Patrick's farewell to the shadow of his mother, the school-teacher and beloved whose shade he had followed into the profession, but, because of Isobel's father's character and his history with her, it is also bound up with Patrick's – and McGahern's – escape from the lingering force-field of his father's influence, an influence that is *repressed* in the novel, only to be *projected* onto Isobel's father. By removing the meeting on the train, however, the revised version severely 'disciplines' the dark energy in the novel that so invigorates the character of Isobel's father and the revised Evatt is a desiccated remnant of his original. Patrick's phrase 'outside the father and the world I now leave' splits this double-barrelled liberation between Isobel and himself, just as in the novel, McGahern distributes his own need between them – to be free of the father *and* of the mother. Is the missing story of Patrick and his father repressed by Patrick or by McGahern? In terms of the narrative invention-construction, was McGahern's 'making' of Isobel a victim of sexual abuse by her father an act of unconscious projection or part of the conscious *reshaping* of his own life into a fictive order? Isobel's journey from sexual abuse and confusion to salvation by the 'talking cure' of analysis parallels McGahern's journey as a writer, despite his belief that 'personal therapy has no place in art'.[44] So is Isobel Patrick's anima-figure or McGahern's?

44   Ibid.

McGahern's revisions also re-focus Patrick's thoughts of his mother. He remembers his broken promise of the priesthood and connects it, implicitly, with his deliberate provocation of his dismissal, and rationalizes this double act of breaking faith with her in language that recalls both Elizabeth Reegan's joy in the quotidian and the young Mahoney's refusal to give up 'the dream of woman' for the 'death in life' of the priesthood (see *L* 1984: 156). Ultimately, both parents haunt Patrick, and it is surely significant that it is another 'father-figure' who plays the role of gate-keeper to Patrick's future. Father Curry does not have the power to grant him a dispensation from the Church's rules – he is merely an errand boy for the archbishop; but McGahern subtly shapes the priest into a potent symbol of the life Patrick has rejected: 'this is what she had dreamed for me – and I shiver' (*L* 1974: 191; *L* 1984: 167]. Even in Father Curry's parlour, his mother's shadow is present and bears witness to his expulsion.

And so it only makes sense that when he leaves with the letter of dismissal in his pocket, having taken his leave of the school, the profession, and his Church, Patrick should be overwhelmed yet again by the traumatic memory of the first leave-taking. The passage subtly connects Father Curry with the priest in his mother's deathroom, as well as with the priest who lectured Patrick at the Training College (*L* 1974: 192–3: *L* 1984: 168) – and, it might be added, with Father Gerald in *The Dark*. The passage completes McGahern's theme and motif of the narrow circle of the priest's 'dubious power' (*L* 1984: 156) in sacred ritual being replaced by an open and secular sacramentality. Patrick imagines Isobel setting the table in their room in Howth for a communion meal of bread and wine. Love is the new faith, predicated on his absolute belief in the mystery of the beloved's otherness. Yet – and this is crucial – the epiphany collapses in upon itself as once again memory intrudes to turn his mind toward his mother (*L* 1974: 193; *L* 1984: 168–9). Clearly, the only real continuum in his life is the love and memory of the first beloved that inform his relationship with Isobel just as they informed his relationship with the black-haired country girl he met at Training College. It has been as well, sadly, a continuum of guilt and grief, and it is these which infect his love for Isobel with the fear of loss and make his future with her uncertain.

What McGahern attempted in the first version of *The Leavetaking* was a first version of his 'supreme fiction', the recovery of the 'lost beloved' in a newfound love, or what he describes in the 'Preface' as the attempt to write a two-part, bi-modal narrative 'to see if these disparates could in any way be made true to one another' (*L* 1984: [5]). That 'these disparates' are the two beloveds is evident from the echo in Patrick's language at the end: 'We will be true to another and to our separate selves'. For McGahern, the 'beloved' is an unknowable other who becomes known and beloved through the self's projection of desire upon her or him. Both versions of Part II show that process to be mutual for Patrick and Isobel, with more detail for Patrick, of course, because the first-person narration cannot transcend its subjectivity. The difference is that the original Part II makes clear that the 'disparates' McGahern sought to make 'true to one another', the separate lives and different backgrounds of Patrick and Isobel, were shadowed by the divorce between the still grieving child and his first beloved, his mother, as well as by Isobel's continuing 'possession' by her father. Symbolically, Patrick's return to Ireland with Isobel, which he explains as necessary in order for him to make the clean break with his past that her presence will force, signifies quite the opposite of this. By returning with a new beloved he brings life back to the dead land and ensures a future there, but ironically, not with her.[45] Isobel's is the blood he brings to quench the shade of his mother, who still haunts Howth Hill where Patrick takes his bride on a honeymoon that is a barely veiled pilgrimage-*hommage*: 'The next morning, Sunday, we walked in the path of the dead across the hill of Howth, and if the only true festivals are festivals of the spirit it was the end of the honeymoon of our love before our life in Ireland began' (*L* 1974: 167).[46] The changed order of the revised version – 'it was the end of the honeymoon of our love before our life in Ireland began, as we walked that morning on

45   The story of Part II of *The Leavetaking* draws on McGahern's life up to the scandal over *The Dark*, his marriage to the Annikki Laaksi, and his firing.

46   'Walking in the path of the dead' is literally and symbolically central to McGahern's *Memoir*. Not only does he describe his literal return to the paths he and his mother walked when he was a child, but the whole narrative is a retracing of her presence in his life.

the same path my dead parents took on their honeymoon across the hill of Howth' (*L* 1984: 144) – does not temper the ambiguity in the passage.[47] We know what the end of the honeymoon of Patrick's parents' love led to, and we also know that Patrick and Isobel's 'life in Ireland' was always precarious at best, not just because Patrick knew that as soon as he married her he would be finished as a teacher there, but also because there is a precarious quality to their love from the beginning because of her father's constant interference in their relationship.

When Isobel joins Patrick in Dublin, they have difficulty finding accommodation in Howth, where they want to live. As they talk on the pier wall, he thinks it may be because the rooms fail to meet her middle-class American standards and he becomes testy. In a perfectly crafted bit of understatement, McGahern has them notice two boys rowing clumsily in the harbour, often missing their stroke and splashing themselves (*L* 1974: 168; *L* 1984: 145). He develops the image in the closing lines of the novel, after alluding to the ending of Arnold's 'Dover Beach', to describe husband and wife setting out for their future together. Theirs is a small boat, however, and the Irish Sea can be very hard on small boats. Isobel, in fact, seems less than fully committed to whatever the horizon conceals and the reader has to wonder if she will ever be able to take charge of her father's deep presence in her psyche. In a passage deleted from the revised version, when Patrick tells her of his confrontation with Evatt on the train, her response is telling: 'I'm so glad you said I loved him, because it was true' (*L* 1974: 167). In the tense moments out on the pier, Isobel expresses her insecurity by asking Patrick if he regrets bringing her to Ireland. The question upsets him. When she tells him she'd rather let him go than for him to stay with her out of a sense of duty, Patrick suddenly finds himself speaking 'out of the shadow of losing her' (*L* 1974: 168–9). Interestingly, McGahern drops this last phrase from the revised version of their exchange, as if by removing the language of shadow and loss he can erase the shadow-presence of the 'lost beloved' at that moment in Patrick's feelings; but it is clear that Patrick's relationship with Isobel will always be shaped by

---

47 In 'Korea', the farmer-father recalls his honeymoon in Howth (see *CE*, 46).

that template of love, grief, and the fear of loss that grief inspires, a fear
McGahern has Patrick articulate in a passage he does keep in the revised
edition: 'For a moment we were as separate from one another as we were
from the sea chopping against the blocks of granite below us, as separate
from one another as we would be in our future deaths. Out of the pain of
that knowledge a fierce yearning for her came that was almost grief' (*L*
1974: 169; *L* 1984: 146). The only difference in the revised version is that
McGahern intensifies the sense of *present* feeling in Patrick's recollection
by changing 'the pain of that knowledge' to 'the pain of *this* knowledge'
(*L* 1984: 146; my italics). But the confusion of love and grief is central to
all McGahern's writing and McGahern's version of Arnold's 'eternal note
of sadness' is the undertow of grief that haunts all love in his fiction. The
feeling of yearning is akin to grief because for Patrick his first experience
of yearning *was* the feeling of grief. Like the earlier image of the boat, this
passage too is building towards the allusion to 'Dover Beach' that closes
McGahern's novel (*L* 1974: 195; *L* 1984: 170–1). McGahern's newlywed
is already thinking of widowhood, his earlier gloom about 'our future
deaths' narrowing to a more specific anxiety about 'the first death'. Loss is
inescapable. Patrick, like Arnold, and like his creator, cannot forget 'The
something that infects the world'.[48]

The final episodes at the school and with Father Curry are something
of an anti-climax and distract from the haunted nuptial ceremony and last
supper that occur in Mrs Logan's rented rooms back in Howth.[49] Ulti-

---

48   Matthew Arnold, 'Resignation', *Poetical Works*, ed. C. B. Tinker and H. F. Lowry
      (London: Oxford University Press, 1969), 52. Arnold's 'Isolation. To Marguerite'
      and 'To Marguerite – Continued' are also apposite here.

49   Sampson sees a more traditional plot resolution and positive character growth in
      Patrick's 'willed neutrality' toward his dismissal and the 'authoritarian society' rep-
      resented by Father Curry (*Outstaring Nature's Eye*, 117), but Patrick's refusal to fight
      back and instead, Christ-like, submit to the bureaucratic process of his expulsion, is
      at best a rationalization of a deeper malaise. He refuses to pit his will against those
      with power, seeing a deeper futility in his situation and circumstances that would
      not be cancelled by any victory. The redemption he seems to think he is moving
      towards actually requires the hopelessness of his conversation with Father Curry
      because Patrick's redemption cannot occur in Ireland, which is the past, but only in

mately, McGahern does not achieve the artistic expression of what was perhaps an unconscious, Dantescan 'Idea' behind the original version of *The Leavetaking*, the joining of what is and always will be sundered, the living and the dead, until he writes his way to a visionary reunion with the 'lost beloved' in *Memoir*; instead, Parts I and II achieve the idea, formally at least, of the separation of past and future, the segregation of grief and hope. Like the pebbled shore of Arnold's poem, the long day that occupies Patrick's narrative present is a liminal zone of sharp recollections and vague presentiments. That the 'argument' within the idea behind the two-part structure of the novel is not convincing emotionally is perhaps due to the overwhelming weight of the past upon the narrator's consciousness, which makes the present so fragile a fulcrum and the future with Isobel seem little more than a feverish dream, weightless, implausible, doomed. What's noticeable about the end of the novel is how ghostly a presence Isobel is, for all her sensual and sexual traces. She is the sound of clothing being discarded, the glimmer of flesh in the darkness, the odour of sex, 'redolent of slime and fish', a server more than a celebrant in Patrick's laconic communion; ironically, she is a much stronger presence in her own right in the novel *before* she marries Patrick. In the conclusion, she is little more than the narrative instrument for his dismissal and has morphed from agent to catalyst, becoming in the process as vague as Patrick's future.

The voice of the closing paragraphs – which McGahern allowed to stand from the first edition – with all its Arnoldian resignation is nevertheless that of an exhausted spirit, perhaps reflecting that this is a book that emerged from McGahern's first experience of protracted writer's block.[50] Ultimately, what the revisions to Part II reveal is that both versions of *The*

---

the 'next world', England, or wherever. The repeated image of him holding – that is, stilling – the 'tongue' of the school bell (*L*, 10; *L* 1984:100) as he goes through the motions of supervision on the playground perfectly captures Patrick's cowed spirit and refusal to speak up for himself.

50   See Kennedy, 'Q. & A.', 9. Maher, however, finds it an 'unusually optimistic ending' ('The Irish Novel in Crisis? The Example of John McGahern', *Irish University Review* 35.1 (2005), 65, but appropriate for a novel 'that seems to offer some hope for the redeeming power of love' (*John McGahern*, 40); see also, Terence Killeen, 'Versions

Leavetaking construct a fictive world that is divided but ultimately brought together, a world of division made whole and a narrator-protagonist who is healed, a revised 'creation', literally and symbolically. This is the 're-shaping' and 're-forming' that matters most for the continuity of McGahern's narrative progress and which is perhaps most evident in his last novel, *That They May Face the Rising Sun*, which with its circular form and symbolic solar centre most exemplifies McGahern's desire to produce a work of 'life written to an order or vision'.

The Completed Circle and the Calmness of the Completed Self

If Part I of *The Leavetaking* is the story of the loss of the beloved, Part II is the story of her recovery; there is an Orphic, mythic dimension to the overall shape of the narrative that persists from the first to the second editions. Maher notes that Isobel is 'in some ways the image of [Patrick's] mother', but it should be clear that any 'beloved' in Patrick's life will be so.[51] Waiting in the headmaster's office before he demands a meeting with Father Curry, Patrick looks out the window toward the nearby girls' school and thinks, 'my love's dark head in that window once. I smiled ironically as I turned away. How many different forms had that love by now taken, by how many different names had I called to her, and yet I was calling still, the room in Howth now ...' (*L* 1974: 184). In the revision McGahern rephrases Patrick's feeling. 'I had to smile as I turned away' (*L* 1984: 160) is softer but does not diminish the impression that for all his love for Isobel, Patrick does not regard her as the one and only beloved because he knows that any beloved will only be a version of the lost original. The passage echoes that

---

of Exile: A Reading of *The Leavetaking*', *Canadian Journal of Irish Studies*, 17.1 (1991), 68.

51   Maher, *John McGahern*, 34.

in Part I where Patrick looks up from the playground to where the girl he met in Training College now teaches in a nearby girls' school and thinks of how Isobel is now the focus of his desire (*L*, 25). But as we have seen, the text in both editions of the novel links the former lover with the beloved mother – thus what is being worked out through the 'triangulation' of the three beloveds is the displacement-replacement of the mother – of death by life. It is a displacement that paradoxically completes her transformation into the inspiring muse – an apotheosis McGahern presents explicitly in the remarkable finale of *Memoir*.

At the end of *The Leavetaking*, however, Patrick's lover-wife remains very much a composite beloved. While the room by the harbour in which she waits for him and toward which he walks seems to have replaced 'that upstairs room' (*L* 1974: 85) where his mother died, McGahern's text signals the continuing presence of the dead beloved in Patrick's life. When he arrives, 'she hands me a white stone, oblong and round and completely smoothed, blue veins running through the stone, cold and soothing to the hands' (*L* 1974: 194). The echo of 'the girl with the emery stone in the hayfields on the side of those iron mountains' (*L* 1974: 86; *L* 1984: 86–7) is unmistakeable. And it should be noted that the echo is a convoluted repetition of fathers and daughters, of broken commandments and violated taboos. Is it significant that Patrick doesn't hear it, however? Patrick seems securely ensconced at last in his dream of woman. And yet, his turning for encouragement to the laconic Arnold of 'Dover Beach' – 'Ah, love, let us be true to one another!' – is occasioned by his gloomy acknowledgment that 'another day of our lives is almost ended' (*L* 1974: 194; *L* 1984: 170). Even when he describes the climax of their passion, McGahern has Patrick ambiguously describe how 'the lingering fire of our loving breaks into a last flame' (*L* 1974: 195). The future is a one way voyage toward 'the first death', the last phrase in both versions of the novel. There is as much eschatology as eros, it seems, in Patrick's thoughts, perhaps because 'the first death' he hopes to 'meet' is that of the 'lost beloved', his mother, a meeting that, as we will see, the Orphic McGahern ultimately *shapes* his career to achieve.

Patrick's return to Dublin is an ordeal he has to undergo if he is ever to become whoever he is. Three times Patrick explains his need to face the music, so to speak, at his school – twice to himself (*L* 1974: 161, 174), and then once to Isobel (*L* 1974: 182); gradually it becomes clear that his leave-taking from the school is related to his leave-taking from his mother. He has stayed and seen it through. This is not what he did nor what he was allowed when his mother was dying in the upstairs room and as a result, he could not keep from imagining what it might have been if he *had* seen it through. That lack of closure kept open the wounds of grief and guilt from the day of the failed leave-taking until this last day in the classroom. But now he *can* say: It happened this way and no other (*L* 1974: 174; *L* 1984: 151). When he meets with Father Curry to receive his formal letter of dismissal, he thinks: 'So this farce is another of the deaths' (*L* 1974: 190), which McGahern revises to 'another of the steps' (*L* 1984: 166). Ironically, his replacement for 'deaths' conceals the connection even as it makes explicit that a psychoanalytical 'process' *is* at work. Patrick had failed to make a 'proper' farewell to his mother, but now he leaves the school 'properly'. As he tells Isobel, 'once I've seen it through ... I can wash my hands then' (*L* 1974: 182; *L* 1984: 158).

Patrick's mock-excommunication from the Church-choked Irish school-system frees him to try his wings, Dedalus-like, in what Sampson describes as 'perhaps McGahern's most Joycean novel'.[52] And yet there is nothing of the fire of Stephen Dedalus' defiance in Patrick Moran, whose 'I won't resign' to Father Curry (*L* 1984: 166) is a pusillanimous *non serviam*.

---

52   Sampson, *Outstaring Nature's Eye*, 20. Sampson also conflates Patrick and McGahern by reading *The Leavetaking* as a portrait of the artist novel, 'a narrative of leavetaking from the shadow of the mother, but ... also a revelation of how intimacy with death, especially her death, prompts that illogical and obsessive desire to create a work of art by means of the recovery of lost time, of "memory becoming imagination"' (*Outstaring Nature's Eye*, 126). The first half of this point describes Patrick's effort in the narrative, the second, a credible hypothesis about McGahern's creative impulse. McGahern does not give Patrick any literary ambitions in the novel. One has to wonder if the blankness of Patrick's future at the end reflects the fact that what McGahern was re-shaping from his life at this point in his fiction was the period that he knew led into his writing block, namely the difficult times in his marriage to Laaksi and its eventual break-up. Maher notes in the conclusion 'a suspicion that memory and art may bring some harmony and healing to bear on existence' (*John McGahern*, 41).

For John Cronin, 'McGahern shares Stephen's ambition to mirror an inner world of individual emotions perfectly in a lucid, supple, periodic prose';[53] but McGahern's lucidity has the texture and complexity of stained glass, a complexity rooted in the supple braiding of life and art, the personal and the fictive. Cronin is right to compare McGahern to Joyce's fictional character because, as with Joyce, the mystery of his craft is in his crafting of fiction out of his life. McGahern presumably would agree that his work is indeed a version of Cronin's Dedalian mirror of the inner world of emotions; he did, after all, claim as his artistic ambition nothing less than 'that clear mirror that is called style, the reflection of personality in language, everything having been removed from it that is not itself',[54] a claim, ironically, that surely invites the reader to see McGahern himself reflected in his verbal creations.

Maher describes *The Leavetaking* as 'a brightening of the landscape' in McGahern's fiction. Cronin describes it, and the novel which follows it, *The Pornographer*, as 'troubled, turbulent, and restless'. Terence Killeen, in his essay on *The Leavetaking*, described McGahern as 'a writer of cycle, of process, of repetition', concluding that 'His medium is not that of change or difference but sameness'.[55] If so, it is the cycle of grief and guilt, the process of self-healing through the re-creative work of narrative *poiēsis*, and a repetition that is as much a compulsion as a desire to get it right, or to get it right by making it right, 'it' being the life lived, suffered, and endured. Finally, a medium is innately dynamic, fluid, changing, and McGahern's writing is the use of language against the inertia of grief, a

53   Cronin, 'John McGahern: A New Image?' in *Irish Writers and Their Creative Process*, ed. Jacqueline Genet and Wynne Hellegouarc'h (Gerrards Cross: Colin Smythe, 1996), 113.

54   McGahern, 'Reading and Writing', in *Irish Writers and Their Creative Process*, ed. Jacqueline Genet and Wynne Hellegouarc'h (Gerrards Cross: Colin Smythe, 1996), 109. Samson links McGahern's particular use of 'personality' in his aesthetic thinking to his familiarity with a passage in the letters of John B. Yeats; see Sampson, '"The Day Set Alight in the Mind": Notes on John McGahern's Late Style', *Irish University Review* 39.1 (2009), 128.

55   Maher, *John McGahern*, 31; Cronin, 'A New Image?' 115; Killeen, 'Versions of Exile', 76.

paradoxical subversion of the rhythms of memory that constantly draw the self backwards by subtly, slowly, gradually expanding the vortex of pain and trauma to breach the circle of confinement and enter or admit a larger world. Remembering his mother's death, Patrick thinks 'My mother had no choice in her withdrawal' (*L*, 31). In a sense the longevity of his guilt was a way of prolonging his grief and refusing to let go of the 'lost beloved'; his mother's involuntary withdrawal is met by the equally involuntary nature of the son's complicated mourning. But *The Leavetaking* is all about the possibility of working oneself out of that 'dead world' and what Patrick discovers in 'the long withdrawing tide of memory becoming imagination' (*L*, 45) is what McGahern himself found in the mysteries of story-making, a way of returning to the past that would lead him out of its thrall.

CHAPTER SIX

Breaking the Moulds – Part II:
The Pornographer (1979)

In *The Leavetaking*, the dying enthral and the dead captivate; in *The Pornographer*, the dying instruct and death liberates. Both novels end with an escape from Dublin: a new Adam and new Eve walk hand in hand toward a better future, with the image in *The Pornographer* slightly – but *only* slightly – more convincing. In 1979 McGahern said that the 'conscious risks' he took in *The Leavetaking* had freed him up to write *The Pornographer* and that 'What is done in *The Pornographer* is basically the same thing started in *The Leavetaking*.'[1] If the two novels comprise a single imaginative effort – the attempt to break out of the moulds that had shaped the making of his first two novels – then McGahern's construction of the eponymous narrator-protagonist of *The Pornographer* may represent some unfinished business with Patrick Moran, another unsatisfactory leave-taking. There is much that links the two stories, in particular, the juxtaposition of Dublin and London settings, rural pasts and urban presents, and romantic and professional failure. In both, a haunted, disappointed lover must defeat internal and external adversaries in order to win a future of unhindered possibility he believes is embodied in a new beloved. There are similar patterns of character and scene – e.g. Patrick Moran's mother and the pornographer's aunt; Isobel and Nurse Brady, the new beloveds; Isobel's relationship with her father and Josephine's with Jonathan; Patrick's 'confrontation' with Evatt on the train and the pornographer's with Kavanagh at the pub in London; the friends and 'advisors', Lightfoot and Maloney; the leave-taking scenes and the funerals. The pornographer trolls the same

---

1   Sampson, 'A Conversation', 15, 16.

Dublin dancehall world Patrick Moran habituated. His night with the woman he picks up at the Kingsway is similar to Patrick's first night with his 'calamity'; in fact, the pornographer seems to have rented the same furnished room, with the same lamp made from a Chianti bottle. Finally, the pornographer, like Patrick, has been rejected by the girl he proposed to and whom he considered his beloved, and his relationship with Josephine is a re-writing of Patrick's affair with the black-haired woman, but with the roles reversed.[2]

At the end of *The Leavetaking*, the newlyweds are about to journey eastwards, back to London and the 'old world', the world of the Father but also of Jimmy and the Plowmans. Although the pornographer and his soon-to-be-bride, the significantly trained Nurse Brady, journey westwards, they too are heading toward an equally old world, that of his dead parents, the neglected family farm, and his dead aunt, but it is a world that also contains the pornographer's vibrant and flourishing uncle, a man obsessed with land and ready cash and with a nose cocked to the winds of change. There is a wonderful symmetry in McGahern's shaping of the aunt's and uncle's presences in the novel. As Mary weakens and shrinks, her brother seems to expand and become more robust; when she dies, he blossoms, buying his own farm and leaving her house for his own. The Ireland of *The Leavetaking* has no attractive or redeeming qualities, no promise of self-fulfillment or hope for an authentic, unbridled, or uncompromised life of mind or body; it is the place of purgatorial suffering that releases Patrick to continue his quest for his Beatrice elsewhere. The Dublin and London of *The Pornographer* are likewise places of purgatorial cleansing where the questing anti-hero is brought to confess his wrong-doings and suffer real as well as symbolic punishment and purgation. But the Dantescan paradigm is less stable in this novel precisely because the narrator-protagonist *is* an anti-hero. The moral gravity that his flaws of character generate counter-

---

2   When the pornographer describes his previous relationship to Josephine, he could be describing Patrick's affair (see *P*, 80). For instances of the pornographer's memories of the 'lost beloved' that are just below the surface in his relationship with Josephine, see *P*, 64, 79, 97; as with Patrick Moran, it is the loss of the 'beloved' that leads the pornographer into his life of casual sex.

acts the narrative's centrifugal energy, and ultimately compromises the attempted upward spiral of the novel's comic-romance conclusion. *The Pornographer* wants desperately to be a novel of redemption.

'This painful becoming of ourselves': *Acedia* and McGahern's phenomenological narrator

The pornographer describes himself as 'dead of heart', looking blankly toward 'the nothing that was the rest of our life' (*P*, 13). He considers his ennui to be an inescapable response to the nature of things. This is silly, of course, and also dishonest. As we come to know more about him, the pornographer reveals himself to be that kind of 'victim' of relationships who is in love with their victimhood, who wears it like a hood and gown at an endless graduation ceremony, their days and nights one long procession through a world whose docility before their performance they expect as their entitlement. Things have happened *to* them. There is no question of personal responsibility. McGahern believed that the narrator-protagonist 'causes as much trouble to himself and to others as if he had set out deliberately to do evil'.[3]

The pornographer's 'emotional idleness' (*P*, 13) is a form of *acedia*. The term derives from the Greek $\alpha\kappa\eta\delta\acute{\eta}\varsigma$, literally meaning 'uncared for', or – what is particularly interesting in relation to McGahern's character – 'unburied'. A cardinal sin in the eyes of the medieval Christian Church, *acedia* was a form of sloth that derived from a spiritual collapse, a turning away from God and His creation, an abrogation of one's responsibilities

3 See Maher, *John McGahern*, 149. Sampson argues that 'In *The Pornographer* the alienated narrator is transformed through intimacy with his aunt's dying and commits himself to the recovery of love with Nurse Brady' (*Outstaring Nature's Eye*, 17). In my view, the pornographer's alienation is itself a *secondary* symptom of a deeper malaise and the septic narcissism that infects his character has barely begun to dissipate by the closing lines of the narrative.

in the created order, an all-consuming 'absence of caring'. In the pornographer's case, past, present and future are flattened out into a featureless
horizon that induces a Beckett-like tedium. McGahern told Maher that
'He falls into that disease, which is a very Irish malaise, that since all things
are meaningless it makes no difference what you do, and best of all is to
do nothing'.[4] Perhaps, like McGahern himself, the pornographer is quite
aware of the spiritual sin, but his condition is more psychological, a spreading numbness of affect, a growing incapacity to feel anything but sexual-
sensory stimulation, although even this is rendered increasingly abstract
by his running commentaries on it. Being with his aunt and uncle for the
day distracts the narrator, takes him out of himself, which he appreciates
(*P*, 19–20). What is noteworthy is that McGahern never has the pornographer confront the 'unburied' emotions causing his condition. The
novel does end with the burial of a corpse, however, and the significance
of McGahern's extended description of the aunt's placement in the coffin,
its removal from the house, her funeral, and the graveside ritual extends
beyond the scope of the immediate narrative and is more than mimetic.
Something else is being buried along with the aunt, another 'corpse' which
has been present all along but unacknowledged by the narrator, 'uncared
for' in the sense of *unattended to* rather than 'not cared about'. It is his
grief over his 'lost beloved', the wound he confesses to his uncle and that
festers, like Philoctetes', in the pornographer's psyche; his pornography is
merely its suppuration into his sense of self. And, of course, behind the
unacknowledged presence of the ghost in the narrator's room is the absence
that haunts all of McGahern's fiction, the loss of the *ur*-beloved that, in a
way, set him on the path to his life as a writer.[5]

---

4   Maher, *John McGahern*, 149. McGahern's language links the pornographer with
    the narrator of the short story, 'The Recruiting Officer', who is aware of 'something
    deep in my own nature, a total paralysis of the will, and a feeling that any one thing
    in this life is almost as worthwhile doing as any other' (*CE*, 69). The pornographer's
    paralysis generates self-rationalization in the forms of pseudo-sententious tautolo-
    gies about destiny (*P*, 32) and growing old (*P*, 33) that belong to McGahern's satire
    of the type and reflect the self-delusion and self-pity that the pornographer's *acedia*
    generates and which he must shed if he is to ever find a way to 'live in love' (*P*, 18).
5   The connection between McGahern's narrator-protagonists' grief over the death of
    the mother-beloved and the sense of loss they experience when rejected by a romantic

Another way of understanding this *acedia* and the particular quality of despair that it produces in the pornographer is to see it ironically, as a form of self-abandonment, a giving up on one's potential, the recoil from the 'painful becoming of ourselves' (*P*, 20). And at the core of this turning away or self-rejection is the psyche's confrontation with Time. *Becoming* is painful because it is dynamic, elastic, the *suffering* of change in one's world and oneself. The 'return' of consciousness upon itself is an apt description of McGahern's form of retrospective narration: the pornographer narrates his story in a phenomenological way, continually analyzing and commenting on his experiences, his reaction to his aunt's dying, his attraction to Josephine and then his repulsion, the sensations of sex, the instinctual nature of desire, the process of writing, the artificiality and hypocrisies of social convention, his own amorality, and so on.[6] McGahern's formative years, intellectually, coincided with the high-water mark in the popularity of Sartrean existentialism. We could say that he took a phenomenological approach as a story-teller from the beginning of his career, with each novel ironically showing 'how meaning comes to be' through the act of questioning it. In *The Leavetaking*, Patrick Moran's narrative seems to take him over the hidden horizon of his life, but the apparent clarity his 'return' upon himself gives to his understanding of his relationship with Isobel does not seem really to free him from his attachment to the past. Similarly, in *The Pornographer*, what the narration reveals is that even though the narrator is continually turning back to analyze his own consciousness, his return to the experience of his loss of the object of his desire does not lead to an understanding of the experience of loss itself as meaningful, as part of *his* lived experience. Quite the opposite, he understands it to have been the erasure not only of meaning but also of its possibility as well.

---

beloved, explicit in the case of Patrick Moran, implicit in the pornographer's, is made by McGahern himself when he describes the end of his relationship and divorce from Annikki Laaksi as 'like a death', and recalls that as he moved out of their apartment he thought of his leave-taking from his dying mother (see *M*, 255).

6   See Emmanuel Lévinas, 'Ethics of the Infinite', in *States of Mind: Dialogues with Contemporary Thinkers*, ed. Richard Kearney (New York: New York University Press, 1995), 180.

A premise of my reading of McGahern's fiction is that the nature of his grief, in all its stages and degrees, dominated his experience of being-in-the-world for the formative years of his life, and that his exploration of the history of that experience through the processes of making fiction, led to a series of novels that ultimately compose a cycle of mourning and celebration. Grief, as the after-shock of loss, is essentially an inversion of time, a crease in the fabric of consciousness that cannot be smoothed, but rather seems to deepen the more it is attended to: the days move forward but the mind lags behind, looking back, transfixed by the moment when the object of desire disappeared from the horizon of possibility, when presence became absence, the past an inescapable present, and the future a hopeless blank. The pornographer tells Josephine that when he lost his lover he lost the possibility 'to live in love' (*P*, 18). The loss of the beloved in McGahern's fiction is the loss of the world of affection that makes the experience of time benign and living meaningful. For Patrick Moran and for the pornographer it is also the loss of those 'eternal truths and essences'[7] that shaped experience into meaning and seemed to guarantee a future of significance.

In *The Leavetaking* and *The Pornographer* McGahern writes novels that begin at a fork in the path he started down in *The Barracks*; each begins, in a sense, where the young Mahoney's story ends, with him about to leave home for Dublin, but each imagines a different future from that point.[8] Following the repression of the story of the mother and the catastrophe of her death in *The Dark*, *The Leavetaking* turns back to face it directly and in doing so McGahern constructs a first-person narrator-protagonist who exorcizes his grief through the *poiēsis* of narration, in the process both confessing his guilt and re-inventing himself as a romance hero who successfully quests for and wins a new beloved. *The Pornographer* explores the other fork in the path. The pornographer's story picks up Patrick's at

---

7   Ibid., 182.

8   Eamon Maher notes 'There are enough similarities between [Mahoney] and [the pornographer] for one to surmise that they could be explorations of stages of development in the same character' ('The Irish Novel', 63).

the point at which he was living for casual sex just before he fell into the disastrous affair that ultimately drove him to London. Like Patrick, the pornographer has been rejected; however, the 'calamity' that befalls him as the result of his dance-hall predations is quite different. Patrick was rejected by yet another lover he wanted to marry. The pornographer's mistake is to get a woman pregnant for whom he feels absolutely nothing but physical attraction and who will not let him go without a fierce and demeaning struggle in which he comes to recognize just what a callous, selfish and self-deceiving person he is. Both novels, however, while they proceed down different forks, ultimately resume a single narrative course in their endings, which sees each narrator-protagonist on the verge of setting out with his new beloved for a horizon he had been too blinkered to see; Patrick, because of his obsessive grief over the loss of his beloved mother, and then of the women he had tried to draft into replacing her, and the pornographer by the *acedia* which erupted within him as a consequence of the same disappointments and which led him into the waste lands of pornography and serial sex.

Where *The Leavetaking* focuses on the continuing presence of absence in the life of the grieving son, *The Pornographer* explores the hollowness – emotional, moral, and spiritual – that follows the loss of meaning brought on by despair. In as much as McGahern's last novel is a wonderful example of a world rendered luminous, intelligible, and fully present in a palpable here-and-now, *The Pornographer*, like *The Barracks*, *The Dark*, and *The Leavetaking*, depicts a life lived in the shadows cast by an experience of absence more palpable than the most sensual of pleasures. For McGahern, the loss of the beloved *is* the loss of meaning; it is a world without the sun. It is why he titled one novel *The Dark* and another *That They May Face the Rising Sun*, the latter title triumphantly announcing the end of the darkness that had permeated all his previous works.

The pornographer's loss of faith in love and life lies behind his life of predatory sex. Explicit descriptions of sexual acts is another line of continuity between *The Pornographer* and *The Leavetaking*, but for the most part, the sex in the later novel is a symptom of an underlying psycho-pathology and thus symbolic. The pornographer's description of his first sexual encounter with Josephine reveals how his *acedia* – but more importantly, the *cause* of that condition – informs his outlook and behaviour. The passage is set up by his recollection of the desire 'to glory in the knowing' (*P*, 37) of the woman's body. Woman is first and foremost a body, a place to be entered and, ironically, 'known'; the 'glory in the knowing', however, is limited to the sensory. It is important to see how this apparent shift in rhetorical register toward a pseudo-Lawrentian sexual mystique is simply an excrescence of the morbid, predatory 'excitement' (*P*, 31) that the dancehall arouses in the narrator. Like the *faux* virtue of his 'honesty' back in his room, when he tells Josephine 'Love has nothing got to do with it' (*P*, 38), it is a mystification of his behaviour that is also symptomatic of his condition. When Josephine gives in to her own desperate desire, he recalls feeling sad rather than victorious. A hollowness haunts his feeling of 'glory' even as he celebrates it.[9] His words of seduction 'hang like an advertisement' in the room, clichés of concern that barely conceal his self-interest; his last words before he has sex with her are 'I won't hurt you', and his first words afterwards are 'I'm sorry I hurt you' (*P*, 39). The human history adumbrated in the scene is out of all proportion to its irony; he has only just begun to hurt her, and, of course, she him. The repetition of 'rest' betrays the pornographer's paradoxical desire to escape time by engaging in the one act that makes us most aware of the body's calibration of its participation in time, coitus. The contrast between his mindless immersion in 'the glory and the awe' of the sex act and his sense afterward that 'we were more apart than before we had come together' (*P*, 39) perfectly captures the cloven nature of his pleasure. Ironically, what he comes to know more palpably than her body is 'the burden of responsibility' that suddenly attaches to such intimacy, and the feeling that there was 'no way to turn to shift it or apportion it or to get rid of it' (*P*, 39). By the end of the novel, of course, he manages to do all three.

9   The sadness of this moment, when both characters 'fall', in a sense, into the trap set by their own emptiness, is recalled, significantly, just before the pornographer meets Nurse Brady at the Metropole (see *P*, 169). The later echo alerts the reader to the pornographer's repetitive-compulsive sexual behaviour and leads us to pay particularly close attention to the stages in his affair with the nurse.

It is important to see the emotional and moral dexterity with which the pornographer achieves that final realignment as a feature of his character that is, in fact, an aspect of the condition that has turned him into a pornographer. It is evident already in the scene of his and Josephine's first coupling when she tells him the story of her first sexual partner, a disappointing and anti-climactic experience with a married journalist. As he listens to her, he 'translates' what she describes into a pornographic tableau in his mind. That is, as she confesses to him the details of one of the most important experiences in her life, he 're-casts' it with his pornographic puppets, Mavis and the Colonel, in the roles of Josephine and the journalist. Her memory becomes his fantasy, which he uses to arouse himself, and then her, as he plays Colonel Grimshaw to her Mavis. The fantasy, however, is infected by the same morbid fascination with flesh that took him to the dancehall, and he describes their naked pursuit of sexual release as an escape from their 'graveclothes' (*P*, 42).[10] Here, suddenly, the pornographer tips his hand: the empowerment he seeks through purely sensual sexual pleasure is a power over death; the 'glory' he exults in is a self-glorification that offers the brief illusion of an escape from mortality.

McGahern presents the pornographer as someone who is not really having sex with a 'person'; this is important because we need to see him at the beginning of the novel as someone who is utterly indifferent to the other, just as later he is willing to limit the price he is prepared to pay to give the other justice. From the outset of their relationship, Josephine is abstracted, dehumanized, and dramatized; rendered absent as a person, transformed into a version of the fictive-fantastic Mavis, for a reason. When he responds to her increasingly importunate pleas for love by repeating that there is no love involved on his part, he is protesting that his pursuit of sex is not a search for love. But he protests too much, and his repetitive-compulsive trips to the dancehalls testify as much to his need for love as his preference for casual affairs confirms his fear of love. He gives matters away when he repeats the same language of denial when he refers to his

10   Note how this is a 'repetition' of Patrick's response when listening to Isobel's sexual history (*L* 1984: 118).

loss of the woman who had rejected him just before he met Josephine (*P*, 42). The pornographer is driven to sex by his condition, and his condition is a consequence of his loss of his beloved, or the death of love. This rationale is explicit when he attempts to break up with Josephine, gently but dishonestly, by suggesting a month's trial separation. He recognizes in her pain what he had gone through before: 'I too had stood mutilated by another gate ... but we endure ... Having ... lived our death, we turn to love another way, in the ordered calm of each thing counted and loved for its impending loss' (*P*, 97). This sense that love, as if by a law of nature, brings about 'loss', recalls the Patrick Moran of *The Leavetaking*.[11] In the pornographer's case, the belief rationalizes his turning to sex without commitment or hope for anything other than a short-lived affair.

The vocabulary of 'instinct' and 'energy' that the pornographer uses to justify his sexual activities as amoral vitalism is another expression of his fear of death; hence its appearance when he thinks about his dying aunt (see *P*, 44).[12] Yet 'energy' is an important value-term in the novel because it relates to the *acedia* which is the pornographer's underlying malaise. His paralysis, what he describes as 'my useless passivity' (*P*, 70), and his pathetic comfort in the delusion that things simply happen *to* him rather than because of his own choices, are symptomatic of the *acedia* that infects his spirit. Wounded, crippled, exhausted – the pornographer is living the life of 'drifting death from hole to hole' (*D*, 56) that the young Mahoney dreaded would be his future. At the very end of the novel, driving back to Dublin with Maloney after his aunt's funeral, the pornographer is able to look back on the fiasco with Josephine and this whole period of his life and describe his behaviour and condition; the language is remarkably similar to Lévinas'. He remembers Nurse Brady telling him that they could have met much sooner than they did if he had been 'paying attention'; 'By not

11   The reference to 'another gate' echoes the scene where Patrick watches the girl with black hair enter her mother's shadow (*L* 1974: 91).
12   The grossest instance of this self-deceit is when he thinks Jonathan will marry Josephine and legally annul all claims he might have on the child (*P*, 151). Later, while waiting for her to leave for London, he continues to use her body for sexual gratification, describing his actions as those of an impersonal instinct (*P*, 136).

attending ... I had been the cause of as much pain and confusion and evil
as if I had actively set out to do it. I had not attended properly. I had found
the energy to choose too painful. Broken in love, I had turned back, let the
light of imagination almost out' (*P*, 251). The irony, of course, is that the
pornographer couldn't figure out that his hunter-like acuity in picking
out willing sexual partners was actually his blind-spot. For Lévinas, 'meaning comes to be ... it emerges in our consciousness of the world' as the
cumulative effect of our acts of attention. But, as the pornographer says,
he was not paying attention because he was unable to. 'Broken in love', his
attention was taken up by his memory's compulsive roll-call of presence
and absence. The *acedia* that spread through his will like a cancer, the
torpor that dulled vision, were the result of something, an effect as well
as a cause. The inability to make distinctions, to draw lines in the moral
sand, leads to failure to make choices, to discriminate, to articulate and
act upon values. The loss of the beloved shattered the world of values, put
out the sun, and with it, 'the light of imagination'. When we meet him,
the pornographer is living without purpose in a world without meaning,
killing time waiting to die. The diminished light of his imagination is not
only evident in his writing pornography, it is evident from his predictably
banal response to his horror of the unlived life – mounting his priapic
charger and setting off in quest of ladies to undress. As a quester, he is an
alter ego of Patrick Moran, a reluctant Gawain who will have to be tricked
into his confrontation with his tough-love confessor, and who will still try
to run away from his penance.

If a failure of attention, not looking closely enough at the experience
of being-in-the-world, is both the symptom of his illness and the cause of
the pornographer's predicament with Josephine, an important part of the
cure is the re-focusing of self in relation to the other, a re-focusing that his
aunt, uncle, Maloney, and Nurse Brady help him achieve. In this respect,
his rationalization of his attraction to pornography as an attraction to
energy and instinctive life, while an aspect of his despair, is a parody of
the attention he needs to give to what is really on his mind – death: 'Now
I wanted to pause and turn and pause and stare and pause and idiotically
smile' (*P*, 44). The prose here captures the existential stutter, the irresolution, the reduction of wisdom to window-shopping, the *mis*-attention that

characterizes the pornographer's dissociated mentality.[13] But pausing and looking more closely – as he is forced to do when Nurse Brady takes him to his aunt's hospital ward toward the end of the novel – is precisely what he must do if he is to get out of the mess he is in.

At the beginning of the story, however, the idiotic smile expresses the pornographer's befuddled state. Afraid to contact the attractive and provocative nurse, he goes to his typewriter instead to concoct his pornographic fantasy of Mavis and the Colonel in Majorca. The pornographer's comments about the writing experience, however, make clear that McGahern is using the character and his narration in a self-reflexive manner. His writing session consumes most of his day, and for the pornographer, this is the greatest boon of the writing activity. But if writing is an escape from time, so is sex; thus there is a kind of 'logic' to the pornographer finding himself sufficiently aroused by his own pornography to return to the sexual buffet Josephine offers (*P*, 51). Again, she is nothing more than meat to accompany the crazy salad of his ennui, and so when she presses him to gratify her need for the romantic-sentimental conventions before intercourse, his feelings toward her begin to congeal into attraction-repulsion – a formation that hardens and becomes more intense as their relationship proceeds to its banal conclusion. As before, the sex is impersonal and strangely abstract, even though the language he uses to describe it is moistly zoological: he watches her undress as if he is looking at a film screen, and when he enters her, 'I went through like any fish feeling the triumph of breasting the hard slimy top of the weir ...' (*P*, 57). The pornographer is able to transcend the personality he is beginning to loathe even as he immerses himself in it. Again, his sexual impulse is more symptomatic than authentic. His desire to find somewhere 'out of time' is what impels him, and we should understand his 'old fear of being enmeshed' (*P*, 58) in a relationship as the fear of being made vulnerable to time by loving someone whom he could lose.

---

13   For a reading of the pornographer's character and situation that combines Sartean existentialism and Irish 'national allegory', see Giuliana Bendelli, 'John McGahern's *The Pornographer* or the Representation of Nothingness: an Attempt to Overcome Irish Parochialism', in Giuseppe Serpillo and Donatella Badin, eds, *The Classical World and the Mediterranean* (Cagliari: Università di Sassari, 1996), 188–93.

Sex, Pornography, and Secular Ceremony

In *The Pornographer*, as Denis Sampson astutely notes, 'The difficulties of behaving as a moral person ... are translated into the difficulties ... of writing a moral fiction'; for Sampson, 'The relationship between writing and moral character is, in fact, the subject of the novel'.[14] There is a metafictive dimension to McGahern's treatment of sexuality in *The Pornographer* that coheres around the literal and symbolic meaning of the novel's focalizing trope – pornography; and crucial to an understanding of this dimension is understanding the meaning of the difference between those passages represented as the pornographer's writing about Mavis and the Colonel and the pornographer-narrator's descriptions of his own sexual actions and experiences with Josephine and Nurse Brady. For Sampson, the moral challenge that the pornographer faces is that of the 'cynical and commercial world' represented by Josephine and his editor-friend, Maloney.[15] But there is a danger in linking these figures by awarding them the same negative valence, for they represent different kinds of danger or error. How should we interpret Josephine? Femme fatale-Venus flytrap? Sinister temptress-manipulator? Desperate, clinging vine? Or a sympathetic 'hapless victim', as Maher views her, with reasonable expectations and demands.[16] In the technical sense, Josephine should be understood as the antagonist in the novel; but the very real tension McGahern constructs between the obvi-

---

14   *Outstaring Nature's Eye*, 139, 141.

15   Ibid., 139.

16   *John McGahern*, 51. Josephine, and women like her in McGahern's short stories, represent what Tom Inglis describes as 'female transgressors' who challenge the 'stereotypical image of a *good* Irish woman' ('Origins and Legacies of Irish Prudery: Sexuality and Social Control in Modern Ireland', *Éire-Ireland* 40.3/4 (2005), 25, 24). Inglis refers to the woman in McGahern's short story, 'My Love, My Umbrella', and the nurse in 'Like All Other Men' (25). It is interesting that the latter character bears McGahern's mother's name, Susan, and tells her sexual partner that she intends to enter a convent after their brief liaison, which recalls Patrick Moran's description of his mother's attempt to break off her engagement with his father in order to enter the religious life.

ous defects, ambiguous motives, and positive attributes of her character, and the undeniable difficulty of her situation in the end, contribute to the novel's considerable moral ambiguity.

Nor is Maloney's character unequivocally negative. As a 'fallen poet', he seems to articulate McGahern's own aesthetic principles;[17] and as a disappointed romantic lover, he is an older version of the narrator-protagonist. He seems genuinely interested in the pornographer as a friend, not just as a lucrative source of copy for his paper. He attends the aunt's funeral and endures her husband, Cyril, for clearly unselfish reasons. Moreover, he embodies and articulates those rare qualities in McGahern's fiction – humour, wit, comic irony, and rarest of all, a spirit of fun; the sections with Maloney are the brightest, the most leavened, in an otherwise sour flatbread of a book. He speaks in a steady stream of irony – at times self-directed, other times aimed at his society, but mostly at the pornographer. However, when the latter tells him that he may have been lucky enough to have escaped 'the whole mess' with Josephine, Maloney's irony has an edge to it that leaves the pornographer cut and bleeding, if unaware of it (see *P*, 133). In his repeated pronouncements as score-keeper for the pornographer's moral 'game', Maloney is a kind of chorus-figure, ironic mentor and foil (see *P*, 164–5). Despite his pseudo-Wildean wit and persona, he actually passes judgment on his friend, welcoming him into the party of the damned.

Maloney is a representative 'type' in the novel, but in this he is as much a symptomatic construction as the pornographer, and what he represents is not clear until the end when the pornographer goes home to the country for his aunt's funeral. More Buck Mulligan than Mephistopheles, Maloney represents an Ireland coming round the economic corner in 1979. When he lectures the pornographer to keep his spirits up (*P*, 124), it is clear that McGahern is using the character for a satire that has much more to do

---

17   Maher notes this as well ('The Irish Novel', 66). Grennan suggests 'a kind of underlying debate shaping the plot' of the novel through 'the recurrent clash ... between the nihilist anger of Maloney, the spoiled poet, and the gradually opening-to-the-world acceptance of the narrator himself' ('"Only What Happens,"' 16).

with the 'new Ireland', or perhaps more narrowly, new Dublin, than with literal pornography. In an allegory of economic self-promotion as national self-abuse Maloney seems to represent the 'new man' rising with the tide of economic reform and the effects of globalization in 1970s Ireland. The pornographer, who depends upon him for his living, considers himself Maloney's better yet regards him as more than his employer, at times even as a father-confessor. At first, Maloney comes across as a figure of utter inauthenticity, of self-conscious, cynical manipulation of a public and world he considers beneath him, if not beneath contempt. But if Maloney is the hollow man *par excellence*, he is wonderfully self-contained, in control, and possesses a heroic amount of humour.

What Maloney represents is one thing, but what pornography represents in relation to the narrator-protagonist is something else altogether. As Sampson suggests, McGahern is trying to write a moral fiction in *The Pornographer*, paradoxically, by actually showing his narrator-protagonist writing conventionally 'immoral' fiction. So how should we unpack the paradox? Perhaps by ignoring the obvious and considering that the moral issues the novel engages have less to do with sex, or sex and writing, than with writing and truth. Remembering his time as an altar boy, the pornographer juxtaposes those ceremonies with his current practice but sees continuities, 'ceremonies remembered, … continued' (*P*, 21). McGahern has the narrator parallel the ceremonial preparations of the priest and altar boys before Mass and his own 'ritual' acts before sitting down to write (*P*, 20–1; see also *P*, 49). For all the ironic self-mockery, the parallel is meaningful. These secular 'ceremonies' continue the sacred ones of his altar-boy childhood. The typewriter rests on an altar-like marble table-top; it is his tabernacle and its keys the doors he must open to achieve the communion he so desperately yearns for with the world he has turned away from because he feels it has rejected him. The stack of untouched white pages sit like unsanctified hosts awaiting their transformation into words with the real presence of flesh. The irony, of course, is that in writing pornography the narrator does not write himself closer to the redemptive relationship with the world he so needs, but only further sequesters himself in a sexual phantasmagoria. In this, the trope of pornography that centres both the narrative and the characterization of the narrator-protagonist reveals its deep connection to the central themes that have coursed through McGahern's fiction from the beginning: the loss of the *ur*-beloved, the broken promise of the priesthood, the rationalization of the choice of the 'second best' profession of teacher-writer, and the 'ceremonial-redemptive' nature of art.

Sex is only a symptom in the novel and it would be a mistake to understand pornography in *The Pornographer* in the literal sense only. Its sexual meaning is not as important to an understanding of the character – or of the book as a whole – as its metaphorical significance; on this level, pornography is a kind of secular sacrilege, the writer's breaking of the most serious vow of his vocation – to write only the truth. The narrator's suggestion of the writer as secular priest is valid, but as he makes it he turns it into a missed opportunity to fathom the depths of his own degeneration; not his sexual 'degeneracy', but rather his fall from the grace of words. The theme of the 'fallen poet' developed explicitly through the characterization of Maloney is important here, and when the pornographer says of him, 'He, *too*, had ambitions of being a poet once' (*P*, 25, my emphasis), the narrator lets slip that he, too, is someone who has lost his vocation.[18] Pornography begins with a fantasy of flesh and becomes debased word. It reverses and parodies the transformation of word into truth which betokens art's profoundest parallels to the Johannine description of the incarnation and the sacramental mystery of Holy Communion. But even more impiously, in McGahern's view, considering how sacred memory is to his creative ethos, pornography is the violation of memory by a false imagination, an imagination which, instead of shaping recollection in a way that releases the truth immanent within memory, distorts it, shapes it to fit someone else's agenda, makes it unreal instead of real, and in the process, commodifies it.

Pornography, ultimately, is McGahern's paramount metafictive metaphor for what he understands to be 'bad writing', namely, the confusion of the fictive and the autobiographical. This becomes clear when we read the story-within-the-story of Mavis and the Colonel on the Shannon (*P*, 153–62). McGahern carefully sets up his effects so that we see that what the narrator is doing in the story is transforming his experiences with

---

18   This marks another point of connection between the pornographer and the narrator of 'The Recruiting Officer'.

Josephine into the all-too-predictable escapades of his sexual 'athletes' (*P*, 21). The excerpt from the story repeats much of the language and specific details of Josephine's and the pornographer's weekend (*P*, 82–90), in the same way, it must be said, that the account of the leave-taking in *Memoir* re-uses the language of the novel. Maloney catches on immediately and also intuits that the pornographer has revealed Josephine's pregnancy in the fiction (*P*, 163). The reader, however, notices more, and because of this experiences the comic effect of the pornographer's exaggeration of life into fantasy. The pornographer makes quite clear that even when he is writing pornography he is aware of its connection to his own experience and because of that, it moves him to reflection. As he comes to the point in Mavis and the Colonel's weekend where he and Josephine had sex, the pornographer recalls: 'I felt sick enough to want to turn away from what I saw, to shout at them to stop' (*P*, 162). The moment of writing he recalls here is an ironic inversion of the moment he 'saw' Josephine and the journalist in his mind's eye as she described her sexual initiation to him earlier in their relationship. Now, however, he was seeing himself.

What McGahern is doing here is using the pornographer, and pornography, ironically, to show how life is taken up, used and transformed in the writing process. When we recognize this, a problematic set of questions arises, however. If what the narrator is doing is to be rejected, not as pornography, but 'allegorically', as 'bad writing', in McGahern's terms (and also in Maloney's, who cannot abide the mixing of life and art, history and myth), what are we to make of McGahern's works that we now recognize fuse fiction and autobiographical fact in exactly the same way? And if Maloney is little more than the editor-as-pimp, what are we to make of his artistic pronouncements, which sound so much like McGahern's?[19] Even though McGahern uses Maloney's pronouncements and then the pornographer's own fitful questions about his practice to frame the first extended passage of pornography in the novel, this does not mean he isn't using the novel to pose questions he takes seriously. If anything, the technique seems to be a masking device McGahern uses to temper the seriously self-referential

---

19   See *P*, 21, 27, 129 for statements that sound very much like McGahern's pronouncements in 'The Image' (1968, 1991); see also González, 'John McGahern', 45.

dimension of the novel. When the pornographer wonders if his readers will be as aroused by his words as he was when writing them, we are right to see this as the effusion of a sensibility prone to self-exaggeration and self-pity, an efflorescence that, like the surfeit of affect that the descriptions of the sexual acts arouse, is itself the obverse of the *acedia* that paradoxically compels it; however, the question, 'are my words to be their worlds?' (*P*, 24) is a serious question that all serious writers must ask, and for McGahern, the mystery of the relation of word to flesh, mind to body, imagination to experience, but most of all, of writing to self-growth, is a central preoccupation of his art. The pornographer admits that what he writes 'inflames' him, sends him to pub and then dancehall to hunt his sexual quarry. But this is merely a parody of the kindling of the imagination that McGahern hopes his non-pornographic art might achieve.[20]

So what *is* McGahern doing with these characters and the meaning of pornography? Perhaps the answer is that for McGahern it is all a matter of how the writer shapes the fiction out of the autobiographical sources and what goal that process serves, the *why* of it all. What is truly 'pornographic' in McGahern's view is writing confessionally for profit. In as much as pornography traduces human sexuality, writing confessionally for profit turns the writer into a kind of pimp-and-prostitute in one, writing to satisfy a prurient curiosity as much as the literal pornographer, but 'hollowing out' himself in the process. 'Mavis and the Colonel Take a Tip on the Shannon' is a metafictive parable within the novel. McGahern is showing how he makes fiction from life by allowing the fictive imagination to take up the life, to hold it close, to catch life from it but then let it go. In the parable, life sparks the imagination to comical sexual fantasy; in McGahern's fiction, however, life sparks the imagination to the alchemy of 'vision' and 'idea'. Even the Colonel, however, speaks McGahern's and the pornographer's language of value in a comically encoded moment, when he instructs Mavis about 'well shaped' people (*P*, 153). As we have seen, McGahern's aesthetic gives priority to the 'well shaped' narrative, the ordering of 'vision' as coherent 'idea', the resurrection of life as art. The Odyssean narrator-protagonist of

---

20   The scene where the pornographer gives his story of Mavis and the Colonel in Majorca to Josephine echoes the 'my words … their worlds' theme (see *P*, 66).

The Pornographer has lost his way and failed in his attempt 'to live in love' (*P*, 18). His affair with the Calypso-like Josephine is a grotesque if banally conventional parody of that desire; his attempt to drown his broken heart and bruised soul in her sea of flesh actually draws him towards the perilous rocks of a wife and child he finds repugnant. He sees his life as a 'farce' (*P*, 66, 67), but actually it is realistic fiction. He needs instruction, Maloney tells him, and he's right. The instruction he needs and receives comes in the form of his aunt's and Nurse Brady's tutelage. Together they position the pornographer so that he is 'ready to start all over again' (*P*, 163), not in Maloney's sense of returning to the way of living that got him into the mess with Josephine, but rather in the sense that has been the hidden *telos* of McGahern's writing from the beginning and that he achieves with the redemptive vision and symbolic resurrection of his last two works.

Medusa and Child: Josephine

The pornographer's understanding of 'this painful becoming of ourselves' gradually comprises both the role of circumstance and the consequences of choice. In his condition at the beginning of the novel, he is prone to allowing the greater influence of the former to excuse him of his own responsibility for his life, seeing himself as a victim of the necessity of loss. His problematic and difficult growth can be measured in terms of his increasing self-assertion against the force of circumstances, and with that, the acknowledgment of his role in his own misfortune. He does not allow Josephine to dress up their situation as simply bad luck that they must now make the best of (*P*, 124). His self-judgment is a positive sign; so, too, is his intuition that by going to London with her, he would be giving up control of his life when greater self-control is precisely what he needs to exercise to escape the *acedia* of will and emotion that has led him to where he is. He needs to 'shape' his life for himself instead of allowing circumstances – or Josephine – to shape it for him.

The pornographer is on the wrong foot from the outset in his relationship with Josephine. On their second meeting, uncertain about inviting
her back to his room, when they do go back for sex he puts on a condom,
and admits to himself he is lying when he tells her he was thinking of her
(P, 56). The pornographer does tell her, before they do have unprotected
intercourse, that he will not marry her if she becomes pregnant; but if
this is McGahern's attempt to construct a moral defence for his protagonist, it is a weak foundation. It is clear he and Josephine speak different
languages and live in quite different moral and emotional universes. She
cannot fathom his justification of casual sex as instinct and he, presumably
because of the intensity of his 'need' (P, 56), ignores the obvious fact that
she is already deluding herself with the romantic-sentimental notion that
he will eventually fall in love with her; moreover, she seems incapable of
believing that he really means it when he says he could never come to love
her (P, 67), and knowingly has sex with him when she knows there is a
risk of pregnancy (P, 90).

How 'sinister' is Josephine? Does the blood on the sheets mean she
was lying when she told him she was not a virgin (P, 44)? Has she been
'hunting' for a husband as much as he has been on the prowl for a one-
night stand? She makes him remove the condom when they have sex the
second time because she feels protected sex is 'a kind of farce' (P, 56), and
at the beginning of their weekend on the Shannon she rebukes him when
he performs coitus interruptus (P, 86).[21] He is as afraid of getting her
pregnant as she is confident – or uncaring – that it won't happen. He is
clearly consciously negligent, but he also seems extremely slow to consider
that Josephine may not share his degree of concern about an unwanted
pregnancy because, if it happened, it would not be unwanted. Resolving

---

21   The pornographer's and Josephine's use of 'farce' becomes a motif in the novel, seeded,
      perhaps, by the narrator's cynical sense of acting a role 'in the play' (P, 39) of their
      first night together, and later thinking of their relationship as a 'doomed charade'
      (P, 70). When he uses the metaphor, it confirms our sense of the inauthentic behind
      his actions as well as conveying his feeling that 'the whole setup' (P, 66), reality, is
      a con; when Josephine uses the word, it expresses an apparently sincere reaction to
      the dissonance between his behaviour and attitudes and her sense of what is real.

to end the relationship after their weekend on the Shannon, and already having escaped the consequences of unprotected sex with her and promised never again to put himself at risk, he nevertheless does just that on the trip and this time the consummation of his bad faith does result in pregnancy. Even though, by the weekend's end, his recognition of her competence as a journalist makes her more attractive, he still intends to end their affair. But in his weakness he tells her only that he wants to separate for a month. Then, at their next meeting, she tells him she's pregnant.

Josephine's pregnancy is more than just a predictable crisis leading to the climax in the narrative. The way McGahern handles the pornographer's handling of it is crucial to the novel's illumination of the narrator-protagonist's character and the credibility of his later resolve 'to live in love' with Nurse Brady. McGahern's intention would seem to be to maintain what he has developed throughout the relationship in terms of the pornographer's heated sexual passion but emotional coolness, and Josephine's militant disregard of the latter along with his explicit disavowals of love for her in the hope that eventually he will come to share her desire for a life together, a hope she might feel warranted by the unequivocal evidence of the pleasure he takes from her body, and the fact that, despite his disavowals, he has continued to see her. The problem with this is that, while McGahern might want us to sympathize with his protagonist's sense of being entrapped by someone who, other than physically, increasingly evokes in him only 'fear and shame and dismay and revulsion' (*P*, 102), based on the pornographer's behaviour, as long as she is only naïve and *not* duplicitous, Josephine's point of view is not unreasonable.[22] Josephine's desire for the happiness she believes a conventional marriage will bring blinds her to the pornographer's growing revulsion. As she describes her vision of their wedding, the picture of the future she sketches brings out a 'cold sweat' in him (*P*, 99), but what is more interesting is that he cannot help translating his situation with her into a 'what if' scenario with his 'lost beloved'.

---

22   Peter White's wife's remarks during the dinner scene reflect this view (see *P*, 112).

The pornographer's fear of becoming enmeshed would seem to be an inverted reaction to his rejection by his former beloved, a rejection he has cunningly reconstructed as a justified rebuke of his attempt to destroy 'her singleness' (*P*, 100). Further, he uses his memories of that relationship and of his suffering at its end to justify his rejection of married life with Josephine as the right thing to do based on this value of uncompromised 'singleness'. The pornographer's description of the failure of the relationship as a kind of death, 'the loss of my own life in the other' (*P*, 104), repeats the sentiment and language of *The Leavetaking* (*L* 1974: 104–5), just as his image of the wedding as 'the funeral of her singleness' recalls Patrick's image of the bride Isobel/his mother walking down the aisle as 'the picture of death'. Patrick Moran thought, ironically, that he owed the beloved who rejected him a debt of gratitude because 'it had taken the sexual death to burn out the first death'; but the pornographer is a seriously flawed version of Patrick Moran – a selfish, rationalizing, ingenuous coward, who is running away from love as much as Moran was searching for it, and who resists facing up to what he is doing and why, and so has not yet reached Moran's point of progress where he can claim to have discovered 'my life late but at last' (*L* 1974: 108). The pornographer's *acedia* has chained him to a wheel of sexual attraction and recoil, of relationships without futures, of passion tipping into fear and shame. Marriage to the pregnant Josephine would seem to present an opportunity to escape this nightmare of paralysis and meaningless repetition. The child is an obvious symbol of hope for the future and release from the past. But McGahern has the pornographer reject this conventional interpretation of the choice she represents by seeing her as a succubus who would possess him body and soul and entrap him in a death-in-life, 'a lived loss' (*P*, 104).[23] In fact, his language suggests that by rejecting her, he is actually doing Josephine a favour by preventing her from achieving her monstrous potential!

23   The trap of marriage to Josephine as the *vagina dentata* occurs later when, after she tells him that Jonathan thinks he should stay in Ireland rather than accompany her to London, the pornographer thinks he may have escaped 'the bared teeth of the loose trap' (*P*, 130).

From the outset in McGahern's fiction there is a clear ethical preoccupation with justice between individuals and a concern for 'the other as
other'[24] in his treatment of love and desire, particularly in *The Leavetaking*
and *The Pornographer*. McGahern told Denis Sampson, shortly after he had
finished writing *The Pornographer*, that questions of Self and Other had
'obsessed me all my life',[25] and the conceptual vocabulary of self and other
recurs throughout his writing. McGahern probably would agree with the
philosopher Lévinas that we most encounter Time when we enter into a
relationship with another person.[26] The core narrative event in McGahern's
fiction – the loss of the beloved – is, in a sense, a crisis in the individual's
relation to Time. Instead of the ground of *becoming*, time becomes something to 'kill', after it has killed the beloved. The pornographer's *acedia* is a
kind of 'wasting disease', a wasting of time, a wasting away. As he is about
to take his chances on the dance-floor, he thinks: 'the shudder that makes
us flesh becomes the shudder that makes us meat' (*P*, 30). The pornographer's sexual antics are a kind of existential panic or hysteria induced by
the crisis of the loss of the beloved which has transformed the dance of
life into a dance of death. Sex becomes the attempt to reconnect to time
through the body of another, but, of course, in a kind of existential irony,
the body of the other can only ever be a reminder of her unknowable otherness, and when possessed, possessed only as a defeat of the self's desire
to possess. For all his sermonizing about sex as instinct, the pornographer
lives in the world of 'meat', and his repeated return to the abattoir-floor of
the Dublin dance-halls, like the degenerate ritual of preparing to write his
pornographic stories, is an obsessive-compulsive fantasy of the presence of
flesh compensating for the absence of the body he most desires but which
is forever lost to him, just as the pornography itself is a pathetic parody
of the redemptive word made sacrificial flesh.[27] It is significant that as he

24   Lévinas, 'Ethics of the Infinite', 186.
25   See 'A Conversation', 15–16.
26   Lévinas, 'Ethics of the Infinite', 187.
27   For the pornographer as sexual carnivore, see *P*, 31, 32, 34; see also his rhetorical ques-
      tion about the nature of his 'art' (*P*, 50). Goarzin suggests that '*The Pornographer*
      should be read as a novel that complements … 'The Image' from a theoretical point

is brought to the point where he must act decisively with Josephine, the pornographer is able to describe his pornography with remarkable clarity to his friend Peter White: 'It's heartless and it's mindless and it's a lie. I'm stuck with it and I'm sick of it, a cold anvil that has to be beaten' (*P*, 109). There is no better description of the condition of the *acedia* that made pornography attractive to him in the first place.

The pornographer has already made it clear what his feelings toward Josephine are: she is great in bed, but her attractions begin to recede as soon as she starts to talk. He doesn't love her, could never love her, and the idea of marriage to her is abhorrent. All his talk about self and other is self-serving clap-trap. One does not need a discourse on the concept of 'singleness' and the sanctity of alterity to justify rejecting Josephine's proposal of marriage. Marriage to her would be suffocating. The issue is really the fact of her pregnancy and any sense of moral responsibility he feels toward her. There is no way McGahern can avoid this 'black hole' in the novel's fictive world and the pornographer's character. Peter White, the doctor-acquaintance the pornographer contacts to carry out the pregnancy test, functions to add credibility to what is really just an embarrassing expense of spirit in a waste of shame on the pornographer's part – and perhaps, on McGahern's as well. White's opinion that his friend should not feel obligated to marry Josephine because she obviously wanted to get pregnant in order to trap a husband may be what the pornographer wants and needs to hear (*P*, 112–13), but it is as unconvincing as it is disturbing precisely because it overstates what we may have read into Josephine's character and exaggerates what McGahern does seem to want us to consider.[28] For all

---

of view, since it shows how literature is but the trace of a real which was lost' ("'A Crack in the Concrete'": Objects in the Works of John McGahern', *Irish University Review* 35.1 (2005), 36).

28   McGahern does have the pornographer admit that he was 'looking for allies' (*P*, 105), and uses the dinner scene between the pornographer, White, and his wife to present a balanced view of the conventional perspectives on the pornographer's situation. White is adamant that marriage would be a mistake, that Josephine probably unconsciously willed the pregnancy, and that she should go to London for an abortion; his wife's point of view emerges from the scene as most reasonable (see *P*, 112–14).

White's eminently rational analysis of the situation and commonsense view of their options, ultimately, if the pornographer is to emerge at the end of the novel as a protagonist worthy of our respect because of a credible change in his condition and outlook – and the structure of the novel as well as the conclusion make clear that that is McGahern's intention – he will have to move forward without such self-serving flummery. He will have to confront his actions and their consequences directly, for what they are, and face as well, his need to decide his future and act upon it.

McGahern attempts such a resolution through the series of decisions and actions that constitute the end of the paralyzing *acedia* that has characterized the pornographer throughout the story. From this point of view, Josephine *must* be rejected – and, in this specific regard only, her pregnancy is irrelevant because she embodies a future of paralyzed entrapment in bourgeois banality, convention, and soul-destroying superficiality. The pornographer may be morally wrong to abandon her, from some points of view, but he is surely right existentially. Marrying Josephine would be a grievous error, a colossal act of further bad faith (on *both* their parts), a shabby, corrupt, contorted act of self-sacrifice (*P*, 112), and two wrongs, moral or sentimental, do not make an existential right. It is no coincidence that, following his dinner with the Whites, and particularly Mrs White's clarification of a way forward for him, the pornographer remarks that his friends had helped him to see that he was not solely responsible for his situation; but the same can be said for Josephine, and the reader knows that really there is only one 'vulnerable single person' (*P*, 114) in the situation and whatever happens, she will most surely suffer the most from the consequences of her relationship with him. However, it is also true that the pornographer cannot and should not take Josephine's moral burden upon himself, and his sense, at the end of the evening with his friends, of having found some room to act – as narrow as it is – is a sign that he is going to end his paralysis.

Bolstered by the support he feels the Whites have given him, the pornographer confronts Josephine with the definitive results of the pregnancy test, the suggestion that she abort, and then, when she refuses, an adamant refusal to marry her. The scene is very well handled, especially the bitter, sweet ending with them returning to the pornographer's room where all

their problems started, and going to bed once more. But there is a facet of
the pornographer's character that emerges boldly in the scene but remains
something of a mystery right to the end of the novel, and that is his attitude
to the child Josephine will bear. The pornographer quite coldly dismisses
the child as someone who will have any relation to his life. Before she leaves
for London, Josephine asks him if he has any interest in the baby and his
reply is instant, firm, and strangely cold: 'None' (*P*, 136). When she tells
him that Jonathan wants him to give up all claim upon the child before he
marries her, the pornographer crows, 'I could hardly believe my luck' (*P*,
151). The novel seems to be hiding something about the pornographer in
all of this, diverting attention from the subject of paternity and fatherhood
by implying that the subject of authentic marriage takes priority.

The *ur*-beloved in McGahern's fiction is the mother; Josephine is the
unwanted mother. Perhaps the real source of the repugnance the pornographer feels for Josephine when she is pregnant is that she has suddenly
become the mother he has always 'wanted' but now intuits that to possess
would be an 'irredeemable' error. Is Nurse Brady, who has had an affair
with an older man, like Isobel, attractive because she represents a kind of sex
that nurses but will not (s)mother him as Josephine's love threatens to do?
Is there something 'missing' in the pornographer when it comes to fatherhood, 'a lack of feeling', as Josephine claims (*P*, 136), that derives from the
troubled history of fathers and sons in McGahern's other fiction? Is there
a fear of being a father? In contrast to the previous novels, McGahern has
decided to provide few details of the pornographer's childhood or of his
parents; they died when he was young and he was raised by his Aunt Mary
and Uncle Michael. But there is a pattern of sorts in the contrast between
the attractions of Isobel, who has had multiple abortions when Patrick
Moran meets her, and the repugnant Josephine, who refuses to abort, and
whose repugnance is certainly bound up with her pregnancy but also, perhaps, with her desire to be a mother. And there is a connection between the
rejected Josephine and the memory of the mother Patrick Moran struggled to free himself from. Are these patterns and connections part of what
McGahern meant when he told Denis Sampson that 'What is done in *The
Pornographer* is basically the same thing started in *The Leavetaking*', and
evidence of how the 'conscious risks' he took in *The Leavetaking* freed him
up to write *The Pornographer*? Is Josephine so repugnant because she wants

to be a mother of someone other than the pornographer? There is a moment in the novel when Josephine's voice sounds positively sibylline. Speaking to the pornographer about his aunt and their baby, she says: 'One person going out of life … and another person coming into life. I suppose that's the story' (*P*, 122). It is tempting to read this as a buried 'clue' or cryptic challenge to the reader on McGahern's part. If 'that's the story', then there is a side to this novel that, like the dark side of the moon, remains invisible to us. The baby remains an awkward presence in the novel, a paradoxically obstructive non-presence that prevents a tidy resolution, a pointedly undeveloped symbol, or a symbol denied, and thus something the reader's attention should not just drop.[29]

After his first visit to her in London, as the pornographer waves good-bye to Josephine from the train, there is a rather surprising passage of recollection and judgment that goes some way to answering these questions. The passage is important for understanding precisely how McGahern's narrative inventing has entered a new phase in *The Pornographer*. It is the only time in the novel that the pornographer gives a specific detail about either of his parents. He suddenly sees Josephine and his mother as the same type of woman:

> There are women in whom the maternal instinct is so obdurate that they will break wrists and ankles in order to stay needed.
> My mother, too, may have been such … . Maybe I had been lucky in my mother's death. Before she could get … properly to work on me she'd been taken away. And was I now acting out the same circle in reverse – leaving her in London with her growing burden? (*P*, 200–1)

There is no greater sign that with this novel McGahern reached a new place in his development than this narrator-protagonist's wondering 'Maybe I had been lucky in my mother's death'. Such a sentence seems inconceivable in McGahern's fiction before this point. Presumably, it was writing

---

29 Goarzin interprets Josephine's pregnancy as 'a metaphor for [the pornographer's] gestation of the real' ('"A Crack in the Concrete,"' 37); Whyte also notes the change in psychological valence of the mother-figure in the later fiction (see *History, Myth, and Ritual*, 176–84).

The Leavetaking that freed him up to imagine a protagonist capable of such a thought. The pornographer is a version of Patrick Moran – and of McGahern himself, of course – but while all three share the experience of having been 'taken from the farmhouse' (*P*, 201) days before their mothers died, by changing the detail of the pornographer being taken to his aunt and uncle in town, McGahern is 'shaping' this character into an even more complex version of the autobiographical pattern he has followed with his previous narrator-protagonists. The pornographer has compared his relationship with Josephine to his former beloved before (and does so again later in this passage), but never to that between him and his mother. The explicit construction of the mother as a threat to the son's independent life is an important development; from showing the constrictions of grief and memory in *The Leavetaking* to constructing the mother-figure as suffocating is a momentous dis-encrypting that confirms our sense that *The Pornographer* is completing a process that McGahern's previous novel had left unfinished.[30]

---

30   Whyte also recognizes this passage as 'a remarkable development in McGahern's fiction' (*History, Myth, and Ritual*, 184). We should remember, however, the element of ambiguity in the language of the leave-taking scene in the previous novel – 'She held me still in her eyes' (*L*, 71) – as well as the mother-shadow motif discussed in Chapter Five. With regard to McGahern's 'progress' at this point, it is worth noting that, while all McGahern's novels invite Jungian readings, *The Pornographer* does so with particular energy. The characters of Nurse Brady and Josephine have many of the qualities and functions of the true and false anima, respectively. Recalling McGahern's description of the dancehall floor and his use of 'amazed' to describe the pornographer's state of mind as he gazed out on it, it is fascinating that, according to Joseph L. Henderson, 'In all cultures, the labyrinth has the meaning of an entangling and confusing representation of the world of matriarchal consciousness; it can be traversed only by those who are ready for a special initiation into the mysterious world of the collective unconscious'. In the myth, Theseus could not rescue Ariadne until he had overcome the monster in the labyrinth. In Jungian terms, Theseus's rescue of Ariadne 'symbolizes the liberation of the anima figure from the devouring aspect of the mother image. Not until this is accomplished can a man achieve his first true capacity for relatedness to women' (Henderson, 117). It is not difficult to recognize 'the devouring aspect of the mother image' in Josephine; by disentangling himself from her, the pornographer frees himself to 'achieve his first true capacity for

McGahern shows the pornographer sensing the origin of his own ennui – his sense of life as merely 'killing time' – in his mother's rush to get to the end of life (*P*, 200); and what is significant here is that, instead of presenting the mother as a figure eliciting grief from the son, in this novel McGahern has converted the grief into its effect, ennui, *anomie* or *acedia*, and projected it onto the mother, ironically, making it a kind of genetic rather than emotional cause of the son's weakness. There is, moreover, a wonderful ambiguity of pronoun-reference in 'leaving her in London with her growing burden' – 'her' referring to (the memory of) his mother as well as Josephine – which even casts some light on the pornographer's passionate coldness toward the baby: if he is leaving his mother behind in the figure of the pregnant Josephine, then symbolically that 'burden' is also himself, or at least the self he associates with his mother, and which he must 'abandon' if he is to ever move beyond his current state of paralysis. The phrasing of 'the same circle in reverse' allows him to identify with his mother – both are figures who abandon those who love them – but also to separate himself from her and thus break from the cycles of repetition that compose his existential nightmare. By leaving Josephine-the-unwanted mother, who is symbolically also the no-longer-wanted mother whose death-abandonment he was still grieving, like Patrick Moran, in the loss of the surrogate beloved, the pornographer is trying to leave 'the cursed circle' (*P*, 201) of love that holds him prisoner.[31] Josephine is, finally, an instrument

---

relatedness to women' in his relationship with Nurse Brady. His aunt's role in this disentangling is symbolized wonderfully in the scene where she takes him to help her 'weed out' the undesirable growths in her garden, a setting as archetypal as the labyrinth and an activity clearly symbolic of psychic hygiene – especially considering the pornographer's *un*enjoyment of it. In my discussion, of course, I concentrate on Ariadne's contribution to Theseus' salvation only because in McGahern's novel, the future of the princess is left more uncertain than in the myth. See Whyte, *History, Myth, and Ritual* (229) for McGahern's admission that he was familiar with and fond of some of Jung's ideas.

31　As soon as she told him she was pregnant, he made clear to her that he had no intention of 'playing the game' (*P*, 68) and in London he tells her that as soon as the baby is born he will 'vamoose' out of her life for good. Metaphorically, 'the cursed circle' is a version of the maze of grief, anger and fear that the Ariadne figure, Nurse Brady,

of abasement, temptation and punishment, the false grail the quester must suffer and then reject. Her attractiveness to the pornographer is a sign of his self-blindness and his 'escape' from her clutches requires him to shed the blinders that keep him from seeing himself for what he is.

Once she has left for London, the pornographer sighs in relief. Danger averted, his mind cannot take off its running shoes and relax into the comfy slippers of self-congratulation fast enough. The pornographer now understands why he could not feel for Josephine what he had felt for his former beloved. Josephine was too easy! What the pornographer loves most is a woman who says 'No'! '[I]t had been ... the immanence of No that raised the love to fever ...' (*P*, 139). Most lovers are terrorized by the *imminence* of No, of course, but the pornographer's phrase expresses his sense of doom – the gloomy fatalism many of McGahern's protagonists bemoan. This is the nadir of his descent into a self-indulgent rationalization of his life of inauthenticity and the high-water mark of his lack of self-understanding. By casting himself as a Dark Romantic who needs 'the immanence of No' to raise his love to fever-pitch, the pornographer can justify his rejection of Josephine as someone whose love of him was immanently deficient. He now even judges Josephine's inferiority to his former beloved *because* she had said Yes when the woman whose loss he still grieves had said No. Masochism is suddenly a virtue. The pornographer now almost celebrates his former beloved's rejection of him as the proof that she was more worthy of his devotion. What is most obnoxious about all of this, of course, is the smug arrogance of the pornographer's construction of Josephine's desire to keep their baby as a weakness of character, proof that the nature of her love was of a lower order than his former beloved's, who rejected him because she did not want them both to be doomed to a life in the warming-oven of bourgeois marriage.

The pornographer is hardly a Byronic all-star, however; as he describes it, he lives a life of boring routine, his days book-ended by hours of verbal

---

will help him escape by showing him that it is actually all an illusion, a projection of his own pain and fear: the monster at the centre is his aunt and death, and by forcing him to confront her and it, she liberates him from himself.

wanking and one-night stands, interspersed by drinking with Maloney or aimless wandering around the city. His abhorrence of 'the normal beat' (*P*, 139) seems out of proportion and even character. He protests too much. And that is the point. As the scenes with his aunt and uncle gradually reveal, this Odysseus is lost and a long way from understanding who he is. Josephine was never going to help him discover that, but that is less a consequence of her character than of the fact that he would never have let her. By the end of the novel, he *is* willing to place himself in Nurse Brady's professional hands, however. At first, the differences between her and Josephine seem insignificant; indeed, Brady's desire for a life of domestic ordinariness (*P*, 174) certainly puts her in sync with 'the normal beat' as much as Josephine was. It is the change in the pornographer's attitude that is remarkable. By the time he tells Maloney, on the drive back to Dublin from the aunt's funeral, that he is thinking of proposing to a woman, the pornographer seems to have moved beyond 'the immanence of No', and his aunt as much as Nurse Brady is instrumental in this development.

The Ariadne of the Cancer Ward: Nurse Brady

It might seem a weakness in the novel that the character of Josephine, the antagonist whom the narrator comes to loathe and reject, is a much stronger, more vivid presence in the novel than her antithesis, who comes to represent the 'right choice' the quester must make if he is to complete his redemptive journey. It is not that Nurse Brady does not come across as a real presence in the story – or at least, as a symbol of the existence of the real presence; the point is that the specific burden of meaning and narrative function that she carries tends to 'thin' her out compared to the wonderful sense McGahern creates of an increasingly 'monstrous' Josephine constantly expanding in physical size and tentacular reach. But Nurse Brady – and McGahern's awkward use of her occupational tag in lieu of a Christian name is perfectly appropriate – is, like Isobel in *The Leavetaking*, as substantial as she needs to be: she is not only the 'prize' for which the quester has been searching, but the 'guide' whom the quester always meets when he most needs guiding: she shows him both the way to the prize and what he must do to win it. Brady, in effect, 'nurses' the pornographer back to life and presents him with his chance at redemption, the chance 'to live in love' that he thought he had lost forever. An inner force seems to emanate from her, challenging him to respond (P, 70).

Nurse Brady's role is composed of the obvious and the less than obvious, the problematically conventional and the conventional that is perennially fresh. What is problematically conventional is her choric function – along with Peter White – confirming the existential 'rightness' (if not moral rectitude) of the pornographer's attitude towards Josephine and their child (see P, 218). Her awkward collaboration with the pornographer in the matter of his rejection of Josephine and their child is necessary because she is clearly both the 'chosen one' and the one who chooses him in terms of his future life-in-love. With Peter White, McGahern tries to present a 'reasoned defence' of the pornographer's position; with Nurse Brady, he simply plays the gender card: this is a woman siding with a man against another woman – it trumps both the man who supports the other woman, Michael Kavanagh, and the other woman herself. Neither trick takes the hand, however, because the only argument that can convince the reader that the pornographer is doing the 'right thing' must originate within the pornographer. And the 'right thing' is as psychologically complex as it is morally murky. He tells Brady that he has kept in touch with Josephine throughout the pregnancy 'as much out of cowardice as anything else' (P, 218). The imprimatur of her approval is her invitation for him to take her back to her residence and share her bed. For the first time, the pornographer experiences sexual anticipation as 'a spiritual lightness' and suddenly he feels very fragile: 'I was entering a new life. I was being questioned, and I had no longer the power to turn away...' (P, 218). Nurse Brady assumes the role of Grail Maiden here. The problematic dimension to her role is offset by what is ultimately more important about it, her function as teacher-guide, the black-haired Ariadne who shows this priapic Theseus the way out of the maze of lust and fear, or in this case, into and out of the night ward of death.

The long episode beginning with the pornographer's coincidentally meeting her at the dancehall fittingly moves to the hospital where they first met and where the nurse can carry out her necessary ministrations. At the dancehall, he is standing appropriately 'amazed' at the sea of flesh washing around him (*P*, 169). Their relationship begins with him noting '[a] taunt, a warning' (*P*, 170) in the echoes of his first meeting with Josephine; nevertheless, he blithely sets off down what he assumes will be the familiar path of sexual adventure. On the taxi ride back to the nurses' residence, however, he suddenly, unpremeditatedly, asks how long she thinks his aunt has to live, and from the beginning his relationship with Nurse Brady is linked to his experience of his aunt's dying. Her direct and honest reply signals her trustworthiness as a potential guide and that her role will be instructive. To court her he must return to her room on the hospital grounds, a journey which further releases his unconscious preoccupation with his aunt's death. As the taxi passes beneath the latter's hospital window, the pornographer thinks: 'The wheel had many sections. She had reached that turn ... the whole wheel of her life staggering to a stop. ... I shivered as I thought how one day my wheel would turn into her section ...' (*P*, 172).[32]

What is amazing about McGahern's *poiēsis* at this point is how this moment of death's presence in the lovers' moonlight is subtly involved with an earlier instance of symbolic memory and imagination in his fiction. The pornographer is struck by a familiar smell that he cannot place, though he associates it with his childhood. She tells him it is the smell of new-cut hay. The echo of Patrick Moran's memory-fantasy of his mother in her father's field in *The Leavetaking* (*L*, 68–9) subtly links the dying aunt, who is based on McGahern's mother's sister, to the death of the mother in the previous novel, which we know to have been closely based on his mother's death. Later, his uncle tells him that as she neared death, he overheard his aunt talking to the pornographer's dead mother (*P*, 236), which further strengthens the buried network of connections between the novels and

---

32   Recalling childhood and the anticlimax of adulthood, the narrator of 'Wheels' thinks of 'all the vivid sections of the wheel we watched so slowly turn, impatient for the rich whole that never came but that all the preparations promised' (*CE*, 12).

between the fiction and its autobiographical sources. Nurse Brady's role
needs to be understood in relation to McGahern's fiction's preoccupation
with the continuing consequences of that original trauma.

The way down is the way up. She leads him 'down a corridor' (*P*, 173)
into the maze; as if in a fairy-tale, it is the third room that is hospitable and
where they begin their foreplay. But then Nurse Brady suddenly sounds
like Josephine: she asks him if he's interested in marriage; he replies in
kind, asking her what she'd do if she became pregnant. In the exchange,
she affirms her desire for domestic life and he admits 'I'd want to marry
you' (*P*, 174). The scene is turning into a job interview and their short-lived
wrestling match is comically pro forma. Significantly, it ends with Brady
asking him if he would like to see his aunt and the episode then moves
to its symbolic centre. Oddly, yet reasonably, he asks 'Why?' Her reply,
that 'It might be fun' (*P*, 174), uses the same word she uses to explain her
desire to be married. Apparently, 'fun' here means more than light pleasure
or transient amusement. She is already teaching the pornographer about
the necessary humour lacking in his life, the joyful acceptance of all the
wheel's sections.

McGahern's language pointedly draws attention to the way Nurse
Brady guides the pornographer to the site/sight he must attend at the centre
of the labyrinth. It is that liminal time between night and morning; they
walk through the dew on the new-cut grass; she has 'a bunch of keys', one
of which opens a rear door into the hospital; suddenly he finds himself
in his aunt's ward: 'I hadn't recognized it, always having come to it from
the other side' (*P*, 175). As he stands in the darkness and moonlight of the
ward, his heart pounding, his thoughts again return to the symmetry of
the 'womb and the grave'. The collocation of birth and death in a cancer
ward reminds us of the connection between birth, cancer and death in
Patrick Moran's thinking in *The Leavetaking* and McGahern's recollections
in *Memoir*. When they leave and return to the field outside, they embrace
and roll in the grass. The scene is a repetition of the wrestling match in the
residence, but now Nurse Brady seems to 'baptize' him in the symbol of
organic process; then she leads him back to her cell-like room where she
continues his instruction in the mysteries of life and death. As he holds her
naked in bed, the pornographer embraces a new disposition, a new attitude

toward life; oddly, considering what has come before in the novel, it is not clear that they have sex, although McGahern provides ironic echoes of the 'glory' the pornographer felt in his first coupling with Josephine, presumably intentional.[33] It is his sudden openness to the 'terrible tenderness' (*P*, 177) of mortal love that marks this as a turning-point in the pornographer's journey. At the beginning of the novel he felt the prisoner of a 'doomed marriage with the body' (*P*, 24). Nurse Brady's taking him to his aunt's sickbed, coaxing him to face the 'truth' in woman's bed of copulation, birth, and death, is necessary before he can accept the truth of *her* bed, and what she teaches is that he must grow up and lie down with mortality, embrace it, love it in a grown-up way if he is to be worthy of her. The 'turn' in this episode is only that, however, a change in direction; the pornographer still has a long way to go before he can see over the horizon to a life of meaning. Before that, he must face the music in London, which he does on the two trips he makes to visit Josephine, the most important being the second, after she has given birth to his child.

When he returns from the first trip, however, he delays visiting his aunt because he is afraid of resuming contact with the black-haired nurse. McGahern has the pornographer reflect and remember in a way that further shows the characters of the aunt and nurse to be 'complementary' in his narrative's symbolic process. As he approaches his aunt's bed the pornographer cannot help recalling 'that clandestine night' (P, 203) that Brady brought him to the ward. There follows a long passage in which the pornographer thinks of himself as a quester – 'We have to go inland ... and there make our own truth' – but more importantly, recognizes that his way forward entails a going back; he will not find what he needs until he confronts what he has lost (see *P*, 203). If his *acedia* has been characterized by his failure to 'attend' to his life – to care *for* as well as *about* what he was doing, this second night-visit to his aunt brings about a new focus. The pornographer is ready to confront his condition: 'And the dark-haired girl, and the woman

---

33   Indeed, the echo of his response to Josephine's body when he first meets Nurse Brady on this crucial night for his future suggests that the pornographer could repeat the same mistakes; compare *P*, 177 and 34.

with child in London, the dying woman I was standing beside … what of them? … What of yourself?' (*P*, 203) His linking of his memory of 'that clandestine night' and the language of quest and learning contradicts his earlier sense of the absolutely solitary nature of his journey. The women he includes in his question *shape* the answer. The question itself signals his turn toward the rebirth he fears, a rebirth which requires the death of his fear of love. If his aunt inspires him to love life, Nurse Brady inspires him to overcome his fear of loss.

When the pornographer tells Brady about Josephine, he gives an honest account of his behaviour, attitude and feelings and she is understandably non-committal when he asks her if she will see him again (*P*, 211–13). When she does, he takes her to meet Maloney. It seems he needs to show this 'father confessor' that he has turned a new leaf and to receive his benediction. And in a sense he receives it when Maloney pronounces his approval of her in language that evokes the image of a new Eve (*P*, 213–14), which is appropriate because Nurse Brady *is* a figure of myth-romance 'shaped' by McGahern for her role in a realistic fiction.

Like Maloney, as soon as we meet her, we recognize what makes Nurse Brady different from Josephine. A care-giver rather than someone who needs taking care of, she immediately challenges the pornographer to approach her. His aunt's comical warning (*P*, 48) is actually coded counsel: Brady's will show the pornographer the 'work' he needs to do upon himself. From the outset, although just as much a figure of erotic attraction to him, she embodies a different quality of eros than Josephine: he cannot get out of his mind the image of 'her strong legs' (*P*, 49) and confident laughter.[34] At first, of course, he thinks about her merely as another possible sexual 'adventure'. To win her, however, he will have to change. When he returns from his first trip to London, even though unconsciously he seems to know she *is* the prize, instead of contacting her he spends his time writing and masturbating to fantasies of her as Mavis. He is a reluctant candidate for re-birth (*P*, 202). But the pornographer will have to 'die',

---

34   Nurse Brady has a similar anatomy to Isobel, at least from the waist down; see *L*, 43.

if he is ever 'to live in love' as he hopes. And when he does make love to her, his language pointedly contradicts his earlier fear; in fact, love is now no longer the 'cursed circle' but an ordeal that makes the lover worthy to enter the garden – an image that once again links his aunt and Brady as nurses to his sick spirit: 'It seems we must be beaten twice, by the love we inflict and then by the infliction of being loved ...' (*P*, 219). The echo of Patrick Moran's remark about his father and how 'the male urge to inflict the seed' (*L*, 65) ultimately led to his mother's death corroborates our sense that writing *The Leavetaking* freed McGahern from the grief and anger that shape the earlier novels. With the character of the pornographer McGahern acknowledges that everyone carries the selfish gene he condemned his father for possessing; indeed, it is not far-fetched to consider the whole pornographer-Josephine plot as a subliminal redaction of that other unwanted pregnancy in McGahern's fiction and life. Nurse Brady is better off not knowing that she is 'an agreeable plant' and proof of 'the lesser truth', but humility – even the pornographer's brand – is a high step up from the cynicism and despair that had him by the throat – if not the genitals – until he meets her. Where before he saw love as trap and prison, now when he regards the nurse's room as 'more cell than room' (*P*, 219), it is that of an anchorite not a prisoner, in keeping, presumably, with the 'spiritual lightness' he felt as she led him to it.

The Aunt, the Uncle, and the Way Home

Part of the narrative magic in the circular form of this dark romance is how we come to see that the agent of change is not only the obvious figure of the aunt, Mary Doherty, but also her bachelor brother.[35] The novel begins and

---

35   Mary is based on McGahern's mother's sister, Maggie, as is the shop Mary lives above across from the station (*P*, 141–2, 239; see *M*, 72). The autobiographical background of the character is clear from McGahern's memoir (*M*, 245; see *P*, 232). Michael is based

ends with both characters, and the image of a man from the west arriving
in Dublin to visit his dying sister, but whose journey begins the process
by which the narrator is re-connected to his home, his past, but most of
all, to the inner self which had gone missing ever since he lost his beloved.
It is the uncle who, following the visit to the hospital, begins to draw the
narrator back to the world of the saw-mill, his aunt's house, and his own
family's farm, all of which figure in the conclusion of the story. The character of the uncle, appropriately named Michael, is the 'messenger' who
eventually impresses upon the narrator the importance to identity of living
rooted in the home place and who challenges the questing hero to take
action against the spiritual torpor and self-conceit that holds him thrall to
a masturbatory sexuality (emotionally the pornographer has not advanced
much beyond the febrile adolescence of the young Mahoney in *The Dark*)
and the compulsive need to find a beloved. What really 'enmeshes' the
pornographer is not women but the repression that distorts this legitimate

---

on McGahern's mother's brother, Pat, and along with his longtime, long-suffering
employee at the saw-mill, Jim, he returns in *That They May Face the Rising Sun*, as the
Shah, the jovial and benign sub-deity of the world of the lake; Jim returns as Frank
Dolan, the Shah's long-suffering and silent employee; the saw-mill is a wrecker's yard
in the later novel. In *The Pornographer*, McGahern refers to these characters' 'narrow
and strong lives' (*P*, 10), by which he seems to refer to the steadfast focus of their lives
on the tasks, routines and relationships which compose, fill and colour their known
world, a world of quality not quantity, despite Michael's pride in purchasing a house
and farm for less than their market value. Their lives are made strong because of this
existential focus; they do not spread themselves too thin nor do they fall victim to
that obesity of spirit and material appetite that often consumes their urban coun-
terparts. It is this moral, emotional, and indeed, spiritual, 'focus' that is missing in
the pornographer's life, an absence that gives his world its skewed 'geometry' (*P*, 18),
evident in his water-spider-like skimming over the surfaces of word and flesh in his
pursuit of something of value. At the end, when the pornographer silently scoffs at
his uncle's sense of self-importance during his sister's funeral (*P*, 231) and laughs *at*
as much as *with* him as he crows over the sharp deal he made for the house and farm
he has bought (*P*, 234), the pornographer's superciliousness is partly cut by the fact
that we know he genuinely loves his uncle and is himself beginning to feel differently
towards his belief that a man needs to live on his own land if he is ever to know who
he is (*P*, 221) – a belief McGahern himself clearly shared.

quest into a predatory hunt for sexual game, a self-confusion symbolized by his rodent-like scuttling between pub, dancehall and hospital in a Dublin of one-night stands, terminal affairs, and the pornography business. But if his uncle shows the pornographer the way home, his dying aunt shows him something just as important for his future: she shows him the world of grown-up love. In her sincere but sharply measured loyalty to the odious Cyril,[36] in her love of her garden, and in her dying conversations with her long dead sister, the pornographer's mother, the character of the aunt shows the narrator how life is bigger than living and dying, and that to love it is to enter that largeness even as it consumes us. The triumph of McGahern's characterization here is that he shows courage without sentimentalizing or abstracting it as 'heroic'; strength without lamenting its inevitable weakening; humour, hope, resistance and resignation, the whole cycle of holding on to and letting go of life, without any dishonesty. She is one of McGahern's finest creations and there is not a false note in her performance.

Like the two-part *The Leavetaking*, *The Pornographer* is a carefully shaped novel with a bipedal rhythm, moving forward through the accretion of counterpointed scenes – especially those between the pornographer and Josephine and him and his aunt.[37] He is attracted and repulsed by both women, and in both cases he is afraid of emotional entanglement and the inevitable experience of loss that follows emotional commitment. Josephine tries to draw him into a future of marriage and fatherhood, a conventional life he considers unacceptable. His aunt invites him to

---

36 McGahern is still settling the score here. Cyril is a character, based on McGahern's father, who all but abandons his dying wife out of weakness, fear and selfishness and then attempts to set things right by purchasing a flamboyant gravestone that is more a monument to his own vanity than a memorial for Mary. Michael's description of the scene between Mary and Cyril, where she tells him off and cuts him loose, not only captures some of the feeling between Maggie and McGahern's father, it also 'speaks up' for his mother who had been abandoned by her husband during her illness and death.

37 McGahern has the pornographer himself notice the connection (see *P*, 134–5). Another instance of effective counterpoint is when McGahern follows the pornographer's description of his dinner with Maloney with Josephine's description of her dinner with Jonathan (*P*, 124–9, 129–30).

'come home', to approach the future by re-connecting to his roots. The way forward found in the way back is an axiom McGahern's whole career explores, of course, and *The Pornographer* is a story of the protagonist's slow discovery of that truth.

One of the more poignant ironies in the novel is that all the while the pornographer is buying and bringing pain-killing brandy to his aunt, he has numbed himself to his own pain. His expressions of reluctance and pique regarding these visits sound the hollowness of his character (*P*, 48, 68, 69). Even as late as his first trip to London he delays visiting his aunt after his return in order to write more Mavis and the Colonel stories, taking advantage of the fact he had told her he would be away for a week, and lying to her when he does see her again (*P*, 201). He promises to visit her at home but only goes down to escape Josephine's daily letters to him. The pornographer's character is not as black-and-white as might seem at times: even with his aunt and uncle, McGahern shows him to be self-centred in his affections, while with Josephine he is often a confused predator.

But it is his aunt's influence that begins the pornographer's re-sensitization. As he hardens toward Josephine, while getting more deeply entangled with her, he begins to soften in his aunt's presence, even though he is usually in a hurry to leave her bedside. The strength of McGahern's technique is in the way he maintains the realism of their relationship, while at the same time gradually developing its symbolism (see *P*, 206–7). As we might expect, the understanding that begins to dawn within him in her presence is an understanding of the relation between big and little things. The understanding is that there *is* no connection except what the human imagination wills, an understanding that, for the pornographer, means that 'joy ... was part of weeping' (*P*, 62). This is the first sign in the novel that his condition is going to change. Eventually, in the closing paragraphs, he will turn to Nurse Brady, but his feeling here serves to emphasize that Josephine was never in the running. His recognition of 'the need ... to give thanks and praise' (*P*, 62) echoes his earlier statement to Josephine about his 'need' for sex (*P*, 56), but also suggests an expansion of his otherwise constricted spirit. (It also links the language of the pornographer's growth to Elizabeth Reegan's.) Following this moment of self-surprise by his aunt's bedside, he spends the next day walking the streets of the city. It is as if merely expending energy on attention transforms the would-be *flâneur* into a quester, his meandering into a search, and the day's ephemera into a prize no less valued because it is ephemeral. It is important to emphasize that the pornographer is in no way moving toward a conventionally religious 'thanks and praise'. The peace of mind he glimpses is more acceptance of things as they are than resignation. Stoical, humanist, his exhaustion here is very different from the spiritual fatigue that characterizes *acedia*. The pornographer is beginning to break out of his doldrums.

In the scenes with his aunt and uncle, the pornographer is brought back to his roots. Her mention of Sticks McCabe summons memories of the town drunk and his uncle's attempt to hide his upset at her condition evokes memories of her outer roughness toward him and his docility toward her, and the changes that came when she married Cyril. When the pornographer takes her flowers he remembers the times he accompanied her to church. To preserve the 'fragile' sense of freedom he feels once Josephine has left for London, the pornographer decides to keep his promise to visit them. He awakes in the room he used to sleep in as a boy. Every sound, sight and smell summons a memory. His uncle takes him out of the narrow crib of his preoccupations to the world of saw-mills and spare parts, farm-prices and country gossip, a world in which a broken heart is little more than a chipped saw-tooth. It is Michael who keeps the pornographer's family house in shape, ready for his return. The world his aunt and uncle evoke in the pornographer's mind is that of the past; once again, it is Time that is his real adversary.

It is his aunt's involvement of him in her dying that works the necessary change upon the pornographer. In the ritual of his bringing her brandy to dull her pain and then drinking with her, he is brought back within the circle of affection from which he had removed himself (*P*, 142). He uses the same language of instinct to explain his fear of deeper emotional involvement with his aunt that he uses to rationalize his sexual relationship with Josephine. But it is 'the instinct for the true' (*P*, 252) that the pornographer will finally have to act upon, and which he does when he decides to propose to Nurse Brady, and he could not make that decision without the gift of his aunt's dying.

When he goes with her to see her garden, she complains to him about the unreasonableness of her condition: 'Just to get a bit better. ... To just go on. It doesn't seem much to ask' (*P*, 143). This is the quintessential complaint in McGahern's writing: change, time, the paradox that 'to just go on' is sooner or later to use up one's time; and writing about the aunt's illness and death in this way must have recalled his mother's dying. With their shared love of nature and the Leitrim countryside, Susan McGahern and her son, too, must have wished that she didn't have 'to leave the garden'. But her departure was the novelist's first lesson that things cannot 'stay as they are'. Everything changes – landscape and love, others and the self. It is quite appropriate, therefore, that it is in the garden the aunt begins to work her crucial influence upon her nephew: 'she said in a voice matter-of-fact enough to be running through a tenant's contract, "... It's only after years that you get some shape on things, and then after all that you have to leave"' (*P*, 144). The 'tenant's contract' is a wonderful touch, a metaphor that quietly blossoms into a symbol of the nature and responsibility of all human presence on earth. But it is the 'shape' metaphor that signals the importance of her speech for the novel. Mary's lament slyly entails McGahern's experience of the old Chaucerian saw, 'The lyf so short, the craft so long to lerne', encoding a self-referential meaning whose didactic import for the pornographer is the message that he needs to take charge of his life, to shape it rather than passively allow it to be shaped for him, but also, in as much as taking charge relates to his life as a writer as well as a man in search of a beloved, to begin the real work of the imagination rather than continue its waste in the production of pornography. As she gradually turns to accept her death, to acknowledge that it is time to leave the garden, the pornographer turns from the lunar wasteland of his emotional life and the airless world of the pornographic imagination toward the world of relationship and responsibility; ultimately, when he decides to leave Dublin and return with Nurse Brady to his parents' farm, he returns to the world of his aunt's garden.[38] When he says goodbye to her for the last time, he

---

38   Crotty writes that 'The protagonist's choice of Nurse Brady over Josephine involves a conscious rejection of the incoherence of urban life and an attempt to live once

is struck by her 'coldness … her perfect mastery' (*P*, 224) of her situation. In McGahern's dualistic world, this coldness is the obverse of the passion for life which had preceded it but which, inexorably, it must displace, and her mastery is her stoical acceptance of the nature of things.

If the turning-point in the novel is the pornographer's turn toward a future with Nurse Brady, the denouement is McGahern's bringing a final shape to the plots of life, death and love he has developed in the story. The juxtaposition of the birth of the baby and the pornographer's final journey to London to end things with Josephine, with his aunt's death and his trip home for her funeral, gives the novel a balance and symmetry of narrative architecture that expresses the 'vision' and 'idea' behind the writing at the level of structural coherence. As in *The Dark* and *The Leavetaking*, McGahern employs another open-ended conclusion; but the 'four square' completeness of the form of *The Pornographer* looks ahead to the kind of formal compact he achieves in *Amongst Women* and the cyclical round of *That They May Face the Rising Sun*.

Following the birth, the pornographer agrees to go to London to talk to Josephine but adamantly refuses to go near her house or to see the child. She shows up at the pub where they agree to meet with her landlord, the Irishman, Michael Kavanagh.[39] The meeting is a realistic fiasco, but it is the archetypal features embedded in McGahern's realism that give much of his fiction its extraordinary resonances. Three times Kavanagh challenges the pornographer and three times he refuses to go with them to see the child. When Kavanagh tries to manhandle him, the pornographer resists and that is when Kavanagh beats him up. The pornographer strikes out

---

again according to the simple codes of behaviour he associates with his aunt and uncle and with his formative years in the countryside' ("All Toppers,"' 50–1).

39   In *The Leavetaking* and *The Pornographer*, McGahern drew on his time in London for his knowledge of pubs and their neighborhoods for details of setting. Likewise, the comment that Kavanagh's wife, a nurse, makes after a strenuous night-shift at the hospital and that Josephine records in her letter to the pornographer was actually something McGahern's sister, Rosaleen, said to him one morning at breakfast when he and Laaksi were staying with her and Breedge and their families in London (compare *P*, 217 and *M*, 253).

at Josephine when she tries to embrace him and then loses consciousness for a moment. The image of him removing his shoes and skulking off into the shadows and finding a dark place to hide in a church doorway, as Josephine and her champion argue, is comic-bathetic. But McGahern clearly intends us to respond differently to the pornographer's epiphany after they leave: hurting from the beating he has taken from Kavanagh, he also feels 'extraordinarily happy' and sees his situation with 'an amazing clarity', as if he is simultaneously outside it and at 'its still centre' (*P*, 229). In spite of what Maloney says later, the beating, it seems, has been his purgatorial cleansing. Like Gawain at the Green Knight's 'chapel', the pornographer has confessed his faults, endured his three strokes, and now carries the scars of his guilt and atonement. The ordeal has freed him from the spell of separateness that his *acedia* had cast him upon him; his new condition is a version of that stoical 'coldness' and 'perfect mastery' he felt in his aunt. His peculiar sense of feeling apart from and yet at the same time deeply engaged in the business of living becomes the basis of the pornographer's existential realignment.

Also like Gawain, the pornographer must display his scars 'at court' when he returns to Ireland only to be summoned to his aunt's funeral. In the medieval romance, of course, the knight explains his scar by publicly confessing to his shortcomings. McGahern's quester has no such allegorical responsibilities, however, and he is able to tell half-truths to his uncle and lie to everyone else. The description of his aunt laid out in her deathbed and then her removal are pivotal moments in McGahern's writing, turning away as they do from the trauma of incompleteness recounted in *The Leavetaking* and toward the great laying-out and funeral scene in *That They May Face the Rising Sun*. In his remarks on ceremony and the value of social ritual, the pornographer reiterates some of McGahern's abiding beliefs: 'The superstitious, the poetic, the religious are all made safe within the social, given a tangible form. The darkness is pushed out' (*P*, 238). McGahern must have re-read this passage sometime before he wrote the paragraphs in his memoir beginning, 'We come from darkness into light and grow in the light until at death we return to that original darkness' (*M*, 36). He returns to the focal image that recurs in all three of his previous novels. What is noteworthy is the way he braids the aesthetic and the social, ceremony and ritual, in the metaphor of 'tangible form', thereby asserting the power and presence of narrative art, fiction, alongside the other forms of story-telling we use to negotiate the various thresholds that mark our time and presence in the world. The social role, compensatory power, and emotional authority of narrative art are comparable, and for McGahern, equal in their capacity to assuage the mind and heart in the face of the darkness as the words of comfort that once flowed from religious belief. The passage thus offers another way of looking at McGahern's preoccupation with 'shape' and 'shaping' in his statements about the art of writing fiction. The making of the story is the making of 'a tangible form': it is a ceremonial act on the part of the writer, a 'mystery' in the archaic sense, and a ceremonial experience on the reader's part, a participation in the imagining of the life of others that illuminates our own potential as well as our limits, opens our eyes to other worlds as it counsels our egos to adjust our attention to those we do live in.

The pornographer's attention to the speech and actions of the people in his former community throughout the funeral episode shows the pornographer's return to the broader social world following the new stance he adopts after his violent break with Josephine. Maloney's surprise appearance at the funeral strengthens the sense that he is everything and more than he seems. Ironically scolding the pornographer for acting foolishly with Josephine, he again acts as a mock-chorus when he announces that fools generally get what they deserve (*P*, 244), the only time in the novel when he seems less than worldly-wise (at least from the point of view of someone who has had a career as an academic). McGahern also uses Maloney's presence to add value to the pornographer's imminent announcement of his return to the community. When he, Maloney and Cyril visit Comiskey's establishment the morning after the funeral to see the elaborate tombstone Cyril has purchased for Mary's grave, Maloney is impressed by 'the old style' of the business – hardware store, undertaker's, stonemason's and bar all in one. The foreman acknowledges that some of the farm equipment he sells is not up with the times and confesses they no longer make the coffins they use; he speaks as well of a passing attitude to business when he explains that the policy of giving free drinks to good customers is not so much good business practice as simple manners (*P*, 244–5). By returning to the

country, the pornographer will be returning to an Ireland that was already
passing away, would last barely another ten years, something McGahern
had discovered for himself by the late 1970s. In his next novel, *Amongst
Women*, the death of the patriarch, Moran, symbolizes the death of the
Ireland McGahern had grown up in, had left and returned to, the Ireland
of his father and mother and of his own childhood and adolescence.

The pornographer tells Maloney he intends to return to work the
family farm. But what is more important is that he says he is looking to his
future with or without Nurse Brady; if she turns him down, he will come
back anyway. No longer obsessed with the search for the beloved, or, conversely, with the fear of loss, he knows 'The life has to be lived ... anyhow...'
(*P*, 251). His paralysis has ended; the *acedia* is over, and for the first time in
the novel McGahern provides the reader with an explicit diagnosis of the
pornographer's former condition: 'I had not attended properly. ... Broken
in love, I had turned back, let the light of imagination almost out' (*P*, 251).
As suspected, mourning for the 'lost beloved' was behind the pornographer's
acedia all the time. Surprisingly, he feels a powerful need to pray – not to
ask for anything in particular but simply to affirm at long last a sense of
connection to the world that he had lost for so long (*P*, 252). The circularity
of prayer here is, in fact, emblematic of the form of the novel itself, which
ends with the pornographer remembering his uncle arriving at the station
in Dublin all those months ago 'at the beginning of the journey' (*P*, 252),
and the narrator's sense of having completed a journey confirms our sense
of the archetypes of quest romance informing character, structure and
setting in the novel. The circular form pushes toward an upward spiral, as
in *The Leavetaking*, but as with the conclusion of that novel, the future
remains vague, the protagonist guarded in his hope, and the beloved still
some way down the road.

As the carefully crafted clasp on the necklace of the novel's circular
form, the most important aspect of the final paragraph is that it is a paragraph of memory, reminding us that for McGahern, the mystery of narrative
poiēsis is the mystery of memory, that what all his retrospective narrators and
narrator-protagonists seek is a solution to the enigma of memory as loss and
return, separation and recovery, the aporia of grief as the 'tangible form' of
absence. Narration, for McGahern, is heuristic; the making of fiction is the

probing of memory until, as with Augustine, confession becomes praise.[40] 'They say that it is the religious instinct that makes us seek the relationships and laws in things' (*P*, 30). But for McGahern, I believe, the instinct to connect is not religious so much as artistic, imaginative. The profundity of his personal aesthetic and narrative quest lies in the *story* he sought, which is the story of meaning itself, and which was found in the mysterious connection of opposites, of life and death, and having and losing. What his career as a writer shows is that the instinct to seek relationships and laws in things was for him the recoil from loss, the positive energy that comes out of grief, the constructive urge that sparks off the flint of heartbreak. It is the instinct to make and tell a story. If this is a religious instinct, then art is religious and organized religion is an attenuated and diminished version of the individual imagination, the herd's abandonment of the solitary quest. Like *The Leavetaking*, *The Pornographer* is a turning-point book in McGahern's growth as an artist because it is a work that successfully fuses the journey out of grief with the open way of narrative.

40 At the end of his memoir, McGahern describes the story he has told as 'the journey out of that landscape [that] became the return to those lanes and small fields and hedges and lakes under the Iron Mountains' (*M*, 260–1). The memoir has the same circular form as *The* Barracks, The *Pornographer*, and *Amongst Women*, and when his novels and memoir are seen together it is possible to see McGahern's career as having been shaped by his struggle to bend the repetitive circularity of grief into the upward spiral of recovered joy, the ultimate shape of the myth he brings to fruition in *Memoir* and *That They May Face the Rising Sun*.

CHAPTER SEVEN

The End of Father History: *Amongst Women* (1990)

With the publication of *That They May Face the Rising Sun* and *Memoir* it
is now possible to get a clearer sense of how *Amongst Women* fits into the
progress of McGahern's writing life and the overall shape of his oeuvre.
The great achievement of the novel is McGahern's successful shaping of his
abiding themes and deeply personal preoccupations into a fiction that maintains its autobiographical core within a vivid carapace of accurate regional
topography and documentary realism. In *The Pornographer* he constructed
a narrator-protagonist who is, paradoxically, both a more complex and yet
freer version of his previous autobiographical narrator-protagonists. There
is an even greater sublimation of the recollective self in *Amongst Women*, a
novel which returns to the family history of the first three novels in order
to bring it to its conclusion, and which appears to silence the expected
autobiographical narrator-protagonist in the character of Luke, whom
the author places in 'self-exile' in London, distant and militantly uncom-
municative, in order to allow Moran and his women to possess the stage.[1]
Luke's 'separateness' from the family (*AW*, 144) and his refusal to return to
Great Meadow signify McGahern's own refusal to return to the passions he
had tapped in *The Dark*. It would be a mistake, however, to confuse tonal
objectivity with moral neutrality and to overlook the element of judgment
that attends McGahern's exploration of individual character and collective ethos in this novel. Eamon Maher describes *Amongst Women* as 'one

---

1   McGahern's strategic-symbolic treatment of Luke is thus responsible for 'that dis-
     tance, that inner formality or calm' that McGahern claims to be his stylistic ideal
     (*L* 1984: [5]). Cronin describes McGahern's achievement in this novel as 'a stylistic
     seamlessness, a tonal serenity not discernible in either of the two preceding novels'
     ('A New Image?' 115).

of the great novels about family life in Irish literature', adding, 'whether that was McGahern's primary purpose or not, [the novel] is an important chronicle of Irish rural family life.'[2] But *Amongst Women* is a great novel about a *particular* rural Irish family rather than about *all* rural Irish families, and its provenance derives from lived experience rather than theoretical abstraction or allegorical historicization. *Memoir* makes abundantly clear that the Morans are *also* the McGaherns, and the great personal achievement of the creative-memorial process that produced this novel is the final exorcism of 'the father' in McGahern's writing.

The Barracks began a process of creative recollection that was a continuous engagement with the two formative traumas in McGahern's life and their long-term effects – the horror of his mother's death, and its sequel, the years spent under his father's rule. With *Amongst Women*, that 'recreative' quest, evident in the cyclical alternation of mother- and father-figures in the four novels that precede it, reaches the first stage of its conclusion, the imagining of the father's death. McGahern's last novel is an oracular expression of his mother's spirit, and it is clear he was not free to write it in the way he did without the 'burying of the dead' which he achieved in *Amongst Women*. The paradoxically grounded lightness of being we encounter in *That They May Face the Rising Sun* suggests that the writer was no longer burdened by the baggage that the other novels had carried.

While *Amongst Women* is McGahern's most 'classically' realist novel, it is nevertheless as confessional as any of his previous works. It is an engagement with the past that clears up the last traces of anger more than grief. Indeed, the way in which grief figures in this novel betokens a new stage of maturity in McGahern's artistry. Like *The Dark*, *Amongst Women* is a confrontation with the father; but by this point in McGahern's life, his father had become, like his mother, a ghost of memory.[3] But unlike *The*

---

2   Maher, *John McGahern*, 116–17.

3   Francis McGahern died in 1977. Like Maher (*John McGahern*, 100), Cronin sees Moran as the culmination of all the father-figures in McGahern's previous writing: 'the perfection of the type, an unforgettable combination of paternal autocracy, embittered nationalism, atavistic piety, twisted love and, probably most of all, a ruinous fear of life itself' ('A New Image? 116).

Dark, which is a profoundly conflicted work of seething rage and deep hurt and a novel that in the end ultimately recoils in fear and shock at its release of such passion and pain, *Amongst Women* is a work of carefully measured and controlled emotion. Whereas *The Dark* glows red hot in the 'darkness visible' of the inferno, *Amongst Women* is luminous with the light of a purgatorial 'cold flame'.

The explanation for this quality of passion made precise by the shaping consciousness of art is, I believe, a creative effort that balances two profoundly important beliefs in a dialectical tension: first, McGahern's belief that he never understood his father or why he behaved the way he did to his children; and second, his belief that what fiction *does* is to make sense of the human experience of life.[4] The greatest achievement of *Amongst Women* is McGahern's balancing of that honesty and that need, while remaining true to both. Ultimately, this novel is an act of dismissal. Like *The Pornographer*, it ends with a funeral. McGahern buries the last of his dead; the school of grief is over. Following this, in his final novel, McGahern heads for the lake and finds portents of the resurrection he had unconsciously sought all his creative life.

The Morans and the McGaherns

McGahern had examined his father and himself in *The Dark*, and while the relationship between Luke and Moran is the deep energy source at the narrative core of *Amongst Women*, it is the story of Moran's influence on Luke's siblings that is told in the novel. Moran's predecessor is definitely the vicious Mahoney of the earlier novel. This needs to be stressed because of the way some critics attempt to ennoble Moran as a tragic figure, particularly at the end of the novel. *Amongst Women* has mythic qualities, but its shape and ethos are not tragic so much as they are in keeping with

---

4   For McGahern on the enigma of his father, see *M*, 226, 271.

the fundamental romance structure that underlies all McGahern's fiction. Moran is not a tragic figure: he is the ogre-miser of fairy-tale, the monster of myth, the parental obstacle of romance.[5]

Memoir identifies Moran, like Mahoney, to be another reconstruction of McGahern's father. But it is not details like their shared devotion to the rosary that are so important, however, as the major thematic strands in the characterizations that derive from McGahern's memories of his father, stepmother and siblings.[6] For example, Moran's war experience in the IRA,

5   To Maher, Moran 'is a different type of man altogether to Mahoney: he is more honourable and secure in his cult of family' (*John McGahern*, 107). McGahern is anything but 'secure' in his family, however; indeed, his paranoid insecurity is why he is such a totalitarian tyrant. He is as insecure as nitro-glycerine is unstable; the slightest hint of a threat to his imperium sets him off. Whatever 'honour' he ever possessed turned long ago to the acid of self-loathing that pools in the corroded brain pan behind his mask of self-importance; he is a man who in his youth brushed up against honour, but for some unexplained reason it did not stick. For other 'positive' views of the character, see Antoinette Quinn, 'A Prayer for My Daughters: Patriarchy in *Amongst Women*', *Canadian Journal of Irish Studies* 17.1 (1991), 88, and Whyte, *History, Myth, and Ritual*, 106. Sampson writes: 'This suffering figure, who is unlikeable for his hatred of life and his contempt for those close to him, gains a mythic stature from the depth of this anguish'; and because of the motif of eating children, he relates Moran to the mythical figure of Cronos (*Outstaring Nature's Eye*, 236). I find Moran to be more Cyclops than Cronos.

6   Details like Moran's Ford and favourite chair are taken from life at the barracks in Cootehall, as is Moran's shaving ritual and the 'pure tenseness' (*AW*, 40) that gripped the house until it was over (compare *M*, 33). Moran's delusion about his mechanical aptitude (*AW*, 63–4) is based on Francis McGahern's (see *M*, 194), as is his preference for Protestants to his fellow Catholics (*AW*, 163; compare *M*, 171–2). Maggie and Mona mock Moran's sub-Jobian laments (*AW*, 9) in the same way that Rosaleen and Monica chant their father's habitual refrain (see *M*, 160, 191, 192). The echo of the children's mockery of Mahoney's mantra in *The Dark* links the two father-figures. Like the other Moran, Patrick's father, in *The Leavetaking*, Moran quarrelled with his wife's sister (*AW*, 48) and McGahern mentions the bad feeling between his father and his aunt more than once in the memoir. Moran raises the question of his remarrying with Maggie (*AW*, 27); in the memoir, McGahern's father raises it with him, and while there is some overlap in the language, the tone of the interview is quite different because of his feelings toward his father (see *M*, 206–7). The Moran girls'

which McGahern develops early in the novel as a clue to the character's damaged personality, is also a hypothesis he floats in the memoir when admitting his father was beyond his understanding (*M*, 226–7). Even more important is Moran's attitude not only to this history but to his past in general; it is clearly based on what McGahern describes as his father's 'refusal of the past' (*M*, 49). The 'inviolate secrecy' that Moran maintains about himself (*AW*, 19) derives from Francis McGahern's 'practically pathological' secretiveness (*M*, 57; see also 35, 47). In Moran's case, his repression of the past is important not so much in relation to his time in the IRA but to the untold story in the novel of Luke's self-exile. Moran's 'compulsion to dominate' (*AW*, 21) is also taken from McGahern's memory of his father, as is Moran's use of the daily ritual of the rosary to ceremonially enact his authority over his children (see *M*, 222–3, 15). Moran 'resented' (*AW*, 49) giving in to Rose's requests for money to decorate the house; he withdraws his support of Sheila's dream to go to university when she wins the scholarship; and his miserliness is based on McGahern's recollections of his father's parsimony (see *M*, 156–8). McGahern does not present any scenes in which Moran beats his daughters, although there are suggestions in the novel that he did when they were young. Rose's mother asks Maggie about this directly, and we are told she lies in reply (*AW*, 34). The memoir, of course, is sadly replete with McGahern's accounts of 'the brutality of the house' (*M*, 159; see also 151). The 'terrible awareness of Moran' (*AW*, 45) that the narrator describes reflects McGahern's memory that there was 'always tension' whenever his father was near (*M*, 23) and Moran's unstable moods (*AW*, 47) derive from his life-model, whom McGahern describes as 'so changeable … so violent, so self-absorbed, so many faced' (*M*, 226). The Moran girls are not *shown* to have been driven to the state of abjection that McGahern and his sisters approached – 'We were made to feel a burden and to feel ashamed' (*M*, 157) – but McGahern describes them

---

trips home for Christmas and Easter are drawn from McGahern's sisters': Rosaleen and Breedge went to London, like Maggie Moran, to become nurses; Margaret and Monica, and later, Dympna McGahern, like Sheila and Mona, went to Dublin to work in the Civil Service (see *M*, 218).

learning to mimic abjection, remaining 'obstinately silent, abject looking' under Moran's accusatory look in order to escape the bully's wrath (*AW*, 68). Moran is never shown doing anything to *raise* his children's self-esteem. As will become clear, their sense of 'separateness and superiority' (*AW*, 135) is a 'negative' virtue of being raised by him, and easily punctured once they leave the bubble of Great Meadow.

There is no sexual abuse in *Amongst Women* but presumably that is because it occurred with Luke, and is one of the reasons he refuses to return to Great Meadow or have anything to do with his father. Like the pornographer's attitude to the baby in *The Pornographer*, Luke's absence and the intensity of his rejection of his father and Great Meadow remain a disturbing mystery in the novel. His behaviour toward Moran seems out of all proportion to the few details of their relationship that the narrator provides and as a result it is reasonable to assume that, as with their predecessors in *The Dark*, sexual as well as physical abuse occurred in their past together. There is a hint of Moran's capability of sexual abuse in the description of his 'kneading hand' on Michael when they wake the morning of Moran's wedding (see *AW*, 39); it is the same prelude to sexual interference that occurs in *The Dark* and that McGahern describes suffering at the hands of his father in his memoir. Like the Mahoneys and like McGahern and his father, Moran and his son sleep in the same bed and Michael's 'uncertain' feelings and quick exit from the room are familiar and suspicious. Another disturbing echo, this time of Mahoney's abusive behaviour in the opening chapter of *The Dark*, occurs later when Moran orders Michael to go upstairs and strip so that he can beat him with a strap. Significantly, Michael tells his lover, Nell, that Moran used to force Luke to strip before he beat him in the upper room. Like Mahoney's, Moran's actions are illuminated by McGahern's belief that his father's physical abuse had a sexual origin (*AW*, 112–13; *M*, 188).

The Morans, the McGaherns, and the Narrator

McGahern's narrative voice in *Amongst Women* marks a dramatic advance in the nature and process of his writing, but it remains a noticeably *directive* voice; indeed, it is because some readers fail to recognize the *direction* the narration gives that they emphasize the novel's achievements as a work of social realism. That emphasis, however warranted, distracts from the way the narration achieves the completion of a profoundly personal process of purgation. McGahern's first-person narrators served him well and in terms of what he needed his story-telling to achieve, he could not have told what he had to tell in any other way; but they could not take him the full distance to where he had to go. The narrative voice of *Amongst Women* is the turning-point he was heading for and Patrick Moran and the pornographer took him to the turn. The sophistication of McGahern's technique in *Amongst Women* is a reflection of the complexity of the recollective imagination that produces the novel, a complexity which sees the sublimated presence of the autobiographical first-person not only *in* the third-person narrator, but also evoked and released in the narrative voice by a subtle ventriloquism in which the fictive surrogate of the author, who is kept off-stage for most of the novel, speaks through the narrator by means of an irregular network of intra- and inter-textual echoes, associations and connections.

An important indication of how far McGahern had progressed in this regard is the description of Sean Flynn and his mother at Sheila and Sean's wedding reception. One cannot help thinking that what McGahern describes in this paragraph could – should – have been a version of *his* wedding, if his mother had not died when he was a child. How different things would have been. He, too, would have disappointed his mother's hopes for him becoming a priest; he would have become a teacher rather than a civil servant, and eventually a writer, and would have been content, as well, with 'the mere life of any man with a woman' (*AW*, 154). But most of all, he would have been able to 'look back' to her in a profoundly different way from that which her death and his childhood and adolescence without her had shaped, because he would not have had to endure the hell that descended upon him and his siblings following her death or spend all those years struggling against the abjection that life under his father's rule made a daily horror (see *M*, 186–7, 197–9). In one of the saddest lines in his memoir, McGahern writes: 'A child can become infected with unhappiness' (*M*, 23). The writing process, story-telling, the making of art, became for McGahern the antibiotic that ultimately eradicated the *anti-life* of the infection which coursed within him. There is no greater evidence that that infection was over, however, than when he takes the mother's dream and her son's disappointment of it, which, as the memoir makes clear, was central to his own relationship with his mother and deeply intertwined with the guilt and pain he felt over his failed leave-taking, and places it all in the life of a minor character like Sean Flynn. This material *had* to be presented in the first-person in *The Leavetaking*; but because of what he achieved from writing that novel, and because of what writing Moran's story was achieving, at this point, McGahern had worked free of this baggage. He gives it away to another character, the character of an 'other', a 'brother-in-law' by the law of fiction, not a surrogate of the authorial self; and in giving it away, he lets go of it.

The moral dimension of this novel is to be found in the profound generosity of the narrative voice's combination of understanding and judgment in the presentation of the Moran girls, Michael, Rose, and even Moran himself, in whose presentation there is also a degree of forgiveness. The narrator 'corrects' the girls' and 'directs' the reader's understanding of things with varying degrees of explicitness, subtlety and understatement. When Maggie lies to Rose's mother about Moran's physical abuse of his children, the narrator intrudes with unequivocal explanatory authority: 'Shame as much as love prompted the denial' (*AW*, 34). The direction is more subtle at the beginning of the novel when the girls want to buck up Moran's flagging spirit by reviving the ritual of Monaghan Day, hoping 'it could turn his slow decline around like a Lourdes' miracle' (*AW*, 2). The simile is an ironic tonal signal: the narrator then steps in to inform us that the girls' enthusiasm for the idea seems to require an equal effort of repression: 'Forgotten was the fearful nail-biting exercise Monaghan Day had always been for the whole house; with distance it had become large, heroic, blood-mystical, something from which the impossible could be snatched' (*AW*, 2). This sounds very similar to nationalist myth-memory of the War of Independence itself. A more pointed judgment comes later in the novel when the narrator describes the girls' relief and gratitude for Moran's sociable behaviour when they visit after Michael has run away to Luke in London: 'they were grateful for anything short of his worst moods, *inordinately* grateful for the slightest goodwill, what they barely would have accepted from an equal' (*AW*, 129; my emphasis). Because of the way the narrator has presented the girls' growth from childhood through adolescence, we understand why they feel like this, but the narrator's language plainly does not intend us to condone it.

The most important instances of narrative direction compose the central theme in the novel, which takes up the effect Moran has had on his daughters' emotional and psychological development, their construction of the myth of 'Daddy' and Great Meadow, and the illusory and pernicious sense of 'superiority' that the myth has generated within their self-image. A reader would have to be extraordinarily inattentive to the narrative voice to think that the novel is an unequivocal celebration of the identity-forming influence of Great Meadow on the Moran children. On the second page McGahern has the narrator declare his colours: 'On the tides of Dublin or London they were hardly more than specks of froth but together they were the aristocratic Morans of Great Meadow, ... Moran's daughters' (*AW*, 2). A lengthier qualification of the benefits of Great Meadow's nurture that more explicitly outlines the nature of the delusion it has generated in the girls comes later when the narrator explains the importance of their weekend visits after they have all left home; the passage illuminates as well an important feature of the narrative voice:

> These visits of his daughters from London and Dublin were to flow like relief through the house. They brought distraction .... Above all they brought the bracing breath of the outside, an outside Moran refused to accept unless it came from the family. Without it there would have been an ingrown wilting. For the girls the regular comings and goings restored their superior sense of self, a superiority they had received intact from Moran and which was little acknowledged by the wide world in which they had to work and live. That unexamined notion of superiority was often badly shaken and in need of restoration each time they came home. Each time he met them at the station his very presence affirmed and reaffirmed again as he kissed them

goodbye. Within the house the outside world was shut out. There was only Moran, their beloved father; within his shadow and the walls of his house they felt that they would never die; and each time they came to Great Meadow they grew again into the wholeness of being the unique and separate Morans. (*AW*, 93–4)

What impresses here is the precision of McGahern's psychological notation – how he shows the reciprocity of need between Moran and his daughters. As the children leave Great Meadow and Moran is left alone with Rose, it is clear her presence is not enough to keep him going. His children had always been the distorting mirror that assured him of his presence in their lives, the sounding board that echoed his rage against life and the world. His family and his acts of aggression against them were what had kept him from collapsing inward into the emptiness at his core. Now when he looks about him into the space they once filled, he feels as if he is an empty presence (*AW*, 91); it is this inward wilting that he experiences the first evening after Mona and Sheila leave for Dublin. As he grows older, Moran comes to rely on his children to provide him with a sense of security against the world and life he had always feared, a fear he used to manage by striking out at those who could not defend themselves against him.[7] In the same way that the narrator's description of the girls' future as 'the living stream they were about to enter' (*AW*, 80) implies that their past home-life has been an immersion in something less oxygen-rich, so 'the bracing breath of the outside' implies a stale and stagnant atmosphere within Moran's house. What the girls receive in exchange for resuscitating a slowly suffocating Moran, a recharged sense of their superiority, is clearly as delusory in the narrator's view as their feeling of immortality is silly.

The narrator wants the reader to recognize that it is an unexamined notion of superiority that the girls hold to and that their selective memories of Moran and Great Meadow reaffirm, and thus it is an equally unexamined sense of 'wholeness' that they take away from the place. Nor does the narrator seem to credit the value of thinking oneself 'unique and separate'; McGahern's previous narrators have usually considered these attributes of

---

7   A passage in the memoir speaks directly to this point; see McGahern on 'The beating, the cries, the shouts, the anger …' (*M*, 197).

an inexorable human condition rather than a cause for celebration. The commonalty of human joys and suffering experienced by unique individuals is a paradox at which McGahern's fiction often marvels. Moreover, what is clear from the novel is that any sense of superiority the Moran girls have developed is a 'negative' superiority derived from their internalization of Moran's scorn, cynicism, bitterness, and sense of injustice suffered at the hands of a world inhabited and run by inferior others. The Moran girls do not feel superior because they spent their childhood and adolescence nurtured by the praise of a parent who told them they were beautiful, brilliant and capable of achieving whatever they dreamt; they feel superior because they have spent their lives listening to Moran run everyone else down.[8] Finally, this passage makes us particularly aware of the distance between the narrative voice and the girls. In his memoir McGahern describes a gap that opened between himself and his younger siblings during childhood (*M*, 178–9) and one can hear this in the novel in the narrator's descriptive analysis of the Moran girls and their feelings toward Moran and Great Meadow.[9] The narrator – like Luke, and like McGahern, presumably – clearly does not share these feelings even though he understands them

8   The narrator also discredits the girls' sense of superiority later in the novel when he describes Maggie's fiancé Mark's surprise at the change that comes over her at Great Meadow (*AW*, 135).

9   This distance is particularly resonant in the effect of the repeated 'They' of the narrator's description of the girls' return for the holiday, as well as in the allusion to the absent Luke in the ironically alliterative and elegiacally cadenced 'all, almost all' (*AW*, 96). Moran's offering up of the Rosary for the absent Luke two paragraphs later exhausts whatever emotional capital the girls' sense of returning to their familiar world might have brought, and the narrator's comment that Moran's 'dramatizing of the exception drew uncomfortable attention to the disturbing bonds of their togetherness' (*AW*, 96) is a rather pointed reminder of McGahern's sense of difference from his sisters in his feelings for his father: what is 'disturbing' about the girls' 'bonds of togetherness' is that they accentuate Luke's absence, and what is 'uncomfortable' about that is that their happiness underscores their *acceptance* of it. The language further undermines the sense of 'wholeness' (*AW*, 93) that the narrator describes as one of the delusions encouraged by the myth of Great Meadow that the girls have constructed together.

and their psychological efficacy as survival tactics. Indeed, as the story unfolds, Luke's physical distance within it seems an analogue for the narrative distance McGahern wants to maintain in order to facilitate the kind of analytical judgment his narrator makes in passages such as this.[10]

Forms and acts of attention are a motif in the novel and structure the narrator's descriptive analysis of Moran and Maggie before she leaves for London. Before he replaced her with Rose, Moran had used Maggie as a domestic 'drudge' (*AW*, 61), and once he agrees to let her leave Great Meadow (which he does when he is sure he will not be out of pocket as a result), he comes on to her as Prince Charming.[11] Before Rose arrived, he had given Maggie little attention and she blossoms under her step-mother's influence; but in getting Maggie out of the house as soon as possible, Rose is as much the cunning manipulator as she had been when courting Moran.[12] The sooner Maggie leaves to take up her life, the sooner Rose can

10   See, for example, *AW*, 145. This sense that the narrator and Luke are on the same narrative plane grows throughout the novel so that, following Maggie's unsuccessful attempt to convince him to visit Great Meadow, the narrator's description of the threat Luke's withdrawal posed to their sense of wholeness is clearly critical of them; the language subtly – but ambiguously – describes them thinking like Moran: 'Together they were one world and could take on the world' (*AW*, 145). The narrator makes clear that he sees the girls as having internalized their insecure and xenophobic father's view of the function of family. The same critical voice is heard when the narrator describes Michael's need to have his sense of identity confirmed by Great Meadow (*AW*, 147). Later, at Sheila's wedding, when Luke repeatedly tells Maggie that he 'will not exist' (*AW*, 152, 155) his words echo this passage and affirm not only his 'amiable separateness' (*AW*, 144) from his siblings but his rejection of Great Meadow as the guarantor of his identity.

11   The narrator's tone here is noticeably directive. McGahern says of his father that, when he wanted or needed to, 'he could charm and seduce us' (*M*, 29).

12   Rose, in her own way, is after *power*, and her calculated manipulation of Moran is part of her campaign to become the power behind the throne at Great Meadow. Robert F. Garratt notes her 'subversive subservience' but distorts the insight by allegorizing and abstracting a very character-specific trait into 'the basis of McGahern's subtle critique of paternalism' ('John McGahern's *Amongst Women*: Representation, Memory, Trauma', *Irish University Review* 35.1 [2005], 126). It is power, not paternalism, that McGahern 'critiques' in *Amongst Women*, and he is hardly 'subtle' when it comes to

consolidate her position in the household and increase Moran's reliance on her. Becoming his 'drudge' is a price she is willing to pay in return for the power over him it will bring in terms of the master-slave paradigm McGahern uses to construct their relationship (see *M*, 263–4).

McGahern's construction and development of Rose's character is on the whole much more positive than his memories of his stepmother in the memoir. For example, in *Amongst Women* the narrator says of Rose Moran that she was totally committed to her husband whom she loved even if she was afraid of his 'darkness' (*AW*, 60), but in his memoir, McGahern describes Agnes and his father *sharing* 'a certain darkness' in their relationship (*M*, 247). (Unlike his father, McGahern's stepmother was alive when he wrote and published *Amongst Women*; Agnes McGahern died in 1998.) Rose's love for Moran is sincere and strong, her devotion and loyalty unquestionable; the strength of the characterization is that McGahern conveys all of this while at the same time showing her acting intelligently, wisely, 'tactfully', to advance and safeguard her own self-interests, and without generating any sense of contradiction or incoherence in the character. Rose is an older, more desperate version of Elizabeth Reegan, but without the imaginative intelligence and sensitivity of that character. McGahern re-cycles some of Elizabeth's thoughts and feelings about her motives for marrying Reegan to describe Rose's hope that Moran represented her last chance for a life of her own (*AW*, 30; see *B*, 210). Like Elizabeth with

exposing Moran's megalomania or Rose's petty counter-campaign. McGahern told Whyte that, as far as he was concerned, *Amongst Women* was 'essentially ... a novel about power' (*History, Myth, and Ritual*, 232). Rose is simply going after power in the way she thinks will succeed and by the end of the novel it has. McGahern described Agnes McShera, his father's second wife, as 'both his slave and master' (*M*, 5); he also described her as his father's 'terrier' (*M*, 219) and admitted that from the beginning he and his stepmother were 'enemies' (*M*, 207). Before marrying Francis McGahern, who was 10 years her elder, Agnes had worked for a stockbroker in Manchester (*M*, 206): before marrying Moran, Rose, who was 'much younger' than Moran (*AW*, 27), had worked for a family in Glasgow (*AW*, 22). Like Rose, Agnes called her husband 'Daddy' (*M*, 215). Moran's treatment of Rose seems to derive from Francis McGahern's 'ongoing war with Agnes' (*M*, 220). An early version of Rose and Moran appears in McGahern's short story, 'Wheels', in *Nightlines*.

Reegan, however, Rose soon realizes that Moran is not what he seemed during their brief courtship, but her vanity would never allow her to admit she had made a mistake (*AW*, 53). After Elizabeth Reegan, Rose is Moran's most complex female character and his achievement with her, considering his feelings for the woman she is based on, is clear evidence not only of the maturity of his technique in *Amongst Women*, but also of how far he had evolved in terms of a *poiēsis* that shaped the personal into the fictive.

Moran's attention to Maggie is more sinister than Rose's, however. 'His instinct was to draw her closer to him' (*AW*, 61) and he does this by changing the form of attention he pays to her, counselling her about life beyond Great Meadow. Unused to this kind of attention, Maggie is smitten: 'Daddy is great', she proudly announces to the others in the house; and their responses are carefully crafted by McGahern's narrator: Rose is silent but visibly pleased; Mona acknowledges Moran can be nice when he wants to; Sheila adds that all their lives would be better if Moran was 'always that way' (*AW*, 61–2). Though present, Michael makes no contribution to the conversation once he realizes it is not about him. The motive behind Rose's pleasure, like her rebuke of Sheila, is ambiguous, like so much of her 'tact' (*AW*, 34). Sheila's remark itself is fitting considering her future relationship with Moran. Mona's tautology more or less expresses the weak form of stubbornness Moran's influence on her has built up. And Michael's silence, like his posture, suggests the extremes of submission and rebellion in his future, as well as the craving for attention that Rose will come to satisfy, only to turn Moran against him.

It is Moran's theatrical manipulation of Maggie and the others that the narrator brings out on her last night at Great Meadow. He ends the obligatory rosary with a special prayer for his daughter's safety out in the dangerous world beyond Great Meadow, intoned with a dramatic emphasis that brings the woman to the brink of tears (*AW*, 62). Following the celebratory farewell feast prepared by Rose, 'Maggie looked at him with the light of love as she kissed him good night. He was her first man, her father, as she faced for London and the further opening of her life' (*AW*, 62). The narrator's tone here connotes, among other things, a recognition of the resilience of the human heart as well as the capacity of the mind, when it must, to repress what it knows in order to let the heart grow. The structure of the second sentence here subtly insinuates that 'the light of love' in Maggie's eyes is as much the backwash of her excitement and anxiety about the future as tears of gratitude and affection. And the irony in '*further* opening of her life', considering Moran's chokehold on her growth, only adds to the sinister resonance in 'He was her first man'. Maggie is a mess and it is Moran who has messed her up. The narrator further directs our understanding of Moran's influence on her when he describes Moran, Rose and Maggie on the station platform. Like Moran, Maggie waits in silence pointedly ignoring the other people around them, while Rose tactfully 'responded to each greeting with warmth, careful to watch that her friendliness did not grate on Moran' (*AW*, 62). There is an unmistakeable note of clarification and judgment when the narrator tells us that Maggie considered the isolation Moran had imposed upon his children to be the source of their 'distinction and strength' (*AW*, 63). One can only hope London will be gentle with her and give her time to find her way in a world Moran has done his best to leave her unprepared for.[13]

With Maggie gone to London, the narrator's attention turns to Mona and Sheila. Both are bright at school but Sheila in particular not only has university potential but also the keen desire to go; however, growing up under Moran has left her with a passive-aggressive personality that will put her at a disadvantage in the competitive world beyond Great Meadow (*AW*, 66). The narrator again directs our understanding of the characters and the world of Great Meadow when he says that the girls used their school homework as a way to isolate and protect themselves from Moran's attention (*AW*, 64). Moran understands Great Meadow to be, like Prospero's island, a refuge from the world he abhors, but ironically it is he who drives his children to seek a refuge from him within it. Both Mona and Sheila see education as a way of escaping their father's house (*AW*, 67). It is a risky venture, however, because the more they concentrate on their

---

13   Maggie is based in part on McGahern's sister Rosaleen, and her ironic remark to McGahern when he visited her in London is sadly relevant to this point: McGahern asked how she was getting on in London, and 'she smiled sadly: "Life in the barracks was a great preparation. Everything here is a cakewalk by comparison"' (*M*, 213).

studies, the more Moran senses he is being placed 'outside their circle of concentration' (*AW*, 77), a feeling that could rebound violently against them. The effect on Moran of the intensity of attention they give to their studies is to cause more cracks to open in the façade of his power. Their anxiety derives from their recognition that their future lives depend upon their positive results, and Moran, in turn, is left 'feeling vulnerable' (*AW*, 77) against a reality greater than the paranoid, xenophobic farrago he imposed on his children.

As they become adolescents and then approach adulthood it is inevitable that they should realize that Moran's stature as the omnipotent deity of the world known as Great Meadow was always a stature based on his power over children and the limited horizons that encircled them, a delusion they could neither escape nor challenge until even he could no longer prevent their seeing beyond Great Meadow to the 'the wide world in which they had to work and live'. This sense of the screen of childhood suddenly falling down to reveal the 'wizard' behind it as no more than an old man, mortal, vulnerable, and in Moran's case, utterly devoid of self-knowledge, is almost comically foreshadowed in the scenes when, while the girls are awaiting their results, he comes in each evening covered from head to foot in the lime he has been spreading on his fields. The image of him chanting 'I'm a boody man' (*AW*, 73) and chasing Rose and the children around the room, however, is grotesquely ironic more than funny. The ogre of fairytale is too powerful an archetype and has been too active beneath the surface of McGahern's characterization of Moran for the scene to be anything but comically sinister. Moran may be becoming a ghost of his former self, but he still has some teeth left. Not until he is defeated in his 'combat' with Michael will he – and we – know that his reign is finally coming to an end.

The narrator also directs the reader's understanding of the girls' love of Great Meadow. Peach's recognition that the women in *Amongst Women* 'are associated with a heightened sensitivity to the beauty in nature' – illustrated by the repeated phrase 'dear presence' – attests to the continuing presence of McGahern's mother's influence.[14] In his memoir, he bears

14   Peach, *Contemporary Irish Fiction*, 90.

witness to the influence of her love of nature upon him as a child and her continuing presence in his lifelong love of the flowers, hedges, lanes and lakes of his beloved Leitrim (*M*, 44–5, 57). This influence permeates his characterization of Elizabeth Reegan at the beginning of his writing life and reaches its apogee in his last novel. It would be a mistake to associate the Moran girls' feelings for their beloved landscape with Moran as some kind of benign deity who has shepherded his children's sensibilities in this respect. The scene in which Maggie and her sisters go out to the fields where Moran is working the day after her return for her summer break is instructive here, and the 'cycle' of mood swings that follow their encounter with him is typical of the unstable psychological weather in Moran's world. It is their evident enjoyment of the beautiful summer morning in conjunction with finding Moran in an apparently good mood that again leads Maggie to enthuse about 'Daddy' and Mona to agree. The narrator then quietly directs our understanding of their feelings: 'The girls in their different ways wanted to gather their father and the whole, true, heartbreaking day into their arms'; but when he enters the house that evening, 'Moran's mood had completely turned again' (*AW*, 81). It is the 'again' that shows the narrator's continuous *attention* in the novel to directing the reader's understanding of Moran and the way he has moulded his children's characters and outlooks. The cause of the mood change is his brooding obsession with Luke.[15]

This epitome of the girls' shared illusion about their lives at Great Meadow is also subtly undercut by the narrator and by McGahern's narrative structure, which follows it with yet another of Moran's deflating mood swings. Maggie's stay strengthens the bond between the sisters and that bond is bound up with their sense of connection to Great Meadow: 'In London or Dublin the girls would look back to the house for healing. The remembered light on the empty hayfields would grow magical ... the house would become the summer light and shade above their whole lives' (*AW*, 85). The narrator's language makes it clear that this is a passage about the emotional power and real psychological nourishment of nostalgia. McGahern is in no way criticizing the characters for forgetting or repressing the

---

15 Note that Rose discovers that feeding this obsession is the best way to ingratiate herself with him (see *AW*, 132).

lives they lived at Great Meadow, of which such moments in the fields were a brief and momentary exception to the norm. But he *is* carefully presenting this kind of memory and its value so that we understand the after-life of the characters' childhood. It should be noted that Moran and Rose are conspicuously absent, indeed, excluded from the passage. McGahern is drawing on his own memories of the close bond between his sisters – a closeness that was forged in reaction and defence *against* their father (see *M*, 159–60, 178–9). With wonderful precision he captures the balance between self and other that composes the girls' happiness at such moments in each other's company and which is a welcome respite, a 'healing', from the pain of becoming that is otherwise life. But the light grows 'magical' in memory because that is the nature and power of nostalgic memory and, when needed, its function, namely, to provide the overarching structure 'above their whole lives'. However, this high-point in the girls' ability to shape memory into a nurse is followed by yet another instance of Moran's treacherous emotional nature.

When Mona and Sheila learn they have done not just very well on their exams, but in Sheila's case, 'brilliantly', Rose congratulates them but Moran throws cold water on their excitement (*AW*, 86). Sheila senses immediately that he is referring to her dream of attending university. When she receives the offer of a scholarship his reserve is as hurtful as when he told them he had not praised them publicly in the post-office for fear of appearing to boast (*AW*, 87; see *M*, 6). Sheila wants desperately to take the scholarship and pursue a medical degree, but, disheartened by the knowledge that Moran would not support her and unwilling to confront him about it, she goes into the Civil Service instead. There is no sense that the narrator is trying to justify Moran's attitude when he proffers the explanation for Moran's treatment of his daughter that he was loath to see her join the class of priests and doctors who had taken power in the land once Moran and his kind had done the necessary killing (*AW*, 88); rather, the explanation only confirms Moran's narcissism. For Moran, the issue of Sheila's future has more to do with *his* past than her happiness; moreover, his perspective is so self-centred that he cannot see that the country he had fought for was now offering his daughter the kind of chance at life he had never had, and so clearly *was* repaying his sacrifice. The whole episode of Moran's reaction to his daughters' academic success and Sheila's career choices – and their reactions to his reaction – is more evidence of the distortions of self and personality that his character has exacted on his daughters. The narrator's judgment is as unequivocal as Moran's behaviour is dishonest. Once Sheila commits herself to a government job, Moran 'courts' her with cryptic suggestions that he might be able to find the extra funds she would need; but Sheila knows her father too well, knows that if she were to respond with hope he would quickly change his mind and never raise the subject again (*AW*, 89; see also *M*, 208).

While McGahern shows Rose and his daughters 'enabling' Moran's tyranny, at the same time he also shows how this is often more a strategy for controlling or deflecting the ogre's rage. The effect is to preserve Moran's narcissistic delusions, of course, and may seem to hinder any possibility of change in the man or their situation, but the novel makes clear that any peace of mind Moran ever had or could have had was fatally broken by Luke's rejection of him years ago. Moreover, Moran's tyranny was established during the years following his first wife's death when the children were incapable of resisting it, let alone preventing it, and had to expend all their energy and intelligence merely trying to endure their father's violent and incomprehensible will (*AW*, 54; see *M*, 159).

The narrator's management of the relationship between Moran and Luke, and indeed, of *his* 'relation' to Luke, is one of the most sophisticated aspects of McGahern's achievement in *Amongst Women*. Luke appears on the opening page of the novel as the exception amongst the Moran children who will not return to Great Meadow. The language implies a history of requests and refusals. Maggie, Mona and Sheila have no sooner arrived with their gifts for the surprise celebration of Monaghan Day than Moran raises the subject of Luke's continued silence in response to his letters, and suddenly becomes morose and withdrawn; we are told that Rose and the girls knew better than to speak Luke's name within Moran's hearing (*AW*, 4). Sampson notes that 'Luke in his absence is more real to Moran than Rose and his daughters'.[16] The repeated image of Moran sitting in the car-chair

---

16   *Outstaring Nature's Eye*, 226. During the excitement of Maggie's return for her first summer holiday mention of Luke sends Moran into another funk that gradually builds into one of his self-pitying outbursts (*AW*, 79–81). The issue of Luke's infuriating refusal to answer Moran's letters is based on McGahern's own evasion of his father's

twiddling his thumbs and staring morosely into space is encoded with the suggestion of his puzzlement by his son's rejection. Whenever he thinks of Luke, Moran thinks of him as wanting 'to get back at me' (*AW*, 63), but McGahern never explicitly tells us why. When she comes home from London, Moran presses Maggie for information as if he was back in the war and interrogating a prisoner. His exasperation, after she tells him all the details she knows, reveals just how much Luke's absence is at the centre of Moran's mystery: 'I don't know what I did to deserve it. ... I don't know why it is always *me* that has to be singled out' (*AW*, 82). Moran doesn't know *what* he wants to know, but he knows that there is something he *should* know and only Luke can tell him. What baffles Moran is that Luke, unlike all his other children, is a mirror in which Moran cannot see himself.

Luke's absence is a thread that runs through the novel as much as the family's daily recital of the rosary and the two motifs are intertwined by McGahern. The rosary motif has a number of features: Moran reaching for the leather pouch that holds his beads, placing the newspaper on the floor to kneel on, and ordering his family to take their positions for the prayer; his offering of the prayer for some family need; an often awkward moment when one of the usual participants' absence causes a stutter in the rotation of the decades; and occasionally, an impromptu closing prayer for effect. The narrator clearly presents this daily ritual as an instrument of Moran's authoritarian domestic regime through which he reasserts his dominance over the family while at the same time drilling them in the exophobic, centripetal focus that sustains it. Yet there is an obvious irony running through the motif that is accentuated on those occasions where one of the participants is missing: when Rose goes to her room following Moran's insult; after Maggie goes to London; and after Mona and Sheila leave for Dublin. Each of these moments reminds us that there has been a gap in the family circle from the very beginning of the novel. Luke's absence from the

---

persistent attempts to correspond with him when he was working in London before attending teacher's college and afterwards during his years teaching in Dublin (see *M*, 213–15).

prayer cycle is the missing link that prevents their family circle from being the symbol of perfection Moran and the girls want to believe it is.

It is important to recognize that from the opening pages and the first reference to the absent Luke, McGahern is quietly informing us that the Moran family is already 'broken' and has been for some time. Late in the novel, the irony in Moran's speaking the cliché – 'They say the family that prays together stays together' (*AW*, 137) – is so extreme it seems a rare instance of McGahern's loss of control, and yet it is a credible statement given the character's lack of self-consciousness and the magnitude of his self-delusion. All the forced prayers have not kept the Moran family together. Luke's absence is such a powerful presence in the novel that its evocation by the rosary scenes results in the rosary itself coming to seem a broken ritual, a dead form, and Luke's story a crucially missing 'mystery' in the novel. The way McGahern conveys that Moran's spoken references to Luke are just the tips of his conscious and unconscious preoccupation with his son is one of the great 'touches' in this novel that reflects the deftness of narrative control as well as the depth of his writing's continuing engagement with its autobiographical sources.

Father History: Moran, McGahern, and Post-Revolutionary Ireland

McGahern's examination of his father's impact on his children is one aspect of the 'father history' that *Amongst Women* explores. Sampson recognizes this when he notes that 'Their love for Moran is inextricably bound not only to their fear of him personally but to the fear of life he has transmitted to them'.[17] But there is a dimension to this 'father history' in which Moran and the fictive world of *Amongst Women* take on allegorical qualities. The hero-worship and female idolatry that abound at Great Meadow,

17   *Outstaring Nature's Eye*, 232.

like birdsong in an abattoir, opens up the novel to other senses of family and patriarchal history: the history of the Irish 'nation', Irish society and culture in the half century from independence to the time of McGahern's father's death in 1977. This dimension of the novel thus picks up the note introduced in the scene at Comiskey's at the end of *The Pornographer*.[18] In his memoir, McGahern is critical of universalizing 'discourses' that abstract the concrete and generalize the particular, associating them with the bogus propagandizing of nationalist ideologues. Referring to the era covered by *Amongst Women*, he asserts that in his experience regional and communal identities took priority over national consciousness, and of the latter, acknowledgement was token rather than deeply undertaken (*M*, 211). It may be here, however, that the Moran family becomes an allegorical figure for the 'Irish family' in the sense of the society and culture of the spirited and idiosyncratic local communities that resisted assimilation into any ideologically constructed notion of the 'new Ireland' even as they smiled at its salesmen (see *M*, 210).

But in as much as the Morans and Great Meadow may represent McGahern's belief in the origin of individual identity in small communities, deciphering the Morans as an allegorical family is a tricky proposition.[19] McGahern's criticisms of the Ireland of his childhood, adolescence and early years as an adult in his memoir and elsewhere *accord* with Moran's, suggesting that, on one level of the characterization, McGahern is using Moran to critique a Dublin-centred postcolonial society and culture by making him the stalwart representative of a particular regional identity and 'traditional' local culture.[20] But on another level, Moran is clearly the *object*

---

18   Sampson describes *Amongst Women* as 'a fable about the society created after independence' (Ibid., 215).

19   Eamonn Hughes notes this even as he constructs Great Meadow as 'a metonym for Ireland'; Hughes regards the novel as more than a political allegory, however, and rejects the notion of Moran as a De Valera-like patriarch ('"All That Surrounds Our Life": Time, Sex, and Death in *That They May Face the Rising Sun*', *Irish University Review* 35.1 [2005], 151).

20   Moran articulates a narrower, more self-interested version of McGahern's views about the failure of the Irish revolution to deliver social and cultural change commensurate

of a critique that reveals the 'community' he centres to be nothing more than an exaggeration of his own ego and a terribly distorting influence on those unfortunate enough to be born within its confines. For all Moran's separation of himself from the *arrivistes* of Church and State that emerged to take power in post-revolutionary Ireland, and which McGahern holds responsible for much of the economic, social, and cultural deficiencies of the Ireland of his youth (*M*, 211), *Amongst Women* clearly depicts Moran and his influence as emblematic of the hypocritical, religiose, repressive, unimaginative, xenophobic, inward-turning, navel-worshippng nationalist-clerical society that McGahern recalls in his memoir.[21] On this level of reading, Luke's self-exile from Great Meadow reflects McGahern's own departure from Ireland following the 'scandal' of his treatment by the clerical-secular compact over *The Dark*, and the girls' and Michael's nostalgic construction of Great Meadow as a source of identity, if it points to anything outside the fictive world of the novel, may point to the urban-bourgeois-nationalist myth of the rural Irish heartland, just as Moran's militant refusal to examine his past except in the severely censored and selective memories he shares with his idolizing daughters may reflect the selectively self-serving version of nationalist history that dominated Irish public discourse for so long in the last century.

There is a way of reading the Morans, allegorically, as a family, however, which is also rooted in the fact that they are obviously a fictive reconstruction of the McGaherns. In his interview with González, McGahern disagreed with the interviewer's unquestioning recourse to Irish cultural

---

with the political changes brought by independence. In relation to the claims of the 1916 Proclamation, McGahern considered the revolution bogus and the new state morally bankrupt and imaginatively moribund, blinkered and hidebound by a dogmatic Church and 19c nationalist ideologies: 'in a way the revolution never happened. ... nothing changed ... women were badly off' (McGahern in González, 'John McGahern', 43; see also *M*, 48–9). McGahern considered *Amongst Women* 'very subversive' because of its critique of the Church's role in prolonging the disempowerment of women in the new Irish state.

21   See, for example, *M*, 210–13. Moran obviously deviates from this conventional set, however, in his admiration for the Anglo-Irish.

mythology to explain the widespread attention given to the family in
modern Irish fiction. In his view, it was not explained by 'the importance
of the family bond in Irish society' but rather reflected 'the narrow development of proper society [in Ireland]. There is no system of manners in this
country. ... I see the family as a sort of interesting half-way house between
the individual on one side and a larger society on the other hand, and one
is not alone, and one is in a society but it's not a true society, since certain
things will be tolerated within a family that won't be tolerated in a larger
society'.[22] The idea that what we see in Moran is a failure of manners may
seem morally and psychologically inadequate to the magnitude of his
character, but if we understand McGahern's interest in manners to derive
from his interest in the 'two things that have obsessed me all my life ... the
Self and the Other',[23] then what *Amongst Women* studies is the particular
set of deformations that characterize the growth of the individuals who
come under Moran's influence, a man who has an instinctive scorn for the
'mere Other' (*AW*, 178). McGahern told Sampson that 'To interfere with
the life of the Other would seem to me like bad manners or discourtesy'.
McGahern's portrait of Moran brings the self/other theme in his fiction
into its clearest focus, suggesting that all along, even in his own surrogate
first-person narrator-protagonists, his exploration of this theme was driven
by the unhealed wounds of his treatment by his father: why would anyone
treat another this way, let alone a father his children? To see Moran's house
as an allegorical 'half-way house between the individual on one side and a
larger society on the other hand' is to read *Amongst Women* as McGahern's
use of the writing of fiction in his personal search to understand the painful process of his own becoming, as well as a novel of broader historical-
moral reference to an Irish society that too long tolerated 'certain things'
within the family that it did not allow in open society. In his memoir, after
recounting incidents in which his father hit him on the head with a shovel,
drove Margaret into a fit, and beat Breedge with a spade, McGahern recalls
bitterly that, while there were beatings almost every day, often watched by

22   González, 'John McGahern', 42.
23   Sampson, 'A Conversation', 16.

the other policeman in the barracks, no one, not even the 'family doctor' who treated the children's injuries ever reported his father's behaviour (*M*, 187, 199). But while these observations belong to the general indictment of the patriarchal institutions of Church and State that tacitly colluded with the life of abuse McGahern's generation suffered at home and at school contained in his fiction, the relation between *Amongst Women* and the memoir shows that both remain less a call for a public inquiry than a personal attempt at truth and reconciliation. Towards the end of his memoir, McGahern records a conversation with his father noting that whenever his father entered a discussion it was with the sole object of dominating and tripping up his adversary, and that if his father felt that his indirect approach was not achieving the desired effect, he would not hesitate to become more offensive and insulting by contrasting other writers' celebrity, success and wealth with his son's. When his father asks him what he hopes to achieve from his writing, McGahern's reply is a key to understanding his whole writing life: 'To write well, to write truly and well about fellows like yourself' (*M*, 263). This is what the thunder in Leitrim once said. McGahern's reply is his *Datta, Dayadhvam, Damyata*: to write well was within his gift; to write well and truly was only possible with sympathy; and to write well the truth about his father required a moral and emotional control commensurate with his talent. *Amongst Women* is the work in which McGahern finally achieved this conscious aim as a writer, but he had been working toward that achievement, consciously and unconsciously, with every word he wrote leading to it. McGahern's recollection and reconstruction of a very particular father in *Amongst Women* does not preclude that process of reconstruction producing a character who is a representative type of patriarch-villain or heroic remnant or pastoral ruin, and many critics see Moran as larger than his textual self. In relation to his textual predecessors in McGahern's fiction, however, Moran's character is best understood as a particular formation of the masculine will and a pathological fear and loathing of others.

McGahern also shows Moran 'enabled' in much of what he does to his children by the institutionalized paternalism of Irish society embodied in the Catholic Church. McGahern himself said Moran 'uses the Church as a form of bullying'.[24] But what the novel shows most powerfully is not the effects of 'Catholic discourse'[25] so much as the actual physical, emotional, and economic oppression of women by a particular form of *masculine will* which, even though enabled by that institution and its misogynistic subordination of women, would behave as it did regardless of such institutional sanction. From what he writes in his memoir, by mid to late adolescence McGahern was distinguishing between the Catholic Church and Catholicism as historical institution and what he would always remember feeling when he experienced the 'ceremony and sacrament and mystery' of his favourite ritual (see *M*, 201).

McGahern's critique of the role of the Church in the continuing subjugation of women is so effective in *Amongst Women* because he focuses it in a single symbol – the rosary. It is such a powerful symbol because it repeatedly shows the women participating in their subjugation; moreover, by making it a daily ritual in Moran's household, McGahern shows the power of the Church to influence the characters' daily lives even though the ritual itself has lost any spiritual significance for them. In as much as the daily recitation is merely an instrument of Moran's will, it also symbolizes the continuing presence of the Church as merely a 'power' in the lives of such communities. The motif and symbolism of the rosary function in another way. Like the novel itself, the rosary is a circular form. The relation between the symbol and the form is ironic, however, because the circular form of the novel spirals upward in the comic resolution of the ending – the death of Moran and the liberation of his family, whereas the rosary goes round and round with no escape and no liberation. The rosary needs to be seen as a ritual symbolic of the centripetal discipline Moran imposes on his family, a circle with him at its idolatrous centre as well as policing its increasingly porous periphery, linking wife and children in a chain of worship he enforces with himself as the focus of their gaze. The rosary's centripetal form maintains the inward-turned perspective favoured by Moran, who constantly demeans his daughters' interest in the

---

24   González, 'John McGahern', 43.
25   Peach, *The Contemporary Irish Novel*, 84.

'wide world' beyond Great Meadow. The calm the ritual seems to bring to the participants, when not merely the heavy eyelids of boredom or exhaustion, is really the numbing of mind and will that is a condition for their acquiescence to Moran's myth that the family circle is a bulwark against the chaos outside, a light amidst the darkness of a historically, as well as theologically, fallen world.

The image and metaphor of the family in *Amongst Women* are thus particular *and* representative; they serve as the alembic of a *poiēsis* which distils memory into the precious grains of understanding. The material of McGahern's alchemy is the same elemental experience he has transformed in all his other novels and the understanding he seeks continues to be as much an understanding of the mystery of his own growth as an individual as of the darkness of the man who, paradoxically, shaped that growth even as he sought to stifle it. When Moran tells Maggie – with Luke in mind – that he held no favourites amongst his children and that he was open to all even if they were not open to him (*AW*, 98), McGahern was drawing on his memory of another one of his father's 'mantras' (see *M*, 231). The irony is that 'family' for Moran *is* all about exclusion and partition, about his paranoid constructions of self and other and the continual separation of 'us' from everyone else; that is how Moran has moulded his family and shaped his children's outlook and ethos, the girls' most successfully. When Sean makes a joke about Michael's bolting for England, Sheila silences his laughter, making it paradoxically clear that while he was 'in' her family he does not 'belong' to it (*AW*, 123). This is another scene in which the narrator's irony and understated judgment of the Morans can be missed by critics ideologically bent on reading the novel as a *hommage* to 'family'. When all the textual peaks and troughs are taken into consideration, *Amongst Women* is not a postcard that will appeal to the *Bord Fáilte* literary critics McGahern might be having fun with when he writes that the fugitive Michael's reception on the ferry to Holyhead suggested that everyone on the boat had either done what he was doing or wished they had (*AW*, 123–4).

The Nobodaddy of Great Meadow

In terms of McGahern's skills in characterization, Michael Moran is his greatest achievement but it is an achievement that follows from and builds upon his previous efforts. The character of Mahoney in *The Dark* is proof of this, but like all McGahern's father-figures before Moran, Mahoney is a monolith in comparison. The characterization that freed up McGahern to write Moran is that which produced the pornographer. McGahern's exploration of that narrator-protagonist's condition would have given him a way into the darkness that is Moran, who is less of a mystery if we think of him as suffering from a form of the same crippling emotional malaise as the pornographer. Moran's *acedia* is memorably expressed in his repeated whine, 'Who cares? Who cares anyhow?' (*AW*, 1, 3, 4, 175, 176, 178, 179), a motif that functions in tandem with his sad belief that 'Together we can do anything' (*AW*, 84). The sentiments are actually counter-pointed twice late in the novel, in scenes that convey the sense that Moran's failure is his failure to make and preserve a *masculine* community – symbolized by his driving Luke, and then Michael, from Great Meadow (*AW*, 108–9, 125). (The overarching irony of the novel's title's allusion to the 'Hail Mary' is its clue to Moran's condition as a self-imposed curse: for he does *not* feel 'blessed [to live] amongst women'.) Moran calls his children 'the troops' and his belief that together they can do anything is based perhaps on memories of his wartime successes as a leader of a flying column. But instead, Luke is a traitor, Michael a deserter, and Moran sees himself to be a victim of betrayal and disloyalty. The symptoms of his *acedia* – he is blind, self-pitying, and will not acknowledge responsibility for his self-disappointment – recall the pornographer. And his bathetically rhetorical 'Who cares?' increasingly illuminates the nature of his condition: *he* should care, care *for* and care *about*. Moran's *acedia* and its consequences go to the heart of his treatment of his family.

Moran's absence of caring – his inattention to the world of the other – is so noticeable because McGahern presents it through a paradox, Moran's cyclopic-panoptic, totalitarian surveillance of his family's every move.

Like the pornographer, Moran is a narcissist. After his wedding, even though the occasion belongs as much to Rose as to him, Moran demands to be the centre of attention (*AW*, 45). Moran is a spiritual miser who steals and hordes his children's freedom. His demand for their exclusive attention to him draws them into his cyclopic world, deprives, disconnects and imprisons them, stunts their growth. The word *focus* derives from the Latin for 'hearth' or 'fireplace', the centre of the home, the 'focal point' of domestic life. McGahern's narcissistic distortion of the family into his magnified self-image turns the house at Great Meadow into a grotesque focal-point for his family's forced attention to the vagaries of his ego. By keeping them focused on him he hopes to keep them from looking to the horizons beyond Great Meadow, or in Rose's case, even her mother's house down the road. This ogre of imagination cannibalizes his children's vision. The narrator subtly reminds us of Moran's voracious appetite for attention when he says that Moran was uncomfortable around people who were enjoying themselves because that usually meant they would be too distracted 'to pay attention to others' (*AW*, 61).[26]

Moran resents it when Mona and Sheila give more attention to their studies than to him; and when Maggie comes home the first summer after her move to London, he is 'bored' because he is not the centre of attention during her visit (*AW*, 79). He resents Rose taking her homemade bread and preserves to her mother, not simply because he is reluctant to give away anything that belongs to him, which he is, but because her gifts are evidence of her attention focused centrifugally, away from him (*AW*, 68). He cannot credit the fact that Rose returns with a greater amount of fresh produce in exchange because he will not acknowledge the value of anything outside his domain. After Maggie leaves for London, as Rose establishes her position in the house, Moran begins to torment and abuse her, finally insulting her in front of the children (*AW*, 69). Behind the cut is Moran's growing realization that his position at the centre of attention is no longer secure; he is in danger of becoming a mere 'figurehead', which is what he has become by the end of the novel. When Rose threatens to leave, he is forced

---

26 McGahern describes how his father resented others' joy and pleasure (*M*, 6).

to give way, and in doing so, he acknowledges her foothold in his house; she had called his bluff, and though their struggle would continue until his last breath, his death and her triumph were inevitable (*AW*, 71, 73). From his omniscient perspective on their relationship, the narrator informs us that their relationship steadily devolved into a 'deepening blindness' (*AW*, 71–2). Now, with increasing irony, the more Rose salves his vulnerability with her ministrations of 'pure attention' (*AW*, 73), like an addict, Moran seems to deteriorate under the effects of his addiction.[27]

At the beginning of the novel, it is clear that Moran is a shadow of his former self. He is losing heart and weary of 'wrestling' with a world he feels has only one focal point, himself, and ironically, one purpose, to mock him (*AW*, 45). From beginning to end the house at Great Meadow is the Cyclops' Cave: 'Amid it all was their constant awareness of Moran's watching presence .... All their movements were based more on habit and instinct and fear than any real threat but none the less it was an actual physical state. They would wash up the same way even if they were not watched' (*AW*, 79–80). This is more than description. The narrator wants us to note the effect on the girls of the years of Moran's abuse; they have so internalized their fear of their father that it now is a permanent, 'instinctive' response to his presence; it is a state of mind, a forced concentration that they experience as 'an actual physical state'. The narrator describes the effect induced by Moran's panoptic surveillance as a kind of vertigo. Moran's miser-like scrutiny of their handling of every article of his property is intensified by his growing realization that he was soon going to lose his daughters to 'the living stream' (*AW*, 80) that coursed beyond the stagnant pond of his personal 'concentration' camp. But until then, the girls are caught and held in his gaze like fish in a net (*AW*, 79).

---

27   McGahern drew on his father's 'ongoing war with Agnes' (*M*, 220) for Moran and Rose's early relationship, as well as the 'honeymoon' period of his father's marriage to Agnes for this particular point in Moran's relationship with Rose; note the language of attention in the memoir (*M*, 216) which corroborates the feeling that the archetypes of myth and fairytale underlie his characterization of the father-figures in his fiction, but also that the concept of attention and a centripetal/centrifugal dialectic inform the characterization and narrative structure in *Amongst Women*.

Moran's bitterness and resentment are products of his inverted world-view. The world – the universe – should care about him. He is the centre of the cosmos, so how can the cosmos *not* orient itself to his will? But like the meadow he repeatedly tries to reach as he is dying, the cosmos does not seem to know he exists. His experience on his wedding day, when the event is both anti-climactic and decentring, a nullity rather than a delight (*AW*, 45), recalls the pornographer's *acedia*. Elizabeth Reegan, too, experiences this feeling. But the difference is that Elizabeth and the pornographer possess sufficient imagination to eventually work through it. Moran does not. Like all bullies, his only strength is violent force, his only recourse is to lash out physically and 'punish' the world for disappointing him, a punishment he exacts upon the vulnerable around him. This is why Luke is such an obsession for Moran and why he turns so suddenly against Rose over the incident of the telegram. Afterwards, when he tries to explain his feelings to her, he almost apologizes, but cannot, and complains instead. Luke's telegram had made him feel as if he 'didn't even exist' (*AW*, 56). Moran cannot abide the feeling that he has become invisible to his son, a non-entity, someone not worth attending to – in a sense, he cannot abide the idea that Luke regards him as Moran himself regards any 'mere Other'. Luke is the Odysseus whose successful act of rebellion has permanently, even mortally, wounded the monster, and ironically, shown his ungrateful siblings the way out of the cave. This Cyclops, however, was already blind.

The possible aetiology of Moran's condition in the pornographer's *acedia* is all the more fascinating if one considers that in one sense the continuity suggests that McGahern is exploring the presence in his own personality of elements inherited from the dreaded father. This is also sensed when one hears Moran's complaint to Rose echoed later in Luke's self-description to Maggie at Sheila's wedding (*AW*, 152, 155). In McGahern's case, the origin is grief; so what was the source in the father? What grief or grievance turned him against life? Sampson describes Moran as 'a disillusioned hero' and 'frustrated religious searcher'.[28] Disillusioned hero and hypocritical man of faith, perhaps, but there is no credible evidence of the

---

28   Sampson, *Outstaring Nature's Eye*, 238.

'frustrated religious searcher'. The war-experience hypothesis is prominent in the opening pages of the novel and harkens back to Sergeant Reegan in *The Barracks* (see *B*, 109).[29] Like Francis McGahern, Reegan went from the IRA straight into the first-intake for the new police force. Moran, however, bought Great Meadow. The war-experience hypothesis is unsatisfactory for a number of reasons. Many people grow up in abject poverty but do not become thieves or, if so, use their background to explain their thievery. Many young men fought in the War of Independence; did they all become Morans? If not, then Moran is a *particular* damaged veteran, and not a figure to be taken as representative of patriarchy in rural Ireland in the first half of the 20c. The war-experience hypothesis risks justifying Moran: he is a victim of historical circumstances, his violent character is understandable, *poor Michael*. At most this line leads to the suspicion that, as Josephine says about the pornographer, there is 'something missing' in Moran, and it could have been missing all along; his war experiences may have contributed to the kind of man he became, but his character was already flawed. Other men with different characters were affected in other ways. Moran's war experience is less significant than a feature of his character that is related to it: his silence about the past.

Like his *acedia*, Moran's refusal to look into his past is another key to his character. Sampson remarks that 'Moran is presented objectively, with the narrative voice rarely entering his consciousness, or, indeed, the consciousness of any other character'.[30] But this objectivity is an illusion created by McGahern's construction of a narrative voice that *shapes* our understanding of Moran as much as it *directs* our understanding of the girls. For example, when the narrator tells us that Moran begrudges any attempt to bring up the past because he requires everyone to inhabit a present that is basically the aura and authority of his own presence (*AW*, 3), he not only reports something about Moran's 'consciousness', but also leads us toward a judgment of that consciousness. (McGahern is also preparing the effect

---

29   For Eamon Maher, Moran 'has been moulded by his environment and by the time
      he spent as a guerrilla fighter' (*John McGahern*, 105).

30   Sampson, *Outstaring Nature's Eye*, 217.

of Moran's death in the closing paragraphs, when time will suddenly seem to 'begin' with the end of the ogre's reign.) There is a great deal of judgment in this novel. It is not just his war experience that Moran does not want recalled; there are other parts of his past he does not want brought to account, in particular, his treatment of Luke. If we can impute an indirect relationship between the 'objective' narrator and McGahern's surrogate in the novel, Luke, then it is the unspoken history of father and elder son that 'shadows' and 'challenges' Moran throughout the novel, *not* his war experiences. As someone who represses memory Moran is the antithesis of McGahern himself, whose whole writing life has been a dredging up of the shadows that challenged not only his peace of mind but also his need to move on with his life. That Moran is drawn from McGahern's memories of his father is undeniable; but some of this quality of the character might express the resistance McGahern had to overcome within himself if he was to shape his experience and history into fiction.

What might appear to be the narrator's refusal to enter Moran's consciousness can be looked at from another angle, however, which might refine the point about Moran's attitude to his past. It may not be a refusal so much as an incapacity to do so. What Sampson sees as a feature of the narrative voice may be a reflection of something in the character that McGahern wants us to consider, namely, Moran's benighted interiority. Moran's secrecy and aversion to recollection and reflection are shadows in the fog of his inner 'darkness', the miasma of narcissistic complaint, envy, insecurity and spite that makes him as much a mystery to himself as to those unfortunate enough to spend large periods of their lives in his presence. The greatest paradox of this man is the enormity of his presence and the hollowness of his character; he is as solid as a mountain, yet a 'black hole' of anti-matter. His presence is a 'dead weight'. This deficit of interiority may also be considered a lack or failure of imagination – perhaps McGahern's best guess at an explanation of his own father's behaviour and character, and the connection between Moran's repression of memory and lack of interiority may reflect McGahern's ultimate view of Francis McGahern. Curious about his father's past, in *Memoir* McGahern said that he consciously decided not to pursue it, believing that a full understanding of the man would require more than just knowledge of his background (*M*,

49). With Michael Moran, however, McGahern does seem to confront the conundrum he faced in his father: either he was born with a defective 'mother-board' or something happened to wipe out his emotional 'software'. The narrator says that Moran 'seemed inherently unable to return' love (*AW*, 6) and McGahern follows this observation with the dramatic 'incongruity' of the women's relaxed breakfast chatter being suddenly interrupted by a shotgun blast when Moran shoots a jackdaw from the front room window. When he tells them that the only men he was ever really close to were those he looked at down the barrel of a rifle, and that he felt closest to them just before he killed them (*AW*, 7), Moran confirms our sense that the war merely hardened an already defective character.[31] The violent eruption of the gunshot prefigures the shock of his final outburst to the women praying at his deathbed. Both 'exclamations' are the desperate attempts of a man at his wit's end, striking back at the circle of women that has absorbed him.

Narcissism is as much about self and other as it is about Self. Narcissism is a failure of imagination, a failure to recognize the other as Other. The narcissist is mirror-man, blind man; and the Cyclops's perspective is, like the narcissist's, reductive, mono-topic, monotonous. The mirror vision sees only the Self, consuming the other as self-image. When Moran looks to the other his outlook consumes, cannibalizes; hence the fee-fie-fo-fum

---

31 Moran's behaviour as he waits outside for McQuaid on Monaghan Day, only to slip into the shadows to watch him get out of the car and approach the house, reinforces this sinister quality; it is the behaviour of an assassin, not a host (*AW*, 10–11); the narrator describes it as something he does 'instinctively'. The instinct is fear, however, and the paranoid need to feel he has the upper hand in any situation involving other people. McGahern shows this feature of Moran's character again when he describes him watching from a hiding spot when Sheila arrives with her fiancé (*AW*, 135); Moran waits until he has sized up Mark as a fool and then, confident of his superiority, approaches them with a supercilious smile on his face. Compare McGahern's description of his father's 'calculated coldness' when meeting a new member of his family for the first time (*M*, 7, 38, 257). Moran's mentality of inhabiting a world of combat, of kill or be killed, also surfaces after he writes a letter to Luke at Rose's suggestion and Luke responds with a brief, impersonal telegram; Moran is furious because it put him out in the open, an easy shot for anyone with a gun or a grudge (*AW*, 51).

eating-the-children business (*AW*, 47, 73, 99). When Rose moves in after the wedding, she soon notices the 'silence and deadness' that descends upon the children whenever Moran comes into the house (*AW*, 53). If they cannot escape his presence, they become 'like shadows' to try to escape his eye. When Moran releases his rage against her over the incident of Luke's telegram, Rose is stunned by his sudden transformation, but her vanity will not let her admit she has misjudged the man she has married. Moran attempts to grind her down into the same state of abjection that he has driven his children. As she talks intimately with him, opening up her feelings to him, with the children listening, Moran turns on her 'in a fit of hatred' (*AW*, 54). She is devastated, and slinks away abjectly to her room. After living with Moran only a short while, Rose begins to fear his 'darkness' (*AW*, 60). Moran refuses to allow the women to take over his life: 'He had never in all his life bowed in anything to a mere Other' (*AW*, 178). The narrator tells us that Moran 'secretly despised' the women who pursued him as a young man (*AW*, 26). Why? Presumably because *he* was the hunter, not the prey, and there is an echo of the pornographer in this aspect of his character.

Moran's narcissistic lack of imagination is total. Following his cruel outburst against Rose and his pathetic apology, he turns inward and spends the evening calculating his personal wealth; the final sum 'appeared to soothe him' (*AW*, 55). Moran ends the day completely self-absorbed, luxuriating in a bath of his own bitter psychic juices (*AW*, 55, 56). Taking stock of his wealth, the miser has no sense of basic human values; he may have permanently damaged Rose's affections for him, so what does he do? He calculates his independent 'worth' if he were to forego the substantial sum she had brought to the marriage and which was always part of her attractiveness to him. Moran is incapable of getting outside the cave of his own ego or of grasping the truth of the kind of family he has made (see *AW*, 12). The narrator develops this sense of incapacitating narcissism into a major strand in Moran's characterization (see *AW*, 22). However, the patriarchal family as a projective fantasy of the patriarch's ego that, when accepted by the family members, becomes a form of group delusion, is doomed by Moran's great adversary, time. As his children grow older and inevitably leave home, his sense of the family becomes insecure and begins to fail him in the same way his aging body seems to betray him. In as much as the family is a 'larger version' of Moran himself, the Moran family is itself a monstrosity, an extreme aberration of a norm.

The climax of the self/other theme in Moran's characterization is wonderful. His last words are other-directed, and characteristically, in the imperative mood: he commands the women praying for him to '*Shut up!*' (*AW*, 180). There is no more fitting epitaph for this pious reciter of the rosary, a man who had never in his life ever respected the 'mere Other' of the world and all its inhabitants, and whose will, if it were to have its way, would silence the universe, so that all he would have to hear was the echo of his own hollowness. Denis Sampson credits Moran with a 'brief epiphany' when he nears death and is amazed that the world will go on without him.[32] But Moran's self-pity makes this merely another instance of the inveterate sense of grievance that stokes his boiler: he cannot learn because he will not learn.

How Can We Blame Him, Was there Another Eden to Lose?

The personal history contained within the allegorical 'father-history' in *Amongst Women* complicates the portrait of Moran, many of whose attitudes toward post-independence Ireland seem to be McGahern's own. Moran's disillusionment with the aftermath of the revolutionary war is

---

32   Sampson, *Outstaring Nature's Eye*, 240; Sampson returns to his point in '"The Day Set Alight,"' 122. Maher too sees the character's insight instead of the narrator's judgment of the character when he credits Moran, who has been 'blind' to such observations until this point, with suddenly 'expressing a universal truth' (*John McGahern*, 105). Maher is aware, however, that 'For most of the novel, we don't get many insights into what Moran is feeling'; McGahern does not develop this character's interiority the way he did Elizabeth Reegan's, which made her bittersweet thoughts about life so credible and poignant.

unequivocal: 'The whole thing was a cod' (*AW*, 5).[33] McGahern echoes these sentiments in his memoir in his references to the repressive collusion of Church and State, the forced economic migration, and the shop-worn propaganda of a smug nationalist establishment in the 1950s (*M*, 211–12, 240–1), but is more specific in identifying the Catholic Church in Ireland as the source of his disenchantment with the 'theocratic' Ireland of his youth (*M*, 48–9).[34] That McGahern should use Moran to engage in a bit of *Kulturkritik* does not mean that we cannot also see Moran's deficiencies to be those of the society he abhors. It is this dimension of the character that made *Amongst Women* such a significant intervention in Irish civil discourse at the beginning of the 1990s.[35]

In relation to McGahern's art of memory, however, *Amongst Women* is a work of fiction that brings to an end a creative process that has always had more to do with McGahern's experience as son and brother, lover and writer, lapsed Catholic and Leitrim landowner than as citizen of the Irish state. As a 'climactic' figure in this creative process, the master of Great Meadow is the demon in the garden, the Cyclops in the cave of his own narcissism, a bitter old man who has set himself against life itself. This is the ultimate paradox of his character and the mystery of McGahern's creation: Moran seems larger than life but the truth is he is very much smaller than life, a miserable homunculus scuttling about house and fields most content when he can infect others with his misery. To read *Amongst Women* as a rural saga or paean to a vanishing Ireland is to mistake features of the

---

33   See also *AW*, 18. The same sentiments are expressed by Reegan in *The Barracks*; see
       B, 27–8, 208–9.

34   See also *M*, 210. Moran's complaint about the forced emigration of his children
       (*AW*, 5) is also echoed by McGahern in his resentment that his generation, which
       was forced to leave Ireland to find employment, was dispossessed of its birthright by
       a complacent, self-regarding urban bourgeoisie whose sense of entitlement rational-
       ized economic migration as something that happened to other people because it was
       meant to (*M*, 209).

35   Maher and Sampson take up McGahern's suggestion that Ernie O'Malley's *On
       Another Man's Wound* and Tomás Ó Criomhthain's *An tOileánach* can be used as
       intertextual maps to the national allegory in *Amongst Women*; see Maher, 99–100,
       and Sampson, *Outstaring Nature's Eye*, 238.

narrative and characterization for the larger structure they support. From beginning to end the novel is a painstaking dismantling of the screen of hero-worship and Mariolatry behind which the 'wizard' of Great Meadow hides the truth of his troll-like nature. It is difficult not to consider Moran as larger than life, however, because the cumulative effect of his words and actions seems to turn him from a character into a 'force' or power, like gravity.[36] At times he seems to give off a preternatural aura. But this is to mystify what the profoundly realistic Moran, if he symbolizes anything, can be said to represent in the abstract – namely, a species of masculine will. And it is this representative quality to the character that expands the 'father history' of the Moran family into a broader patriarchal allegory of nation, state, society and culture.

Moran's admission that it would have better if there had been no war (*AW*, 6) points further than post-war disillusionment with the nationalist dream. What is really behind his lament is his recognition that for men like McQuaid and himself the war was the only time in their lives when they felt and were truly free, not afterwards (*AW*, 6). Once the killing stopped, once the power of life and death was taken from him, Moran could not get used to the demands suddenly placed upon him by peace.[37] Moran's position during the war gave full rein to his will: he gave orders and was obeyed, he killed when he wanted, lived from hand to mouth, took what he needed – but most of all, he killed and got away with it. 'Things were never so simple and clear again' (*AW*, 6), he says. It is understandable, then, that after playing God like this he would turn Great Meadow into an island within the island and rule over it with the ruthlessness with which he led his flying column – brooking no opposition to his will. Allegorically, Moran's will is the will-to-power of his generation of nationalist patriarchs. As a young warrior-hero, he assumed an identity of aims and values between his will and that emerging collective. But he was quickly disabused. 'Hard men' like him and McQuaid were pawned off with medals and offers

36   Rose's attraction to Moran is that of an ambivalent moth to a flame (see *AW*, 58).
37   See McGahern's speculation about his father's war experience; he figures his father was happiest then because his violence, cunning, and self-concern would have been given complete expression (*M*, 226).

of careers as policemen, while the power went to those who would have gotten it anyway, the new state gombeen-men (*AW*, 8). Holed up like an outlaw in Great Meadow, Moran wants to stop time, but it is a 'time' that he helped start. Oppressive, tyrannical, cruel, manipulative, fickle, unpredictable, deceitful, cunning, voracious, homicidal, misogynistic – there is nothing positive or redeeming about his character. The bones of affection he throws his children have already been picked clean to feed his ravenous self-love. Moran is infantile – a man-child – a festering clot in time, a case of individual and collective arrested development, a pathological history and a history of a pathology.[38] He is a rottenness that must be expunged if a new model of family and state is to grow. His refusal to examine his past is a powerful reflection of the institutional and public resistance to confront the past – indeed the institutionalization of repression and the pathology of denial that characterized Irish society and culture until cracks in the dam began to open in the late 1980s. And McGahern is one of the giants of modern Irish fiction upon whose shoulders younger writers like Roddy Doyle, Dermot Bolger and Joseph O'Connor stood as they levered these cracks into fissures in their work of the 1990s.

McGahern shows that the consequence of the will-to-power that drives Moran is ultimately a hollowing out of the self. The novel also examines the threat to the future his type represents by looking at his effect on his children. On the second page the narrator describes how for the girls every detail of Great Meadow 'was pure binding' (*AW*, 2), and the rest of *Amongst Women* can be said to be a deconstruction of that apparently positive, but actually ambiguous value, a 'binding' that is really a form of 'bondage'. Great Meadow is less a surrogate republic than an ever-diminishing patrimony, a marriage of convenience, a squandered Eden. It was never a democratic republic. Sampson says 'Moran's offspring do not really want childhood to end'.[39] Luke is the glaring exception to this, but even for the others, the desire is fitful and usually comes when they have been charmed and seduced yet again by the father who had only a short while before abused

---

38   The narrator actually describes Rose and the girls sharing this view of Moran (*AW*, 131).

39   Sampson, *Outstaring Nature's Eye*, 223.

them. The desire should be seen as a version of Moran's own desire to stop time. In the children's case, his attitudes arrest their growth toward confident independence and nurture instead the fantasy of a life in which time stands still and the 'wide world' is held at bay. Their fear of change reflects their lack of confidence and their anxiety about the world outside Great Meadow that is not ruled by their father's will. When he marries Rose, Moran admits someone from that world into the 'magic circle', and thus, until they see how easily she is absorbed into their lives, they are afraid of the future she ushers in (*AW*, 38). Rose soon dispels their fears, but it is clear the children are permanently infected by Moran's fear of change.

What McGahern shows is that Great Meadow and the kind of family and family life it symbolizes cannot last, nor should it. It will end with Moran. Broken from the beginning, the Moran family is corrupt and corrupting at its patriarchal core. Moran instils his xenophobic paranoia into his daughters, in whom it takes the form of a 'sense of separateness and superiority'. The ugliness this occasionally results in is exemplified when they turn against Michael's English wife (*AW*, 171).[40] However, even the Moran girls themselves suffer a breach in the ranks when Sheila berates Moran for insulting her husband for his view of his Civil Service job as a form of drudgery. McGahern then uses the couple to have the narrator show how the 'family' that Moran has shaped in the image of his own misshapen self perceives a threat to its integrity in any behaviour that suggests a member may also feel allegiance to someone outside it. There can be no other loyalty.

Sheila was always the daughter with the most spirit, cowed as it was for most of her childhood and adolescence; and even though she rebukes Sean when he makes a joke about a family member when they are courting, once they are married she turns fully to him as her future. They spend the second week of their honeymoon at Great Meadow helping Moran take in the hay. Sean is unused to the hard work and is soon ready to quit. Sheila sympathizes with him and takes him aside to work at their own pace. They soon start playing more than working and the narrator describes how the

---

40   The connection between Moran and McGahern's father is evident when the narrator explains the girls' attitude to Michael's wife (compare *AW*, 172 and *M*, 197).

others are made uncomfortable by the newlyweds' pleasure in each other (*AW*, 165). When, eventually, the couple leaves the field and returns to the house, the others watch them disappear inside and cannot avoid imagining their love-making. The idea of them having sex in the house is as sacrilegious as their love for each other is 'selfish' (*AW*, 165–6). But the suggestion they are taking umbrage at this patent disrespect for Great Meadow is clearly dishonest; they are simply, understandably, envious of the lovers.[41] What really disturbs them, as they fantasize about Sheila and Sean, is the challenge to their own values posed by the couple's implicit declaration that love, sex, and pleasure are higher on their scale than bundling hay and playing their roles in 'Daddy's' self-interested idyll. The way the others feel towards the newlyweds is yet another example of how they have so internalized life under Moran's regime that they cannot see that the true 'selfish absorption' (AW, 166) is that of Great Meadow and its dictatorial master, a self-absorption that Moran shows to be 'inviolable' even with his last breath. Sheila, the narrator tells us, is the daughter who will work out the most pragmatic relationship to her family and her memories (*AW*, 167). For all her love of 'Daddy', even before he dies, Sheila decides to keep her children away from him (*AW*, 170). Mona's and Maggie's capacity for self-deception about Moran and Great Meadow continues to the end, however. Mona comes home from Dublin every weekend but is treated as little more than a live news broadcast for the increasingly reclusive Rose and Moran (*AW*, 169). When Maggie's marriage with Mark hits a wall and she comes home with her children for support, she does not experience the affirmation and reaffirmation the narrator once described as the effect of Moran's welcoming kiss. Instead, he makes it plain she and her children are not welcome; intending to stay six months, she leaves after two (*AW*, 169).[42]

---

41 Quinn's ascription of an Oedipal attachment between the girls and Moran makes this 'envy' particularly complex. For Quinn, when Sheila leaves the field with Sean, she 'violates ... this latent incestuous relationship with Moran, the perpetual virginity of her daughterhood' ('A Prayer', 88).

42 For the source of this turn in Maggie's life in McGahern's sister, Breedge's, and the origin of Moran's behaviour in McGahern's father's, see *M*, 230–2; even the quotation from the letter Moran writes paraphrases a letter McGahern's father wrote to him (compare *AW*, 109 and *M*, 231–2).

Where the *Poiēsis* Leads

In a way the ending of *Amongst Women* recalls that of *The Dark*: there appears to be a sudden softening of tone towards the monster. It is perhaps less of a problem in *Amongst Women* because of the differences in narrative voice and subject. In *The Dark*, McGahern employs a predominantly first-person focus to present the narrator-protagonist's struggle to survive against his father and at the same time discover enough about himself to make a decision about his future; in *Amongst Women*, the third-person voice results in a different focal length that, while keeping Moran at the centre of the frame, provides equal clarity of detail for his context and co-habitants. Their feelings about his dying are ambiguous yet credible precisely because of what McGahern has shown about the dynamics of the family bond in the novel. Given the overwhelming history of defeat that their relationship with Moran embodies and the contorted victories of the master-slave syndrome that that history came to produce for them, it is hardly surprising that the daughters still look affectionately at the dead fingers that once curled into fists to hit them, all the while walking proudly through the world as the monster's offspring. But there is no mistaking that, in spite of the Gothic frisson of Maggie's 'He'll never leave us now' (*AW*, 183), what leavens their steps as they walk back from Moran's grave in the final paragraphs is the slave's sense of freedom at last. As McGahern wonderfully insinuates, some are on the verge of dancing, an impulse they might even have been stifling as they stood at the graveside.

The apparent tonal shift actually enters the novel well before the ending, at the point where Moran's 'defeat' is recognized by his daughters following Michael's escape to London – an escape carried out with their help. In this respect, the story-within-the-story of Michael's childhood and adolescence: his cosseting by Rose, his refusal to study at school or work at home (except in his garden), his hormonal explosion and affair with Nell Morahan, his hand-to-hand combat with Moran, and finally, his running away to join Luke – forms something of a pivot in the novel's structure. It stands out because it is so clearly a continuous narrative with a single focus, whereas what comes before and after its thirty pages focuses on Moran, the girls and Rose. The effect of Michael's story thus affects the shift in tone that follows it, and its focus on the father-son relationship may be the key to understanding that effect and indeed its function in the work.

To begin with, McGahern clearly wants the reader to connect the episode of Michael and Nell at Strandhill with the earlier episode of Moran taking Rose there following their argument. This is signalled when Michael tells Nell about coming with his family on a summer holiday and Moran forcing the children to sell turf door to door (*AW*, 106); his account contrasts with Moran's version to Rose and points up Moran's blindness as well as selfishness. Michael's description of feeling humiliated by his father in the turf-selling incident matches McGahern's account of this experience in his memoir (*M*, 180–1) and the connection – in conjunction with Moran's admission to Rose that following this holiday, Luke stopped coming to the seaside on family holidays – further establishes Luke as McGahern's 'surrogate' in the novel, physically separated from the family but a continuously acknowledged presence in their individual and collective consciousness in a way that parallels McGahern's sublimated, 'objective' presence in the narrative voice. The two outbreaks of violence between Michael and Moran clearly recall the scenes in *The Dark* when Mahoney terrifies his naked son in the opening chapter and later when the boy stands up to his father; thus McGahern's return to the violence and abuse of *The Dark* in *Amongst Women* is a return to his memories of his own suffering at the hands of his father as well as what he knew of his brother Frankie's conflict with him. When both Michael and Sheila connect these incidents to Luke's history with Moran, the Luke-McGahern connection is further strengthened.[43]

---

43 With the exception of his affair with Nell, the details of Michael's story, from his unhappiness following his sisters' departure through his truancy, fight with his father, and running away to Dublin, are all found in McGahern's account of his younger brother Frankie's adolescence and abrupt departure from home (see *M*, 233–9). What is interesting is that, having 'removed himself from the novel', McGahern redistributes his role and actions in helping Frankie among Sheila and Mona; even some of the dialogue between McGahern and Frankie in the memoir is similar to that between Sheila and Michael (compare *M*, 233–4 and *AW*, 116). It was McGahern who went

Finally, Michael's story focuses on Moran's relation with a son after the concentration on his relations with the girls and Rose; this again leads toward the 'untold story' of his relationship with Luke – and Luke will become not only more prominent in the novel after Michael's story, but just as that story literally led to Luke, Luke will actually return to Ireland for his sister's wedding and a physical meeting with Moran in the final movement of the novel. Michael's story 'explains' Luke's absence in Luke's absence to tell it himself. But its deeper role in the narrative is to provide the bridge for Luke's return and, in the wedding episode, McGahern's final exorcism of the father in his fiction.

The tonal shift enters the novel abruptly as Moran returns from driving Mona and Sheila to the station the weekend after they put Michael on the boat-train to London. The girls are feeling mellow because Moran had been so uncharacteristically nice the whole time, behaviour which moves Mona to utter the Moran girls' refrain about wonderful 'Daddy'. We know that the previous instances of these expressions of love have been carefully managed by the narrator to reveal the ambiguous nature of the girls' emotional states and the complexity of Moran's influence upon their characters. By this point, Mona's and Sheila's statements read like mottos for t-shirts to be sold at future Moran family reunions. The reader knows Moran for what he is, knows he drove Michael from the house, and knows as well that for all his immaturity, selfishness, and weakness, Michael is the way he is and does what he does because of his nature and the intransigence of Moran's. So we are ready for the other shoe to drop after the girls' teary-eyed backward glance at the 'special glow' of the train station. But it does not drop. Instead the narrator turns to describe a despondent Moran walking his land, 'field by blind field' (*AW*, 129), not only looking over his real estate but also reviewing his life: he is angry, he feels betrayed, his time is over, and he understands nothing of what has been his life, a life he has given

down to his father and Agnes at Grevisk to negotiate Frankie's return to home and school, and he, Margaret and Monica put Frankie on the boat-train to Rosaleen in London. The details of Luke's life in London that Rosaleen reports to the family actually describe the beginning of Frankie McGahern's career once he settled in London.

to Great Meadow; but what, now that it is over, has it given back to him? He is a nothing, a nobody; the land does not even know he exists, and he walks it 'like a man trying to see' (*AW*, 130). But what's happened? There has been no sign of such an interior life in the character up to this point. Why now? What's McGahern up to? Should we expect Michael to 'pull a Mahoney' and write home saying, 'Sorry, Daddy, I wouldn't have been brought up any other way or by any other father – but I'm still not coming home'? No. The tone is changing but not the narrator's fundamental attitude to the character. At first it might even seem that McGahern has lost control of the narrative voice; it seems almost 'sympathetic'. But to feel sympathy in the prose would be an inappropriate projection on the reader's part, soft-headed as much as soft-hearted, because unwarranted, *unearned*, by McGahern's language.

The tonal shift in the final movement of the novel marks an intensification in the narrator's attempt to *understand* Moran, but no abandonment of the narration's correlative need to *judge* the character, and in both McGahern holds to the cardinal points that have been his compass throughout his construction of the character – narcissism, paranoia, blindness, and the lack of both imagination and self-knowledge. Thus, in the faux-epiphany, Moran's 'sense of betrayal and anger' (*AW*, 130) is no surprise. Life, like his sons, has let him down; the world, like them, owes him more than this. His feeling 'of never having understood anything much' is the only quantum of truth in the moment, as illuminating and as ephemeral as a firefly in the failing light of the scene. If he had ever tried to understand anything, Moran might not feel so angry and betrayed. His narcissism is unflagging. He *is* a failed patriarch; his land will pass out of his blood-line because his sons have turned their backs on him, on the farm, and on the life, but mostly on *him* because for them *he* is the land and the life.[44] His

---

44   Compare Moran's crowing to Rose and the girls, after they have helped in the haying
     (*AW*, 84) with McGahern recalling his father (*M*, 216). Moran repeats the sentiment after Michael helps him dose sheep, remembering as well his dream that Luke
     would one day take over Great Meadow (*AW*, 108). The scene is a reprise of one in
     The Dark (see *D*, 150), but here it is the reference to 'the eldest son' that is telling.
     McGahern records his father's 'dream' for them in his memoir (*M*, 214, 216).

narcissism remains his only way of centring his consciousness, and so when he tries to imagine someone else farming his land after him, he cannot. He cannot 'see' anyone in his place because he *is* the place; without him in the picture, there is no picture.[45] The failure of imagination is a blindness induced by his own selfishness. The narrator describes him as 'like a man trying to see', but it is clear Moran's case is hopeless. And from beginning to end McGahern's characterization of him has rested on the mystery of his own father, of whom he wrote in the memoir, 'A life from which the past was so rigorously shut out had to be a life of darkness' (*M*, 271).

If there is a sympathetic quality to the tone of the final movement of the novel, it is the sympathy that follows from understanding; but sympathy does not co-opt judgment. It is in this final movement too that McGahern introduces 'outsiders' to Great Meadow and their reactions to Moran and his household are an important reminder to the reader that there *is* a world of other families beyond Great Meadow. Mark O'Donoghue's feeling that Great Meadow is more a war zone than a home (*AW*, 135) means Maggie's nostalgic waxing of her memories of the place when they return to Dublin has no credibility for him; moreover, his observation that she completely loses the 'air of separateness and superiority' she has in Dublin when she returns to Great Meadow corroborates our sense that the narrator does not mean us to credit the girls' belief that Moran 'affirms and reaffirms' their superiority every time they go home to see him. The narrator also continues to point out the girls' need to delude themselves when he describes how Moran's gruff acceptance of Mark would soon become a generous familial embrace in Maggie's mind (*AW*, 140).[46] Moran is increasingly described as

---

45   Moran is not the omphalos of Great Meadow in his own estimation only; Rose and the girls see him as the 'magnet' at the centre of their world as well (*AW*, 131).

46   Mark's daily intake of alcohol leads him to feel flattered by his connection to Great Meadow (*AW*, 139), and blinds him to Moran's scorn for him. In his memoir, McGahern's father's grudging endorsement of Breedge's engagement to Con O'Brien, on whom Mark O'Donoghue is based, is given in the same words Moran speaks to Maggie, and McGahern's comment about Breedge's reaction echoes the narrator's about Maggie's (see *M*, 221). Correspondences such as these between the memoir and the novel strengthen the argument that McGahern's narrator is not as objective

a tired old man, but his miserly selfishness remains as potent and as hurtful as ever. Sheila had always wanted a traditional wedding in her local church, but Moran refuses her; he cannot stomach the idea of parading up the aisle before people he has never respected, let alone providing them with food and drink afterwards (*AW*, 150). In the same way that he responded to her desire to go to university to become a doctor, Moran is incapable of seeing that Sheila's wedding is about her happiness, not about him. But Moran is incapable of caring about another's happiness except to the extent that it will affect his own. Through Rose's diplomacy, he gets his way and agrees to attend the wedding at a hotel in Dublin. Disappointed in the forced change of venue, Sheila gets her own back by inviting Luke without discussing it with the family beforehand (*AW*, 151).

Moran's and Luke's long awaited re-union at the wedding is an anti-climax in spite of the suspense. They avoid each other throughout the day but it's clear that Moran has to work harder at it (*AW*, 155). When everyone is making their farewells, though, Luke, seeing Moran standing like St. Sebastian at an archery competition, makes the first move. His sisters fear an outburst of the violence they have all grown up with and which presumably explains some of what lies behind Luke's rejection of his father; but nothing happens because Moran cannot leave the narrow circle of his self-delusion and Luke will not re-enter it. Nothing happens and everything happens, because the wedding has also been 'The Last Supper' of the Morans of Great Meadow as a family. After this the patriarch will swiftly move toward his last resting place in the deluded memories of his daughters. Luke does not upstage his father's performance of the injured party but simply thanks him for the day, as if he were any polite guest thanking the bride's father whom he does not know. Moran is clearly taken aback by his son's approach and by his words, which politely but pointedly do not acknowledge any filial motive or even relation.

---

in the sense of non-judgmental as some critics of the novel believe. For the source of the Maggie-Mark relationship in that of Breedge McGahern and Con O'Brien, see *M*, 221, 230–31). Like Moran, McGahern's father did not go to their wedding.

'*Shut up!*': The Death of the Patriarch

As Moran approaches death McGahern describes a changeless character
within a deteriorating body. When Rose tries to get him to recall their first
meeting at the post-office, his antipathy to self-recollection persists (*AW*,
173). Like any bully, so much of Moran's presence and authority derives
from his physical power and the commission or threat of violence. But
as his body deteriorates with age, that presence and authority wane. The
girls notice it first, then Rose, then others. When the postmistress, an old
adversary, openly mocks Moran behind his back, the narrator describes
the tone of mockery in the general laughter as revealing that Moran had
never been credited by his community with the superiority from which he
scornfully regarded it (*AW*, 173). When he and Rose visit the bank, they are
ignored and then fobbed off by a fool of a provincial manager whose self-
importance, ironically, recalls Moran's in his heyday; but Moran does not
rise to the bait and lets him get away with the insult: 'Who cares anyhow?'
(*AW*, 175) The world of 'mere Other[s]' he had built Great Meadow to
escape was getting to him at last. The house becomes a cell and in their
need to flee Great Meadow they escape, ironically, by driving around the
countryside and unknowingly retracing the same roads Michael and Nell
took to escape school and Moran all those years ago. Yet Moran remains
the miserly, miserable, fickle, obnoxious nag he always has been, hunched
over his account books at night, and to the end, tormented by his grief
over Luke.

   Like Oedipus, Moran dies blinded by the violence he has done to
himself; he blinded himself to life long before his death and when he dies,
he is still blind to the wrongs he did to others. When he decides to write
a letter to make his peace with Luke, he writes as the injured party. While
it is clear that some part of who he is senses his role to be more than that
of the injured party, Moran remains utterly incapable of *seeing* the truth
of what he is and what he has done to his children. As he labours over the
letter, 'Some of his old fire and anger returned as he wrote' (*AW*, 176), but
like a shard of broken glass, the letter reflects the obscurity and confusion

of a severely stunted self. Luke recognizes the symbolic meaning of the letter as gesture, but he really has moved on; his father's studied moral and emotional chicanery leaves him untouched. The narrator does not describe him stopping to think about Moran's crude rhetoric: the self-pity hidden in the opening gambit, followed by the sly feint toward compliment in the quotation; the protection from the vulnerability that compliment opens by the use of another's voice; the shift to the 'neutral' authority of a third person and a third-person report of her 'wisdom' before the dramatic shift to the self-pitying crux – 'I am dying' (*AW*, 176) – and the generosity death brings such a person, and so on. Moran's instinctive tendency to hide in the bushes, whether it is waiting for McQuaid or watching Maggie arrive with her fiancé or writing to the son he has alienated, remains strong to the end; he will not allow himself to be drawn into the open. So even though his rush to the confessional here is so precipitate and difficult for him he seems to fall into the garden with the effort, he quickly gets up, dusts himself off, and ends this momentous treaty with little more than a shrug – 'who cares anyhow?' (*AW*, 176) His instinct for self-protection never lets up.

The letter to Luke would be a remarkably sophisticated text if Moran were not Moran. As it is, it is a passage of pure genius on McGahern's part and must have cost him dearly. The understated rhetorical balance of Luke's reply – 'There was nothing to forgive' (*AW*, 176) – closes the circle on his father as if he were closing the eyes of a corpse. It also ushers in McGahern's closing of the circle of the novel's form. Maggie invites Luke to return to Great Meadow to help the girls' revive Moran's spirits by celebrating Monaghan Day as they did when they were children and Luke refuses, knowing full well that his father's letter had asked the same thing of him. This is where the novel began, with Moran surrounded by women determined to save his life, but it is a life he has already given up on.

McGahern's description of the girls' desperate effort on behalf of 'their beloved' (*AW*, 178) recalls, of course, his use of 'my beloved' to refer to Patrick Moran's mother in *The Leavetaking*. The echo, however, only accentuates the distancing effect of the third-person pronoun and is a pointed reminder of the gap between the narrative voice and the girls, a distance confirmed by McGahern's plangent lament in his memoir, 'I had but the one beloved' (*M*, 133). At the end Moran wants only to get free of the women and the house (*AW*, 178). He keeps trying to get out to the meadow, which puzzles Mona, who thinks 'He must see something there' (*AW*, 179). But what would Moran 'see' at the end of his life? Is it the family working at hay time? Is that his happiest memory? The dissolution of the individual in the mindless oblivion of collective labour, the unconscious wholeness of the beast? The 'troops' all putting their backs into it, realizing his vision of the peaceable kingdom? Or is he baffled by the meadow's otherness, its enduring indifference to him and his vision, its being before and after him, his conquest and empire merely shadows passing over the grass?

Recognizing the quality of McGahern's narrative voice is essential if one is to respond accurately to his characterization of Moran and his representation of the family, particularly at the end of the novel. When the narrator says that in all his life Moran had never recognized 'what an amazing glory' life was (*AW*, 179), the narration does not say *Moran* thought or felt this. One can argue, of course, that it is implicit in the free indirect style McGahern employs, but that style of narration is notable for the subtle ironies it allows to emerge in the seam between the narrative voice and the character's perspective. It can be argued that it is the narrator who is telling us what Moran is on the brink of realizing but which remains beyond his capacities of imagination and feeling; after all, there is little evidence of the former in the novel before this, and Moran's feelings remain leashed to his solipsism. Moran could never have sensed that he was part of a great mystery because he could never have imagined himself or Great Meadow as anything less than the whole. His life was a 'ferocious' (AW, 173) effort to maintain a life apart from others and the 'wide world': for Moran, *they* were the unwanted parts *he* had severed. Moran remains the occluded heart of the novel, and there is a metafictive dimension to this multi-dimensional character; like Roddy Doyle's Charlo Spencer, in *The Woman Who Walked into Doors*, Moran is 'that "force" without which there can be no story, but which remains *beyond* the story's capacity to know'.[47]

47   Dermot McCarthy, *Roddy Doyle: Raining on the Parade* (Dublin: Liffey Press, 2003), 188.

The patriarch of Great Meadow leaves the world not with a bang nor with a whimper, but with contradictory commands, as befits his inexhaustibly fickle and autocratic nature. First he tells the women to say the rosary, then, after they have begun, to '*Shut up!*' Moran does not reach that point where, like Conrad's Kurtz, he judges himself and earns our respect as Kurtz earned Marlow's. Moran does not die reviewing his life and uttering the equivalent of 'The horror! The horror!' He never sees who and what he is, what he has been, what he has done to those who were in his care. There is no such 'victory' for him. However, his '*Shut up!*' is as enigmatic as Kurtz's last words. Is it that he has had enough of this pious charade of prayer? Is it that he cannot abide someone other than himself centring the ritual? Is it that the lifelong tension between his misogyny and his need of women, ironically embodied in this Mariolatry, has finally reached its *terminus ad quem*? Whatever its meaning, his last command, an attempt to silence others, is a fitting epitaph for this man who never heard anything but what he wanted to hear, and who understood only what he needed to justify his acts and rationalize his beliefs. And it is equally fitting that the women, finally, should not obey him. They keep on praying, and distracting him, presumably, from fully concentrating on the moment of his extinction.

This well-intentioned, or perhaps merely instinctive, veto is also a sign of the shift in regimes that the narrator describes in the closing paragraphs of the novel. The description of the 'new order', which is clearly matriarchal-sororal, is a final instance of the coherence of the narrative voice and perspective in the novel. Throughout, these have been shown to be 'objectively judgmental', so to speak, particularly in the passages describing the girls' sense of superiority and the myth of Great Meadow they construct for themselves. To say the narrative tone has been critical of them would be too strong; but the tone does communicate an 'understandable distance' between the narrator and the characters. The narrator's sense of being *outside* the group of mourning women who walk out of the graveyard runs through the description of their suddenly – and perhaps, ominously – growing strength. The closing sentence in the passage – 'it was as if each of them in their different ways had become Daddy' (*AW*, 183) – when read in relation to the narrative and narrative voice that have preceded it, only confirms the un-bridged, and presumably, unbridgeable distance between the narrator and the women. What underscores the sense that, even though he understands their feeling, the narrator does not credit it, are the many echoes in the passage of the earlier ambiguities in the narrator's descriptions of the girls' relationship with Moran and to Great Meadow. He was 'their first love' (AW, 183) recalls the narrator's ambiguous explanation of Maggie's feelings when she was leaving 'her first man' (*AW*, 62) for London.[48] We have already seen how their sense of 'allegiance' to Moran and Great Meadow could be turned against them when Sheila and Sean are 'ostracized' following their defection during the haying. Also, the narrator has shown through Maggie that the feelings of affirmation and reaffirmation the girls felt when they came home to Moran and Great Meadow were as easily dispelled while there as their sense of superiority when away from it. Moran's 'central' position in their lives and psyches attests to the centripetal focus of his influence and his demand that he be the centre of their attention. Given all these echoes, there is little to celebrate in the narrator's observation that 'it was as if each of them in their different ways had become Daddy'. If it meant that each of them had become, finally, the centre of their own lives, perhaps there would be; but why would anyone want to be the Moran presented in this novel?[49] The passage is also undercut by

48 The theme of Moran as the false animus-figure in the girls' development is worth considering: has Moran's 'unbroken presence' in their psyches – a presence the passage now emphasizes through the sinister image of their internalization of his memory – actually affected their ability to have fully mature relationships with the men in their lives? Does the novel suggest that the girls' instinctive reaction to exclude others from 'their own closed circle' extends unconsciously to their husbands? Maggie's attraction to Mark may be explained in part by his apparent difference from her father, but it is shown to be ultimately a 'bad choice' for her, and the novel makes clear that when she is back working in the fields with Moran and her sisters, she forgets her married life, her husband, and even her child. Mona never marries and the relationships she does have are always with older men. Sheila seems to have achieved the most psychological distance from her father, but even she remains problematically 'centred' by Moran's role within her psyche.

49 Their internalization of Moran's presence may be understood as a feature of the Hegelian master/slave paradigm that McGahern seems to allude to in his description of Rose and the girls' positions in the house (see *AW*, 46). McGahern told González

what precedes it, the openly disrespectful comment heard at the graveside, as well as the description of the two politicians looking back at Moran's grave and mourners 'in undisguised contempt' (*AW*, 183).

Forgiveness but not Forgetting: McGahern, the Narrator, and Luke

It would be a mistake to read Luke's 'nothing to forgive' (*AW*, 176) as a reprise of the young Mahoney's 'I wouldn't have been brought up any other way or by any other father' (*D*, 191). The problem with the earlier protagonist's judgment is that it lacks credibility; insufficient time and experience had passed for him to have achieved the equanimity in his explanation (see *D*, 150). By keeping Luke away from Great Meadow and present only as a wound in Moran's memory that will not heal, McGahern builds a sense of the son's having achieved and carefully preserved an emotional detachment equal to his physical distance from his father. But the 'amiable separateness' (*AW*, 144) that describes Luke's relationship to his sisters and their

that *Amongst Women* 'is also about how women in a paternalistic society create room and power for themselves' ('John McGahern', 43), which puts a much brighter face on their situation than the novel actually seems to present. While Quinn seems to recognize Moran's erosion of his daughters' sense of self-worth and the pathological impact that Great Meadow has had as 'a disabling fantasy' on their characters, she misreads the narrative voice – and renders much of her analysis of the novel incoherent – when she concludes that 'The narrative endorses Moran's centripetal attraction by scarcely ever focusing on life outside Great Meadow' ('A Prayer', 88–9). The novel begins with a vivid juxtaposition of Great Meadow and the outside world in the reference to Monaghan Day (a reference to a bustling cattle market that figures in McGahern's last novel) and ends with the wedding in Dublin; in between, the motif of Luke's self-exile in London, the girls' leaving home and the men they meet and marry, Michael's escape, all show that the larger world is constantly breaking through the dyke Moran has put up to keep it out. As for endorsing Moran: nothing could be further from this novel's deepest truth.

husbands does *not* describe his relationship with Moran, and his 'There was nothing to forgive' does not mean he has already forgiven his father so much as he has grown beyond the need to forgive him. Luke's wounds *have* healed.

Rose's remark to the girls that Moran was 'secretly grieving for Luke' (*AW*, 143) is worth contemplating. Considering the power of grief in McGahern's life and its enduring presence in his *poiēsis*, it is significant that he would make this the affliction that has kept Moran in pain throughout the novel. It helps us to understand how, in terms of McGahern's career, *Amongst Women* could be such a liberating achievement for him. Rose's diagnosis of Moran's condition carries weight because the narrator has presented her in a balanced way and because of where it comes in the narrative. In terms of how I have read McGahern's fiction, this sudden illumination of Moran's character shows how with this novel McGahern's art of memory had evolved to the point where, by using grief as the paradigm for the Moran-Luke relationship, McGahern was projecting his own wound into the fictive figure of his father, and in doing so, finally separating himself from this particular demon in his past, moving on. Rose's insight implies that Moran knows he has 'lost' Luke forever, that in a sense, he is already dead to his son. This explains why their meeting at Sheila's wedding is so strange. Ironically, it is Moran who behaves as if he is seeing a ghost. Luke shakes his hand as if Moran is merely someone he has just met and knows he will never see again. 'I hold no grudge. ... But I have a good memory' (*AW*, 143), Luke tells Maggie when she criticizes him for never visiting Great Meadow, and the statement is icily cold. Thus his 'There was nothing to forgive' is more dismissive than generous: he is announcing that nothing his father thinks or does matters to him. And if Moran is already dead to Luke, it explains why he does not come home for the funeral – nor even reply to the telegram informing him of it (*AW*, 181). Moran's grieving for Luke is the ultimate ironic reversal in McGahern's fiction, ultimate because it is a turning back that is a final turning away. *Amongst Women* finishes the therapeutic work of making fiction out of the memories of his father.

A major source of narrative energy in both *The Dark* and *Amongst Women* results from the centrifugal-centripetal dialectic of children and father, with the narrative interest in each novel being the reverse polarity of the other: *The Dark* focuses on the centrifugal struggle of the son, on the painful becoming of the self; it is a story of rebellion, psychologically dynamic and tumultuous. *Amongst Women* focuses on the centripetal force of the father; it is a story of emotional atrophy and spiritual morbidity – and for all its violence, it is static and sclerotic. Both novels end with McGahern's characteristically ambiguous glimmer of new beginnings. For all Moran's complaining about the 'new Ireland', he was one of its fathers. He helped make it. And if his children were to have any hope of making it a better Ireland for themselves and their children, he *had* to die. McGahern suggests this in Sheila's decision to restrict her children's exposure to Moran (see *AW*, 170).

Moran never grows out of his *acedia*, but he dies from grief. McGahern *makes* him die from it. Through Luke, he kills him with the same pain McGahern felt all those years ago and for all the years after, a pain all the more intense because of his memory of his father's selfish abandonment of the son's dying beloved. In a very uncharacteristic moment in one way, but one typical of his bathetic evasion of responsibility in another, Moran says to Mark, who has just told him all that Luke said in his meeting with him and Maggie when he refused their request to visit Great Meadow: 'There are people who say we have had other existences than our present life. If that is so I must have committed some great crime in that other existence. That is all I can put Luke down to' (*AW*, 148). If one reads McGahern's *Memoir*, and then reads through all McGahern's novels in chronological order, Moran's remark strikes one as something between uncannily comical and profoundly true. In a post-modern fiction it would be the moment when a fictive character becomes aware of his origin in the author's imagination – or in Moran's case, his author-son's memory, and realizes that it is, in fact, his son who has placed him in this ring of hell *amongst women* because of what he did in another life to the woman who remains his son's image of his only beloved. Moran is the way he is and suffers what he suffers because of what Francis McGahern did to his first wife, his children, and especially, to his first-born son. And in writing Moran, McGahern was righting those wrongs, and with that justice brought to an end the purgatorial phase of his writing life.

CHAPTER EIGHT

The Completed Circle:
That They May Face the Rising Sun (2002)

McGahern's last novel surprised many of his readers. Eamonn Hughes, for example, thought it 'in many ways an inexplicable novel' because 'it seems to break with, rather than emerge from, any trajectory or pattern' coming out of the earlier work.[1] Yet McGahern could only have written *That They May Face the Rising Sun* when he did because it was the evolving nature of the creative-memorial process that produced the earlier fiction that led to the solar vision at its core, a vision he records in his memoir and that bided its time until the long eclipse of the first five novels had completed its cycle. The spiritual and emotional well-spring of *That They May Face the Rising Sun* is the spirit of Susan McGahern, and at an appropriately cardinal moment in the narrative – Easter morning – her voice is actually heard. McGahern began his career as a novelist trying to imagine her death; he ended it with two works that celebrate her memory and spirit, and paradoxically, his last novel is a paean to the very cycle of life that is the focus of his animus in the early work. 'Of all the books I've written, it was the most difficult', he told one interviewer; 'It was fifteen hundred pages long at one stage'.[2] The creative struggle, the original length, and the many continuities with the preceding works suggest this last novel is something of a 'summa'.

The rural setting and landscape are familiar, as are the concerns and character-types: families remain the focus of attention, and family remains

---

1 Hughes, "'All That Surrounds Our Life,'" 147.
2 Kelly, 'High Style', 5.

'the moral unit' McGahern uses to calibrate his social world.[3] There is a sinister sexual tyrant, an irascible bully, and an eccentric uncle; there is even a pair of lovers who have left previous selves and painful histories to begin their lives anew in the heart of the country. The train journey to the unnamed town that Joe Ruttledge recalls making with his mother to do the shopping is the same journey Patrick Moran remembers and that McGahern describes in his memoir (*L*, 59–63; *M*, 71–2). The train station and signal box are the same as in *The Pornographer* and *Memoir* (*RS*, 227; *P*, 141–2, 239; *M*, 72). The Monaghan Day market that figures in *Amongst Women* is described in vivid detail here (*RS*, 216–4). The Shah, Ruttledge's beloved uncle, and his long-time employee, Frank Dolan, reprise the pornographer's saw-mill-owning Uncle Michael and his long-suffering employee, Jim.[4] Ruttledge remembers escaping from a small farm through education, like Mahoney at the end of *The Dark*, and intimates that he has been hurt in love like Patrick Moran and the pornographer (*RS*, 19, 7); he and his American wife, Kate, met in London, recalling Patrick and Isobel. The themes in this novel are also familiar: emigration; modernity, modernization, and change; spousal abuse and violence in the school system; the power, hypocrisies and interference of Church and State in the lives of people who pay lip service to the authorities but live according to traditional-communal mores; and finally, the vision of human 'being-in-the-world', expressed a few times in the novel, but most memorably by the Shah: 'The rain comes down. Grass grows. Children get old .... That's it. We all know. We know full well and can't even whisper it out loud. We know in spite of them' (*RS*, 150).

The narrative voice is similar to that in *Amongst Women*, but the focalization is less intense. The effect is an 'enchanting' narrative and narration, a continuous progress through the time and space of the lakeside world and

---

3   McGahern lauds this feature of Ó Criomhthain's *An tOileánach*, a work that influenced his shaping of his novel's world and community; see McGahern, 'What Is my Language?' *Irish University Review* 35.1 (2005), 7.

4   The Shah's name in the novel is Joe Maguire (*RS*, 161), which is somewhat awkward considering that the owner of the central hotel, whom the Shah is constantly visiting, is Mrs Maguire (*RS*, 169) but not his wife.

its community.⁵ What anchors the narrative voice is its sustained attention to the natural world and landscape – indeed, the setting soon emerges as the central 'character' of the novel; yet the lack of a single subjective focus of narrative interest also makes this McGahern's most 'social' novel. The continuity with his earlier fiction in this respect is with the pornographer's epiphany at his aunt's funeral: 'The superstitious, the poetic, the religious are all made safe within the social, given a tangible form' (*P*, 238). Seeing through the 'tangible forms' of communal life to the ethos and spirit those forms manifest results in some of McGahern's best writing in the long account of the Monaghan Day cattle market and the descriptions of the birth of a calf, the town at Christmas, and the laying out of Johnny Murphy's corpse. It is the public, social world, not the inner, subjective world of the grief- and guilt-haunted self that occupies narrative interest in McGahern's last novel. The narrative perspective exemplifies McGahern's ideal of respect for the sanctity and *otherness* of people. Community, friendships, histories, comings and goings, deaths and entrances, living-in-place and being-in-the-world form the plot of the novel, which is encapsulated in the title itself. The episodic narrative structure is a perfectly observed process of 'orientation' – of the Ruttledges but also of the reader – to the promise and peace of *home*. Indeed, the orientation achieved in *That They May Face the Rising Sun* is nothing less than the positioning of the self in time and place, the coming to feel *at home* in the world. McGahern's last novel is thus a fitting terminus to the ontological quest that his narrative *poiēsis* always was, a quest thrust upon him by the loss of home he experienced with his mother's death and his removal to the father-world of the barracks.

The great triumph of this final work is a consequence of McGahern having written his way through to what Eamon Maher aptly describes as 'the right way of conveying the image that is at the heart of his creativity',

---

5　Denis Sampson calls it a 'poetic narrative': 'In the end, its technique affirms a vision of life's essential movements that is not to be understood by human intelligence or to be explained in terms of socio-historical formations. This vision rests on a sense of the human embedded in the natural' ('"Open to the World": A Reading of John McGahern's *That They May Face the Rising Sun*', *Irish University Review* 35.1 (2005), 136.

the image of the 'lost world' of childhood, the world of his beloved.⁶ In *That They May Face the Rising Sun* McGahern in a sense takes the walk he imagines at the end of *Memoir* (*M*, 272), playing Jamesie to his mother's Mary, and telling her all the parish gossip. The 'Image' that emerges is not the image of the 'lost beloved' in *The Leavetaking*, nor of the visionary reunion of *Memoir*; it is the 'total image' at the level of narrative form of a whole, self-contained world of imagination. McGahern himself felt that he had created 'a whole, completed world'⁷ in this novel, and what is significant is that by the end of the work it is clear that, for him, death *completes* this world. The world-image of *That They May Face the Rising Sun* is the polar opposite of that presented in *Amongst Women*; there McGahern presents an image of a 'lost world' in the sense of a morally and emotionally fallen world, with Moran the patriarch who has squandered his gift and sundered himself, ironically, from the life-sustaining knowledge of the feminine world that surrounds him and that could nourish his being. Too miserly to feed even himself, Moran's life was a slow death by starvation, an emotional and spiritual famine he blamed on everyone else. But the *nostos* of *That They May Face the Rising Sun* is an archetypal turn away from the father and back to the mother-world; the 'lost world' is recovered.

For some, *That They May Face the Rising Sun* is McGahern's 'most optimistic' book, 'a celebration of, rather than a lament for, a way of life that is passing'; for others, it is definitely a lyrical lament, a 'swan song to rural Ireland'.⁸ But it is worth emphasizing that McGahern himself resisted this historico-sociological approach and directed attention instead to 'the spirit of the personality in language, the style'.⁹ Read from this perspective, this novel emerges as the crowning act of an art of memory which always expressed the process and struggle of the self to shape experience into language and language into a narration that expressed and embodied what he described as 'this painful becoming of ourselves' (*P*, 20). McGa-

---

6   *John McGahern*, 98.
7   Ibid., 159.
8   Kelly, 'High Style', 5; Maher, 'Irish Readers', 134; see also Maher, *John McGahern*, 121.
9   Maher, *John McGahern*, 145.

hern told Shirley Kelly: 'I've always thought that one of the functions of the writer is to celebrate and to praise. ... Maybe that doesn't come across in my earlier work, but all the writer can do is write what he has to write at the time'.[10] McGahern's recognition that he was unable to write a work of praise and celebration until *That They May Face the Rising Sun* supports the argument of this study that what McGahern worked through, stage by stage, through the act of writing, namely, the Complicated Grief and anger he felt following his mother's death and during his life with his father, was resolved by the time he finished writing *Amongst Women*. He wrote *what* he had to *when* he had to. From the absolution of the son in that novel, McGahern was able to turn to the sun rising in his last, to resurrection. What is redeemed is nothing less than 'Time' itself, and for McGahern the resurrection occurs only in the mind through the grace and power of the imagination and lasts only as long as memory does.

The Novel, the World, and a Concentric Art

Eamonn Hughes argues that McGahern 'freed himself' from plot in this novel through a 'repetitive style' which 'denies the passing of time, the motor of plot'.[11] But the opposite is the case: time *is* the plot in the novel, and McGahern shapes it into a *comic* plot. A series of scenes, vignettes, and portraits introduce the *dramatis personae* – Bill Evans, Patrick Ryan, John Quinn, Jimmy Joe McKiernan, Jamesie and Mary Murphy, Joe and Kate Ruttledge, the Shah – and through them, McGahern's usual themes: the violence of Irish political and social history; the 'new class' of doctors, priests and *petit bourgeois* that emerged following independence and the civil war; emigration; institutional abuse; the hollowness and hypocrisy of Church and State; rural courtship, and spousal abuse. Gradually, the

---

10   Kelly, 'High Style', 5.
11   Hughes, '"All That Surrounds Our Life,"' 158.

story behind each character is extruded and their relationship with the Ruttledges developed. The pace is organic, the proportion asymmetric, as if each character must grow in the garden according to its own rhythms, the novel's rhythm and form emulating the growing cycle in nature. Like a well-made play but really more like a well-planted garden, everything that is introduced in the opening scenes is gradually brought 'to fruit' (*RS*, 177) later in the story: the comic banter about the un-necessity of belief climaxes in Ruttledge's measured admissions of the reality of happiness; Jamesie's announcement that his brother is about to come home from England for his annual summer holiday ultimately 'blossoms' in Johnny's death the following summer, and Ruttledge's involvement with that death brings further resolution not only to the issue of faith, but to his fear of death and loss; Bill Evans' arrival introduces the history of institutional abuse and the collusion of Church and State in the story of the 'homeboys', and when Bill refers to Patrick Ryan, not only is that character's increasingly sinister role in the Ruttledges' life intimated, but the symbolism of the unfinished shed Ryan is responsible for is 'seeded' into the narrative. The second section introduces the characters and stories of the Shah, Joe's uncle; Jimmy Joe McKiernan, auctioneer, publican, funeral director and IRA chief; and John Quinn, a figure of Olympian libido. Repetition shapes the narrative's circular world; repetition denotes cyclical time; and 'repetition' connotes sameness, but that is not the sense of the world or time that McGahern presents here. There is newness in the sameness, new energy in the round, a spirit of continuity and renewal. The opening paragraph of the novel is repeated, word for word, when the story has reached the end of the 'narrative year' that extends from summer to the following Easter; in fact, not only the opening paragraph but the first three pages are recycled (*RS*, 238–9). The repetition establishes a circular shape, and the effect accentuates the novel's 'comic turn' toward its conclusion. The final movement of the story makes an upward turn toward the redemptive spiral of romance, a turn signalled by a sudden act of oracular quotation.

Circles within circles: the narration is as patterned as a choral dance in classical drama, moving centrifugally, then centripetally, out from and back to 'the still centre' of the lake. The lake centres the concentric worlds of action and experience, moving outwards from the lakeside community of the Ruttledges and Murphy's, Ryan and Quinn; to the town and the Shah, Frank Dolan, Father Conroy, Luke Henry's bar, the Central Hotel and Mrs Maguire; then to Dublin and Jim, Lucy and Margaret; and finally, to London and Robert Booth. Early in the novel, Ruttledge and Patrick Ryan are putting up the rafters on the shed they are building. The passage can be read as a metafictive parable. What Ruttledge describes to Ryan – 'how the rafters frame the sky. How the squares of light are more interesting than the open sky. They make it look more human by reducing the sky, and then the whole sky grows out from that small space' (*RS*, 68) – is a version of McGahern's credo of the artist as the maker of meaningful order; it is a precise statement of how art is the 'reformation' of *aesthesis*, the perception of the external world by the senses, into the *aesthetic*, the perception of meaning and beauty in order. For McGahern, the making of narrative 'frames' the disconnected accidents of life, 'shapes' them into pattern and symmetry, connecting leaf, branch and sky into a composition of foreground and background, creating in the process the illusion of a managed order and manageable universe by 'reducing' the immensity that surrounds and permeates each life to an intelligible human scale, the terrible beauty of finite borders and the infinite unknown they push against. This is how the randomness of experience in a world that is oblivious to us is given meaning, is brought within the ambit of human value and made 'more interesting' by the artist, and how, as a result, the universal is projected from the particular, as 'the whole sky grows out from that small space'. The exchange between Ruttledge and Ryan glosses McGahern's approach to narrative form in the novel, his concentric shaping of the characters' stories – the circles within circles of the lives, experiences and relationships – into a narrative mandala with his gaze fixed on the immoveable certainty of the world symbolized by the lake that all the characters orbit, like planets around a sun.[12]

---

12   Sampson reads the rafters passage as 'one of the few moments in the novel when the non-believer Joe Ruttledge articulates an idea of aesthetic perception as a principle of order and meaning in the continuum of time' ('"Open to the World,"' 144).

We see this concentric shaping in the synchronizing of death and harvest, endings and new beginnings, showing the continuous rhythms of change in everything natural and human. When the cat brings in a dead hare to Kate the scene serves as prologue to the extended haying episode, which is described in loving detail, a hymn to the natural rhythms and beauty of the land and the satisfaction of physical labour upon it. For all its similarity to the scenes in *Amongst Women*, however, the description of the haying in *That They May Face the Rising Sun* differs noticeably in tone and effect: the 'community' here is that of two families, the Ruttledges and Ryans, helping each other, not that of a single family in neurotic isolation from others. McGahern follows the haying scenes with Ruttledge hearing that the Shah has decided to retire and John Quinn to marry for the third time. The narrative method links natural processes and human feelings and decisions in a single flowing medium, a narration that emulates time itself, paradoxically, in its unconscious containment of the world that has invented it. 'The time comes ... when we all have to move over', the Shah tells Ruttledge (*RS*, 118), and the descriptions of them walking the fields together, looking out to the Iron Mountains where the Shah's life began, and where, of course, McGahern's mother's life also began (*RS*, 35–6), express McGahern's sense of easing into the inevitable (see *RS*, 119, 356). That life long ago completed its cycle; now the Shah's is moving into the next segment on the wheel that is completing yet another ultimate revolution. And yet the paradox is that there is no ending in the completion. As Kate says, 'The past and present are all the same in the mind', (*RS*, 73). This is a truth that has coursed through McGahern's writing ever since *The Barracks*, where McGahern presents Elizabeth's dead lover, Halliday, to be as much of a presence in her life as her husband. McGahern affirms his mother's presence in his own life and in the imagining of this novel with every reference to the flora and fauna of the landscape, but especially, with every allusion to the sun, a motif that achieves its richest expression in the grave-digging scene at the end.

In the final phase of this first 'act' in the novel, McGahern shapes the natural cycle of harvest and the human cycle of retirement into an emotional and aesthetic consonance with the bittersweet heartbreak of mother-love. Ruttledge is helping Jamesie and Mary stack hay in their barn when their son, Jim, and his wife arrive to pick up their daughter, who has been staying with them. Jim is an allegorical character – a younger version of McGahern himself, someone who used education to escape from life on the family farm to a career in Dublin, only to feel uprooted and spiritually starved in the nation's capital. But it is Mary who is the real focus of McGahern's attention in the scene. Love and loss, the emotional dyad that pulses darkly and powerfully through all McGahern's writing, are here folded wonderfully into the mysterious fabric of time. Mary seems to recognize for a moment the 'strange and substantial' shape (*RS*, 125) that her own life has taken, palpable as the ache in her breast and yet somehow beyond the grasp of understanding. The 'scattered years of change' cannot be 'gathered in and kissed' (*RS*, 125); she'll never hold again the brilliant little boy she and Jamesie made and raised, even though she can still see him there in front of her. Mary seems mesmerized by the real presence of time in its wholeness, by the paradox that time is always whole and always continuing. McGahern's mother didn't live to see him as a man with a wife, with the life he eventually made for himself. What he imagines here is the mother's feeling of the duration of her son's life as *inseparable* from her own living yet ultimately happening without her. Time as change is sensible; this is the undeniable, not-to-be dulled ache of loss; but this is not the loss of absence: Jim is there before her, 'in the flesh'. Perhaps that is the meaning of 'There is only flesh' (*RS*, 125). Even if she were to take him in her arms now, Mary could not take back the whole of him she knows and feels and carries in her mind, but which is beyond her having in time in the flesh. In time, there is only flesh, the stages and phases of a body's being in the world, *in* time, and *in time with* the world. Only in the mind, in memory, in the imagination that is memory, is there a wholeness that time cannot outrun or leave behind. Like the earlier allegory of the rafters, this passage bears directly on our understanding of McGahern's fully developed art of memory.

The alternating current of centripetal-centrifugal energy in the narrative is a manifestation at the level of structure, imagery and motif of the life-death dialectic that has always energized McGahern's story-telling. The dialectic moves between the poles of consolidation and dissolution in a circular-cyclical rhythm. One of the great achievements of McGahern's narration in this novel is its fusion of human and natural time-senses into an intuition of history as an endlessly unfolding present. 'History' in *That They May Face the Rising Sun* is broached in the Jimmy Joe McKiernan-Troubles references, then subtly undermined in the turn on nationalist myth-time that emerges in McGahern's play on the 'Easter Rising' in the Easter episode that begins the novel's final movement, and finally deconstructed in the comic play with clock-time in Jamesie's house in the final pages. The story ambles gently from summer to summer, ending with Johnny's death. The sense of time as a cyclical 'dance' of natural and human rhythms emerges with the repetition of language at the beginning of the Easter episode and again with Johnny's second visit. In the first instance, the sense of renewal that attends the season gives way to an ominous foreshadowing in the death of the black lamb, a premonition of Johnny's death later that summer.

The description of Easter morning repeats the description of the morning that opens the novel but adds the reference to Easter to denote the progress of time; then suddenly, there is a passage of apparent speech: '"On such an Easter morning, as we were setting out for Mass, we were always shown the sun: Look how the molten globe and all the glittering rays are dancing. The whole of heaven is dancing in its joy that Christ has risen"' (*RS*, 238). Someone has spoken, but McGahern does not tell us who. It makes sense to hear Joe Ruttledge remembering Easter morning as a child, for we know Kate was raised an atheist; but if it is Joe's voice, he is something of a ventriloquist's dummy, for McGahern is actually quoting *his* mother's voice directing the children to the Easter morning dance in heaven (see *M*, 11). Thus the circling back within the novel is itself encircled by a second, more expansive, and *extra*-textual retrospective cast. The text here is 'strange', 'weird': the quotation marks announce an 'annunciation' that is also a resurrection, not of Christ but rather of McGahern's 'beloved.' McGahern's appropriation of his mother's language of belief and praise for a remembering, but as we know, no longer believing, Ruttledge, frees McGahern to engage in the 'impiety' which he then puts into the scene. On his way to Easter Mass Jamesie bursts into the Ruttledge house with a parody of an invitation to participate in the Christian ritual of renewal. The allusion to the Easter communion in the image of the chocolate bar initiates the dance of language by which McGahern displaces the Christian mystery of Easter with his own myth of death and resurrection, a myth he gives full expression in his memoir. This whole passage is a personal-secular 'mystery' that emanates from the heart of McGahern's art of memory, revealing the autobiographical muse at the core of this, his apparently most 'impersonal' novel.

Jamesie's greeting, like so much of his banter and actions in the novel, has the air of theatre and play. Because he sports an Easter lily on his lapel, Ruttledge asks him if he supports the IRA. Jamesie's reply completes the linking of Christian myth and nationalist myth-history through the allusion to the histories of violence each has been responsible for (*RS*, 239); this also evokes the secular history of post-revolutionary Ireland that has been a satirical theme in McGahern's writing ever since *The Barracks* and which is continued in his last novel through Patrick Ryan's and John Quinn's scorn for guard, priest, doctor and teacher. McGahern has this secular history and its appropriation of the Christian myth of blood sacrifice – as Jamesie says, 'The dead can be turned into anything' (*RS*, 244) – more or less hi-jack the Easter episode when Jamesie and the Ruttledges hear the IRA drummers gathering on Glasdrum for the annual march to commemorate the 'martyrs' who died in a Tan ambush during the War of Independence. Jamesie and his father witnessed the action and saved one of the wounded survivors, Big Bernie Reynolds, and Jamesie's account of the ambush and of the reprisal killing of an innocent Protestant farmer (*RS*, 239–43) leads into Ruttledge's sarcastic suggestion that a ventriloquist's dummy with a looped recording of 'Hello' would be a more appropriate memorial than what the local boffins have erected (*RS*, 243). McGahern continues to express his disgust for the men of violence as Jamesie and the Ruttledges walk out to see the parade on the main road and he describes the effect of the IRA colour party and the marchers with placards and posters of Pearse, McDermott and Sands as 'somehow sinister and cheap' (*RS*, 244). McGahern's take on republican nationalism and Jimmy Joe McKiernan, the leader of the provisional IRA in both the North and the South, is that it and he are just another form of power-mongering. Instead of a movement, McGahern seems to see his father, the bully who had to dominate all around him; instead of a dream, he sees self-delusion, craven deceit, and hypocritical cant (*RS*, 245).

The way that the Easter section ends is emblematic of McGahern's 'shaping' of the narrative as a whole. Out on the road, Jamesie and the Rutledges run into Patrick Ryan and Big Mick Madden. Madden is described as a bully, and Ryan, an aging bantam who thrives on confrontation, eggs him on against Jamesie. The outing suddenly turns unpleasant, and Rutledge leads Kate and Jamesie back to the lake. The final paragraph rounds on the language that began the section. The irony McGahern has built into the echo in the last sentence – 'A child could easily believe that the whole of heaven was dancing' (*RS*, 247) – undoes the apparently benign sense of the imagery in the opening paragraphs and the allusion to his mother's proclamation. Ruttledge – like McGahern – is no longer a child, and long since has lost his childish belief in his mother's faith. And what Christian heaven would dance to the Provos' fife and drum? The section ends circling back, ironically, on its beginning, just as the section itself began by circling back on the beginning of the novel: circles within circles, a concentric art. Later in the novel, when Jimmy Joe McKiernan and Big Mick Madden appear at Johnny's removal and the grave-digging scene, we see even more concentric ripples extending from this section. And when Ruttledge takes Johnny's still warm hand to begin washing his corpse, and thinks, 'It did not take an ambush to bring about such quick and irrecoverable change' (*RS*, 272), the ripple effect of McGahern's concentric art is felt in the moment's blending of 'history' and truth, the 'national' and the individual, and the 'religious' and the secular into the irreducible, un-transcendible reality of human vulnerability to change.

Following the Easter episode Ruttledge himself is 'ambushed' by death in the very next scene when the black lamb is crushed because of his impatience and haste dosing his flock. When Kate hears the ewe calling for its missing lamb, McGahern turns the episode into a parable of memory (*RS*, 250–1). Kate's attempt at consolation ironically affirms the centrality of memory to human consciousness. The death of the lamb clearly symbolizes loss, McGahern's familiar demon. When Jamesie breezes in, he dispels their gloom by calling them back to the world of continuous becoming which is their life; 'The beauty of that instant in the sun could only be kept now in the mind' (*RS*, 251): mind and memory, for McGahern, the place and agency of resurrection.

In the Heart of the Country: The World of the Novel

In *Memoir* McGahern describes the farm he bought when he returned to Ireland in the 1970s as the centre of a circle with a ten mile radius that contained the world of childhood memory (*M*, 267). This 'mother-world' is very much the template for the fictive world of *That They May Face the Rising Sun*. McGahern has given the centrifugal-centripetal pattern of his own life to Joe Ruttledge's. After leaving Ireland in the mid-1960s, McGahern returned eventually to live not far from the Aughawillan graveyard where his mother lay, and where, eventually, he would be buried with her. In his memoir McGahern describes his neighbours as enthusiastic, free-spirited and full of playful wit (*M*, 261), and in doing so he describes Jamesie and the Shah, Patrick Ryan and John Quinn, and the other characters in the novel. Like the Shah, McGahern's uncle, Pat McManus, was a frequent visitor at his farm, and his amiableness, humour, stubbornness and hearty appetite are all celebrated in that character (see *M*, 261, 263). The Shah, like McGahern's mother's family, hails from the Iron Mountains, and he had an older brother and sister who won scholarships, like Jimmy and Susan McManus (*RS*, 35–7, *M*, 45–6); he also once owned and operated a saw-mill, like the uncle in *The Pornographer* and like Pat McManus. He is a figure of wealth and independence who enjoys the 'power' these afford, and like Uncle Michael in *The Pornographer*, enjoys it when others acknowledge his successes. Also like Michael, the Shah considers his bachelor state to be ideal.[13]

In the same way that the Shah is based on McGahern's uncle, Joe and Kate Ruttledge are thinly disguised versions of John McGahern and his second wife. The details of their arrival at the farm by the lake and their life there match those recounted in *Memoir*. Ruttledge's memory of the train

---

13   See *RS*, 40. The Shah's words repeat the pornographer's comment about Michael; in fact, Ruttledge's whole conversation with the Shah at this point is almost word for word the same as the pornographer's with his uncle (compare *RS*, 40 and *P*, 17–18).

ride to town to shop with his mother is based on McGahern's memory of trips he and his mother took from Aughawillan to Ballinamore. While Maher finds 'no strong central consciousness to hold our attention' in *That They May Face the Rising Sun*, he senses Ruttledge to be 'McGahern's mouthpiece … the friendly but detached observer, the "seer," the prophet' whose 'insights are born out of a carefully nurtured vision of existence that is anchored in the local but reaches the universal'.[14] Ruttledge is not all that 'detached', however, but rather close to the Shah and Jamesie, intimately involved in their lives, and not merely observing them. He arranges loans for the transfer of the one's business, and washes the body and digs the grave of the other's brother. Ruttledge does not write the letter for Jamesie and Mary so well that they say he perfectly captured their feelings about Johnny and his request to live with them because he is a detached 'seer' and 'prophet', but rather because he is so close to them, to the community, and to the manners and mores of their world. Ruttledge is McGahern's 'mouthpiece', to be sure, expressing his aesthetic values and even method, as well as his attitudes to the Church, Catholic dogma, and nationalist politics. And in all of this McGahern is building on the style of narration he developed in *Amongst Women*; for the triangulation of the narrator, Ruttledge, and McGahern replicates that of the narrator, Luke, and McGahern in that novel.[15]

One of the first things we learn about Joe Ruttledge is that, like McGahern, while he misses the ceremony and ritual of the Catholic mass, he no longer believes in the faith of his childhood (*RS*, 2). Later, we learn that he studied for the priesthood but then abandoned it and went to England (*RS*, 39). Ruttledge's refusal to attend mass becomes a comic motif in the novel; Jamesie constantly chides him, less for his religious dereliction than lack of interest in people, 'the whole performance', that his absence on Sundays shows. As he says, 'None of us believes and we go' (*RS*, 2). Maher finds Ruttledge to be 'undoubtedly a deeply spiritual man', and as he also

---

14   Maher, *John McGahern*, 123, 136.
15   Grennan also notes a similarity between the third-person voices in *Amongst Women* and *That They May Face the Rising Sun* (see '"Only What Happens,"' 26).

considers the character the author's 'mouthpiece', this implies that McGahern is expressing his own spirituality through the character. The nature of
the spirituality to be found in this novel, however, is expressed more by the
structure and form of the narrative, than by anything Ruttledge says, and
it is important to note that McGahern himself resisted Maher's point in
the same way he rejected reading the novel in terms of an elegiac sociology.
McGahern denied that his attention to natural details and landscape in the
novel expresses *any* spiritual values or experience.[16] 'Spiritual', because of its
transcendental connotations, is perhaps the wrong word; 'religious' may be a
better choice, as long as we emphasize its disconnection from any organized
religion and especially the Catholicism and Church of McGahern's youth.
Discussing the community and world of Ó Criomhthain's *An tOileánach*,
McGahern praised E. R. Dodds' observation that 'religion grows out of
man's relationship to his total environment, morals out of his relations to
his fellow man'.[17] This meaning of religious draws on the etymology that
derives the word from the Latin *religare*, 'to bind fast', as in monastic vows.
For McGahern, someone's religious nature is what nurtures and is nurtured
by the sense of belonging to another, to a family, to a community, and to
the earth they make their living on. One of the strongest features of *That
They May Face the Rising Sun* is the way it conveys the bonds that grow
and bind the Ruttledges to Jamesie and Mary, that strengthen between
Ruttledge and his uncle, and that blossom between the Shah and Kate.
It is the Ruttledges' bond with the place, the lake-world their home, that
most embodies the 'religious' power in the book.

But if the religious-spiritual outlook in the novel needs careful qualification, the political views are clear. *That They May Face the Rising Sun* contains some of McGahern's most explicit criticism of southern republicanism
in his fiction. Ruttledge's scorn for the men in balaclavas is another motif,
along with the comic-satirical references to the two detectives permanently
stationed in the alley beside Jimmy Joe McKiernan's bar. McKiernan has

---

16   See Maher, *John McGahern*, 135, 159.
17   McGahern, 'What Is My Language', 7; McGahern also quotes the passage in his last
      published work, 'God and Me'.

been linked to murder, mutilation and mayhem and has spent years in prison in the North (*RS*, 284). Ruttledge recognizes the presence of both the idealist and the ruthless pragmatist in the man's character, but there is no suggestion he has any respect for the former and he is unequivocally hostile to the latter. Ruttledge also expresses disgust with the southern politicians who allow McKiernan to function with impunity as the chief of the provisional IRA in the North and South (*RS*, 136). There is an interesting consequence to McGahern's decision to treat this theme through the device of a motif, however. As a result of being random and dispersed among descriptions of the town at different times of the year, the references to McKiernan's republican passion are contained and indeed overwritten by the bustle and business of everyday life in the community, and as a result the narration captures the way this political issue is simultaneously acknowledged but ignored by the people, in the same way that they pay lip service to Church and State but do what they want anyway. The narrator never enters McKiernan's bar; it is a world he has no interest in, except when it slithers out to invade the public world he lives in – as in the bombing at Enniskillen, at which he expresses revulsion (*RS*, 225). Ruttledge tells Jamesie straight out that he has no time for McKiernan or his kind, and then tells McKiernan to his face that he has no interest in his cause and objects to the violence he uses to advance it (*RS*, 283, 286). Like most people in the community, however, Jamesie and Mary are in awe of McKiernan; and when he shows up to personally remove Johnny's body to the church, they believe only Ruttledge is capable of entertaining him.

Mary and Jamesie Murphy: are they Baucis and Philemon or gods themselves? They welcome the Ruttledges to the lake-world but also 'test' them, and at the end of the novel they vanish like angels or divinities into the light at the top of a hill (*RS*, 296, 298). It is possible to see the couple as the elegiac core of the novel, vanishing into the evening half-light in the closing lines like the rural ethos and community the novel celebrates through them. But while Jamesie is most definitely Ruttledge's Virgilian guide, he *doesn't* 'know the whole world' as he claims (*RS*, 7, 296), even if Ruttledge humours him by agreeing that he does; nor does his bottomless bag of old saws, clichés and 'folk wisdom' make him the Silenus of the lake-world. Jamesie is a joker, teaser, and mimic, but McGahern often shows him at a loss, panicking, or in quick and quiet retreat from people and situations where his blarney and uncontrollable curiosity are unappreciated or unwelcome. An aspirant Fool, Jamesie is really never more than a would-be Puck. Bill Evans, Patrick Ryan, and even Jamesie's daughter-in-law are immune, if not even hostile, to his 'charm', and when he utters such pseudo-profundities as 'There's nothing right or wrong in this world. Only what happens' (*RS*, 56), it is clear he enjoys listening to the sound of his own voice more than he does thinking.[18] (His favourite pastime, after all, is watching *Blind Date* on the telly.) But if he is no wise man Jamesie *is* the 'unconscious' angel who guides Ruttledge through the lakeside world by luck and by example, instructing him as much through the display of his shortcomings as by his manifest and real virtues. 'And you have been my sweet guide', Ruttledge tells him at the end of the novel (*RS*, 296), and perhaps his most important lesson to Ruttledge is his 'attention' to the particulars and events of the everyday world around him – comically yet seriously celebrated in his passion for gossip (*RS*, 121).[19] This quality is the hallmark of that generosity of imagination – openness, curiosity, interest, the vulnerability of self to other – that emerges as a primary value in McGahern's writing and which is the polar extreme of the *acedia* that deforms other characters in his fiction. Jamesie is enthralled by life, by 'the whole performance' of man and woman, bird, beast and flower.

Jamesie is a surprisingly sentimental-romantic creation for this novelist, but then *That They May Face the Rising Sun* is full of surprises. Who would have thought John McGahern could be funny? Of course, his dry

18   What lay behind Jamesie's would-be wisdom is probably McGahern's sense of him as a character out of *An tOileánach*; McGahern admired that Ó Criomhthain 'never examines why people behave in such and such a manner …. What happens is all' ('What Is My Language', 5). A glaring and authoritative contradiction of this view in the novel, however, is Ruttledge's view of McKiernan, his kind and his cause.

19   Ruttledge calls Jamesie an angel when he suddenly appears behind him in the field where the Shorthorn is in labour, and it's clear that Jamesie has indeed been acting as Ruttledge's 'guardian angel', watching the cow while Joe was away in Carrick with Patrick Ryan (*RS*, 53). Later in the novel, when he lifts her out of her gloom over the loss of the black lamb, Kate also describes Jamesie in angelic terms (*RS*, 252).

wit is legendary, but until this novel an essay on humour in McGahern's fiction would have been a depressing task. But *That They May Face the Rising Sun* is different from anything before it. Hilarious is too strong, perhaps, to describe the scene of Patrick Ryan chased by a swarm of bees after trying to 'cut a button' (*RS*, 71) near the Ruttledges' hive, but funny it is; as is the scene of the Shah delivering Ruttledge's boxes of wine in a covered cattle-trailer so that no one would know his nephew was such a prodigious consumer of the grape, and hectoring him and Kate to move the wine into a back room of the house so no one will see it, all the while tut-tutting sincere moral concern at his nephew's imminent decline into alcoholism and lakeside bacchanalia (*RS*, 58–60). So, too, is the image of the Shah and Ryan exchanging mock ecclesiastical 'blessings' all the while slagging the other to Rutledge (*RS*, 61–3). The description of the Shah on holiday at Burtonport, walking through the hotel lobby on his way to his daily swim attired in an anti-deluvian swimsuit and becoming the 'star attraction' the other guests turn out to see every day, and then spending his evenings anxiously chaperoning Monica in the hotel bar, is also comical (*RS*, 101).

Like a regular breeze from the mountains, humour is a continuous presence in the world of this novel, ranging from broad slapstick to subtle irony, from the satirical to the pathetic – as in Ryan's description of Big John Madden's comment on dying (*RS*, 280). But as in the latter instance, McGahern's technique remains an expression of a dialectical vision and temperament which present a world that is 'complete' by virtue of the balance of the contraries that compose it. There should be no mistaking the many passages of natural description in *That They May Face the Rising Sun* as setting and maintaining a tone of bucolic bliss. There are dark tones throughout, beginning in the first section with the stories of the exploited and abused orphan, Bill Evans, and the deceived lover, Johnny Murphy; Evans reappears regularly throughout the novel to remind the reader of the shameful social history his life represents, while Jamesie's description of Father Conroy's misinformed eulogy for Johnny at the end is a reference to the theme of emigration and the scorn with which the 'new class' looked down upon those driven to England for work (*RS*, 295). The balance and integration of contrasting images and moods, the dramatic yet coherent juxtaposition of a world of natural and social order along with the natural and human forces that threaten to pull it down, a juxtaposition that occurs whenever Bill, the ghost of an Ireland *not* long past, enters the Ruttledge house, demanding tea and drink and cigarettes, or, more sinisterly, whenever Patrick Ryan or John Quinn appear, reflect the full maturity of McGahern's narrative art.

Along with Jimmy Joe McKiernan, Ryan and Quinn occupy one end of a moral spectrum with the Shah, the Ruttledges, Jamesie and Mary at the other end. But while this might suggest hard and fast moral positions or identities that is not what the reader encounters in the novel. Rather what we encounter in all the characters is a realistic mixture of qualities, strengths and weaknesses, understandable and baffling, attractive and repugnant. In keeping with his admiration for Ó Criomhthain, McGahern is less concerned with individual morality than with the collective ethos of the community.[20] Thus even the villains have their moments of goodness: Quinn helps to dig Johnny's grave; Ryan eventually returns to work on the shed; and even Jamesie and Mary have their failings – as with their treatment of Johnny. The latter is a telling instance of McGahern's narrative integrity. Jamesie and Mary are without doubt emblematic creations in the novel; as individuals and as a couple, they symbolize all that is good and decent in people who have spent their lives close to the land. They have opened their home and hearts to Ruttledge and Kate, who have responded in kind, and each couple has great affection and respect for the other. And when the 'problem' of Johnny's request arises, the narrator proffers a painstaking explanation of Jamesie's and Mary's predicament in terms of the manners and mores of their rural world, 'a language that hadn't any simple way of saying no' (*RS*, 186). This is sympathetic to the couple's plight, but it is also clear that what McGahern has Ruttledge do by writing the letter is quite simply tell Johnny 'no': even though it is his family home, he cannot come back and move in with his brother and sister-in-law. The narrator informs us that, as Ruttledge delivered the letter, he needed to 'reassure' himself

---

20 McGahern praises Ó Criomhthain's respect for 'the values of his society as a whole' ('What Is My Language', 3).

that he was doing the right thing (*RS*, 188), and afterwards, on his walk
home, when a heron in the moonlight spooks him, the narrator's sense of
guilt over his role in the affair is clear (*RS*, 191). The final talent that levels
the balance here is the effect of Jamesie's and Mary's ingenuous claims in
the closing lines of the section, that 'It couldn't have worked any better';
'And Mister Singh stood by him in the end' (*RS*, 194). Jamesie and Mary
are good people, but their goodness is real, flawed, human: Jamesie does *not*
stand by his brother, Mary refuses to live with her brother-in-law under any
circumstances, and they both refused to make room for him in the home
that was as much his as theirs. Later, when we hear of Johnny's version of
his decision to remain in London, it is sadly ironic (*RS*, 259).

    While not as important a character as Patrick Ryan, one cannot ignore
the equally theatrical but more priapic John Quinn, who arrives to welcome
the Ruttledges to the neighborhood in the second section of the novel. His
real purpose is to ask them to find him a woman. Newly married themselves, he thinks Kate should know someone who would be interested in
becoming his partner. Duplicitous, cunning, a false charmer, a 'performer'
like McGahern's own father, Quinn married Margaret Sweeney to get her
parents' farm and more or less raped her on her wedding day in full view
of the wedding guests and her parents (*RS*, 28). He drove the latter to
early graves and eventually – after eight children – Margaret as well. His
relentless search for a 'housekeeper' after her death recalls McGahern's
account of his father's in *Memoir*. There is an almost Chaucerian quality
to Quinn: he is slightly larger than life, like a character out of folk- or fairy
tale who ultimately gets his comeuppance. Kate and Ruttledge immediately
find him repulsive, and their judgment of him does not change; but like
all in the lake-world they accept him for what he is, or as Sampson puts
it, they 'accept his nature as a given'.[21] McGahern tempers what we know
about this unctuously odious man's predatory sexuality and spousal abuse

---

21   For Sampson, all the characters seem like 'medieval humours': 'the lecherous Quinn,
     the curious Jamesie, the hungry Evans, the shrewd and taciturn Shah, the lost emigrant
     Johnny, the actor and procrastinator Ryan, the returned native Ruttledge'; Sampson
     describes the novel as a 'morality play' ('"Open to the World,"' 139).

by showing him to be a father who stands up for his children against the abusive schoolteacher, 'Missus Killboy', and who continues to have his children's love and respect long after they have left home; he also shows up to help dig Johnny Murphy's grave. Like the more enigmatic Ryan, Quinn is also treated comically; every time he greets someone, the reader cannot help chuckling, and his sexual questing is so persistent it takes on a 'mock-heroic' quality. Ryan, too, for all his darkness, is occasionally humorous and sociable, although Kate is never comfortable in his presence. But that is the nature of the world McGahern has envisioned, a place of sunshine, moonshine, and all the varieties of light and shadow in between. And given this, it should be no surprise that McGahern includes death in this world; what *is* surprising is just how much death he does allow. Jackie, Bill Evan's employer-abuser; Jimmy Joe McKiernan's cousin, the woman who lived in the house the Ruttledges bought; Margaret Sweeney and her parents; Mary's father; Jamesie's father; Edmund Ryan; the men killed in the ambush; Taylor Sinclair; Big John Madden; Johnny Murphy – not to mention the cattle, sheep, black lamb and hare: there is a lot of death in *That They May Face the Rising Sun*, more than in any other of McGahern's novels. Yet the world of the novel is overwhelmingly *alive*, perhaps because of the 'Lady of the Lake'.

The Lady of the Lake

The world of *That They May Face the Rising Sun*, as in all McGahern's novels, is an amalgam of memory and imagination, recent memories as well as memories taken from the 'mother lode' he kept in the deepest recesses of the archive, and which he brought into the explicit light of day in his memoir. The descriptions of the lake-world that pulse through the novel are a slowly building hymn of celebration and thanksgiving for his rediscovery of the continuing and remembered world of his mother's love, those brief childhood years he had lived with her inside the magic circle that contained

Ballinamore, Lisacarn, and Aughawillan, and his rediscovery of that land-scape when he settled at Foxfield. Symbolically, the centre of the fictive world of *That They May Face the Rising Sun* – the lake, and within the lake, the heron island – is the spirit of McGahern's beloved, Susan McGahern. In his memoir he makes clear that he learned his love of the countryside, of the flora and fauna of the lanes and lakes that surrounded him and his wife, and that he describes in the novel, from her. *Memoir* is a celebration and thanksgiving for what he describes as the abiding influence of her love in his life, a presence he believed 'saved' him from his father. *That They May Face the Rising Sun* is a complementary act of homage. The spirit of the woman who initiated him into the beauty of the life of the region informs his narration from beginning to end, and centres its concentric circles of character, setting, and action, all of which cohere around the lake and the spirit that emanates from the recurring passages that describe it. Eventually, it becomes clear that the centrifugal-centripetal pattern in the narrative emulates the structure of McGahern's own life-journey, as well as the rhythms of memory and imagination that have ebbed and flowed through his *poiēsis*.

The paean to the lake-world begins in the first section, with the description of the lane from the Ruttledges' house down to the lake, its 'steep banks ... covered with foxgloves and small wild strawberries and green vetches' (*RS*, 14). This is the first of what becomes a choral motif of passages that describe the reeds at the lakeshore, the swans, the shoals of perch that ripple the surface of the water, the island in the middle where the herons nest, Gloria Bog in the distance, the open sky, and the Iron Mountains on the horizon (see also *RS*, 35–6, 42, 119, 150, 177, 236). The passages usually occur when Ruttledge walks his fields with his uncle who, when he looks towards the mountains, looks to where his life began. In such passages, McGahern is looking at where *his* life as an artist began, under the tutelage of his mother. In *Memoir*, he imagines walking with his mother again and taking her down to the shore Ruttledge walks with Kate in the novel (*M*, 272). The imagery of bones and shells, the otters, and the Iron Mountains is the same as in the novel. The lake centres the novel in same way that his memory of his mother centres his memoir.

Perhaps this is why McGahern has given the 'reminding' voice of memory in the novel to the two important female voices. Mary says that 'People we know come and go in our minds whether they are here or in England or alive or dead' (*RS*, 115). Kate earlier articulates McGahern's abiding commitment to the art of memory and the quest for the 'Image' – the 'picture in the mind' – of the 'lost world' (*RS*, 73). The recurring actions of driving and walking around the lake, leaving and returning to the lakeside world, are the ultimate emplotment of the dialectic that shaped McGahern's writing life: the centrifugal/centripetal dialectic of memory itself. The circular form of *That They May Face the Rising Sun* deploys this dialectic through the shape given to the narrative by the seasonal cycle and the works and days of the rural calendar.

When we 'hear' in retrospect – as the memoir allows us to do – the voice of McGahern's mother in Ruttledge's memory of Easter morning, the spirit of the mother is revealed as a 'real presence' in the novel. Kate's and Mary's reminders serve as premonitions, in a sense, of this moment. Later, when Patrick Ryan explains the reason for placing the coffin in the grave with the deceased's head to the west, the linking of resurrection and the rising sun does not express any belief on McGahern's part in the faith of his child-hood, but rather the sense that as an artist he has finally managed to become a priest of the imagination after rejecting the priesthood he had promised to his mother. The only resurrection McGahern believes in occurs in human memory. What this climactic moment in the novel connects is the *image* of the rising sun and the truth of a life recovered through memory become imagination. The title of the novel connotes a desire to bring the dead to life through a celebration of the spirit of life that they manifested for their time, and which does not pass away with them as long as there is a memory to keep it alive. Teeming with life, the lake in the novel symbolizes memory itself, the rich archive McGahern has drawn from, consciously and uncon-sciously, for everything he has written; and the descriptions of Ruttledge living beside it, walking round its shores, studying its life and life-cycles, his view always centred by the heron island at its centre, are McGahern's subtlest metapoetic images of the writing life for him. With *That They May Face the Rising Sun* McGahern finally mastered the art of memory by imagining something completely new out of what he had always known.

'Sergeant Death' and His Unfinished Shed in Co. Leitrim

While Johnny Murphy's death does not come as a surprise in the novel, Ruttledge's volunteering to lay out his corpse does. The impulse comes from somewhere and something inside Ruttledge that he was not aware of until that moment. Jamesie's reaction – 'Will you be able?' (*RS*, 271) – suggests Ruttledge will face a test. It is a test he wants to face. Ruttledge seems to be asking for something from Jamesie and the community gathered in the house. To be 'admitted', perhaps. If Ruttledge has been perceived as an outsider until this moment, this will take him across a threshold. He would always be 'different' and 'special' and a bit 'above' the locals, perhaps, but this will bring him inside their world as much as Jimmy Joe McKiernan. And at the end of the episode, Jamesie, without asking, includes him in the grave-digging party. Although Ruttledge's offer is a public overture and the action he performs a public-communal ritual, his motive seems deeply personal; nor does he really understand it until afterwards. The laying-out scene is one of the best things McGahern ever wrote, and along with the grave-digging scene, provides closure to much more than just this novel.

Ruttledge and another volunteer, Tom Kelly, are given whiskey before beginning, along with the paraphernalia necessary for the preparation of the body. Johnny is still warm when Ruttledge touches him; just a few hours before, they had been together in Luke Henry's bar and Ruttledge is in awe of his sudden and irrevocable going. The description of their removing Johnny's clothes, cutting away his undershirt and pants, closing the ears, nostrils and rectum with cotton wool – is perfectly measured; the shifting rhythms of short statements, list, dialogue, and longer periods capture their physical movements as they work on the body. The effect is far from clinical or minimalist, however, as it builds to an elegiac climax: 'To see him naked was also to know what his character and clothes had disguised – the wonderful physical specimen he had been' (*RS*, 272–3). Eamon Maher is spot on when he says this 'is a spiritual experience for [Ruttledge] and constitutes one of the key moments in the book';[22] but again, it is 'spiritual' in the sense of McGahern's non-transcendental spirituality, his reverence for the sanctity of the human, and his 'religious' sense of the bonds that bind us all in the acts and experiences of our coming and going. McGahern has made a point of keeping the scene and moment rooted in the innate comedy of the circumstantial, not for any dramatic juxtaposition of high and low, but rather to affirm the sense that the human experience of ultimate reality comes in the medium of the banal. After moving the naked body onto the floor, Kelly begins to give Johnny his last haircut; the door suddenly bursts open and Ruttledge has to leap up to close it before anyone can see into the room. With people getting restless outside, they cannot get Johnny's dentures to stay in his mouth; no matter how much cotton wool they pack into the cavity, they keep popping out. Abandoning perfection, they are forced to settle for bulging cheeks: 'We did our best', Ruttledge tells Kelly (*RS*, 275).

Although Jamesie and Mary praise their effort and the wake goes off successfully, Kelly is right and they *are* criticized – by Patrick Ryan, the man everyone had expected to do what Ruttledge had volunteered to do, and who arrives to find that he has been replaced. 'Were you that greedy to get stuck in?' (*RS*, 277) he asks Ruttledge, and the insult is loaded with unconscious insight because Ruttledge's action *did* have something to do with getting 'stuck in', but with death as much as with the community of mourners. When they are alone and Kate asks him how he had felt working on the corpse, Ruttledge can only tell her: 'I'm not sure except I am very glad to have done it. It made death and the fear of death more natural, more ordinary' (*RS*, 279). The fear of death, loss, and change, if not the question of last things, has run through all of McGahern's fiction. In this episode, the *natural* spirituality that courses through the novel and which is most explicit in McGahern's descriptions of the lake-world, expands to encompass the *human* world: death is not tragic, but natural; the fear of death is not an extraordinary fear, but a fear as ordinary as the fear of heights, of snakes, or unpredictable bullies; and sudden and irrevocable change is,

22   *John McGahern*, 126.

like sunrise, an ambush only if we foolishly expect darkness never to give way to light. But this is an odd moment in the novel because we have not had any prior indication that Ruttledge *was* afraid of death; it is as if he is speaking for someone else or someone else is speaking through him.[23]

Who the 'silent partners' behind Ruttledge's admission might be is suggested when Kate brings up Patrick Ryan: 'Did you ever see anything like that entrance?' (*RS*, 279) and her theatrical metaphor cues Ruttledge's allusion to *Hamlet*: 'Sergeant Death appeared and found he had arrived too late' (*RS*, 279).[24] We might feel that an allusion to the famous play that begins with the son confronting the ghost of his father is long overdue in McGahern's oeuvre, but it was only in *The Pornographer* that McGahern had put Death in its place, and in *Amongst Women* he had laid the ghost of his father to rest. So here it is Ruttledge's ability to laugh at 'Sergeant Death' that is significant, because Ruttledge's fear of death and his need to stand up to Patrick Ryan are not unrelated. It is no coincidence that Ryan calls his house the 'Tomb', and anyone who has read McGahern's memoir will recognize characteristics in 'Sergeant Death' that recall Sergeant Francis McGahern. Both are physically attractive men with the personalities of 'performers'. In his memoir, McGahern describes his father as an actor, and he makes Patrick Ryan a respected amateur actor in this community. When Ruttledge asks him if he is happy, Ryan replies that he has no sense of interior continuity: 'That's why I always liked the acting. You are someone else and always know what you are doing and why' (*RS*, 203). McGahern thought his father's 'happiest role was in the IRA' during the War of Independence because it allowed him to exercise 'his propensity for violence' with impunity (*M*, 226). Ryan is the same kind of man but without a script. According to Jamesie, Ryan asks Ruttledge to drive him to Carrick to visit his brother in hospital simply to save face and not incur the talk of his neighbours. The scene is particularly well-written and shows an apparently

---

23   Referring to McGahern's achievement in this novel, Sampson writes: 'the *timor mortis* which has constantly unnerved McGahern's characters is abolished' ('"Open to the World,"' 143).

24   See Hamlet's reference to 'this fell sergeant, Death' (*Hamlet*, V. ii. 325).

gruff and insensitive Ryan heartlessly 'torturing' his brother, yet perhaps merely being clumsy and unhelpful with his feelings; afterwards, in the bar on the way back, Ryan is a different man, socially gentle and affable, and shows himself to be another kind of 'performer' (*RS*, 50–1), a charmer like John Quinn and Francis McGahern. Ryan constantly mocks Jamesie's mannerisms and curiosity, mostly, it seems, because Jamesie's good spirits and humour rankle his own miserable nature, recalling McGahern's father's jealousy of the joy of others. Ryan goads Ruttledge – prying into his and Kate's lack of children, for example – and tries to run down Kate's drawing because it does not bring her any money – just as McGahern's father goaded him about his modest success as a writer. However, Ryan's strongest connection to McGahern's father – and to Moran in *Amongst Women*, for that matter – is found in the narrator's reference to Ryan's narcissism and volatile temperament (*RS*, 65); also, with that fickleness, there is an ever-present threat of violence – 'a seething, barely restrained urge to strike out and wound ...' (*RS*, 67). Like McGahern's father, Ryan needs to dominate whatever situation he finds himself in.

But if McGahern's relationship with his father does inform and energize his construction of the Ruttledge-Ryan relationship, what is important is how he fits the relationship into the total shape of the work to counterpoint the relationships Ruttledge has with Jamesie and the Shah, both of whom counterbalance Ryan's 'power' in the lake-world. Patrick Ryan can be charming as well as aggressive, humorous as well as acerbic and rude, friendly as well as brusque and offensive. McGahern constructs him, like John Quinn, as someone who is as much a 'pillar' of the lake-world as the Shah or Jamesie. Ryan remains a sinister character from beginning to end, but to expel him, like the scapegoat in a Shakespearean comic romance, would be to traduce the human truth of the work. What Ryan represents in the novel is something *in* the world – and *in* Ruttledge – that McGahern now accepts as *necessary* to make both world and character complete. Returning from Johnny's wake, after his confrontation with Ryan, Ruttledge decides not to tell Kate that Ryan is coming to finish the shed; then in the closing lines of the novel, after Ryan appears and orders Ruttledge in Kate's presence to meet him the next morning to purchase the last of the building materials, when asked by Kate if he will simply tell him to forget the job, Ruttledge plays for time (*RS*, 298). His indecision and irresolution do not necessarily mean that he has taken up the manners of his chosen community; rather, his whole approach to Ryan and the kind of man he is has been an oblique firmness, an indirect confrontation rather than head-on head-butting. As a result we are constantly seeing McGahern – and Ruttledge – control or corral the darkness Ryan symbolizes. If Ryan mocks Jamesie, Jamesie also mocks Ryan; the scene in which Ryan needles Ruttledge about having no children with Kate is followed immediately by the scene where Ruttledge, Kate and Jamesie help the Shorthorn calve – another extremely well-written episode in the novel (*RS*, 52–5). Ryan insults the Shah to Ruttledge, but Ruttledge replies immediately, defending his uncle, and forcing Ryan to turn away. Ryan hurts Johnny by throwing up his mistake in leaving Ireland for London, and then excuses his bad manners by describing himself as a truth-teller. Ruttledge immediately corrects him: 'The truth isn't always useful'; and when Ryan truculently asks what is, Ruttledge does not miss a beat: 'Kindness ... understanding ... sympathy maybe' (*RS*, 75–6). Ryan keeps Ruttledge from his brother's funeral – which hurts him; but Ruttledge then displaces Ryan when he prepares Johnny's body for his burial, angering Ryan. Ryan's rudeness to Ruttledge, when he and Kate are welcoming Johnny home from England, is a violation of the ethos of guest and host, but Ruttledge stands up to him in his way, drawing attention to the breach in manners even as he allows it, leaving Ryan feeling exposed and nonplussed (*RS*, 84). What Ryan represents will always be present in the world and men like Ruttledge will always fear it. But it is a 'natural' presence and an 'ordinary' fear that can be contained and controlled, by wit and the language of wit, as Ruttledge does – or by art, as McGahern shows.

Ultimately, the relationship between Ryan and Ruttledge coheres around the symbol of the unfinished shed which, as the best symbols do, resists translation or reductive paraphrase. The unfinished shed becomes Ruttledge's unfinished business with Ryan, and that may symbolize McGahern's conscious or unconscious sense of unfinished business with his father; their 'business' together might even express an unconscious recognition of a connection between his father's destructive influence on him and his own creative processes and life as a writer; the unfinished shed may symbolize the unfinished nature of all art or McGahern's fear of finishing what he knew would be his last novel. The unfinished shed may or may not symbolize any, all, or none of these. Perhaps Ruttledge simply has come to prefer the view through the open rafters, the vision of how 'the whole sky grows out from that small space' (*RS*, 68). At the very least, the image of the unfinished shed seems to express the vision of the world that McGahern has shaped into the fictive world of the novel – an open, continuing, unfinished yet complete world, a gathering of the living and the dead.

Johnny's death and Ruttledge's washing of the body compose the first part of the climax of *That They May Face the Rising Sun*. The second part is the grave-digging scene and together they achieve a wonderful symmetry. Fear gives way to humour, flesh to bone, and 'Sergeant Death' appears in both scenes; in the first, he challenges Ruttledge to assume his role in the world he has chosen to make his home, and in the second, to accept the burden of knowledge entailed in that choice. McGahern describes the setting in a way that gathers the whole world of the novel to the graveside (*RS*, 279–80). The allusion to the Easter Sunday gathering brings the varieties of history and myth that have been present in the novel to the moment, but also brings a reminder of the potential for confrontation between Ryan and Madden and Ruttledge and Jamesie. The priest's cattle recall the Monaghan Day market episode and the bees the humorous scene with Ryan and Kate's bees. The sounds of traffic evoke the world of the Shah and Dolan at the scrapyard and the view to the family home in the blue mountains.

Past, present, and future suddenly come together when they uncover the bones and skull of one of Jamesie's family, which he gathers into a plastic bag (*RS*, 280). The abstractions of history and myth, nation and dogma suddenly scatter before the power of this homely image of ancestral presence and connection. Big Mick Madden looks over at his own father's grave and recalls his long and painful dying. 'All the antagonism he held towards Jamesie had disappeared', we are told (*RS*, 280). With a wonderful touch, McGahern confirms the sudden community that forms between them by having Patrick Ryan recount the humorous story of Big John Madden's difficult death. The gathering of the bones complements the scene of the washing of Johnny's body; the humour demystifies death, affirming that, even though it is a man's painful dying they are remembering, such a death is still 'natural', 'ordinary'. The grave-digging scene comes to its 'point' when Patrick Ryan realizes he has made a mistake in laying out the grave: 'We have widened the wrong fucken end' (*RS*, 281). When Ruttledge asks what difference it makes, Ryan's answer explains the title of the novel:

> 'He sleeps ... so that when he wakes he may face the rising sun.' Looking from face to face and drawing himself to his full height, Patrick Ryan stretched his arm dramatically towards the east. 'We look to the resurrection of the dead.' (*RS*, 281–2)

Perhaps this is why McGahern made Ryan an award-winning amateur actor, so that he could have Ryan deliver the climactic line theatrically – which draws immediate applause from Jamesie – but at the same time undercut the moment through the image of Ryan as an overdone ham. John Quinn is moved enough by Ryan's performance to remark that 'it'd nearly make you start to think' (*RS*, 282), which presumably explains why Jamesie, a few days after Johnny's funeral, asks Ruttledge if he believes in an afterlife. We know that, like his creator, Ruttledge does not, and he says so, adding, 'I suspect hell and heaven and purgatory – even eternity – all come from our experience of life and may have nothing to do with anything else once we cross to the other side' (*RS*, 294). This is McGahern's 'last word' on the question of life, death, and the afterlife, a final, resounding rejection of the faith of his childhood. But it is left to the reader to complete the answer to Jamesie's question with what the novel itself provides. *That They May Face the Rising Sun* does not affirm belief in the Christian concept of resurrection, but it does affirm 'the resurrection of the dead' in memory – and it is this which makes the novel the culmination and crowning achievement of McGahern's art of memory. The statements Kate and Mary make about the mind and memory; the 'allegorical' passage on the rafters; the poignant realization that 'There is only flesh'; and the gathering of the bones in the grave-digging scene, all come together to 'explain' the process, method and achievement of McGahern's novel. Metafictively, Ruttledge's question to Ryan is a question about narrative shape and form; the correct alignment of the coffin, like the successful re-formation of memory through the incarnation of idea in the words of personal vision, is critical if 'We look to the resurrection of the dead', which John McGahern very much did, but only as the ultimate achievement of his art of memory.

The Completed Circle: Clocking Out

That They May Face the Rising Sun is McGahern's most symbolic work of fiction. From the 'heron-priested' island at the centre of the lake to Rut-tledge and Ryan's unfinished shed, to the clocks and clockmaker at the end of the novel, McGahern has shaped his usual naturalism into a softer, more evocative, at times, poetic prose. The symbolism of the clocks and telephone poles in the closing pages is an interesting conjunction of the obvious and the encoded. The telephone poles that suddenly sprout up around the lakeshore signal modernity and change, but what is important is how the people welcome the change and do not feel threatened by it. Continuity in change is the abiding faith this novel affirms. This seems to be the point in the story of the Shah's retirement and sale of his busi-ness to Frank Dolan. As they wait in the lawyer's office, Ruttledge and his uncle stare at pictures of the town from years ago, noting how much it has changed (*RS*, 211). But there's change and there's change, it seems. Ruttledge and Mrs Maguire worry about the Shah's decision; however, the Shah welcomes the change in his life, and by selling to Frank he knows that the business will continue to be run as it has always been; indeed, Frank loses his chance at a bank loan because he refuses even to pretend to commit to the changes in business practice that the bank policy requires for the loan. He intends to keep things exactly the way they are, and after the sale goes through, the Shah continues to go to the scrapyard as before, but now as Frank's employee. It is a revolution, but a benign change of order, like a change in seasons, which is in fact the model of change that structures and informs the novel.

The symbolism of the clocks in the Murphy house is more complex and much richer. The nature and experience of time is a preoccupation throughout McGahern's fiction, and indeed, Jamesie's and Mary's clocks have migrated from Father Gerald's rectory in *The Dark*. A clock also fig-ures prominently in *The Leavetaking*, in the scene where the young Patrick imagines his mother's funeral. Are the clocks in the priest's house and later in Jamesie and Mary's a surreal multiplication of this clock, that McGahern describes in the novel and memoir 'telling' the time, tolling the minutes of the day of the mother's funeral, the clock that the little boy and young McGahern take under the stairs and then outside into the bushes, staring at its face like the face of their 'lost beloved', as if that face had become the face of time itself, time lost and never to be again? Yet as the boy stares at the clock it becomes a portal into the world of imagination, through which he 'sees' the funeral he was forbidden to attend, and paradoxically, memorializing the wound of absence while at the same time initiating the mystery of recovery.

Telling time: like the unfinished shed, the clocks may have a deeper meaning related to the nature of narrative itself. 'They'd have a tale to tell if they could speak', Mary says (*RS*, 293). There is an important dialectic running through McGahern's fiction which can be expressed using a phrase from the earlier fiction where his grief and anger dominated, leading to the *acedia*-inflected perspective on existence as merely 'killing time'. One way of understanding the overall process and shape of McGahern's evolving art of memory is to see the shift in the narrative drive from 'killing time' in the early novels to 'telling time' in the later, and to see the act of writing itself as his struggling with the wound of loss. From the outset McGahern's fiction sites this struggle in the act of narration itself, with all his novels attempting to transform the experience of an inhuman absolute, Time as overwhelming loss, into the experience of time as the consciousness – and acceptance – of what is natural and ordinary. McGahern's displacement of Time by time is cognate with his loss of faith in the Catholicism of his youth and his development of his own version of a secular humanism in its place, and all three are bound up not only with his decision to pursue a career as a writer of fiction, but with the ways his story-telling evolved over the span of his writing life.

As image, the clocks all out of sync, striking their chimes before, on, and after the mark, is comical; as a symbol, the image of their being 'set right' at the end is metafictive. Some of the humour derives from the sense of excess in the image, the suggestion of a parody of time-consciousness itself. There is a quality of overkill in the image: this is McGahern 'killing time' with a vengeance; except that it is clearly all so tongue-in-cheek. By making time so plural, the clocks connote not so much the relativity and arbitrariness of clock-time as its almost ornamental or decorative function in the life of the house and its inmates. Mary looks upon them as a comforting sound, like the 'voices' of companions (*RS*, 99). McGahern reduces the music of the spheres to the gentle cacophony of a farmhouse. Time becomes the music of the serendipitous, the entertainment of the accidental, a novelty, a joke, as Jamesie says (*RS*, 99); 'real time' in the novel is natural – diurnal, seasonal, organic, mortal – the life cycles of bird, beast and flower into which those of man and woman are absorbed. The clocks in Jamesie's and Mary's house – a house that holds the dead Johnny and where Ruttledge goes and ends up washing the dead, a task he is given unexpectedly by his 'guide', Jamesie – are, appropriately, still when he performs that ritual which he tells Kate afterwards took away his fear of death. After this, in the final paragraphs of the novel, Ruttledge and Kate witness the clocks being set 'almost right' by the beautiful, crippled clockmaker who may be McGahern's most cunning representation of the daemon within him, the story-telling, time-mastering, damaged demiurge within all his writing. For if the natural form of the seasonal cycle in *That They May Face the Rising Sun* signifies anything, it is how narrative produced by the art of memory not only 'keeps time' but 'corrects' it. *That They May Face the Rising Sun* is the finest achievement of McGahern's art of memory, surpassing the complexities of grief and guilt in *The Leavetaking*, guilt and atonement in *The Pornographer*, and even his masterwork of absolution, *Amongst Women*. It represents a higher order of artistry, perhaps, because in it McGahern uses the muse of the past to focus on a *still living* world; to show, in effect, a way of 'being-in-the-world' that is as fulfilling as it is un-deluded.

Another distinctive element in this novel, joining the humour and explicit politics, is the admission of the possibility of happiness. In *Memoir*, McGahern writes: 'A child can become infected with unhappiness' (*M*, 23), and the memoir proceeds to show the sources and history of his own infection. But in his last novel, McGahern has Ruttledge, on three occasions, affirm his undeniably real sense of feeling happy. The first admission comes as he returns to the house and overhears the Shah and Kate, the two people he loves most; but 'As soon as the thought came to him, he fought it back, blaming the whiskey. The very idea was as dangerous as presumptive speech: happiness could not be sought or worried into being, or even fully grasped; it should be allowed its own slow pace so that it passes unnoticed, if it ever comes at all' (*RS*, 182–3). No matter that Ruttledge recoils from his bliss as soon as he savours it, as if the drink were too hot and scalded his lips; it does not matter because the 'word' is out. Happiness, as Ruttledge thinks of it, is like the heron suddenly rising from the darkness into the moonlight, a gift. The second occasion involves Patrick Ryan, of all people. When Ruttledge visits him in his 'Tomb' on Christmas morning, Ryan asks him if he is happy. Ruttledge's answer is still guarded: 'I'm not unhappy.... That, I believe, is about as good as it gets ...' (*RS*, 203). His reply suggests Ruttledge has taken his earlier self-reprimand to heart. No hubris here. But he *is* speaking to 'Sergeant Death', after all, and his understatement needs to be understood in that context. Admitting he is happy to Patrick Ryan would be inviting ridicule. The third occasion where McGahern has Ruttledge think about happiness results in a statement that splits the difference between the warmth he felt seeing the Shah and Kate and the reluctant expression of a positive by a double negative with Ryan. Later in the Christmas season, Ruttledge thinks: 'The days were quiet. They did not feel particularly quiet or happy but through them ran the sense, like an underground river, that there would come a time when these days would be looked back on as happiness, all that life could give of contentment and peace' (*RS*, 206). The way McGahern's focalized narrator expresses Ruttledge's feeling is revealing. McGahern describes Ruttledge putting his present feeling into the past by imagining a future when he would look back to this present, as if happiness can only be something one has had, and can be known, only *in retrospect*, once it has passed. The formulation, its temporal-emotional structure, precisely describes the perspective McGahern takes on the happiest time in his life in his memoir, those few years of childhood before he lost his mother. Ruttledge's thought thus adumbrates McGahern's art of memory, the career spent following and drawing from that 'underground river' of conscious and unconscious recollection, that source of his fiction which, symbolically, was all the time flowing towards the lake of this last novel.[25]

Ruttledge's location of happiness in memory recalls Patrick Moran's ideas about memory and imagination in *The Leavetaking*: 'Two worlds: the world of the schoolroom in this day, the world of memory becoming imagination; but this last day in the classroom will one day be nothing but a memory before its total obliteration, the completed circle' (*L*, 35). *That They May Face the Rising Sun* completes the cycle of experience, memory, and imagination that structures the process and history of McGahern's writing life. Patrick Moran is Ruttledge's closest 'ancestor' in McGahern's fiction. Ultimately, the art of memory is the art of metamorphosis: memory must become imagination if the past is to continue to live in the present. The concentric worlds of *That They May Face the Rising Sun* are the same worlds found in McGahern's other fictions, where narrator-protagonists like the young Mahoney, Patrick Moran, and the pornographer struggle through their quests, journeys described by Isobel as 'The painful going inwards ... circle by slow circle' (*L* 1974: 133). In his last novel, McGahern reached the final inner circle of his journey, and discovered there the world of memory completed and redeemed by the imagination, a world both familiar and new, knowing it as the place where he had started from but understanding it for the first time. 'Everything that had flowered had now come to fruit' (*RS*, 177).

25   See Grennan's remarks on McGahern's use of 'would' – 'a tense poised between past, present, and future' as expressing McGahern's ceremonial-ritual sense of life in the novel ('"Only What Happens,"' 23, 27).

Violence, Dislocation, Truth and Vision

In his Preface to *Creatures of the Earth* (2006), his last collection of short stories, John McGahern wrote: 'The imagination demands that life be told slant because of its need of distance' (*CE*, vii). For me, this is further confirmation of the connection between imagination and memory that I have attempted to trace in McGahern's creative activity; the need for distance may have to do with perspective on the particular and the shaping of the latter into a larger vision, but it most certainly also has to do with the breathing space between the life experience and its recollection that McGahern found necessary before the past could be re-imagined. But the distance his imagination needed to open was the distance his memory sought to close and that tension is what powers McGahern's art of memory. In his review of *Creatures of the Earth*, Karl Miller proclaimed McGahern's *Memoir* to be 'at least as satisfying, in its candour and imaginative fervour, as any of his stories' and went on to ponder: 'What does art add, in this case, to autobiography? The answer should make room for the thought that the memoir and the variously gifted novels and stories are all of them art. They drink from the same well'.[1]

Indeed, McGahern's short stories tell the same story of grief, guilt, and anger as the novels and many readers before Miller have noted the connections between them. Patrick Crotty, in fact, considers 'Wheels', from *Nightlines* (1970), to be the 'key' to all McGahern's fiction.[2] In it, there is bad feeling between the step-mother, Rose, and the narrator, which is modelled on McGahern's own relationship with Agnes McGahern; the

---

1   Miller, 'Dark, delightful country things[:] John McGahern's austere eloquence', *Times Literary Supplement*, 8 December 2006', 20.

2   Crotty, '"All Toppers,"' 43.

father's relationship with the son is similar to that of Moran and Luke in *Amongst Women*, and as in that novel and *Memoir*, the narrator describes the father becoming his wife's child. The father's background in the *Gardai*, his letters, and his desire to sell the farm and move to Dublin to live near the son, are all recounted in the memoir, and the narrator recalls rowing on the river, which also figures in *The Leavetaking* as well as *Memoir*.

A related story, 'Gold Watch', from the U.S. edition of *Getting Through* (1980), also provides a 'key' to the map of McGahern's fictive world or what the narrator describes as 'the bitter school of my father' (*CE*, 136): the latter sits in a car-chair he has placed beside the fire, like McGahern's own father in the memoir and Moran in *Amongst Women*, and like the stepmother in 'Wheels' and in that novel, the character in this story is also named Rose; the family farm that the son returns to is called 'Big Meadow', and he returns in the summer to help with the hay, like the Moran children. The scene between the girlfriend and the father is a version of the meeting McGahern describes between his father and Annikki Laaksi in *Memoir*.[3] The son-narrator remarks in this story, 'after enough suffering a kind of iron enters the soul' (*CE*, 139). 'A Slip Up', from the same collection, has an old man remembering his childhood walks around the lake with his mother, prefiguring both the recollections central to the memoir and the setting of *That They May Face the Rising Sun*. Also in McGahern's first collection, 'Korea' has a father-figure who is a former IRA man like Reegan in *The Barracks*, Michael Moran, and Francis McGahern, and the honeymoon in Howth that he remembers is re-used in *The Leavetaking*, when Patrick Moran imagines his parents there; the son remembers going to a football final with his father, which McGahern also recounts in *Memoir*; and when the father asks him about his plans there is an echo of Mahoney in *The Dark*. Like Mahoney and Reegan, Moran and Francis McGahern, the father in 'Korea' is selfish and 'calculating'. The narrator in 'The Recruiting Officer', also from *Nightlines*, has similar symptoms and suffers from the same ailment as the protagonists in *The Dark*, *The*

---

3   See Laaksi's comment on her first exposure to Francis McGahern in Conway, '"A calculating, control freak"'.

Leavetaking, and especially *The Pornographer*: 'something deep in my own nature, a total paralysis of the will, and a feeling that any one thing in this life is almost as worthwhile doing as any other' (*CE*, 69). The father in 'Sierra Leone', in *Getting Through*, complains to his son that his second wife takes things from his house to her own family, which is a complaint Moran makes about Rose in *Amongst Women*, and he tells his son that he wants to disinherit her, which McGahern records his own father considering in *Memoir* (*M*, 263–4). The setting of 'Oldfashioned', in *High Ground* (1985), is similar to that in *The Leavetaking*, and the farm the father buys from the estate is based on McGahern's father's purchase recounted in *Memoir*; the gossiping Guard Casey appears again in the memoir, Annie and Lizzie in the Post Office reappear in *Amongst Women*; the father is ex-IRA and a Garda Sergeant, like Reegan and Francis McGahern and the father-figures in earlier stories; the fire at Rockingham House is described in the memoir. The Kirkwoods of 'Eddie Mac' and 'The Conversion of William Kirkwood' in *High Ground* are drawn from the Maroneys who played such an important role in McGahern's adolescence and to whom he expresses his gratitude in the memoir; the Garda Sergeant Moran in the story is also based on his father.

The pattern of connections continues into McGahern's last works: 'Love of the World', first published in 1997, is set in the same 'world' as *That They May Face the Rising Sun*, where 'Nothing much ever happens' (*CE*, 336); the 'quiet' is the same quiet that Jimmy Joe McKiernan asks Ruttledge about in that novel; the love of 'news' that is an important feature of Jamesie Murphy's characterization is a characteristic of people in general 'here', and there is a scene in which the narrator watches a football game on television that contains the same remark that Jamesie makes in a similar scene in the novel; finally, the story and novel both have characters named 'Kate Ruttledge;' and, moving in the other direction, the character of Bill Evans in *That They May Face the Rising Sun* is drawn from the 'homeboy' material of 'Christmas', a story in McGahern's first collection. Even a shallow trawling of the connections between McGahern's stories, novels, and memoir such as this suggests that McGahern's short fiction is a product of the same creative-memorial processes that resulted in his novels.

In the Preface to *Creatures of the Earth* McGahern describes how his stories were inspired by quotidian banalities as well as surprising discoveries from out of the past, and how all the stories went through 'many workings' (*CE*, vii). This study began with my feeling that this phrase needed parsing. What was the 'work' that was writing for McGahern? He tells us that 'The most difficult [stories he wrote] were drawn directly from life', but that none of his stories 'seemed to work' if they were not 'reinvented, re-imagined and somehow dislocated from their origins' (*CE*, vii), and this study has been an attempt to understand just what McGahern's writing did when it 'worked' for him. The 'work' of writing for McGahern was, of course, the creative activity itself – the struggle with words, structure, form; but as his own description makes clear, this struggle was itself merely the continuation and ultimate resolution of the prior struggle to wrestle the idea, experience or memory into articulate shape. The 'work' of writing may ultimately have been the written work, the published article, but the 'work' that produced the novel was as much the 'working through', 'working up', 'working over' and 'working out' of memory as narrative as it was the crafting of language. The argument of this book is that the finished product only 'worked' for McGahern if it was a successful product of that other 'working through' and 'working out'.

This point is supported, ironically, by McGahern himself in his Preface to *Creatures of the Earth* when he discusses two stories that had given him particular difficulty over some years. Obviously, he was unable to get them to that point of resolution where they 'worked' for him; not surprisingly, they were stories about his father. Each one seems to have contained something, some kernel of feeling, some seed of meaning, that he was unable to give up on until he had brought it out into the light of narrative. It was not until he was working on *Memoir*, however, that he realized that the core of each story was 'essential' to his representation of life in the barracks with his father in that work, and that to use the scenes in any other way would have been a mistake: 'No matter what violences or dislocations were attempted, they continued to remain firmly grounded, obdurately what they were' (*CE*, vii). McGahern's contradiction of himself here is dramatic. In the previous paragraph he asserts that his stories 'never seemed to work' for him 'Unless they were ... somehow dislocated from their origins'; then he confesses that he had failed to complete the two stories about his father precisely because he had attempted such 'dislocations'. It is important to note here as well the polysemy in McGahern's language of 'violences' and 'dislocations': his first order of reference is aesthetic, to his recognition of his error in craft-judgement; but we may see this also as a tacit admission that he was disregarding the deeper levels of the 'work' of writing from which his most successful recuperations of the past had always issued. Furthermore, the language of 'violences' and 'dislocations' is, as we know from *Memoir*, directly associated with his father, who 'dislocated' McGahern when he brought him as a child from his mother's farmhouse to the barracks following her death, and who, according to McGahern, subjected his children to many instances of violence in the following years. The coincidence here of the aesthetic and the autobiographical, the business of writing life and the work of life-writing in McGahern's language, is striking.

What I hope I have made coherent in this study is the way McGahern's writing is an art of memory that from the beginning set out to work through these formative traumas of his life by transforming them into the order, unity, and coherence of narrative art, or, in his own words, the 'truth' of 'a central idea or vision of life' (*CE*, viii). McGahern's total body of work ultimately expresses a creative process that is mythopoeic in motive and scope and articulates a myth of loss and recovery that is both profoundly personal and universally compelling. In speaking for himself, he may often have spoken for a generation, but in his fiction, John McGahern also articulated a most singular vision.

Bibliography

Works by John McGahern (in order of publication)

'The End or the Beginning of Love: Episodes from a Novel.' (1961). *An Anthology from X: A Quarterly Review of Literature and the Arts, 1959–62*, ed. Patrick Swift and David Wright. Oxford: Oxford University Press, 1988. 153–63.

The Barracks. (1963). London: Faber and Faber, 1983.

The Dark. (1965). London: Faber and Faber, 2008.

'The Image (Prologue to a Reading at the Rockefeller University).' *The Honest Ulsterman* 8 (December 1968): 10.

Nightlines. London: Faber and Faber, 1970.

The Leavetaking. London: Faber and Faber, 1974. Rev. ed., London: Faber and Faber, 1984.

Getting Through. London: Faber and Faber, 1978. New York: Harper and Row, 1980.

The Pornographer. (1979). London: Faber and Faber, 1990.

'Preface to the Second Edition.' *The Leavetaking*. 2nd edn, rev. London: Faber and Faber, 1984.

Amongst Women. London: Faber and Faber, 1990.

'The Image' (rev. version). *Canadian Journal of Irish Studies* 17 (1991):12.

'Reading and Writing.' In Jacqueline Genet and Wynne Hellegouarc'h, eds, *Irish Writers and Their Creative Process*. Irish Literary Studies 48. Gerrards Cross: Colin Smythe, 1996. 103–9.

That They May Face the Rising Sun. London: Faber and Faber, 2002.

Memoir. London: Faber and Faber, 2005.

'What Is My Language?' *Irish University Review* 35.1 (Spring/Summer 2005): 1–12.

Creatures of the Earth: New and Selected Stories. London: Faber and Faber, 2006.

'God and Me.' Village.ie. 28 December 2006. 28 July 2008. <http://www.village.ie/Ireland/Feature/God_and_Me:_an_essay_by_John_McGahern/>.

Criticism, Reviews, Interviews

Adair, Tom. 'Darker side of Irish charm.' Rev. of *Memoir*, by John McGahern. *The Scotsman* 10 Sep 2005. 28 July 2008. <http://www.arlindo-correia.com/101105. html>.

Bendelli, Giuliana. 'John McGahern's *The Pornographer* or the Representation of Nothingness: An Attempt to Overcome Irish Parochialism.' In Giuseppe Serpillo and Donatella Badin, eds, *The Classical World and the Mediterranean*. Cagliari: Università di Sassari, 1996. 188–93.

Brown, Terence. 'Redeeming Time: the Novels of John McGahern and John Banville.' In James Acheson, ed., *The British and Irish Novel Since 1960*. New York: St. Martin's, 1991. 159–73.

Collins, Pat. *John McGahern: A Private World*. RTE, Hummingbird/Harvest Films, 2005.

Conway, Isobel. '"A calculating, control freak," claims the first wife of late author John McGahern.' *Irish Independent* 28 May 2006. 28 July 2008. <http://www. independent.ie/opinion/analysis/a-calculating-control-freak-claims-the-first-wife-of-late-author-john-mcgahern-130514.html>.

Cronin, John. '"The Dark" Is Not Light Enough: The Fiction of John McGahern.' *Studies* 58 (Winter 1969): 427–32.

———. 'John McGahern: A New Image?' In *Irish Writers and Their Creative Process*, ed. Jacqueline Genet and Wynne Hellegouarc'h. Irish Literary Studies 48. Gerrards Cross: Colin Smythe, 1996. 110–17.

Crotty, Patrick. '"All Toppers": Children in the Fiction of John McGahern.' *Irish University Review* 35.1 (Spring/Summer 2005): 42–57.

Deevy, Patricia. 'A light in the darkness.' *Irish Independent* 30 December 2001. 28 July 2008. <http://www.independent.ie/unsorted/features/a-light-in-the-darkness-512368.html>.

Devine, Paul. 'Style and Structure in John McGahern's *The Dark*.' *Critique* 21.1 (1979): 49–58.

Douglas-Fairhurst, Robert. 'Memories from the shadows of the past.' Rev. of *Memoir*, by John McGahern. *Daily Telegraph* 25 September 2005. 28 July 2008. <http:// www.telegraph.co.uk/arts/main.jhtml?xml=/arts/2005/09/25/bomcga225. xml>.

Foley, Michael. 'The Novels of John McGahern.' *The Honest Ulsterman* 8 (September 1968): 34–7.

Freyer, Grattan. 'Change Naturally: The Fiction of O'Flaherty, O'Faolain, McGahern.' *Eire-Ireland* 18.1 (Spring 1983): 138–44.

Garfitt, Roger. 'Constants in Contemporary Irish Fiction.' In Douglas Dunn, ed., *Two Decades of Irish Writing*. Cheadle: Carcanet Press, 1975. 207–41.

Garratt, Robert F. 'John McGahern's *Amongst Women*: Representation, Memory, Trauma.' *Irish University Review* 35.1 (Spring/Summer 2005): 121–35.

Goarzin, Anne. '"A Crack in the Concrete": Objects in the Works of John McGahern.' *Irish University Review* 35.1 (Spring/Summer 2005): 28–41.

González, Rosa. 'John McGahern.' [Interview] In Jacqueline Hurtley et al., *Ireland in Writing[:] Interviews with Writers and Academics*. Amsterdam: Rodopoi, 1998. 39–50.

Grennan, Eamon. '"Only What Happens": Mulling Over McGahern.' *Irish University Review* 35.1 (Spring/Summer 2005): 13–27.

Holland, Siobhán. 'Marvellous Fathers in the Fiction of John McGahern.' *The Yearbook of English Studies* 35 (2005): 186–98.

——. 'Re-citing the Rosary: Women, Catholicism and Agency in Brian Moore's *Cold Heaven* and John McGahern's *Amongst Women*.' In L. Harte and M. Parker, eds, *Contemporary Irish Fiction: Themes, Tropes and Theories*. Basingstoke: Macmillan, 2000. 56–78.

Hughes, Eamonn. '"All That Surrounds Our Life": Time, Sex, and Death in *That They May Face the Rising Sun*.' *Irish University Review* 35.1 (Spring/Summer 2005): 147–63.

Kamm, Jurgen. 'John McGahern.' In Rudiger Imhof, ed., *Contemporary Irish Novelists*. Studies in English and Comparative Literature, Vol. 5. Tubingen: Gunter Narr Verlag, 1990. 175–92.

Kearney, Richard. 'A Crisis of Imagination: An Analysis of a Counter-Tradition in the Irish Novel.' In Mark Patrick Hederman and Richard Kearney, eds, *Crane Bag of Irish Studies*. Dublin, Blackwater, 1982. 390–402.

Kelly, Shirley. 'The writing keeps the cattle in high style.' *Books Ireland* (February 2002): 5–6.

Kennedy, Eileen. 'Q. & A. with John McGahern.' In James P. Myers, ed., *Writing Irish: Selected Interviews with Irish Writers from the* Irish Literary Supplement. Syracuse University Press, 1999. 3–9.

Kiberd, Declan. 'Fallen Nobility: The World of John McGahern.' *Irish University Review* 35.1 (Spring/Summer 2005): 164–74.

Killeen, Terence. 'Versions of Exile: A Reading of *The Leavetaking*.' *Canadian Journal of Irish Studies*, 17.1 (1991): 69–78.

Lee, Hermione. 'Everything Under the Sun.' Rev. of *That They May Face the Rising Sun*, by John McGahern. *The Observer* 6 January 2002: 16.

Maher, Eamon. 'The Irish Novel in Crisis? The Example of John McGahern.' *Irish University Review* 35.1 (Spring/Summer 2005): 58–71.

———. 'John McGahern and his Irish Readers.' *New Hibernia Review* 9.2 (2005): 125–36.

———. *John McGahern: From the Local to the Universal*. Dublin: The Liffey Press, 2003.

———, and Kiberd, Declan. 'John McGahern: Writer, Stylist, Seeker of a Lost World.' *Doctrine & Life* 52 (February 2002): 82–97.

Malcolm, David. *Understanding John McGahern*. Columbia: University of South Carolina Press, 2007.

Mangan, Gerald. 'The Long Road Home.' Rev. of *Memoir*, by John McGahern. *Times Literary Supplement* 28 October 2005: 26.

McKeon, Belinda. '"Robins Feeding with the Sparrows": The Protestant "Big House" in the Fiction of John McGahern.' *Irish University Review* 35.1 (Spring/Summer 2005): 72–89.

Miller, Karl. 'Dark, delightful country things[:] John McGahern's austere eloquence.' Rev. of *Creatures of the Earth: New and Selected Stories*, by John McGahern. *Times Literary Supplement* 8 December 2006: 19–20.

Molloy, F. C. 'The Novels of John McGahern.' *Critique* 19.1 (1977): 5–7.

O'Dwyer, Rianna. 'Foreword.' In *History, Myth, and Ritual in the Fiction of John McGahern: Strategies of Transcendence*, by James Whyte. Lewiston, NY: Edwin Mellen Press, 2002. xi–xv.

O'Hagan, Sean. 'A family touched with madness.' Rev. of *Memoir*, by John McGahern. *The Observer* 28 August 2005. 28 July 2008. <http://www.guardian.co.uk/books/2005/aug/28/fiction.features3>.

Paratte, Henri-S. 'Conflicts in a Changing World: John McGahern.' In Patrick Rafroidi and Maurice Harmon, eds, *The Irish Novel in Our Time*. Lille: Pr. De l'Université de Lille, 1976. 311–27.

Peach, Linden. *The Contemporary Irish Novel: Critical Readings*. New York: Palgrave Macmillan, 2004.

Quinn, Antoinette. 'A Prayer for My Daughters: Patriarchy in *Amongst Women*.' *Canadian Journal of Irish Studies* 17.1 (1991): 79–90.

Rogers, Lori. *Feminine Nation: Performance, Gender and Resistance in the Works of John McGahern and Neil Jordan*. Lanham: University Press of North America, 1998.

Sampson, Denis. 'A Conversation with John McGahern.' *Canadian Journal of Irish Studies* 17.1 (1991): 13–18.

———. '"The Day Set Alight in the Mind": Notes on John McGahern's Late Style.' *Irish University Review* 39.1 (Spring-Summer 2009): 122–8.

———. 'The Lost Image: Some Notes on McGahern and Proust.' *Canadian Journal of Irish Studies* 17.1 (1991): 57–68.

——. 'A Note on John McGahern's *The Leavetaking*.' *Canadian Journal of Irish Studies* 2.2 (1976): 61–5.

——. *Outstaring Nature's Eye: The Fiction of John McGahern*. Washington, DC: Catholic University Press, 1993.

——. '"Open to the World": A Reading of John McGahern's *That They May Face the Rising Sun*.' *Irish University Review* 35.1 (Spring/Summer 2005): 136–46.

Schwartz, Karlheinz. 'John McGahern's Point of View.' *Éire-Ireland* 19.3 (Autumn 1984): 92–110.

Sennett, Tracey. 'Rhythm, Images, and the Fiction of John McGahern.' *An Gael* 3.2 (1976): 1–13.

Sheehy Skeffington, Owen. 'The McGahern Affair.' *Censorship* 2 (Spring 1966): 27–30.

Smyth, Gerry. *The Novel & the Nation: Studies in the New Irish Fiction*. London: Pluto Press, 1997.

Tighe Ledwidge, Grace. 'Death in Marriage: The Tragedy of Elizabeth Reegan in *The Barracks*.' *Irish University Review* 35.1 (Spring/Summer 2005): 90–103.

Toolin, Michael J. 'John McGahern: The Historian and the Pornographer.' *Canadian Journal of Irish Studies* 7.2 (1981): 39–55.

Updike, John. 'An Old-Fashioned Novel.' Rev. of *The Pornographer* by John McGahern, *New Yorker* 24 December 1979. Rpt. in Updike, *Hugging the Shore: Essays and Criticism*. New York: Knopf, 1983. 388–93.

Van der Ziel, Stanley. '"All This Talk and Struggle": John McGahern's *The Dark*.' *Irish University Review* 35.1 (Spring/Summer 2005): 104–20.

——. 'John McGahern: An Annotated Bibliography.' *Irish University Review* 35.1 (Spring/Summer 2005): 175–202.

——. '*Memoir*, by John McGahern.' [Review] *Irish University Review* 35.2 (Autumn/Winter 2005): 463–9.

Whyte, James. *History, Myth, and Ritual in the Fiction of John McGahern: Strategies of Transcendence*. Lewiston, NY: Edwin Mellen Press, 2002.

Other Works

Abraham, Nicolas and Torok, Maria. *The Shell and the Kernel: Renewals of Psychoanalysis*. Ed. Nicholas T. Rand. Chicago: University of Chicago Press, 1994.

———. *The Wolf Man's Magic Word: A Cryptonomy*. Trans. Nicholas Rand, with a Foreword by Jacques Derrida. Minneapolis: University of Minnesota Press, 1986.

Adams, Hazard. Ed. *Critical Theory Since Plato*. Rev. ed. New York: Harcourt Brace Jovanovich, 1992.

Arnold, Matthew. *Poetical Works*. Ed. C. B. Tinker and H. F. Lowry. London: Oxford University Press, 1969.

Bowlby, John. *Attachment and Loss*. 3 vols. New York: Basic Books, 1969.

Carruthers, Mary J. *The Book of Memory: A Study of Memory in Medieval Culture*. Cambridge: Cambridge University Press, 1990.

Derrida, Jacques. 'Foreword.' In Nicolas Abraham and Maria Torok, *The Wolf Man's Magic Word: A Cryptonomy*. Trans. Nicholas Rand. Minneapolis: University of Minnesota Press, 1986. i–lxxii.

Duff, Jacques. 'Grief and the Grieving Process.' *Behavioural Neurotherapy Clinic* (2005). 1 August 2008. <http://www.adhd.com.au/grief.htm>.

Eliot, T. S. *The Complete Poems and Plays*. London: Faber and Faber, 1969.

———. 'Tradition and the Individual Talent.' *Selected Prose of T. S. Eliot*. Ed. with an Introduction by Frank Kermode. New York: Harcourt Brace Jovanovich, 1975. 37–44.

Ellmann, Maud. *Elizabeth Bowen: The Shadow Across the Page*. Edinburgh: Edinburgh University Press, 2003.

Ferriter, Diarmaid. *The Transformation of Ireland*. New York: The Overlook Press, 2004.

Foster, R. F. *Luck and the Irish: A Brief History of Change from 1970*. Oxford: Oxford University Press, 2008.

Freud, Sigmund. *The Freud Reader*. Ed. Peter Gay. New York: W. W. Norton, 1989.

———. 'Mourning and Melancholia.' *Standard Edition*, v. 14. Trans. and ed. James Strachey. London: Hogarth Press, 1958. 243–58.

———. 'Remembering, Repeating, and Working Through.' *The Standard Edition of the Complete Psychological Works of Sigmund Freud*, vol. 12. Trans. and ed. James Strachey. London: Hogarth Press, 1958. 147–56.

Frye, Northrop. *The Great Code: The Bible and Literature*. New York: Harcourt Brace Jovanovich, 1982.

Head, Dominic. *The Cambridge Introduction to Modern British Fiction, 1950–2000.* Cambridge: Cambridge University Press, 2002.

Heidegger, Martin. 'The Question Concerning Technology.' *Basic Writings.* Ed. David Farrell Krell. New York: Harper & Row, 1977. 287–317.

Henderson, Joseph L. 'Ancient Myths and Modern Man.' In Carl G. Jung et al., *Man and His Symbols.* New York: Dell Publishing, 1964. 95–156.

Holmes J. *John Bowlby and Attachment Theory.* London: Routledge, 1993.

Hurtley, Jacqueline, et al. *Ireland in Writing[:] Interviews with Writers and Academics.* Amsterdam: Rodopoi, 1998.

Inglis, Tom. *Moral Monopoly: The Rise and Fall of the Catholic Church in Modern Ireland.* Rev. ed. Dublin: Dublin University College Press, 1998.

——. 'Origins and Legacies of Irish Prudery: Sexuality and Social Control in Modern Ireland.' *Éire-Ireland* 40.3/4 (2005): 9–37.

Julian of Norwich. *Revelations of Divine Love.* Trans. Grace Warrack. (1901) *Christian Classics Ethereal Library.* 1 June 2005. 30 July 2008. <http://www.ccel.org/ccel/julian/revelations.xiv.i.html>.

Jung, C. G. *The Archetypes and the Collective Unconscious.* Trans. By R. F. C. Hull. 2nd ed. Bollingen Series XX. Princeton, NJ: Princeton University Press, 1968.

Kandt, V. E. 'Adolescent Bereavement: Turning a Fragile Time into Acceptance and Peace.' *The School Counsellor,* 41 (1994): 203–11.

Kavanagh, Patrick. *The Complete Poems.* Ed. Peter Kavanagh. Newbridge: The Goldsmith Press, 1990.

Kearney, Richard, ed. *States of Mind: Dialogues with Contemporary Thinkers.* New York: New York University Press, 1995.

Kersting, Karen. 'A New Approach to Complicated Grief.' *Monitor on Psychology* 35.10 (2004): 51.

Kristeva, Julia. 'Strangers to Ourselves: The Hope of the Singular.' *States of Mind: Dialogues with Contemporary Thinkers.* Ed. Richard Kearney. New York: New York University Press, 1995. 6–13.

Lévinas, Emmanuel. 'Ethics of the Infinite.' *States of Mind: Dialogues with Contemporary Thinkers.* Ed. Richard Kearney. New York: New York University Press, 1995. 177–99.

McCarthy, Dermot. *Roddy Doyle: Raining on the Parade.* Dublin: Liffey Press, 2003.

Pater, Walter. 'Conclusion to *Studies in the History of the Renaissance.*' In Hazard Adams, ed., *Critical Theory Since Plato.* Rev. ed. New York: Harcourt Brace Jovanovich, 1992. 644–45.

Plato. 'Symposium.' *The Great Dialogues of Plato*. Trans. W. H. D. Rouse. Ed. Eric H. Warmington and Philip G. Rouse. New York: New American Library, 1956. 69–117.

Posner, Michael. 'Of Mothers and Sons and a father long gone.' *Globe and Mail* 8 Mar. 2007: R1–2.

Rand, Nicholas. 'Translator's Introduction: Toward a Cryptonomy of Literature.' In Nicolas Abraham and Maria Torok, *The Wolf Man's Magic Word: A Cryptonomy*. Trans. Nicholas Rand, with a Foreword by Jacques Derrida. Minneapolis: University of Minnesota Press, 1986. li–lxix.

Ricoeur, Paul. 'The Creativity of Language.' [Interview] In *States of Mind: Dialogues with Contemporary Thinkers*. Ed. Richard Kearney. New York: New York University Press, 1995. 216–45.

———. *Memory, History, Forgetting*. Trans. Kathleen Blamey and David Pellauer. Chicago: University of Chicago Press, 2004.

———. *Time and Narrative*. Vol I. Trans. Kathleen McLaughlin and David Pellauer. Chicago: University of Chicago Press, 1984.

Riggs, Pádraigín and Vance, Norman. 'Irish Prose Fiction.' In Joe Cleary and Claire Connolly, eds, *The Cambridge Companion to Modern Irish Culture*. Cambridge: Cambridge University Press, 2005. 245–66.

Segal, Eliezer. 'From the Sources: Bare-Bones Burial.' 29 July 2008. <http://www.acs. ucalgary.ca/~elsegal/Shokel/021219_Ossuaries.html>.

Storey, Mark. '"Bewildered Chimes": Image, Voice and Structure in Recent Irish Fiction.' In Gerald Dawe and Edna Longley, eds, *Across a Roaring Hill: The Protestant Imagination in Modern Ireland*. Belfast: The Blackstaff Press, 1985. 161–81.

Vansina, Jan. *Oral Tradition as History*. Madison: University of Wisconsin Press, 1985.

Whalley, George. *Aristotle's Poetics*. Trans and with a commentary by George Whalley. Ed. John Baxter and Patrick Atherton. Montreal: McGill-Queen's University Press, 1997.

Worden, J. W. *Grief Counselling and Grief Therapy: A Handbook for the Mental Health Practitioner*. 2nd ed. London: Springer, 1991.

Yates, Frances. A. *The Art of Memory*. London: Routledge and Kegan Paul, 1966.

Yeats, W. B. *The Collected Poems of W. B. Yeats*. Ed. Richard J. Finneran. Rev. 2nd ed. New York: Simon and Schuster, 1996.

Index

Reimagining Ireland

Series Editor: Dr Eamon Maher, Institute of Technology, Tallaght

The concepts of Ireland and 'Irishness' are in constant flux in the wake of an ever-increasing reappraisal of the notion of cultural and national specificity in a world assailed from all angles by the forces of globalisation and uniformity. Reimagining Ireland interrogates Ireland's past and present and suggests possibilities for the future by looking at Ireland's literature, culture and history and subjecting them to the most up-to-date critical appraisals associated with sociology, literary theory, historiography, political science and theology.

Some of the pertinent issues include, but are not confined to, Irish writing in English and Irish, Nationalism, Unionism, the Northern 'Troubles', the Peace Process, economic development in Ireland, the impact and decline of the Celtic Tiger, Irish spirituality, the rise and fall of organised religion, the visual arts, popular cultures, sport, Irish music and dance, emigration and the Irish diaspora, immigration and multiculturalism, marginalisation, globalisation, modernity/postmodernity and postcolonialism. The series publishes monographs, comparative studies, interdisciplinary projects, conference proceedings and edited books.

Proposals should be sent either to Dr Eamon Maher at eamon.maher@ittdublin.ie or to oxford@peterlang.com.

Vol. 1   Eugene O'Brien: 'Kicking Bishop Brennan up the Arse':
          Negotiating Texts and Contexts in Contemporary Irish Studies
          ISBN 978-3-03911-539-6. 219 pages. 2009.

Vol. 2   James P. Byrne, Padraig Kirwan and Michael O'Sullivan (eds):
          Affecting Irishness: Negotiating Cultural Identity Within and
          Beyond the Nation
          ISBN 978-3-03911-830-4. 334 pages. 2009.

Niamh S
was here.